Growing One's Inner Wisdom - To the Max

Or, discovering just how to full bloom even more gloriously than the lilies of the field

Dr. Lynn

Balboa Press books may be ordered through booksellers or by contacting:

Balboa Press
A Division of Hay House
1663 Liberty Drive
Bloomington, IN 47403
www.balboapress.com
1-(877) 407-4847

ISBN: 978-1-4525-7654-1 (sc)
ISBN: 978-1-4525-7655-8 (e)

Library of Congress Control Number: 2013910950

Printed in the United States of America.

Balboa Press rev. date: 7/03/2013

BALBOA
PRESS
A DIVISION OF HAY HOUSE

The Front Cover Image

This image is very much based upon Dr. Carl Jung's book 'The Secret of the Golden Flower', wherein Dr. Jung points to the most Beaut-I-Ful Far Eastern many thousand petaled - ancient Golden Lotus Flower archetypal metaphor. Insofar as it has been use since earliest recorded history to convey our human most possibility to so fully Bloom every cell within our very own unique - positively huge many thousand petaled completely whole body nerve fiber inter-connected - seemingly unlimited information storage capable nervous system. In such a way as to thus enable us to thus enter into our now pure energy quantum level attuned & thus actual apparently without limits - whole being Awakened Awareness Field. We become fully Conscious of our greatest possible hu-man potential. Which is to link our selves completely up within that most unlimited, non-local Unitary Intelligence Field of All. We end up accessing a state of totally free non-separate unbound, full-on in At-One-Ment with the Source of All – truly Loving Co-Creative Consciousness. Or that place of our greatest well beyond ordinary, actual Tap Our Source Empowering King-Dome of Heaven Found, true great Wisdom Intelligence Place - we all have With-In.

To take this under-standing which 'The Secret of the Golden Flower' attempts to point us all toward, yet another step further. My own sense of this possibility we all have within was most beautifully alluded to, by that way Beauty-Ful being known as Jesus the Christ. In his famous Sermon on the Mount when he admonished us all to look to the Lilies of the Field - in order to help ourselves much better whole being 'Grok'. That neither 'toiling', which is to say remaining stuck in our half wit only, constantly trying to so called rational/logical keep ourselves justifying, our less than whole conscious ways of behaving our selves forth, alone. Nor remaining endlessly spinning off into some mere so called feeling and emotional other half of our brain dominated, tangent by itself alone. Are ever likely to help us to sense our Self's as fully enabled to Bloom even more Glori-Us-Ly, than any Solomon or for that matter Salome, in all his/her finery. In other words, no matter how much we may choose to stay halfwit locked into, either so called conventional small mind linear sequential rational/logical 'toiling' only, or for that matter seemingly endless emotionally 'spinning'. In such a way as to constantly pit one half of our brain power, in opposition to the other half. There is no gathering of mere material wealth, power, & every kind of seeming glory, by itself, no matter how half wittedly we may attempt to justify such narrow band mind focus. Which can ever help us pass through the most sacred 'I' of that 'Needle', said to enable us to enter into our very own King-Dome of Heaven within. Which is of our own unique human potential to actually now Be, truly Whole Brain indeed whole Being Lit Up and thus full of the most actually Non-Separate from One-Ness in It-Self - truly way One-Drous found De-Light. In the greatest sense of our Hu-Man/Woman most possibility to FIND that very Now - Full-On Consciously Wake-Ful - Intelligence Bloom - such as we All of Us have access to 'WITHIN'. Insofar as will just take all those response-abilities required for us to 'ACTUALLY BE-IN' this place of our totally 'NOW TOTALLY GOLDEN - FLOW ZONE FOUND FULL FLOWERING WITHIN'.

Chapters

First A Short Forward to the Initial Half of the Book

It seems the time has come for Hu-Man/Woman-Kind to way more fully understand, that at the most basic level of our being, we are more than anything pure energy generating systems. And that we have been designed/evolved to become aware of ourselves as the sort of Radiant Light pure Energy attuned Beings, that can emanate a field of true found En-Lighten-Ment all around ourselves. In this respect 2 of our greatest great wisdom spirit teachings were: Make thine 'I' single, and thy body shall be filled as if with light. And become as a candle flame unto your self"! Inasmuch as this is our greatest gift toward becoming enlightened. In other words learning to integrate our sense of self into a single whole unified being, and we will begin to actually experience our self as a being akin to a Field of Light. The first 4 lessons are therefore, very much dedicated to the importance of taking some greater awareness time, to learn how to better ground our sense of ourselves. Within our much more pure radiant energy awake - now way more quantum Super Light speed attuned Shining Spirits.

In such a way that these innermost characters we all have within, keep helping us to so expand and thus elevate the greater sense of our very own Super Light attuned Awareness potential. That we may now find our self's able to enter the Huge Quantum Level Pure Energy Field of non-locality. That we may thus find our greatest possible sense of our Self's, more and more enabled to operate our intelligence as if non-separatively connected. Except now at quantum Super Light speed in relation to all that we may choose to study and become excellent at. In the very senses implied by Carl Jung's concepts of synchronicity, as well as in terms of the more general idea of finding our more in our flow zone enabled sense our Self. Wherein as if in a now way perfectly serendipitous, inner dimensional attuned place. We suddenly not only find ourselves in exactly the right place, in the right moment in time, tuning into exactly whatever next level of information seems to be required to help us be enabled to actually realize our dreams. But we seem to be able to operate within the very sort of way more expanded aware place, wherefrom we begin to process so many more bits of information per moment. It begins to seem like time itself - starts to slow down for us. Thereby enabling us to make much more here and now grounded intelligent decisions, with respect to whatever intentions we may find ourselves choosing to help our greater sense of Self, be most fully enabled to manifest.

In other words, agreeing to take some time each day to develop this kind of more non local Tap Our Source expanded awareness within our self. Is every One's initiating step toward becoming the very sort of Magical, way more now In Our Flow Zone, truly empowered sort of Adult. Which we all have within us and thus actually deserve to be! The very sort of Magical Adult who is going to find One's very own sense of One's Self ever more empowered to help realize - whatever very best dreamed for intentions, One may keep choosing to put in front of ONE'S SELF. Based on our very own way more, truly here and now embodied and thus inwardly grounded Awarenesses, of our very own highly individual and unique best senses - of our Self. Inasmuch as this is the very best way for all of us to help arrange for that positively great life for our Self's, we so much keep longing for.

Chapter 1

To Begin: Let's Re-Kindle Some of Our Most Precious Early Memories - To Help Re-Set Our True Innermost Wisdom Oriented - How To Have A Positively Great Life - Stage

(Starting Out By Way of Introducing Our First 3 Lesson Set of Greater Wise-Dome of Awareness Oriented Methods - Designed To Help Fully Enliven The Way More Optimally On And Up Feeling & Emotional And Thus Truly Full of 'Life Energy' Side - Of Our Greatest Possible Whole Nervous System Integrated - Capabilities)

Chapter 2

Lesson # 1 – Agreeing To Constantly Come Back Fully Embodied All Home Inside & Thus Optimally Grounded Present - Within Our Very Own Innermost Here & Now Present - Sense of Our Selves

Chapter 3

Lesson # 2 – Now For Diving Totally Core Energy Inside Every Emotion - As Our Best Way To Light Up Our Vital Energetic 'Radiance' - Even More

Chapter 4

Lesson # 3 – So That We May Thus Learn To Total House Clear Every Last Byte - Of Any Old Energy Contractive & Thus Ultimately Inner Held - Negativity Based Self Sabotaging Self Doubt

(Next Our Second 3 Lesson Set of More Truly Wise-Dome of Awareness Oriented Methods - Designed To Help Totally 'Liberate' The More Big Mind Lit Up & Thus Way More Truly Brilliant Solution Generative Enabled Side - Of Our Whole Nervous System Integrated - Capabilities)

Chapter 5

Lesson # 4 – First – Going On From Here To Keep Supporting Our Most Extra Ordinary Sense of Pure Light Spirit Radiance - Always Expanding From Here 'To Infinity & Beyond'

Now a Short Forward to the Second Half of Our Book

Beyond becoming aware of One's greater sense of Self, as a being of Light. The continual practice of ever more grounding our own sense of self, into this Uni-Versal most Super Light, Is going to keep on expanding us into what ultimately going to amount to, a state of Dissolution within this Greater See of Light. Or, into a state of wherein our individual Light, will begin to merge within the great to Infinity & Beyond Oceanic Super Light, which ultimately is of One-Ness or God-Ness Itself! In this respect imagine that we all of us are like One Individual Light Bulb in an Ocean of pure Energetic Current. And that the way this great Ocean of pure energy get's to know the endless rainbow of infinite possible ways, it can keep on consciously lighting itself up, or not. Is through how we our self's choose to light up the various colors of our rainbow light within this great Ocean that is of One-Ness or God-Ness It-Self. In other words the way God-Ness without prior preference, get's to know the whole range of what it is capable of? Is through how we our self's with our own innate given freedom, may keep choosing to behave our self's forth within this great Ocean of One-Ness.

Here's the great rub, once you your self get to know in the Gnostic sense, that you are a most intimate part of the Great Singular most essentially Mysterious never completely knowable in an Agnostic sense Hologram we have been referring to as God. And that within the very core root of this great Hologram out of which all things manifest, is no thing any less than at very core, infinite Peace & Love It-Self. This next group of awareness techniques are therefore, going to be all about changing how you will now choose to behave your self forth. In the direction of One becoming as an instrument of this infinite - essentially Boundless Ocean of Peace & Love. All hail Om Shanti Om, Buddham Gachami, Lehiam, Halleluyah, Allah Akbar, Wakan Tanka Ho - to this same Great Mysterious One-Ness or God-Ness principle which resides within the very Heart Core of all so called things, indeed all Creatures Great & Small. As well as to all those pathways which have the possibility to lead us into a true sense of En-Lighten-Ment. That we may NOW find our most whole being Tap Our Source connected, and thus truly able to fully Bloom, Made in the Image of this Great Mysterious Source - Brilliance Within. In such a way as to thus enable our selves to Co-Create the most ever ongoing evolving - nevertheless Holographically Big Picture Integral - kinds of Hum Love Resonant Solutions! Such as will end up singing glory Halleluyah, Hosanah in the Highest with the utmost respect to our possibility to now live in total Loving Harmony! Within this Biggest of All Pictures - as Yes We Can!

Chapter 6

Lesson # 5 – Next Re-Claiming Our Inner State Of Pure Innocent Like - Yet Way Greater Unlimited & Therefore Truly Most Blessedly Magnificent - Far More Adult Awake Found - One-Der

Chapter 7

Chapter 8

Chapter 9

Chapter 10

Chapter 11

PREFACE

HOW WOULD 'YOU' LIKE TO BECOME A REAL WHOLE BEING EMPOWERED - & THUS WAY TRULY FUL-FILLED - MOST MAGICAL FOUND ADULT?

Welcome You Therefore All Aboard! - OUR GREAT QUANTUM LEAP HUMAN EVOLUTION REVOLUTION - VIA THIS NEW EVOLVE OUR MOST TRANSCENDENT HUMAN CONSCIOUSNESS - BOOK

Heare ye ALL then this! And we like to use heare in the old English sense! Inasmuch as this old usage contains within it, both the verb to hear with our ears. As well as the verb to be here, in the much larger sense of our possibility to be totally here and now present within this very moment. With respect too which, it is being said very much as a consequence of a number of very special convergent factors, by more and more leading edge visionaries. Mankind appears to be on the verge of a quantum leap wake up call in human under-standing, aimed at the very heart of each and every One of Us. These factors include the fact that more and more of us have come to experience various natural forms of mind expanding teach-nology. Which when conjoined with the constantly expanding outer world global information explosion, we have all been bearing witness to over the past 50 years. E.G. such as the internet, fantastic search engines, modern computer programs and computer games, the development of 3 D holographic computer posted imagery, instant social media postings, other high speed communications devices including digital camera's. When this trend is then combined with leading edge understandings about the quantum field in relation to pure energy oriented physics. In conjunction with what we now know about how to facilitate an intimate connection to this field, via all the various self help mind expanding means. We have in the context of more modern psycho-biology, been designing to help way more fully develop that purest possible most expanded awareness principle, which we all have within each of ourselves.

The great news is that more and more of us are actually discovering, just how too find our natural 'Philosophers Stone' or great Wise-Dome of greater awareness attuned place, we all have within. Which is to say, that totally drug free 'inner expanded awareness' place, wherein it is possible to end up being far more great Big Mind solution generative awake, than most of us ever dream possible. Very much as a consequence of us discovering just how to now way more fully operate, that most One-Der-Ful, giant wizard computer processor, we all have within. To such a degree that we become so whole nervous system lit up to that King-Dome of Heaven place within - this very moment. To such a degree more and more of us are finding ourselves suddenly able to function, much like Alice in Wonderland, as though we are 10 ft tall. As though we have turned into the twinkle, twinkle little Stars, we were all meant to be. In such a truly pro-found way, that we clearly find ourselves becoming the brilliant shinning in every respect, super stars we each of us each in our own unique ways, are all meant to be. Within which we can sense, that we have become exactly like the little engines. Who now know exactly how Yes, We-Can - solve every problem that ever comes our way. Yes we can improvise our way through any situation that may ever arise. In ways that are going to be far more loving and peace-ful, than we have ever before even dared to dream possible. Exactly in the sense that more young people are becoming multi-millionaires today by the time they reach full adulthood, than ever before in the history of Human Kind. Precisely because they have found their most One-Der-Ful, Yes, I now know exactly how I-Can - Wizards Within.

What this book is all about therefore, has everything to do with providing all who may choose to read it. With a like never quite like before, greater consciousness awakening guide. With all due respect to finding that inner most Wise-Dome which we all of us already have - within. Much in the very same sense that Eckhardt Tolle in his A New Earth book, refers to the idea that every One's ultimate purpose here, is first & foremost to become fully conscious. In the huge sense that the more fully conscious any of us may choose to become The easier it is going to be for us to go about manifesting, the greatest possible ongoing series of have a great life oriented outcomes - we can possibly manage. As such, it involves remembering '9' count them, '9' secret aspects of our own inner intelligence principle - which in greater truth we all already know about! But yet which most of us have long forgotten, and which in thought, word, and deed, we most unfortunately for us, have actually been so called educated out of! Very much as a consequence of the various dogmatic, mostly belief based, in marked contrast to actual experiential teachings. So many of these fear based controlling, and most unfortunately for us in many cases actually essentially psychopathic, elitists. Are thus constantly putting out there, via the multiple forms of information dispersal they have for centuries arranged to maintain control over. In ways that allow this elitist minority to keep us in mere half witted checkmate. To the point where the greater masses of us become much like global village idiot peons, way too overly vulnerable to being used mostly to these elitist's, self interest ends alone. When in greater truth, we really should all, know so much, way much, better!

Fortunately for all of us, our old ways of holding down and restricting our greater both individual and collective human potentials, are in the process of being cracked wide open, and ultimately broken down. I say fortunately for all of us, because the great underlying truth is, that we all of us are actually far more brilliant that we have ever dared to give ourselves credit for. What's more we are actually capable of inventing a world full of prosperity and abundance for all of us, beyond even our wildest dreams. Because you see, the moment 'we the people' finally fully get it, that it is precisely by way of our ability to build a Tap Our Source bridge between ourselves and that virtually unlimited, full of to infinity & beyond quantum energy, Big At-One-Ment Field - Itself' - we all find ourselves living within. This will be the moment we will finally see, we already have all the energy and brilliance required, to produce abundance and prosperity for everyone. This is the moment we are going to see such an explosion in way more brilliant holographic solutions, and ongoing sustainable product production. We are finally going to realize, that Yes We-Can actually manifest, everything we ever long for. All it is going to take is for us, to finally wake ourselves completely up, into being all that we can all be. To sense what this greater potential we all have within, is most essentially all about.

First, let's look at our possibility to get totally past, All Self Debilitating Fear & Inner Held Self Sabotaging Doubt!

Next time you for example, notice some-one acting mean & resentful, full of hate for this & that aspect of life, perhaps at times including you your very own self. Who thus caught in some internal conflict, appears to be all tied up in various kinds of knots, and all those endless accompanying rounds of pain & suffering grief, that tend to follow. Now know that such a person must be very afraid of all kinds of unresolved feeling & emotion. So rather than let your self buy into such fear and debilitating self doubt, much better to let any such fear based person know that there is a way out, along with just how it is possible t exit from such a core unfulfilling, basically fearful, disempowered way of living. Next time you notice some-one attempting to hoard and accumulate. Who chooses to live their life based on greed and self aggrandizement, as though we cannot invent enough to go around, as though they are somehow better than you or I. And therefore must be more special forms of being, even though they must also come out of that same One & Only Source. Which can be experienced to exist at the very root of all that is in process of being Created - heare? Know then that such people must be very afraid, that they don't have access to that inner, way more supra-logical brilliance required. To enable them to help keep manifesting enough, for every One of Us. Next time you notice some-one who shows practically no, or at best very little, heartfelt gratitude. For all the many special gifts they have already been provided with. And who thus keep themselves closed to the possibility of offering a helping heart, from the very core of their most fundamental At-One-Ment place within. In ways that can help to empower every other toward that & richly deserved inner place of prosperity & abundance manifestation, which comes with the finding of self empowerment. Know that they must be very afraid, that they will loose their separate sense of power, the moment they help lend their heart toward helping every One - to be equally powerful - each in their own right. When just the opposite will be true, the more every one of us is able to find our true sense of well beyond ordinary, Big Heart guided empowerment, we will all be so much better off. Which in turn makes it pretty much an oxy-moron, for any One to keep holding on to this hugely ridiculous, separation fear.

In this much greater respect it is ever more being said, 'We all of us are at the dawn of the age of Aquarius'. 'We are on the verge of quantum leap in human consciousness'. The very sort of dawn & leap that is going to help us all to realize, we are in thought, word, & deed, all children of the very same One-Ness. In other words, Koo, Koo, Kajoob, "We in our purest Wake-Ful-Ness, actually are the Eggman & every other animal we may ever fully whole being 'Grok' in the metaphoric form of famed Walrus!" We in other words are our neighbors, even our enemies, as a part & parcel of thy larger most transcendental sense of our selves. Within this huge humongous realization, what now, are we going to continue to want to hurt and harm - Good Godness itself - in the form of it's various most One-Der-Ful manifestations? Or will we finally choose to grow up into wanting to co-create that Eden, we have been promised? Wake, wake up, all you good people, neither you, or any 'One' else, is separate from what we have been referring to as God. It is time to get over letting fear rule us, and much rather learn to rule over it, whatever form it may choose to take. 'Heare Ye', in this huge realization about our most intimate connection to One-Ness, we have precisely the grand hope for humanity.

In total marked contract to the above - Imagine One's Self now much rather Choosing to Grow One's Greatest Possible Found Inner Sense Of -

'Life', or the Optimization of One's Feeling & Emotional based – intelligence

- **By way of You now Being able to shift From** - **way** too much inner conflict, discord, stress, anxiety, turmoil, overwhelm, various forms of self doubt, self loathing, self sabotage, and a life filled with seemingly endless emotional problems
- **Toward you now being full of** - life energy, harmony, balance, vitality, flow, and ability to live in your flow zone of, endless self confidence, self love, and beautiful positive emotions to the point of feeling very little of the above, just a life filled with endless possible great solutions

'Liberty', or the Optimization of One's Rational/Logical based – intelligence

- **By way of You now Being able to shift From** - staying way too stuck in your

4

head alone, the limitation of mere 7-8% brain use 'thinking', & thus small narrow mind attachment entrapment in your egocentric mere half wit mostly outer world oriented mind by itself. Which in turn tends to lead to constant limitation; trying; forcing; pushing; & endless either/or attempts to keep controlling to your ends alone

     - **Toward you now being full of** - an ability to mobilize your capacity for way more whole mind lit up, 'In-Sighting'. Which in turn involves your ability to keep vision seeing your way optimally great solution forward. In other words keep on flashing up precisely those ever greater, ever expanding actual whole person fu-filling solutions. Such as are most likely t help you actually realize your most clearly motivated from core inside of you - various dreamed for intentions

'True Found Happiness', or the Optimization of One's Heart Caring/Loving based intelligence, the very core center of every One's potential to actually find the Heaven here on Earth, we all so much long for

     - **By way of One now Being able to shift from** - too much in separation aloofness, cold hearted loneliness, seemingly constant grouchy-ness and endless bitchy not enough of this or that complaining-ness, etc., etc. And thus seemingly endless rounds of cynicism accompanied by a constant lack of true heartfelt - joy based Ful-Fillment

     - **Toward Us now being full of** - a huge Heart-Felt love and gratitude for the gift of your life. Accompanied by a constant appreciation for those willing to come half way into co-operative ventures with you, & especially for your ability to actually help empower others toward their own greatness. rather you constantly trying to control every other you can. And thus finally a new found ability to help your self actually realize the truly ongoing happy state of inner Ful-Fill-Ment, that you so much long for

See the whole point all my dear fellow Hu-Men/Women, there can be no greater satisfaction & thus sense of whole being found Ful-Fill-Ment - life. Than to help empower other some One's to find their own innermost sense of 'Life', 'Liberty' and 'True Found Happiness.' Or in other words exactly those most inalienable of human right's which America's founding fathers so brilliantly pointed us toward! For within the deeper reality of this great human adventure, the more we learn to empower not just our self. But also our sense of actually being able to hear only One-Heart-Beating, within our neighbor's 'as thy very same Greater Sense of One's Self'. The more we will be able to spread our living within At-One-Ment Love & thus greatest sense of empowerment. Into both our inner as well as outer, real whole being Ful-Fill-Ment found investment banks. Besides this is the only way it is ever possible for any of us, to actually realize the true inner found Happinesses we every singular most One of us - keep longing for.

Before Proceeding Further – We'd Like To Introduce You To Our 2 Most Incredible Guiding Forth - Constant Inner Wisdom Seeking Characters! Every One's Innermost Truly Magical Found - 'COSMIC CHARLIE' or 'QUANTUM KATIE' – WITHIN

Whom we the authors have invented, as our means to help reveal what amounts to our already existing innermost Wise-dome place = such as is to be found With-In. And thus Who already reside within the very core of each and every one of us. In other words both quantum Katie, or cosmic Charlie, depending on your particular gender. Are meant to represent the very best of whomsoever each of us in our inner most core, might truly most love to grow ourselves all up, into being. If we were to no-longer hold any fear or self doubt inside of us. As such they represent that truly magical inner wisdom child we all have within us, fully now able to grow all up into that magical most true miracle generative enabled adult, we all long to be. Please note, we have designed our illustrated characters to be somewhat androgynous as well as racially diverse, so that you may see them as you your self. From within your own, inner child like imagery based, sense of much larger than normal in fact cosmic level found, total belly laugh place of innermost divinely connected humor?

In other words, see each of them as that most full of zip, zap, zest, & zing awake & alive, truly brilliant manifest our very best intentions great solution generative enabled, totally heart caring in our flow zone way capable. Far out here way edgy magical, yet fully grown all up totally present adult royal Hu-Man/Woman Being-Nesses, that we all have within us. Whom we have all had encounters with from time to time. Yet whom most of us just don't know how to bring to the forefront of just who it is we really might most want to be, all the time. And thus quite simply, keep longing to come to the surface of our very Essences - way more often.

In this huge respect, picture them as that very sort of feeling & emotional way more in your flow zone attuned person - within you. Who has had glimpses of being so full of 'life' awake, so totally on attuned brilliant within the present moment. That you have at times found yourself able to actually be in exactly the right place at the right time; choose precisely the best course of action in the best possible moment; perform at your very most excellent totally in your flow zone potential; attract those most profound circumstances most likely to help you move brilliantly forward with whatever intention set projects, you may be choosing to be involved with bringing forth to fruition. All in such a way as for us to end up being in a place of the most profound, radiant found Joy-Ful-Ness, at least for a while.

Next let's go on from here to image our 2 innermost you characters, helping you to find your most 'real liberty found' truly free & thus actual whole brain lit up all at once completely open ended, actual supra rational logical creatively inspirational way. Of actually being ongoing enabled to keep on inventively generating, the very sort of positively great whole field embedded, and thus most holographic integral solutions. That are going to help you best bring into fruition, positively all of your inner most vey best dreamed for intentions.

Finally picture these characters who are really the essence of you, helping you to find your most well beyond ordinary transcendental, actual way larger than usual And therefore most effortlessly full of love caring empowered found vortex of pure super-lightness in being - we all have been gifted with within. In other words find that truly whole Being Conscious of One-Ness Essence place - we all have inside. Most likely to help every singular most One of us, including of course you your very own well beyond ordinary, in truth extraordinary Tap Your Source enabled sense of your most expanded possible Self. That we may each of Us now actually Know of that 'Everlasting True found Happiness Place'. Which is all about totally now Full Consciously Loving all that One's Life is all about - such as can only found Core Inside each and every One of Us.

Which is to say, your very own most sacred Quantum Katie & Cosmic Charlie within task - in the context of this self help book. Is going to be for this 2 characters whom you already have within you, to help guide each and every One of us into finding our very own sort of Some-One's - With-In. Who would now find ourselves fully able to keep improvising inventing our greatest possible senses of our Self's - constantly ever ongoing forward. In ways that are going to help us actually be enabled to actually Ful-Fill every single One, of our very best intended, dreams. If you would like to take workshops focused around helping you to more fully internalize essentially the same processes described in this book - Go to greatlifetechonolgies.com or his new site evolve.com, and register for one of Tom Stone's workshops either by him or by one of his certified trainers in your area, even order his 2 great self empowering books, Vaporize Your Anxiety, & The Power of How. Or go to trulyconscious.com, and check out the Aspen Decew's incredible self help workshops, including her dvd recorded self help lessons. Even invite one, or their certified trainers to come present. Certainly as I and many others already know, you will end up being truly grateful!

Warning – Please Proceed with Extreme Caution

How can we ever even expect to find our King-Dome of Heaven within, unless we begin to agree to take some day each day to keep journeying - inwards? Given this, inasmuch as all references to our inner most core awake, natural high elevated truly most consciousness spaces, can only be conveyed meta-phorically or para-bolically. In the greater sense of supporting every One of us to actually clear our way into being as truly full of 'Life' and at the same time totally Liberty' free, in the sort of direction that can enable us to be as 'True Happiness' found - as we possibly can. Please understand that we have simply done our best through a combination of both written text and creative imagery. To point toward ways you can keep growing your greater sense of self, ever on and up. Into what is going to amount to your ever more ongoing - flow zone of At-One-Ment. As to just why we must be willing to take a certain pilgrimage or journey of awareness - in order to find our inner most flow zone fulfillment enabled Wise-King-Dome of Heaven within? This can never to our mere human satisfaction - ever be fully explained. Nevertheless, lest we continue to live at least half our lives or more, as if condemned to living in the pits of a seemingly endless - caught in various degrees of pain & suffering - personal hell! The necessity of us being willing to take such a journey appears to be a what's so, with respect to our possibility to live our lives most optimally forward toward the actually realization of all the fulfillments we could ever long. In the context of this under-standing, what is therefore going to help you the most! Is for you to agree to both look into and then keep awareness practicing what each self teaching metaphor - is pointing toward within you. In such a way as to let each metaphorically guided lesson permeate and percolate all it's way into the well beyond ordinary - inner most Soul/Spirit essence. Of who you have most exquisitely been designed /evolved within the very core of you - to way more Joy-Fully than you ever dreamed possible - be.

(Special Note - To the extent you may want to try & 'think' your way through Dr. Sereda's various books, you may find his writing style challenging. On the other hand to the degree you can just allow his words to keep flowing through you, in such a way as to just let them keep compounding into the development of ever greater levels of helpful In-Sight - within the very core of you. You will most probably end up totally Loving what he helps to reveal, in relation to your very own possibility to find your greatest possible - Hu-Man most potentials.)

Chapter 1

To Begin: Let's Re-Kindle Some of Our Most Precious Early Memories - To Help Re-Set Our True Innermost Wisdom Oriented - How To Have A Positively Great Life - Stage

To help you get your very own journey started, in relation to your much greater Tap Your Source way more SELF EMPOWERING - potentials. Such as you will find offered by our 2 most Inwardly You Orienting, guiding forth characters - 'Quantum Katie & Cosmic Charlie'. Picture yourself as a very young Cosmic Charlie, or for that matter Quantum Katie, retreating into your dreams each night. Wherein you would create the most wonderful pictures with respect to how much you loved being a human born child. You see, for most of us, our earliest dream years were truly magical. Constantly giving us glimpses of what it might be like, to live right inside the very pot of gold. Said to exist within an endless rainbow of everywhere all around us - truly bless-ed Garden of De-Lights. But more than this we would also dream about how much we longed to some day become as fully grown up unto ourselves - Adults. Now truly most One-Der-Fully Awake - to this Underlying / Beyond Lying Super most Light Source - we could sense to be at the very Core Root - of All Things.

Fortunately for us in our so dreaming, we ended up setting the stage for receiving some of the most fantastic, modern guiding light, wise-dome teachings. Any growing all up One of us, could ever hope for. In the huge sense that, what our inner most Quantum Katie's & Cosmic Charlie's within. Are ready to discover about our selves, in terms of realizing each of our most full-on potentials. Involves internalizing various levels of inner wisdom that we all already actually know about. Based very much on memories of those earliest Awarenesses, we are about to outline in this introductory chapter. It's just that within the context of our everyday living, and everyday teaching. It's like we keep having been taught to ignore and keep forgetting about, what our deeper innermost essence already knows. So, let's follow this how to have a positively great life oriented journey toward unveiling what we already know, within our inner most selves. As we point each of our very own unique selves in the direction of becoming as the most Effortlessly - now actual full-on Radiant All Lit Up Empowered - completely independent Whirling Vortices of this nevertheless Same Singular most endless Non Locally at a Distance - to Infinity & Beyond Inter-Connected possibility to Tap that One Super Light Source. Which can be sensed by all of us to be at the very root of all creatures - indeed all things great & small.

For example: in our earliest years, many of us would dream about ourselves out of body spirit flying over our favorite backyard garden, somewhere out behind our own house, pretty much every night. Wherein we could sense how each unique plant out there, each bird, each frog, each lizard, even our favorite pet. Would have it's own unique harmonic life song vibration, that it would love to keep on singing all through the night, indeed all through it's very life. As well as its own rainbow of colors, that it would radiate all around itself every moment of it's existence. As if to say, "Oh please won't you love me most beautiful <u>human</u> creature - made of the very same underlying/beyond lying, rainbow Source of true De-Light. Out of which everything we used to once See, including our self, appeared to be so made. In the huge sense of our own potential to be of Joy-Ful service, toward the manifestation of all that happiness we can feel. Every time we might 'truly get' just how much we in our own particular uniquenesses, love to be Loving toward every Source made every other thing - we ever experience out there or in here in the context of living our lives ever forth."

Even beyond this, sometimes even during our daytime when we would feel especially blessed. We would find ourselves be able to jump outside of our so called normal sense of our self... into our great overseeing well beyond ordinary, way Bigger flying spirit body sense of our Self. Wherefrom our lofty, pure spirit soaring perch, we might find our Self's looking over all the various rainbows we could see. For as far as we could see! Wherein our truly Big Picture much greater Wise-Dome of Awareness sense, such flights into our pure soaring spirit body. Would help us to much better realize, that who we our greater soaring beyond body spirit really must be. Is Some-One so much larger, than the mere limiting dream we would usually be encouraged to dream, when we were regular daytime so called normal not so large spirit, awake. In fact the awareness of this huge sense of self was so well beyond ordinary profound. We all of us hoped that we would never forget this vision of our much larger sense of our truly magical, most One-Drously free and unbound - Out of Body - Beyond Body much Bigger sense of our Self.

Illustrative Image # 1 – Our Inner Child Within - Once Having Spirit Soared over our very own Most Memorable - Truly special Garden of Here & Now Fully Aware - De-Lights

A vision of our selves as very young, nevertheless also potentially fully adult Cosmic Charlie's or Quantum Katie's - within. Having had early life out of body experiences, wherein we were once were able to sense our spirit body selves, clear out of body able to now soar in relation to our ability to over see certain garden of delight areas. In such a way as to in this way actually experience the positively magical, pure energy radiant quality of a rock, a tree, a frog, a bird, a flower and even a dog. All singing their particular vibrant pure spirit energy songs of happiness, from within their very own unique, nevertheless same quantum Source connected, core essences! In the much larger sense that to extent we at times, become way greater than usual, actually peak experience lit up pure energy aware - at times in our in later life's. Such that we may even have ended up finding ourselves blessed with glimpses of this same magical level of overseeing awareness, we once were most blessed to experience in our earliest years. But which far too many of us, have long since chosen to completely forget!

So Let's Start by Acknowledging that it is going to take a certain 'seek & ye shall find' subtle most effort of our awareness - to help us regain that king-dome of heaven state - which is of our now most inwardly amazing all lit up - spine tingling sensed within - true found 'grace'

In the Greater Sense of our now agreeing to fully engage in Our very own ever more quantum jumping mouse attuning journey - toward re-uniting with the more unlimited To Infinity & Beyond hum sound energy - of our 'one & only true singular most 'Source'

1

Here's an even more Joy-Ful example of what amounts to, every single One of Us'es very favorite early life dream! Which is to say, what we all loved most in our early years, was when we would be so cuddled in our mother's or father's arms. And they would rock us so sweetly while they sang their own inner felt love hum song lullaby, with such tender loving care to us. It would be like we would melt into that most special place, wherein it would seem like there was only but - 'One' huge singular heart beating. Such that once snuggled into this place, we would feel so safe, we would know we could now fall asleep each night. Into our own particular dreamland... as if in the arms of love itself. Almost as though this love place, was way bigger than mom or dad's love - in It-self. Actually it was such a great feeling that whenever we would fall asleep in this way. The moment we would awake next day, we would now grounded now deep inside our very heart core - most fully alive sense of ourselves. Could now safely jump in and play, just exactly whatever it might be we would most love to play, for the whole rest of our next day. For in truth, based on this great feeling, our great big hope truly was, that the living out of our lives could always be very much like this.

And indeed later in life when in having the utmost fun, with our very best of friends, we would sometimes find ourselves as if so here and now presently grounded. The moment some One of us would point to the true evident reality of any such moment, we would start to roar from within our very core with such a profound sense of laughter. It would for a while be, as though there would be the sound of Only One Belly Laughing. Even sometimes in the context of a particularly great Magical performance, only the sound of One Hand Clapping. Out of our utmost respect and gratitude for the sheer genius we may have been most blessed, to have just Witnessed.

Illustrative Image # 2 – Our historical Experiences of only 'One' Heart Beating Here - Or even of only 'One' Belly Laughing

Most of us as Quantum Katie's & Cosmic Charlie's have also had early childhood memories. Of having been so loved in certain moments of our lives, by either one or both of our parents. We have felt our heart's melt into a place wherein we were actually able to experience the pure Loving-Ness Presence - of only 'One Singular' - no-longer in separation - 'Heart Beating' - Heare? A special qualitative greater awareness attunement, many of us have had the good fortune to in later life re-experience. Like for example within the afterglow of our very best adult peak love making moments. As well as when we have cracked up totally with the very best of our friends - into suddenly being able to sense the place of Only One Belly Roaring! Even when we have been to some truly spectacular performance in some area of human endeavor! Only to find every one of us simultaneously / synchronistically seemingly endlessly clapping - to show our utmost respect! As though there might be only One Hand moving us, to keep on expressing our most profound heartfelt appreciation for such an inspired performance! It is then, precisely these early childhood and later life experiences, which help us set the stage for growing ourselves all up into ever better under-standing the most profound place of - true At-One-Ment found Wisdom.

2

MOST ONE-DER-FUL MEMORIES THEREFORE
OF ONLY ONE HEART BEATING - AS WELL
PERHAPS ONLY 'ONE' MOST DE-LIGHT-FUL
BELLY LAUGHING - WHENEVER ALL HERE

(Starting Out By Way of Introducing Our First 3 Lesson Set of Greater Wise-Dome of Awareness Oriented Methods - Designed To Help Fully Enliven The Way More Optimally On And Up Feeling & Emotional And Thus Truly Full of 'Life Energy' Side - Of Our Greatest Possible Whole Nervous System Integrated - Capabilities)

Chapter 2

Lesson # 1 – Agreeing To Constantly Come Back Fully Embodied All Home Inside & Thus Optimally Grounded Present - Within Our Very Own Innermost Here & Now Present - Sense of Our Selves

First, let's examine the underlying Rationale for Have A Great Life Lesson - # 1

Please note as we proceed with each chapter, we will do our level best to explain the modern scientific basis for each successive most sacred, grow your self ever up, great life LESSON that follows. By way of attempting to provide you with a basic brief outline in relation to the hugely sensible... modern knowledge based rationale. Which can be under-stood to underlie each lesson we provide.

We know for example from early childhood studies, that children can go inward to describe what it feels like for them to be fully present inside, pretty much any area of their bodies. We also know from studies of our most self actualized, very happiest & most joyful... older citizen's. Who still sparkle with a sense of truly life affirmative... zip, zap, zest & zing - life radiant energy. That one of the most distinguishing features of such more self realized, or, more fully whole being actualized people, is that they seem able to live much more here & now present, inside the whole of their bodies. We refer to this phenomenon in terms of their having found a way, to be optimally embodied within them selves. Which is to say, optimally here and now Grounded within the full-on Open-Ness of all aspects of their very own Whole Being Present - Nervous Systems. This embodiment within our own nervous system ends up in other words, being one of our most important core foundational qualities - which enables us to create a truly Ful-Filling life for ourselves.

On the other hand, we also know that the vast majority of us seem to keep losing this sense of our inner most sense of inner found light-ness in being. To the point where we become overly vulnerable to having periods of extreme blues, even at times way dark nights of the soul. Such that by the time we reach the age of retirement, many of us have not only lost our vital sparkle. But also our very ability to sense that everything is made of the very same Super Lightness in Being - we once all came in here with an ability to clearly sense.

Image # 3 – Acknowledging That We At Times - Experience Our Self's Falling So Down - We feel as if Totally Lost in a place of such Darkness - We sense very little of De-Much-Greater-Light

Image of Our Selves as young growing ever more up Quantum Katie's or Cosmic Charlie's, noticing that we at times. Tend to keep falling from the grace of this light. This has everything to do with us pretty much inevitably having suffered various forms & degrees of pre-verbal - fear based primal trauma. The very sort of trauma's which tend to keep compelling us, toward shutting our vital energetic sense of ourselves ever more down. From being fully inwardly light spirit present, in touch with the more pure radiant lit up alive aspect of innermost feeling and emotional nature. The result of this energy losing process, is that we tend to ever more keep dampening our sense of vitality more & more down, as our year go by. To such unfortunate degrees we tend to keep descending into ever more compounding and complicated lost spirit pain body suffering states. Such that by the time many of us reach adulthood, more and more of our very sense of ourselves, begin to feel as if cut off from not only the awareness of our very own inner light. But also from the very same Light Source which resides within all other sentient beings. To where what we now experience, is an inner presence that is way too so lost. We at certain critical times -experience ourselves living within a state of exaggerated inner darkness, even having huge dark night's of the soul. Which at the worst of times, can build into such intensively felt negative states, we quite virtually begin to feel as though we are living - as if condemned to our own private hell. In such an intensively felt way, that we begin to perpetrate all manner of bad behaviors.

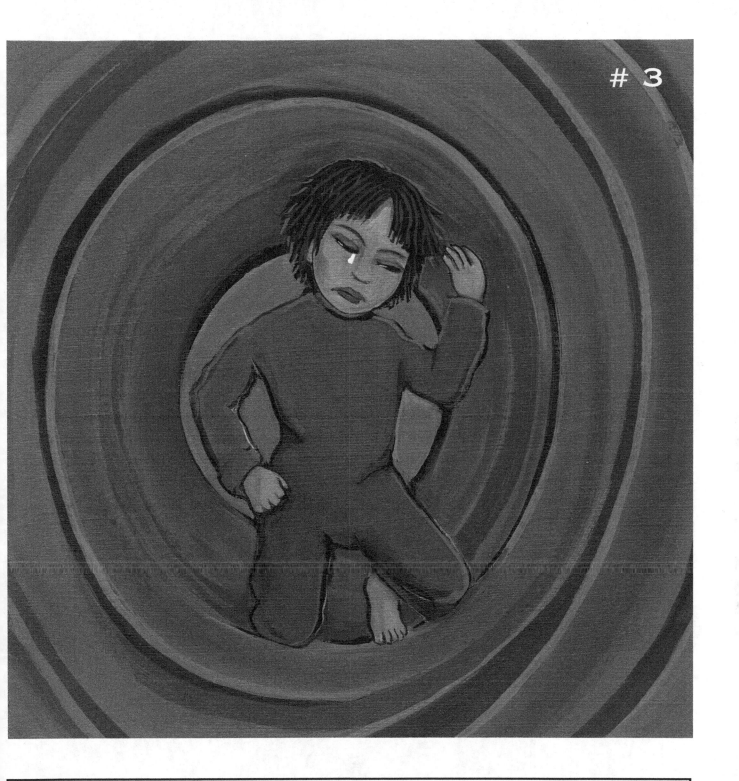

3

OUR PRETTY MUCH INEVITABLE **TENDENCY** TO KEEP FALLING FROM THE GREATER GRACE - OF OUR HIGHER <u>HU</u>-MAN/WOMAN POSSIBILITY TO KEEP LIVING MOSTLY IN - DE-LIGHT

In this greater sense the whole point at this first level of awareness guidance. Is going to be to help your adult within, come into a place of under-standing. Or, being able to so stand... so within... the everywhere here and now presence... of the whole of your very own right now... sensing and feeling body. You will thus begin to realize, that it is exactly by way learning to be everywhere inside open to your own energy sensitive bio system - within your self. Which is in turn, precisely what going to best enable you to stay in intimate everywhere all around you, now holographic connection with the world on the outside of your self. In terms of whatever areas of interest you may be involved in experiencing, and thus choosing to play your self forward within - this very moment.

Most fortunately for all of us, our greater reality is the moment we truly get this! The more aware we will become of just how it is, that the practice of certain ancient body opening techniques, in conjunction with say yoga, stretch, or various martial art katas, or even sufi body movement exercises. Along with ever more aware deep whole body present inside our rhythmic inhalative / exhalative ongoing process of breathing. Have been designed / evolved to help su to sense and grow this feeling of energy awake aliveness and thus pure lightness in being, within our sense of our self's, to our positive max. Is there really anyone of us out there/here, who wouldn't love to learn how to grow this feeling of aliveness, to the point of being able to sense full-on de-light inside ourselves, every moment of our existence here?

Now For Quantum Katie & Cosmic Charlie's First - How To Begin Orienting Toward Greater Wisdom - Lesson # 1

SUPPORTING OUR MUCH GREATER POSSIBILITY - TO ACTUALLY BE MOST OPTIMALLY INSIDE EMBODIED & THEREFORE AS HERE & NOW PRESENT - AS YES WE-CAN POSSIBLY BE

OUR INITIATING INNER KEY THEREFORE - TOWARD US BEING WILLING TO START RE-CLAIMING OUR MOST WELL BEYOND ORDINARY - SOUL FEELING BASED WAY GREATER SPIRIT SHINNING - LIGHT

One day as he/she was growing more up - young Charlie/Katie's inner wisdom awareness - noticed! The more he/she might wake up into each newly arriving day. In such a way as to experience him/her self being everywhere more present inside, this truly most beautiful very body temple, which he/she always everyday found him/her self living within in, every single moment of his/her life. The more he/she would find his/her body become so fully awake alive as a consequence of such natural clearly inside him/her self attuned awareness. He/she could now begin each way more fully here and now grounded - special most day way better able to radiate as his/her very own magical lamp of light. Exactly as he/she remembered sensing various other being-nesses do, in his/her earliest spirit soaring aware dream states.

Such that, in beginning to start helping him/her self really re-gain this quality of being more fully present inside of him/her, which was once so natural to him/her Self. He/She began to practice remembering to be as fully embodied as possible right inside every part of the truly incredible, indeed most One-Der-Fully unique, most precious completely whole body energetically alive, truly sacred bio-system. He/She had found him/her self gifted with, ever since having arrived here on this most magical planet earth. By way of making an agreement to at least once a day, in each unfolding moment for a certain limited period of time, say 12-20 minutes. Keep better sensing his/her own greater awareness principle, becoming more fully grounded present inside of ever bit of him/her self - every right now - centered around his/her process of breathing. As a positively great means to both help him/her self come back more home, inside of him/her self. As well as a great means to practice becoming optimally self healing relaxed with just being here way more fully present, for no reason at all.

Key Supportive Image # 4 – So how about we Now Agree to help ourselves Arrive much more Inside our Bodies - With each exhaling breath in order to help turn our Inner most Glow Lights - Way more Back On & Shinning Up - Within Our Self's

In order to take advantage of what we all once knew when we first came into our most de-light-ful bodies here! Image you your self as a young Cosmic Charlie or Quantum Katie. Now being taught in conjunction with each exhaling breath, just how to keep encouraging the light of your inner here and now present gravity grounding - inner biology relaxing - Greater Awareness. To arrive exactly right inside of every byte millimeter area of your hands, feet & skull! In such a way that you at the same time now notice any small sensations of energy buzzing, whirling, dancing in various places inside your hands, feet, and skull, with each exhaling gravity grounding breath you take. Then from here once you get a sense of being more truly present inside the most distal parts of your body. Notice just how you can progressively support your self to slowly extend the light of your awareness, kind of like an ever growing warm fluid entering into the next progressive areas of your body. First by way of streaming this inner awareness from you feeup your legs into your pelvis, then from your hand up your arms into your shoulder sockets, finally from you face and skull down your throat unto your upper spine, between your should blades. All the while continuing to sense what it feels like to encourage a whole cacophony of buzzing, whirling, sensations, to keep growing, inside of each of these parts of you all at once, every moment you can. To such an aliveness felt degree, you can now extend this warm fluid like awareness to now flow all the way into your very core, belly and chest, even right into your whole spine. Insofar as you keep relaxing deeply inside of your self with each exhaling breath. While you at the same time keep grounding all your growing body of sensations to the gravity core of mother earth. In such a way that you discover just how you can now experience your whole body starting to enter into a place, that is now inwardly ever more both deeply earth grounded, while at the same time way more inwardly sensational alive present. With all internal bodily functions becoming ever more harmonically all together totally relaxed - hypo metabolically slowed down. In terms of you being way more present whole being integrated inside of your here and now sense of your self.

(**Accompanying Explanatory Note** - Research into young children's capacity to enter inside of their bodies has shown, that they usually have no problem entering into pretty much any area of their bodies, with the light of their pure inward sensing - awareness principle. So why not you?)

EVERY EXHALATION - NOW RELAXING INWARD TO HELP OUR GREATER SENSE OF SELF - TO THUS KEEP ON ARRIVING EVER MORE AWARE PRESENT - INSIDE OF US

Key Supportive Image # 5 – Now it's time for Greater Lighting ourselves Everywhere All Up - From our very Core insides All Out - With each expansive inhaling breath

Once you begin to get a sense of how to be more present inside of your self with each relaxing exhaling breath. Image your self as a young Cosmic Charlie or Quantum Katie - now being taught in conjunction with each inhaling breath. Just how to expand the ever growing light of your very own body relaxing, here and now present grounded, greater awareness. Exactly right inside of every byte area of your core body spine, belly & chest! Such that once well established in your core, now notice just how you can agree to progressively support your self to slowly extend the light of your awareness bit x bit - out into your limbs and up into your throat, right back into your hands, feet, & face skull. In such a way that you thus discover just how you may with each inhaling breath, experience your whole body all at once. Be in a place that is now inwardly ever more present, buzzing lit up inside with a greater sense of your life force. As the means to guide your self into a ever more deeply earth grounded - way rest-ful state. Wherein your internal body functions get so hypo metabolic slowed way down, you start to find your self going into a deeply here and now grounded present - totally organ integrated harmonic - way hibernative like self healing state - of whole body deep relaxation. In such a way that this ends up becoming a huge qualitative means at your disposal, to help your whole sense of self to best heal, from all kinds of stress based forms - of psychosomatic illness. In such a way that after 12-20 minutes of such practice you begin to sense your self now totally refreshed, rested.

(Accompanying Explanatory Note – Inasmuch we agree to take the time to learn this deeply relaxative, hibernative like internal organ slowed down state. Scientific research shows there may be no better way to help our selves stay optimally healthy and vital. It has even been said in this respect, that we can learn to slow ourselves so barely breathing down inside, we can learn to capture the equivalent of 2-3 hours sleep in 12-20 minutes. Certainly it has been shown that when athletes develop this ability, their muscles recuperate far more quickly, than so called normal. In such a way as to enable better performance the next day. Which is exactly why it important to take advantage of this ability we all have. By way of guiding our young children from as early an age as possible, into discovering just how they can re-gain their ability to be fully present embodied. With the light of their awareness, shinning in every part of their bodies, all at once.)

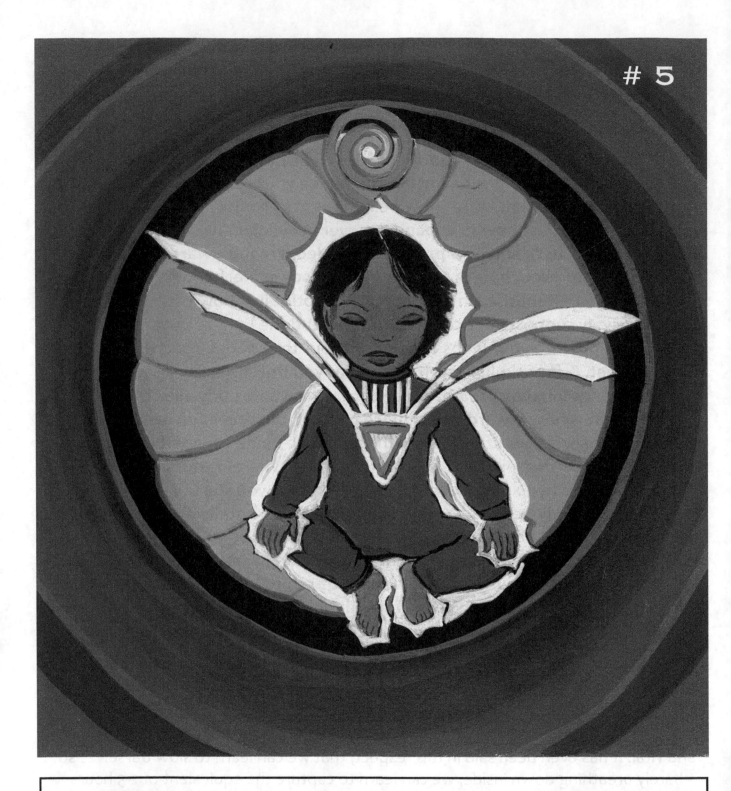

EVERY INHALATION - TO HELP EXPAND OUR POSSIBILITY TO BE EVER MORE INWARDLY PRESENT WITH LIFE SPIRIT - NOW ENABLED TO EVER MORE FULLY GLOW ALL AROUND US

Supportive Image # 6 – In order that we may in this way help Make - Our Inner Most Singular Unified WHOLE BEING I - Wake Up In Such A Way - As To Now Way More Continuously Glow

From here, image of your self as a now ever growing all up Cosmic Charlie or Quantum Katie, continuing to support your greater sense of your more spirit light awake self. Starting to really get it, that you actually can learn to live in a way, which is ever more totally light of awareness grounded centered present - within every part of your now more whole lit up filled with grace - most precious given body temple - all at once. Very much as a consequence of day by day practicing this ever more inwardly present, while at the same time deeply relaxative self embodiment way of bringing your self - more and more home inside your self. Over and over again, often in conjunction with some form of physical exercise, like yoga, or tai chi, or even various forms of dance exercise. Until such time as it becomes easier and easier for you by way of this using breath awareness technique, to be more and more grounded inside your whole body. And thus for you to be inside the sensation of this pure energy coming more and more alive within the whole of every part of your being - with each successive body grounding - expanding ever more inside inhalation and relaxing ever more inside exhalation. In the context of each and every ongoing inhaling and exhaling, ordinary day to day breath, you now take.

(**Accompanying Explanatory Note** – The great news is that we all came in here with this ability to be breath grounded present, everywhere within our whole bodies, all at once. In this respect it is said that babies breathe all the way out into their very toes, their finger tips, the very tips of their skull, and even to the tip of their very own nose. Which enables them to laugh or cry non-separatively with every part of their very beings, knees, elbows, both cheeks, and even their very backside bottom end flows, all at same time. In other words we already have an early life imprint, of what it is like to be fully present everywhere inside of ourselves, and thus have an internal image of what it is like to deeply embedded embodied everywhere inter-connected all at once - fully present within ourselves. Based on this old knowing, it is therefore just a question of helping ourselves to remember what it is like to be wholly light of awareness embodied present, once again. Now however as the growing ever more up, way more brilliant shinning, fully whole embodied Joy-Ful found Adult beings, we have been most exquisitely designed / evolved - to be.)

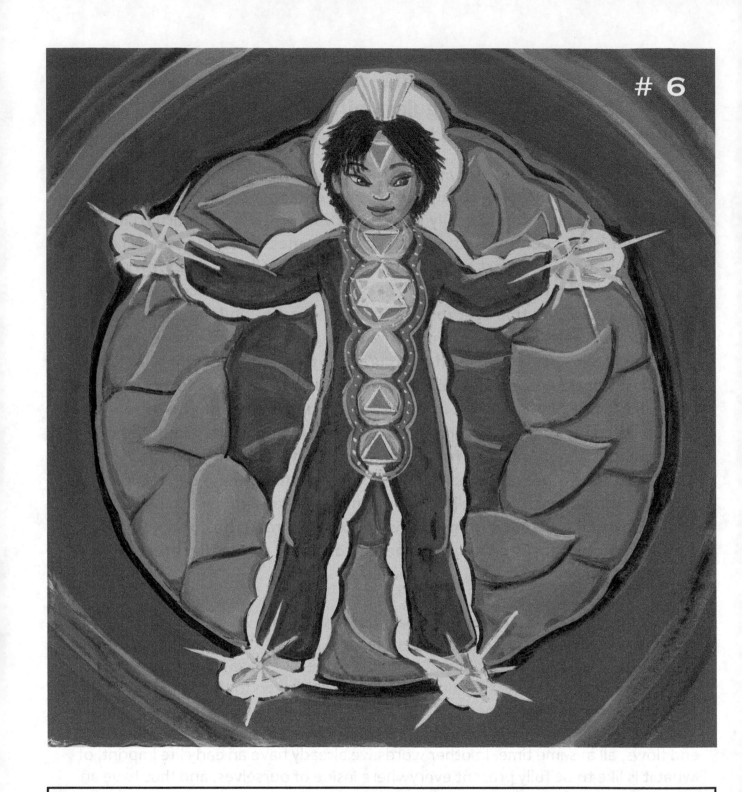

6

WOW LOOK AT YOU - HELPING YOUR VERY OWN NOW EVER MORE TRULY CORE PRESENT LIGHT - START TO WAY MORE FULLY SHINE

Fortunately, for our ever more inwardly growing up characters, this was something Katie or Charlie began to choose to support inside their very own senses of their self, from this moment on. By way of learning some stretch, while breathing in & out into One's whole body, supportive postures. As a great means to help ground them/our selves more inside of their/our bodies, on a regular basis. (And which people in other parts of the world would also support themselves to learn, by way of internalizing various yoga postures, including the practice of making a salutation to the sun each morning. As wells as the practice of various martial art kata's, including the related practice of dragon breathing, even other forms of celebrative dance & breathing, including by way of sufi breath opening movement, and various other forms of absorbing the energy of the sun - exercises. In order to help them/our selves start each day, in this more embodied present way.)

(Please note – For the sake of simplicity from this point on, we will now refer to our 2 characters mostly in the masculine Cosmic Charlie gender. As a female, all you have to do is substitute Quantum Katie as you read forward. Which is exactly why some of our images are made showing the male gender, and some the female, with many somewhat ambiguous.)

Hence before long, thanks to this kind of regular practice which would focus on Charlie remembering to be totally breath grounded present inside, within this more embodied sense of himself. Charlie began to feel more and more alive each day! To the point where this play himself forward way of being more present inside of himself, in relation to each new day. Was beginning to be just as rainbow magical as his earliest remembered nighttime dream life - used to be. So magical that he began to experience his purest most aware sense of him self, getting not only lighter and lighter shining radiant, in the context of him just being himself each day. Much as though his more singular integrated sense of his 'I-Am within', was now being as if filled with light. But also very much as consequence of this process of inward embodiment, finding himself being way more attuned to the magical pure energy glow world all around him, within which he lived. So much so he began to increasingly One-Der, is this how our sense of being 'alive', is really supposed to be for us?

To which his very own inner wisdom self replied, Yes, "Charlie my boy or for that matter Katie my girly girl! Now you are really starting to get it right, cause it goes something like this! This very body you find your self always living within, is the only permanent always home, you will ever 'live in' for the rest of your life. What's more, the more you learn to live right inside of this very body, your most permanent home. In such a way as to make thine inner awareness 'I', single or fully present integrated unitary present, within the whole of your self. The more and more comfortable with living within the positively huge energy generating system you are,

30

you will now find your self becoming. And thus the more you are going to as a now, way more 'lit all up' awake being, find your self able to keep on generating all the energy you require. To help invent your self ever forward, into this most One-Der-Ful, singular most super light filled world. Such as you now will keep finding, exists within everything you ever experience all around you, particularly in relation to your very best dreamed for... play your self ever forward... set intentions. Whatever intention set dreams, you' your self may keep choosing to keep putting in front of yourself. For in truth, what this very body your most core permanent home, appears to be all about. Is to help you be as a field of quantum super light attuned radiant presence, unto your self. Insofar as this the best means you have to help invent the truly great life, you may find your self most longing for. In other words 'Life' itself it can be said, appears to be all about one huge infinite ocean of energy. And your very own innermost attuned & thus empowered ability to invent your self ever more brilliantly forward. Within the context of all the energy & super light brilliance - you can support your self to experience - in relation to this giant One & Only super light field."

(Further Note – In order to help you fully internalize this process of re-awakening your internal present luminescence super lightness in being - within. You may want to listen to Dr. Sereda's - Basic Body Grounding Intro to the Self Healing State - free you tube video Here. Wherein he encourages you to learn how to park your whole body into a Deeper than Sleep - Total Hibernative like State. Of fully here and now Grounded Embodied Present - Way Whole Brain Awake alpha enhancing & Thus Profoundly Self Healing Presence. Complete with an accompanying ever slowing down drumbeat in the background, to help simulate your very own ever more relaxing - heartbeat. As well as an accompanying video to help you way more fully under-stand the huge sense of such regular daily practice.)

(Special Note – Beyond this, we have created a special prayer unto One's self. To help grow the very essence of just who we all really most are within our self - to the max! What follows therefore, is our first such prayer to be re-read occasionally until fully internalized - into One's greater sense of self!)

First Life Energy Enhancing Prayer Unto One's Self - Choosing to Be Full of 'Vital Life Force Energy'.

"Which to say, deeply embodied with that great Mysterious inner I-Am who resides within the very innermost essence of me. Resides some-one who now way more constantly chooses to live within each moment of my existence. Totally present inside of every aspect of this ultimate home here my body, all at once. Such that the more I begin to sense every part of me, more and more able to function in a state of optimal all at once... full of vital life force harmonic attunement... within every part of me. Now the whole of me, cannot help but radiate my own presence as a field of light, my very birthright. Fortunately for me, my greater reality appears to be that, the Who-Am, that I-Really-Am within me, is no-thing other, than a whole body hologram. The very sort of hologram, that lives inside an ever larger series of to infinity and beyond holograms, which exist all around me. Such that the more I learn to appreciate being able to live fully alive inside the most incredible energy generative hologram, that I-My-Self-Am. The even better news is that, the more attuned to the presence of every other holographic thing, which comes into existence within this huge field of existence all around me, I thus support my self to become. The more this helps me to be optimally aware of how I may best choose to move and play forth my own personal presence! Within that world of never ending presents, which keep arriving into my existence all around me, within what amounts to my very own whole field, of purest here and now Present Awareness! That most precious great Wise-Dome gift, which I will more and more come to appreciate, insofar as these have a positively great lessons keep unfolding for me, within the very core of me."

Chapter 3

Lesson # 2 – Now For Diving Totally Core Energy Inside Every Emotion - As Our Best Way To Light Up Our Vital Energetic 'Radiance' - Even More

The Underlying Rationale for Have A Great Life Lesson - # 2

Beyond taking some time to help ground OUR awareness way more INSIDE, what amounts to our very own whole inter-connected unique human bio-system, all at once. When it comes to the next level of our possibility to be even more inwardly present, within the very core of what amounts to our most incredible consciousness oriented - whole being awareness mobilized - nervous system. We now know as we have already pointed to in our just prior lesson, that the many Autonomic Nervous System or ANS connected organ complexes inside us, are actually designed/evolved to help each of us generate all the vital energy we require. To help us keep on inventing for ourselves, the positively great ful-filling lives we each of us keep longing for. In other words, inasmuch as it is precisely the inevitable generation of these various organ based vital energies inside of us, that keeps creating the experience of us being able to keep putting these inner biological generated energies of ours, more fully into motion. Through the mobilization of the more CNS outer body musculature managing aspect - of our whole being mobilized nervous system. Then every way we may ever choose to put our vital energies in motion through the mobilization of our more CNS managed outer body musculature. Is inevitably going to result in us experiencing some sort inwardly felt constant 'emotional' feedback experience. In relation to just how we keep choosing to put our own energies in motion in our first place. With respect to every given here and now present moment of our ever ongoing - behavioral choice based existence.

Which is to say, within the context of this under-standing about the way our more ANS vital energetic generative and thus more e-motional side of our intelligence appears to be designed to work for us. Our huge human bottom line is, that it is really quite impossible for us to avoid having what are referred to as e-motions, or having our vital energies set in motion. Even if such feelings be related to us continually choosing to either try and keep avoiding having certain emotions, or to keep putting all of our emotions aside, as if to pretend too ourselves we are not really creatures of feeling. To such a degree we now start to experience ourselves as either: not feeling much of anything; or alternatively huge inwardly felt charges of pent up unresolved negative e-motion. With the result given we keep choosing to keep trying to put our e-emotional nature aside, in some more strictly cold evasive so called objective unemotional oriented way, only. Being that we will no longer have much positive emotional passion left to put behind whatever we may be choosing to do with our lives. In such a way that we are now going to keep ourselves going down into ever more negative states of our possible e-motional spectrum, more and more moments of our lives. Precisely because of the fear based tendency to keep ongoing avoiding this key vital energetic, or e-motional aspect of our nature.

In order to carry this knowledge as just how our inner organ based, vital energy generating, essentially emotional nervous system. Seems to have been most exquisitely designed / evolved - to help us fulfill an ever ascending hierarchy of inner longings - within ourselves. There are 2 very important aspects related to the operation of our vital energy generational system, it becomes most important for all of us too much better under-stand. First, we now know within the context of modern E-Motional nervous system based knowledge, that our hierarchy of various ANS plexus Organ-Izing sites in our bodies. Starting from the base of our spine - up - appear operate within us. In such a way as to help vital energetically motivate us, toward our innate potential to keep inventing various levels of fulfillment for ourselves. Exactly in relation to how each of these unique core plexi Organ-Ized vital energetic potentials, we all have inside of each and every One of us. Tend to create vital energy based - behavioral choice oriented fulfillment motivation inside of us - in our first place.

I.E. This hierarchy of built in vital energetic motivation, includes our ability to generate Ful-Fill-Ment in relation to all those E-Motions, or ANS aware ways of setting our own vital energies - In Motion. We tend to experience with all due respect to our attempts to seek: Sexual / Sensual Ful-Fillments - via the co-ordination all those Sacral Plexus vital energy generative organs - we have the possibility to regulate. Through the Wise-Choice-Use of all those ongoing embodied senses of Sexuality/Sensuality related E-Motions - we keep finding ourselves feeling; 2.) Doer / Entrepreneurial Ful-Fillments - via the co-ordination all those Lumbar lower Gut vital energy generative organs - we have the possibility to regulate. Through the Wise-Choice- Use of all those ongoing embodied senses of Doer/Entrepreneurial related E-Motions - we keep finding ourselves feeling; 3.) Great Friendships / Relationships Ful-Fillents - via al those vital energy generative organs - we have the possibility regulate. Through the Wise-Choice-Use of all those ongoing embodied senses of

Great Relationships related E-Motions - we keep finding ourselves feeling; 4.) Special Loving Caring involved feeling & emotional Ful-Fillments - via all those vital energy generative organs - we have the possibility to regulate. Through the Wise-Choice-Use of all those ongoing senses of Heart-Caring related E-Motions - we keep finding ourselves feeling; 5.) Way Articulative & Communicative able to effectively express ourselves Ful-Fillments - via all those eyes, ears, nose & throat vital energy generative organs - we have the possibility to regulate. Through the Wise-Choice-Use of all those Communications related E-Motions - we keep finding ourselves having; 6.) Truly amazing Intuitively Visionary most In-Sight-Fully able to see our way effectively forward Ful-Fillments - via all those various Mid Brain Plexi like structures most preciously designed / evolved to help us co-ordinate our overall hierarchy of both outwardly and upwardly oriented vital energies. In such a way as to support all our energies combined, being way more able to flow up our whole vital energetic generative hierarchy, through into our whole brain field. In the sort of directions, that are going to end up helping us light up our so called right brain lobes integrated within our left brain lobes, our frontal forebrain lobes integrated within our rear brain occipital lobes, in all directions all at once. Into states of now much more whole brain lit up & thus much bigger picture positively Brilliant way more Holographic Visionary, Solution Generative Capabilities. We all have the possibility to regulate through the Wise-Choice-Use of all those Wanting to See our way Effectively Forward related E-Motions - we keep finding ourselves having.

7.) & Finally that very kind of actual real experiential truly Spiritual / Reverent found Under-Standing based Ful-Fill-Ment we all long for. Via our ability to openly flow positively all of our vital energies all up - into all 4 hemispheres of our Now much more Wholly Integrated Brain Organ - all at once. In such a way that we begin to greater Wise-Dome of awareness actually realize, that positively everything we ever experience. Is always most intimately entangled within this Huge unlimited At-One-Ment Field - of pure pre-formed to Infinity & Beyond inter-connected / inter-twined Quantum Level Energy. To such a degree we now find ourselves able to inwardly bow our inner most Spirit in true Reverence to every aspect of this Great At-One-Ment Mystery - we all find ourselves most blessed to be living within. Inasmuch as this is all rational/logical justification excuses aside, the very best fully awake to the Great Mystery of One-Ness awareness place we all have within. To now help ourselves actually find ways to live in total whole being found & thus truly Joy-Filled Loving - Harmony. With all that this Great Singular most everywhere present great Mysterious At-One-Ment Field - has to offer. And which we all have the possibility to elevate our sense of ourselves into, through the Wise-Choice-Use of all those E-Motions we keep finding ourselves having.

Here's the thing, the moment we get this huge inner truth about the importance of the inevitable feeling & emotional nature of ourselves! This will be very the moment we will now see that it is simply impossible for us not to have feelings & emotions, with respect to our most essential vital energetic nature. What's more, this will be the same moment we will finally begin to see, that inasmuch as there is no human fulfillment we could ever long for. Which cannot be subsumed under at least '1' of these '7' vital energy areas - we all have within us. You could well now say, it is like at least half of our more full-on awake more whole being integrated intelligent - brain power. Seems to have been most exquisitely designed / evolved to help each of us develop, what we have just referred to as our possibility to realize various levels of more whole being oriented - 'inner emotional' fulfillment within each of our own unique senses of our self's. Particularly in the sense that it is exactly such inner Wake-Ful-Ness in relation to what amounts to this more emotional side of our nature, which seems to form the very basis for that most exquisite sense of vitality, we have the possibility to keep experiencing at ever more profound levels, throughout the whole course of our lives. Whenever we feel the most truly e-motional open to our ability to sense our own vital energy based 'life' force, or lack thereof. In such a way that can best enable us to fully mobilize those various aspects of our own inner energies in those very directions - most likely to lead us into ever higher hierarchical levels of fulfillment - within ourselves.

It is in other words our e-motions, which create the very tree of life power cord, vital energy juice we actually require. To best help ourselves feel as full of life force energy motivated within ourselves, as we possibly can. In order for us to go on and create all those levels of great life fulfillment for ourselves, we so much keep longing for. In relation to just what it is that these key vital energy generating sites, keep calling out to us from inside of ourselves - to find some way to fulfill for ourselves in our first place. As if to say "please inner most me, won't you listen to me enough to help me, find some way to ful-fill this or that inner organ based aspect - of me! Very much as a consequence of what these energies keep calling out for - from inside the very core organs of us - in our first place." This in turn implies, to extent we ignore emotional education, it is like choosing to leave half our intelligence behind. Particularly that part of ourselves which gives us the very inner most felt zip, zap zest, & zing vital energy juice, that has been designed / evolved within the unique human bio-energetic systems that we are. To help us manifest all the various inner emotional Ful-Fill-Ments, we keep longing for from within ourselves in our first place.

Here in the face of this understanding about our inevitable emotional & thus potentially full-on & up - vital energetic nature. Is the huge problem that we all of us face, particularly in relation to our ability to progress toward our potential to actually fulfill this whole hierarchical range of our own basic - inner most vital energetic and thus essentially e-motional callings. It becomes most important for each of us to finally get it, that in the face of all the respective emotional fulfillment longings we keep having. We actually have '2' main ANS based ways to help ourselves generate all the vital energy we require - to help us keep pursuing the whole range of fulfillments we seek. Or explained another way, we have '2' main emotional nervous system based ways, to help put ourselves in the sort of position most likely to enable us. To help ourselves keep manifesting the whole range of e-motional fulfillments, we all so inevitably keep longing for.

Way # 1.) First we have our old most primitive ANS based sympathetic side or hot energy way of generating vitality. Triggered mostly by fear and the immediate flushing of adrenalin plus other related hyper stimulants first into our primitive take immediate survival action oriented, pons & cerebellum. And then throughout the rest of our core plexus organized biology: 1.) In such a way that we instantly start zeroing all of our overall brain focus, including our visual focus, in on some immediate narrow band threat sensed problem. Insofar as we sense such complete immediate problem solving orientation, seems 'on pain of some real survival threat' to be required. 2). While we at the same time pretty much instantaneously start both rapidly speeding up, as well as contractively constricting, certain related key plexus organized organ sites - within our bodies. In a ways we perceive as being most related to certain given emotional fulfillment oriented organ complexes. we feel being most immediately threatened within our inner core. 3.) Such that what starts to happen inside of us, is that we instantly begin to constrictively hold this speeded up adrenalin motivated energy, inside of ourselves, within such perceived to be threatened or emotionally challenged, key organ sites within ourselves. 4.) To such a degree that this sympathetically motivated energy once set in motion, tends to very, very, quickly build, into the sort of huge inner flash balls of highly flared hot e-motion inside of us. 5.) Which in the face of some real survival threat emergency, are in turn actually designed to pretty much compulsively. Drive us very, very, quickly into taking immediate, 'so called fight or flight' survival oriented, completely instantly reactive - life saving action. Mostly in relation to some key core organ site aspect of our selves, which we in some way of another 'feel' to be seriously threat challenged.

Unfortunately for us to the extent we keep resorting to this more primitive side of our emotional energy generating system. As our main line means to try and keep helping our selves - keep generating all those emotion based vital energies. We not only require but also very much actually desire, to help ourselves find ways to actually fulfill ourselves. Particularly when we 'are not actually', I repeat 'not actually' being survival threatened in relation to any given one of these key fulfillment seeking areas, we all have within us. Our huge human problem is, that insofar we keep allowing such contractively inner held in essentially 'hot flare button balls' - of fear based compulsively over-reactive - emotional energy to persist. These unresolved flared up emotions, are very much what tend to result in us not only growing some aspect of our pain and suffering body. Especially with respect to those prior listed, '7' vital energy generating emotional areas, where we feel the most fearful. And therefore within which we start to feel the most persistently flare button reactive and therefore emotionally 'don't know how to fulfill this or that aspect of our self – vulnerable'. Our bottom line is that it is precisely this very sort of persistent specific organ contraction induced stress, associated with constant adrenalin motivation. Which is over time, what tends to keep breaking us down into various states of specific organ related dis-ease. Mostly within the most emotionally fear based vulnerable, won' somebody either help me or take the blame sympathy seeking vital energy generative areas inside our selves.

Even beyond this, insofar as adrenergic motivation is actually designed to help us very quickly build up a flare ball of energy inside of us. In such a way as to then compel us into taking some sort of immediate emergency, so called either 'fight or flee' survival oriented action. In the face of some powerful fear based - emotional response evoking situation. The inevitable result of this kind of relentless vital energy innervation, is that sooner or later seemingly endless resort this kind of emotional flare ball energy, is going to in more human terms. Compel us into taking what I refer to as a more habitual pattern, of either more 'hyper fighter macho tough' extrovertedly - constantly wanting to blame others for our feelings. Or alternatively to take a more habitual introverted 'fleer avoider wimp depressive' blame ourselves oriented stance, in such a way as to compel us to try and shut our own energy down. Which is to say, take the very sorts of over reactive types of e-motional based action, with respect to which we start feeling either more 'wimp depressively driven' to shut ourselves down, very much as a consequence of the prospect of loss of emotional control. Or with respect to which we may begin to feel more 'hyper fighter emotionally driven, to more overtly react outwardly towards others, in ways that are completely out of control'. Even when we are not actually feeling survival threatened, And the worst that would happen to us if we were to just relax, is that we would end up having some powerful, completely energy filled - e-motion.

Such that every time we allow ourselves to resort to either of these compulsively driven - 'hyper fighter' or 'wimp depressive, modes! In the face of what might very well amount to yes potentially powerful emotive, nevertheless actually non-survival threatening, situations! Our unfortunate bottom line is that we end up loosing our own vital energy. I.E. Every time we 'hyper fighter' blow out over react, in such a way as to try and blame some one else for howsoever we may be feeling. We not only tend to feel burned out, often for days and weeks afterwards. But we also are likely find ourselves feeling badly, in relation to the ways we just behaved badly. Not to mention the endless problems that keep arising for us, insofar as we keep setting up the conditions for more bad feelings to keep coming our way in our future, based on our bad 'hyper fighter' based behavior. Whereas whenever we resort to the more 'fleer avoider wimp depressive stance', what we keep doing is trying to shut our own feelings, and thus our very own vital energies, way down. By way of constantly self contractively making our own selves wrong, and thus beating ourselves down for whatever we might be feeling. To the point wherein what we keep taking ourselves bummer state - down into, is less and less vital energy being available inside of us. To help us orient more toward whatever respective emotional fulfillments we may be longing for. Not to mention the fact that every time we blame ourselves, we become more and more vulnerable to ever deeper rounds of strong emotion held way deep inside - depression. In such ways that either way, whether we habitually resort to the 'hyper fighter' or 'wimp depressive; mode, we keep setting up the very self sabotaging conditions for ourselves, To feel even more badly and less and less vital energetically alive - in our future. To an eventual point where what we over time begin to feel, is either way too hyper fighter burned out, or alternatively fleer avoider, wimp depressed stressed out of it, to feel enabled to move more forward toward whatever we really want. Besides our bottom line is, we tend to make our very worst decisions, every time we resort to either one of these way over reactive modes - of feeling compelled to behave badly.

Unfortunately, the energy mode most of us have been trained / conditioned to use. Is this sympathy seeking, 'I have been wronged and am therefore hurting' - most primitive fear based contractive and thus over reactive - survival oriented mode. Which we then feel is what gives us the rationalized justification, to keep on acting badly in relation to our fear based me, me, alone, most childlike sympathy seeking perspective. In fact so much so, that we begin to invent all kinds of endlessly streaming inside our heads, 'so called rational / logical' 'little mind based thought patterns'. To supposedly help us justify these essentially fear based means, to supposedly help us keep moving forward, no matter how badly we find ourselves behaving. This is so much so, that majority of our world population is actually addicted to this mostly adrenalin way of emoting, or alternatively the suppression of our mostly adrenergically innervated emotions. While we at the same time tend to keep letting our 'little narrow based mind' based rationalizations and justifications run rampant, pretty much completely out of control inside of us. To supposedly help us keep distracting ourselves, from whatever we might really be feeling inside the very core of us!

On the other hand, the positively great news for us all! Is that we all have an alternate far more long term e-motionally grown up - totally now solution oriented as opposed to problem focused only - ANS based Way - # 2. To help ourselves generate all the completely non-stressful, way more constantly ongoing streaming flowing - vital energy we require. In such a way that can much better big mind awake orient us toward the invention of the very kind of more holistic intelligent solutions.

Far more likely to help us to keep on moving our selves forward, in relation to whatever core being emotional fulfillments we may find ourselves longing for. Especially in the context of the vast majority of those everyday emotionally challenging situations, when we are not actually being survival threatened. And thus within which we able to create the sort of more emotionally open awareness inside, which can enable us to experience whatever we may be feeling. This alternate way then, has everything to do with our ANS or emotional nervous system ability, to effectively mobilize what is known as our para-sympathetic side. Or above us anymore feeling like we keep 'needing' to seek sympathy side - of our core body emotional and thus vital energy innervative - nervous system.

Fortunately for us, our para-sympathetic more adult solution oriented mode, which operates by way of us triggering the release of cholines, seratonins, meltonins & endorphins throughout our mid brain emotional regulating system. Which then in turn very quickly release related hormones within other plexus organ-ized sites throughout our body! Is able to kick in whenever we can stay grounded enough in our emotions, to actually allow ourselves to experience them, from within a place that is beyond or above fear. This shift into our more para-sympathetic mode ANS in turn, not only begins to enable our vital energies to be able to flow all up into all '4 hemispheres' of our neo cortex more all at once. But at the same time changes the way we now generate vital energy in the various core organ sites throughout our body.

In such a way that: 1.) First of our whole brains, begin to open light up into being able to process way more bits of information per moment. With the result that we start to experience ourselves being able to be way more present, with whatever we are feeling. 2.) While at the same time our internal organs especially focused around our heart & lungs, but also including our whole arterial system, pretty quickly start to slow down cool, and get much more soft and open - actually flowy. In such a way that these key organ sites along with our other vital energy generative areas, begin to pulsate in the sort of more relaxed rhythmic inter-co-ordinated with each other ways. Which are now much steadier, and more powerfully stronger. With the result that in the context of this more relaxed and open mode, all the key areas over the whole our bodies, are better able to receive a much steadier ongoing stream of now more fully oxygenated nutrient rich blood flow. 3.) To the point where this nutrient enriched while at the same time oxygenated blood flow in turn, now begins to help us generate by way of burning nutrients, a more ongoing steady stream of various plexi related - self empowering energies. In a way that make our vital energies now way more constantly available to us, over the course of much longer periods of time. 4.) On top of this, inasmuch as there is no longer any key organ constriction required to help us generate this more flowing type of energy, this alternate para-sympathetic mode ends up being totally stress free. With the important result, that we end up reducing the probability that we will develop some form of psycho-somatic based - core body debilitating illness - in relation to any sympathetically held in energies. While we at the same time, keep enabling our core organs to stay way more optimally healthy, & thus full-on vital energetically radiant supportive to us. In the sort of direction that keeps helping us, feel way more able to fulfill whatever goals we may be setting in front of ourselves over any longer run. In marked contrast to the inevitable vital energy loss, which tends to happen whenever we resort to our more sympathetic adrenalin mode.

5.) Beyond this, choline & endorphine innervated energy generation tends to broaden our field of vision rather than constrict it. In such a way that we start to shift our focus in the direction of looking for way more holistic solutions, rather than staying so stuck in narrow band problem focus. In relation to our being now much more enabled to become way more 'in our vital energetic flow zone' - actually whole brain lit up, optimally creatively inventive brilliant. With respect to what are now going to amount to our much more whole being oriented - fulfillment goals. 6.) Such that, whenever we find our vital energetics more optimally flowing - within this way more whole brain lit up 'zoned in way of being'. Many people report the experience of time slowing down, much as though one has entered a slow motion movie. Precisely because we are now able to process way, way, more bits of information per moment, kind of like a new wave quantum level holographic computer might. This slow motion phenomenon in turn seems to give us the sensation of having much more time to make the most effective in the moment decisions possible. Compared to others, or even ourselves, whenever any of us might be operating on the basis of much more sympathetic side innervated - speeded up fast time. Wherein processing within such a narrow band only partially lit up time / space, we far too often find ourselves constantly feeling pressured, as though we have very little time, to make an effective decision.

7.) In other words, whenever we are able to help ourselves make this shift into our beyond fear, well above demanding sympathy, far more 'zoned in way of being'! By way of discovering just how we may non-evasively dive into the pure energy which can be said to underlie any ongoing e-motion, we may find ourselves having. As opposed to letting our selves get all too caught in the seemingly endless little mind based, self conflictual resistive spin of what amounts to some so called undesirable unwanted negative emotion. Very much as a consequence of us continuing to hold the sort of continually rationalizing and justifying 'thoughts', that keep us being essentially 'mostly unwilling' to totally feel whatever vital energy based emotions, we keep resisting in our first place. The moment we support ourselves to make this shift into a way more core relaxed and open way of emoting. The more we will end up feeling like we are now able to function within our way more big mind awake, and thus far more optimal peak performance magical, totally now 'in our flow zone' way of being. In other words find our self's in this flow zone way - actually enabled empowered to perform at our very best. Pretty much in the same way topnotch athletes describe, whenever they find themselves able to access their 'zone'. In marked contrast to us continuing to hold the more 'sympathy seeking' point of view, which keeps declaring unto ourselves that either somebody else must be responsible for how 'we ourselves' are feeling? Or if not some other, then it must us who are the one's too blame, in such a way that motivates to keep putting our own selves down? Either way, no small wonder we continue to perform badly? Which is exactly what this whole lesson is going to be about, helping you to discover just how to make this shift into your higher end more solution oriented emotional nervous system, on a more and more regular basis.

(Note, it is important to be aware that is precisely people caught up in either of these emotionally evasive styles, i.e. 'hyper fighter macho tough' or 'fleer avoider wimp depressive' - who are most vulnerable to becoming addicted. With the type of drug or addictive behavior most likely to be sought after, being dependent upon whatever counter active to one's habitual avoidance pattern, supposed quick 'vital energy supposed fix hit'. Such a 'lost to their greater more energy open spirit' - type of person might be looking for. Which in turn implies, the best way to help any given type of person to transcend their addictive compulsion. Will be to help them shift into much more non-evasive ways of being with the energy of their emotions. In such a way that they will begin to feel way more grounded ongoing full of energy alive enough, to no-longer feel compelled to toward some sort or another of mere temporary addictive - supposed quick fix. Sorry the moment we under-stand the basics of how our e-motional nervous system has actually been designed / evolved to help us? There is not other way than for us to finally learn how to fully grow all on & up, the e-motional aspect of our intelligence!)

Here Specially For You - Is Every One's Greater Wisdom Oriented - Lesson # 2

HOW TO BEST GROW ONE'S INNERMOST FEELING & EMOTIONAL SENSE OF EVER MORE OPTIMALLY FULL-ON POSITIVELY UP - TRULY ALIVE VITAL ENERGETIC RADIANCE

SECOND INNER SENSED KEY TOWARD RE-CLAIMING OUR WELL BEYOND ORDINARY - EVER GREATER INNER CORE BODY & THUS SOUL BASED - TRULY ALIVE LIVING SPIRIT

Insofar as he kept choosing to grow his way ever more Up, Cosmic Charlie's very own inner most wisdom place within. Began to notice that on certain days and in certain ways, something going on in his life would challenge the Be-Jesus, the Yahweh, the Krishna, the Buddha, the very Allah, even the Wakan Tanka completely out of him. In moments like this, his most child like over-reactive fear based self, would become either an unruly, trouble-making angry, way too 'hyper fighter' wild thing. Throwing his energy around at others as though they were somehow to blame, for how 'he' himself might be feeling in such challenging moments. Or alternatively, an inwardly withdrawn, stubborn little 'wimp depressive' resistor, stuck inside himself in a downer state of internal log jammed hurt, and seemingly endless rounds of pain & suffering. Who would simply refuse to come out and play, rather than reveal his inner most feelings, to others. Usually whenever this would happen, he would find his little mind racing so away on him, like some runaway train. He could sense his constantly yaking way too out of control so called rational mind, compelled to keep projecting forward the worst possible future doom and gloom outcomes, based on old past memories of similar bad experiences. To the point where he would now find him self feeling even more horrible, than he did before he would allow his own negative fear based thoughts to get the better of him. With the result that he would soon find himself filled with all kinds of hateful and resentful, even raging revengeful emotions, whether directed at others or him self. In such a way that before long he would not longer feel the presence of his greater Light, shinning anymore around him.

On days like this, it was like he would feel so unable to take full response-ability to face certain powerful emotions going on inside of 'him self'. His end result would be that these kinds of fear based inwardly reactive emotions would begin to carry him into places wherein he would begin to feel so overwhelmed by his feelings. He would far too often find himself losing control over himself. There were times such feelings of hurting inside would become so huge, to a point where in his blaming and projecting, he would find some devious a way to hurt whomever might get in his way. Unfortunately when these negative feeling would at their worst, he would even at times find himself hating and hurting his best friends. Indeed anyone and everyone including his most dearly loved one's who might get in his path. Other times when things weren't going his way, he would become so frustrated and lost, outright bored and restless antsy - in relation to his hurts. It seemed there was would be a gigantic pounding flare button growing inside of him. Which would then trigger all the twisting, ugly driving him crazy, emotions he hated to have within him self. To such a degree he might even blame himself into a hell hole of depressive despair. Unfortunately there were times such feelings would grow so big and heavy with each passing second, Charlie could hardly bear it anymore. Stuck inside such a place, it seemed his only choice would be to either lash out at others, or equally other than wise retreat inside to a place that was totally down in the dumps. The truth was having feelings like this didn't REALLY make Charlie or for that matter Katie feel very Cosmic or Quantum about him/her self, at all! At times like this, Charlie/Katie would start to 'think', that life wasn't so great, after all. More like a potential 'hell hole', than any kind of Heavenly Garden of De-Lights!

Then one day Charlie's inner wisdom had a truly magnificent breakthrough moment. Thanks to some material he found himself reading on how our emotional nervous system has been designed / evolved to help us. He began to better under-stand just how whenever he would feel some so called negative, more fear based emotion. It was like certain of his organs, would tend to contract inward in such a way as into build his own vital energies into a huge held inside of him - flare button of e-motion? Such that this holding of the energy of his own emotions inside of himself he now began to better under-stand, is what would turn into his own pain and suffering body - inside of himself! Wherein very much as a consequence of in one way or another hurting so badly, it would begin to feel like he was being driven into ever more nasty states of negative held emotion. "Whah, Ahah, now I really get it," he now found himself saying! "Every emotion that I ever have, is simply energy that wants to be set free, in such a way that it can radiate totally on out of me! This makes me wonder if there is a way, I can learn to enter the energy of such held in emotions, in a manner that will help me to set the energy of such e-motions - way more free. Without me becoming far too frequently flare button compelled, and thus driven into being so e-motionally over-reactive with my own energies? That I start taking myself down into some negative either lash out any other or myself - and thus ultimately self destructive way of being? Reinforced of course, by my own runaway 'little mind thoughts', wherein I constantly keep myself trying to rationalize & justify ways to keep evading the energy of my emotions? In such a way that tends to result in the persistence of the very unwanted feelings, I don't want to keep experiencing in my first place!"

"Man oh Woman, Charlie/Katie's own inner Wisdom, could be heard to release a huge sigh of relief! For you to now begin to see this, is positively huge for you my great Wisdom oriented children!" But Charlie/Katie weren't quite yet finished, with internalizing the full power of this Realization. For the moment they found themselves getting this first part, it just took one more moment for them to finally realize. "This tendency to over-react out of control with our e-motions, is then exactly how we each of us over time. Tend to keep losing not only ever greater amounts of what amounts to our own vital energy supply. But this inward contraction against our own feelings, is also precisely how we now at the very same time tend to turn, such resistively feared emotions into so called negative emotions in our first place." See the point, Charlie & Katie now found them selves saying unto themselves. "Our so called negative emotions, are in other words simply nothing other, than our own fear based ways of choosing to keep on self resisting. And thus keep our selves in inner conflict with our own vital energies. Whether we keep choosing to lash out and blame some other, or keep choosing to go more inward to try and self blame ourselves, based on the flare button build up of such resisted emotions, inside of ourselves. In conjunction with us choosing to focus on our most negative, worst case doom and gloom possible, future outcomes."

In other words, Charlie Katie continued! "Our huge most vulnerable, self destructive bottom line, in the face of our human most potential to have nothing more than powerful emotions. Is that rather than learn how to face into our inevitable feeling & emotional and thus vital energy filling nature - fully? What we other than wise tend to keep doing, is to keep resisting the stream of our own inner most felt emotions. Such that very much as a consequence of us resisting our own more true felt, and thus more real in the moment, inner emotional nature. Our own inner held vital energetic pressure begins too build into places wherein, we now find ourselves more and more way too under pressure - e-motionally vulnerable. To the point where we feel ever more compelled to either more outwardly 'hyper fighter; keep lashing out or alternatively 'wimp depress' keep shutting our own selves down, in the face of various powerfully challenging emotional situations. In the complete non-sensical belief, that it is somehow better for us to become self destructive out of control wild things, rather than actually face directly into whatever emotion might be coming up for us, in any given moment. Such that very much as a result of us feeling too much resistive pressure, not only do we over time end up feeling sicker and sicker inside the core of ourselves, especially in relation to those vital energetic areas wherein we feel the most emotionally fearful that we won't be able to fulfill ourselves. But we also because of our self destructive behaviors, begin to feel less and less competently able to move ourselves in those very directions that might help us find. Precisely those inner vital energetically motivating fulfillments, we may most long to fulfill."

Which is to say, what our very own Charlie/Katie's within, began to realize for our selves like never before. Is that most of us tend to keep creating far too much negative emotion based hoopla, constantly going on inside of ourselves. When 99.9999999% of our time here, our bottom line probability is, we are actually not being survival threatened. What's more 99.9999999% of the time, our future projected worst case scenarios will never happen. 99.9999999% of the time the very worst that might happen to us, given of course we can sense that we are not really truly being survival threatened. Is that we would end up giving birth to some very powerful vital energy based emotion. Which we have for one supposed reason or another, developed some sort of old fear based resistive preference, not to experience. With the result being, whether we try to 'blame' ourselves, or make someone else 'responsible' for howsoever we may be feeling, even keep on endlessly 'projecting', seemingly endlessly worrisome negative outcomes into our future. Either way, the moment we choose to go to the 'past' or 'future' within our little yak, yak, endlessly yakking minds, in the face of some resisted emotion. Rather than more wisely choose to face into the here and now energetic felt wave, of any such powerful emotion. This is exactly how we tend to keep ourselves way too constantly self sabotaging ourselves. Simply because, we have been led to believe we won't know how to in the moment, feel completely through whatever emotions may be arising for us, without resort to 'fight or flight' based compulsion. Even though these emotional 'hyper fighter' & 'wimp depressive' avoidance & denial modes, never do seem to help us create effective fulfillment oriented - solutions.

Such that in our now finally really sensing the much greater sense of this new realization, about the basics of our own feeling & emotional nature. Through the medium of our very own Charlie's and of course in the very same way Katie's, inner most wisdom within. How could One now, not help but find One's Self becoming very inwardly excited. Simply because One's very own being, was likely getting very tired of far too frequently - feeling hurt! And then either lashing out to harm others to where some other, would then lash out back at One's own Self, in what could become an endless stream of emotional in fighting. Or feeling so stuck inside One's own hurt, One would constantly make One's Self wrong, even beat the insides of One's self up. In such a way One would thus become vulnerable, to being stuck in seemingly endless rounds of wallowing within One's own pain & suffering. Besides Charlie had been reading that our emotional nervous system, has another, much more relaxed expansive, grown up way. To help us all feel enabled to generate, that very vital energy which underlies every emotion we might ever find our self's having. In such a way, that our own energy might become more available to us, to help our self's feel able to come up with much more constructive solutions, to the many inevitable emotional challenges that keep coming our way. So our Charlie/Katie within, decided to experiment with taking full-on responsibility to face totally into, what would amount to the pure energy of his/her very own emotions. Whenever some emotionally challenging situation might in some way or other, either challenge his more intelligent possibilities, right on out of him. In a similar, but nevertheless even more direct feel into the very center of the energy of one's emotions, way, than our modern psychotherapeutic movement has heretofore been pointing us toward. Now however, well before his old way of continuing to go contractive and thus either 'hyper fighter macho tough' or 'fleer avoid wimp depressive' - reactive - could take compulsive hold of him/her.

"So, to begin creating this inner shift toward non-avoidance of his feeling & emotional nature within himself, the very next time Charlie/Katie found him/her self raging his/her eyes and belly out. Screaming at his best friend, perhaps even someone in his own family, feeling one of those fury filled tantrums where he wanted to blame everyone else, or even himself for how he was feeling. Something about his own inner wisdom said, "Hush, Charlie my own dear childlike ranter & raver inside. Stop for a moment, I want you to now take a few moments to peer investigate totally within, in such a way that you may now completely feel what is bothering you so?" "I am so frustrated & resentful angry, I can hardly stand it, Charlie's inner most emotional essence shouted!" To which his very own greater inner wisdom replied. "I have been through such trials & tribulations with you many times, Charlie my dearest. Now it is time to share something with you, which within the very essence of your SELF, you already know. And which in so knowing, you can now actually use to help your self once and for all, get rid of every such horrible feeling. So that yes, you can return right back again into that One-Der-Land of those happy times, you so much loved to rave about, when you were so much younger."

"Let's look at it this way", his/her own inner wisdom most gracefully continued. Imagine your inner flare button emotional demons, arising within you much as though they are just like those bad creatures, that keep coming up. In one of those computer games we all of us in this modern high tech world, so much love to play. Within which we can be absorbed for hours, and stay up well beyond bedtime!" Charlie nodded, yes it WAS very true! "Well consider this, his own inner wisdom having yet another stroke of genius like insight, kept going on! "You already know of the magical sense of that 'Inner Light' you can feel, when everything is going well? Such that whenever these great light shinning positive feelings, are totally happening for you. You end up feeling so Spirit Alive spectacular, you NEVER want them to stop. Well, I ask you, is this Inner Light you can sense so different, than the light you have learned to control with your joy stick, when you are playing demon zapping in some of your favorite computer games. Such that when you might learn to properly laser light focus your own Light Within. You could very well make it possible for you to blast out those little demon like figures, that keep poping up everywhere on your own computer screen within - poof into oblivion?" "Is it then I ask you, just possible that by way of you learning to use the Overseeing Light present Watcher, who is really controlling the laser light in the various computer games, you so much like to play? Or that OBE watching your self aspect of your most light present sense of self, such as we have already pointed to in our first chapter? Which now can enable you to learn to watch your self dive totally, into the very core center of your feelings? With your very own now inwardly feeling core focused - Laser Beam of Spirit Light in such a way as to help make your own inner negative emotional demons, 'vaporize poof' into nothing? Much in the same way you do, when you play those silly outside of your self oriented only, modern computer games you so much love to play?"

"Well, Charlie dear", inner wisdom said. "How about you now support your wisest possible place within, to get a hold of this inner most light? Which you are of course increasingly discovering - resides both inside - as well as all around you? Very much as a consequence of the embodiment practice you have agreed to internalize within you, based on the just prior first lesson! As well as in conjunction with your early childhood awareness experiences, which have already made you well aware of this Inner Light you have within! In such a way that you can now begin to sense, just how you can focus this light into your very own inner laser light joystick. Exactly into the very center of that pure emotional energy which relates to whatever hurtful flared inside of you emotion, you may still find your self having. With such deadly zeroed into your core focused accuracy, that in a series of subtle ongoing 'demon fighter like' energy flash outs. Any given inner contractive based flare button you may be choosing to now laser lock focus into, within some core point of intensely felt hurt which you may find your self still holding inside of you. Will now start to go 'poof, vaporize, dissolve'! In the huge sense of you now discovering just how, yes you can blast, expand the energy underlying any such emotion completely on out of you, into oblivion. Each & every moment you find yourself willing to focus your very own inner light, right within some still felt byte, or still hurting piece however small. Of what amounts to your own resisted held in energy and thus flare button contained inside of you, hurt & pain body engendering, negative felt emotion you may ever find your self having."

"Such that once you truly get this incredible ability to zap every one of your flare button emotion held energies completely out of you. Whenever anger, frustration, resentment, or any sense of I can-t, I don't know how to feel completely through this or that resisted emotion. Including all other forms of negative emotional malaise, raise their ugly flare heads inside of you. You will now be able to practice using your very own inner light, to zap right on into, every such self destructive emotion. For whatever time it might take, say for 3-4 minutes, even up to 20 minutes plus. Just in the same way you have patiently learned to zap virtual legions of bad guys. In all those favorite computer games you are likely to keep playing, for hours on end! To the point where you feel like you will have cleared, released, the energy underlying some old flare button driving you crazy, inner felt e-motion. First in relation to some particular chosen area of flare button held energy, within you. And then once you realize what it feels like to no-longer have a particular flare button, continuously vulnerable to flaring within you anymore. Now on into every other area of pain and suffering held energy, you may find still bothering you, within you."

"Certainly" inner wise-dome went on! "We now know within the context of our of our relatively recent, modern psych-therapeutic, emotional healing, movement. The moment we learn to face our feelings fully, head on directly. To such an inwardly intensive, e-motional energy flow through, now fully open degree, that we actually feel them completely through. The more we help our e-motional energies to fully let go and release all out, with respect to whatever feelings we may be having. Our greater reality is, the more the energy at the very root of our emotions becomes more freely able to flow through us. The more that energy will turn into the sort of field of radiant light, that is now way more likely to both emanate and thus remain available all around us. As well as ascend up our whole body embodied nervous system. in such a way as to help awaken us into our potential for experiencing much more Big Mind awake states of consciousness. In the form of the sort of ongoing spine tingling inner energetic presence, which will tend to inspire us into much more whole brain states of optimally De-Light-Ful solution generative function. Other than wise, insofar as we continue to resist feeling completely through certain so called undesirable emotions. In such a way as to thus keep ourselves convinced we do not know how to feel, even hate to feel fully through all the various e-motions that inevitably keep coming our way. The inevitable consequence of us holding on to our resistance patterns, is that we will via our law of attraction, tend to keep ourselves repeating precisely those similar kinds of emotional scenarios. We keep resisting & hating to experience in our first place, over and over again, ad nauseum. Until such time as we take the time, to face our resisted feelings - full-on. And thus help clear ourselves of them - once and for all. To the point where in our no more holding such resisted e-motions, we are going to stop attracting them toward ourselves over and over again."

"WOW", the greater wisdom being within Charlie, found him self saying unto himself, NOW with a glowing twinkle within his eyes. Insofar as he felt himself starting to 'really get' this whole new magical way of learning to be way more grown up, in relation to his own vital energetic potential. "You mean to say I can stop running & re-running all those past flare button based pain & suffering stories, I keep holding onto inside of me. Which, insofar as I tend to keep repeating them to myself and all my friends, over and over again, far too often keep me hurting, my own insides so? And which tend to keep re-compelling me into the very sort of reactive states, which keep taking me down way too often?" Charlie felt lighter already! "It's like you, my own greater wisdom within, are telling me that I have the power to vaporize all those negative emotions that keep coming up on my OWN inner computer screen, just like I have learned in all those video games, I often find myself so much liking to play?"

"Oh yes, yes, Charlie, and won't it be great fun?" In fact Charlie/Katie's own inner wisdom, in smiling an even larger whole being smile glow. Was now realizing this would be such a true De-Light, he was now finding him self wanting to start playing this game, inside of his very own self right now. As means to come into much greater flow zone harmony, with his very own found ever greater growing inner wisdom place within. What's more he could now really sense, that learning this new way of being with his emotional nature, was certainly going to take some daily practice. To get to the point where he might find himself fully able to lock completely on and into, al the various flare button emotional targets, going on inside him self. In such a way that he would now be way more open to feeling fully into and all the way through to completion, any given waves of vital energy filled feeling that might keep arising for him. On a much more ongoing, way more here and now attuned to his emotional nature, basis. Rather than keep allowing himself to stay stuck in his 'head' alone, constantly replaying some long past 'little mind' based stories, about how he was once similarly so deeply hurt, somewhere in his past. In such a way that the constant repetition of these same old stories in his 'head' alone, would seem to do nothing more. Than keep reinforcing the re-triggering of some old sense of hurt inside of him self, over and over again, in a way that would never lead to completion and resolution. Simply because yes he now knew, that every time he might sense such a reactive flare button demon cropping up anywhere, inside of himself. This would be cannon fodder for him to now practice developing his new found no-longer e-motionally evasive - laser beam of light - hone in skills. In such a way as to help himself able to feel totally on into, any such over reactive flare button emotion, to his optimal max. Until such time as he would get so good at this new way of dissolving out his old tendencies to lose awareness of his feelings and thus control over his/her emotional nature. There would be positively no more flare button demons, left anywhere inside of his or her much greater sense of Lightness in Being Self, anymore! To keep him attracting more and more of what he didn't anymore, want to keep on experiencing!"

"So how shall we know whenever we our self's are being such going against our greater feeling & emotional life force, locked into seemingly endless rounds of negative emotion - 'demon seed players'? Inner wisdom within went on to inquire? "First and foremost by the constant anger, hatred and resentment any given one of us will keep feeling inside of our self. In conjunction with the way, we will keep trying to both blame while at the same time constantly worry our way: either more pro-jectively 'hyper fighter outward, or alternatively more intro-jectively 'wimp depressive' inward. In relation to every held in flare button emotion, that may ever come our way. Like for example, whenever we might find our self continuously declaring that everyone else but us, is somehow responsible for the internal emotional dynamic mess, we keep finding our own self's in. The very sort of emotional dynamics wherein One might be motivated to call some-one else an A-Hole, a Dick, a Son-of-B, or in Katie's case, even A-Bitch, A-C, or perhaps even a Witch. When in terms of any larger more energetically open potential to move such emotional based energies ever more up - in the direction of creating some great potential inter-personal solution. These name callings could all be taken to be signals, that One's own higher order Quantum Katie or Cosmic Charlie within, is in all probability behaving in some mirror image fear based way. Directly in relation to whatever bad behavior One might be experiencing in others. In marked contrast to any possibility to decide to be some-one way more willing, to take whatever feel to the core responsibility might be required. In such a way as to now stop reacting for moment or two, as a much better means to feel through One's own underlying - either hyper fighter or wimp depressive - fear based retort. I mean how many times have you seen some-one you know, angrily lashing out at some-one else whom they feel has wronged them. In such a way that they themselves start demonstrating the mirror image of the very same fear based contractive & thus over-reactive emotional dynamic, they keep angrily and resentfully blaming some other for. In exactly the sort of way our world wide 'macho tough' and 'wimp depressive' oriented cultures, tend to 'think' of as being somehow 'smart ass' appropriate! Was the rhetorically reply, that was to come from deep within!"

"With our human downfall bottom line duh being", inner wisdom kept expounding! "That as long as any of us keep our self's constantly locked into, any such habitual resort to this unkind of fear based smart ass retort. All we will ever feel our self able to constantly backward looking 'See', will be potentially worst case scenario - self fulfilling prophecy negative outcomes. In relation to all the various situations, that life will keep on bringing our way. And thus by the way, we will tend to keep putting most of our energetic focus on holding various kinds of I-can't pessimistic, and thus persistent no I won't co-operate rallying against forms of constant resistance. Toward any kinds of situations that will keep fear triggering us, into the possibility of having some defensively resisted emotion. Always in conjunction with the way we will keep dwelling on seemingly impossible to solve, endlessly imagined survival threatening, problems, In such a way that we will tend to keep saying, why even bother to attempt to move forward. While we based on your own emotional fears, will at the same time keep attempting to control and manipulate others in our life, mostly toward our own personal ends only. As a means to keep trying to protect our self's from having any kind of emotion - we would prefer not to have. Rather than focus on developing our ability to mobilize our way more well beyond ordinary, fully emotionally capable side. Of our clearly more in our low zone, forward moving vital energetic potentials. In such a way that we might now start supporting our much wiser ongoing human possibility, to keep on inventing ever better holographic as opposed to me, me, either / or only, my point of view alone. Ways for humanity as a whole to move ever more creatively forward."

"Golly Gosh Gee', Charlie/Katie could be heard to exclaim. "It seems clear that the persistent avoidance of One's vital energetic nature, is actually way more 'stupid', than it is in any way real solution generative smart. Inasmuch as this is exactly how we all tend to not only keep losing the very energy we require. To keep moving our selves way more great solution forward, in the face of what amounts to some resisted by both sides - underlying set of emotions. By way of us continuously setting such seemingly endless rounds of emotional dynamic based conflict, in perpetual over reactive motion! Whereas to actually be willing to acknowledge to our own self's whenever we ourselves are being some sort of fear based reptilian - overly reactive blockhead. Is going to be a very difficult pill for many of us to swallow? Simply because it takes far more courage to fully feel the energy of whatever we ourselves may be feeling, from a place that transcends compulsive over reaction. Than it does to keep evasively blaming, or other than wise keep-on little mind projecting negative outcomes, with respect to any given emotionally challenging situation?" "What a novel evolutionary approach for us to take, Charlie could now be heard to muse to himself deeply within the very core of his now ever growing up - sense of himself?"

Supportive Image # 7A – Of Every One of Us Learning to Grow Up Our Very Own Laser Light Ability To Enter Into Every Wave of Old Resisted Feelings Inside - In such as way that we now Might Agree to Inner Surf Right On Through the very Pure Energy Core of All our various Old Inner Body Held - Pain & Suffering Sites

All in order that we Might in this way Help our Self's totally Vaporize - All those fear based contractive Emotional Patterns we have a Tendency to keep Holding Within Us - Completely out of our much greater sense of ourselves Forever!

Picturing every singular most One of us, learning to now use the more adult intelligent developed watching ourselves light - of our own inner awareness principle. In such a way as to concentrate this light into the sort of pin point focused laser beam, we can now then use to help us feel / enter exactly right on into, our ability to surf directly with the waves emanating from right within - the pure felt energy core. Of some powerful flare button held in emotion - which we keep finding is in some pain body way or another - continually over whelm upsetting or bothering us. In ways that keep leading us into far more emotional conflict, than we ever really want to keep on experiencing! Always choosing to focus on only one pain & suffering body area - at a time! As the best means we have to begin expanding / dissolving / vaporizing any such particular held in pain body energy. Which we ourselves are the one's who keep holding by way of our own fear based defensive oriented contractions. To now be gone, right on out of our selves - forever!

(**Accompanying Explanation** – A whole body of recent, new revolutionary face directly into our feelings and emotions, evidence. Is now showing us that whenever we make an agreement to face non-evasively, actually head on directly into the pure core energy, of some formerly feared, and thus continuously inwardly resisted, emotion. We by way of the repetitive application of this dive right into the core energy of any such feeling, inwardly directed awareness, process. Not only begin to release the vital energy at the root of any such formerly held in emotion. But we via this same dive totally in process, actually begin to dissolve / vaporize the very pattern of contracting we once took on - completely out of our fear based sympathetic side emotional nervous system, forever. In such a way that we thus help ourselves elevate ever more ongoing regularly, into the much higher more positive ends of our more whole being intelligent potentials. In order that we may far better enable ourselves to create the sort of way more holistically integral solutions for ourselves, that we all of us so much keep longing for.)

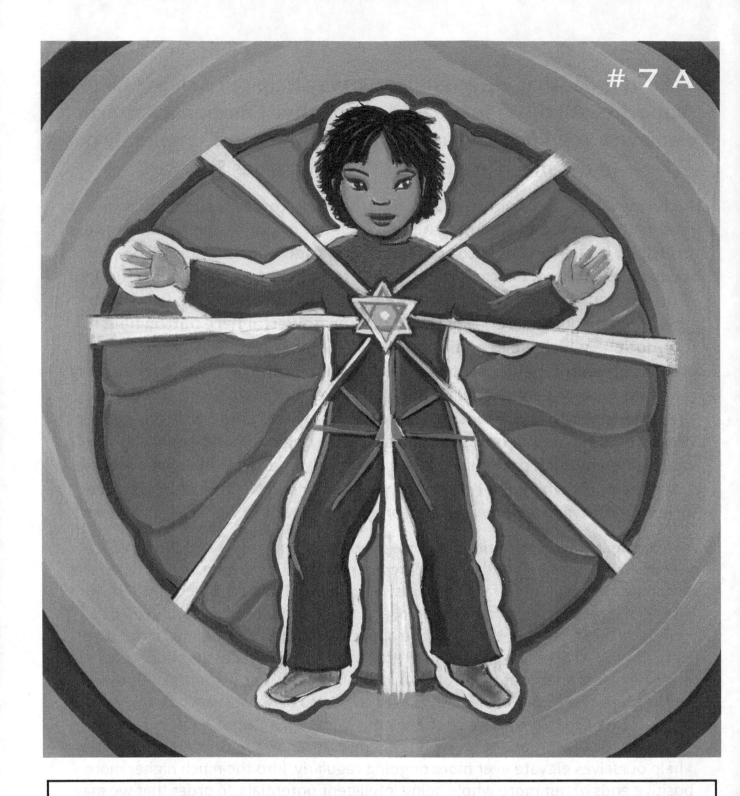

**EVERY US - AGREEING TO PURE ENERGY LASER
LIGHT FOCUS ENTER - RIGHT ON INTO THE CORE
FELT ENERGY OF ALL OF OUR OLD VARIOUS PAIN
& SUFFERING HELD WOUNDS - ONE POTENTIAL
CORE BODY RELEASE AREA AT A TIME**

Illustration # 7B – The Feel to the Core Technique Magnified to Help us All Now much more Fully Get - Just how we may best Use this Feel Fully Through Awareness Method - To help Release Ourselves totally Clear Past all our Old Inner Body Held - Pains & Sufferings

Refined image of each of our self's as Quantum Katie's & Cosmic Charlie's. Learning to full-on focus our laser wave beam of inner light - right-on into the very core center of some given, old pain body wound over and over again. In such a way that we may begin to feel the inner subtle, wave surf all of our e-motions ability involved, with respect to just how we may enter beyond the outer bounds of our old - can't you see I've been hurt - stories. Where from within the pure core centered energetic calm of these old inner held hurts. We can now begin to allow the pure energy of any such formerly resisted e-motion, to much more easily keep on light flashing all out of us. Until such time that there is no more held in pain body hurting energy left inside. But the new found freedom of any given vital energy area to be able to keep radiating any future related felt feelings and emotions - way more clearly on and thus all out of us. From within a place that will now be well beyond anymore felt childlike 'need' - to keep on contractively holding. What amounts to our own inner generated vital energies - within our Self's!

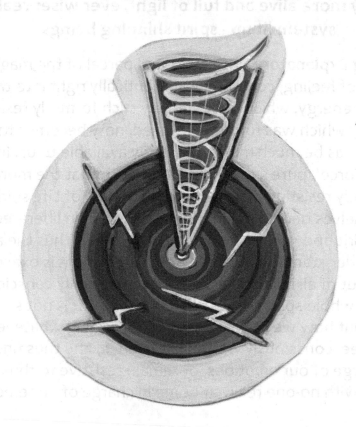

7-B

56

Now For Illustration # 8 – Inasmuch as feeling Fully Radiant Through every Old Such Inner Held Felt Hurt - Is our very best Way to Encourage Our Light Energy Spirit to Now Much Better Shine - Even More

Image now showing this very same Quantum Katie or Cosmic Charlie - within us. Having so learned to expand the pure energy of any powerful, formerly resisted, and thus held in emotion. By way of our agreeing to enter / feel the pure energy core at the very center of any such felt emotion, so authentically fully through. The energy of that old formerly resisted e-motion, is now going to be fully free to radiate out beyond the body of our more limited sense of self. In the form of pure radiant light or energy now in motion - which is to say e-motion. In such a way that the more we practice this, the more we are going to find ourselves shifting from feeling any negatively held emotion, like hating to feel this or that, or even powerfully resenting something, or someone else. To now totally no problem, actually lovingly being able to feel the true relaxed and open real authenticity - of whatever now fully consciously in charge felt emotion - we may in any moment find arising within us. In such a way that we will finally find ourselves much more clearly able to realize - that learning to fully feel whatever emotion may be coming up for us in any given moment. Is exactly how we support ourselves to become much more radiant, way more alive and full of light, ever wiser real whole nervous system lit up - spirit shinning beings.

(**Accompanying Explanatory Note** - Part and parcel of the magic of this new revolutionary way of feeling, completely authentically right into the core center of the pure inner felt energy, which underlies any such formerly resisted emotion. Is that the very energy which was formerly resisted, now becomes fully free to radiate all around us, as well as be much more constantly available to us. In the form of now vibrant full of 'Life Force', pure super light spirit! Such that the more we clear our old patterns of pain body resisting, the more and more full of Life spirit vibrant, we are going to find ourselves becoming. In other words, when liberated, our emotions become our spirit body, when held in our pain body. Thus the ability to fully internalize the under-standing of this lesson is so huge, it is exactly how we help ourselves climb out of all black holes, into becoming fully conscious In charge of ourselves - big light whole spirit beings. Which is to say, it is not so much about what we feel, as it is about how we choose to go about feeling whatever we are feeling. I.E. We can either feel consciously without resistance, and thus find ourselves in the driver seat in charge of our emotions, or remain resistive to thus stay lost out of control - with no-one really at home in charge of our emotions.)

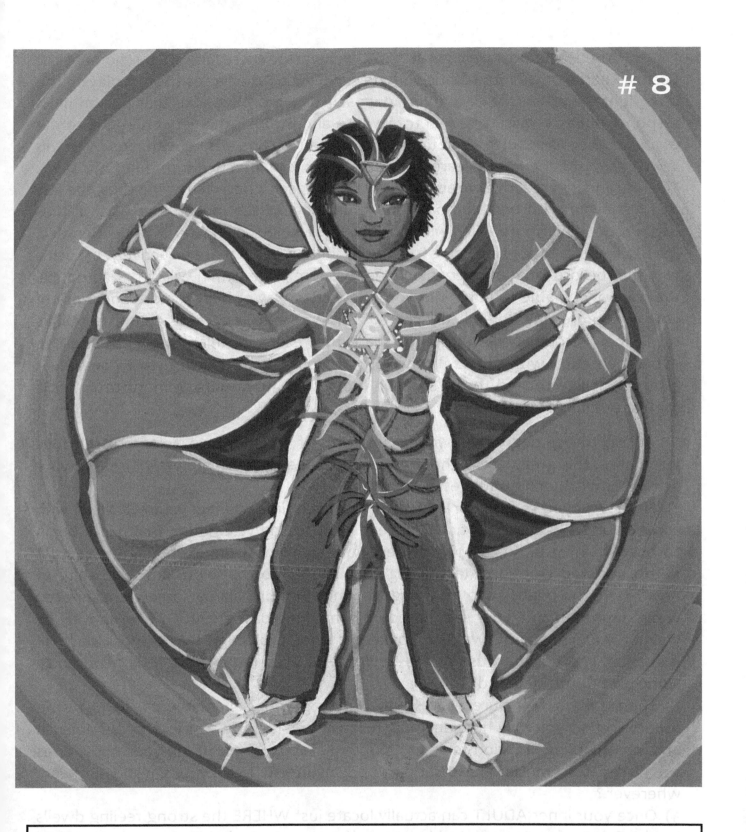

FEELING FULLY THROUGH EVERY OLD FEAR BASED WOUND - OUR VERY BEST WAY TO KEEP SHINING FORTH OUR VERY OWN NOW MUCH MORE CLEARLY SENSED - RADIANT LIFE SPIRIT

"Here is the positively great news my dearest every One's! The moment the Cosmic Charlie or Quantum Katie within every One of us - agrees to start playing this laser light game - inside of our very own self. The more we take that human most response-ability required, to feel totally into and through the very energetic center of any of your flare button emotions, such as we may find arising within us. With this laser beam of light we are learning to use ever more effectively inside of our self's. The less and less reactive we are going to find our self's becoming. And thus, the less and less filled with hurt and pain body suffering. Which means that we will thus begin to feel evermore, filled with positive joy. Like our own vital organ generative, life force energies are beginning to flow through us much more effectively. In such a way that before long, our very own inner wisdom place within will began to notice. We will now be able to enter into your 'flow zone way of being', more and more of your ever more One-Der-Ful - time here." This was so truly exciting, that every One's own inner wisdom now wanted to share the results of this inward investigative experimentation with others. In the form of some great tips to help whomsoever else, might like to find their very own 'flow zone way, more & more often, as a regular ongoing 'way of being."

"So to the degree you your very own self would like to help your self fully internalize, this great laser light of awareness super game completely inside of your self, inner wisdom now suggested:
1) First, "Ask you self to more clearly notice each time you feel your self filling with some strong, negative emotion. The very sort of negative emotion that might begin to overwhelm you. To the point where you might most unfortunately for you, let such a resisted emotion, start taking your energy down, down, down. In spite of how often you might keep on trying to either lash out blame someone else, even wimp depress blame your self, based on some long past event. Or alternatively by way of you constantly wanting to keep future projecting, worst possible case scenarios. Precisely because of this tendency to keep letting your little mind go to some past or future based story.
2) Then, take a few pure witnessing, watching your self moments, to just stop inside. So that you may here and now more clearly identify, just exactly HOW. Such an overwhelming emotion feels for you, and exactly where inside your body, does such a resisted emotion hurt? Is it pain bodying in your belly, your chest, your head, wherever.?
3) Once your inner ADULT can actually locate just WHERE the strong feeling dwells inside. Take a few inward, inside your self moments, to help calm and your Child within. In a way that can help your ADULT to contact the energy of your identified flare feeling - itself. Which you feel to be at the root of your negative, hurting feeling emotion… much more head on, directly.
4) Now ask the inner light of your watching your self feel whatever you may be feeling - greater-awareness principal. To now dive right into that core center place,

exactly where the energy of your so called particular hurting feeling resides. In such a way that you begin to give that energy, all the free space you can. To keep coming on out and releasing, radiating all out of you, in the form of the vital energy, that it really is. Or alternatively as we shall learn in the very next lesson. Find your way to keep expanding the energy of that feeling, past the very outer boundaries of however far out you can sense the energy - of whatever emotion you may be feeling wanting to be free to radiate.

5) From here keep asking your far more capable ADULT watcher within, to keep feeling and allowing whatever particular emotion you will have identified, to keep expanding out from your core. Until it fills the room, the whole neighborhood, even the entire state in which you live! Support your Inner Wisdom to finally truly realize that you actually have the 'Super Awareness Power' it takes, to help this kind of pure awareness release - actually happen for you? From a pure awareness place that is well beyond anymore compulsive 'need' - to resort to any unkind of over reactive - reaction. Keep encouraging this pure flare energy expansion to keep happening. Until such time as you no-longer feel any flare button charge left inside of you. In the much greater found sense, wherein your much more grown up ADULT can actually say with a real, heartfelt - 'Yes'! My innermost truth is I now fully 'get', just exactly how I-can help this much greater sense of energetic expansion, happen for me. To an inner still point, where I no-longer feel any emotional charge left inside of me - anymore.

6) Now you are ready for your final observations. Which involve noticing just how the particular feeling you chose to focus diving totally into, with your laser light beam, has likely changed for you? Has it for example become so less intense, it can hardly be felt anymore? Are there any pieces of that bad hurting feeling still left, floating around any other edges of feeling, inside of you? If so, ask your self to keep diving into the inner most energy essence of any last bad feeling resido-do, such as you may find still remaining anywhere around the original core feeling. With respect to your possibility to clear every last byte of the negative emotion, you started with. Until such time as every last remnant of emotional hurt or pain, is all gone, to where you no-longer feel anymore negative charge left anywhere, inside of you. Only the ultimate Peace-Ful-Ness, which now exists within the very core of that aspect of you.

7) Then take a few final moments to help your inner most ADULT MAGICAL WISDOM - Over Seeing Self, completely under-stand. That in thought, word, and deed you have just transformed some old negative feeling into a beautiful, huge ball of light. Now free to radiate from the very core of you - into the everywhere field of light - that can be sensed to exist all around you! With the great celebrative news being... you will have now just discovered, the true locus of the Super Power it takes... to bring your self back into a state of feeling De-Light once again! Anytime you may in so noticing the recurrence of some old flare button, so choose to under-take this self clearing, feel to the core process!

"Well dearest innermost me, the truly great Love of my life", inner wisdom found him/her self now saying, unto his/her greater found sense of SELF. Let's do our best to sum up, what we have just learned here. "This exercise repeated, whenever a meltdown arises, will free your Inner Child, from staying stuck and endlessly little mind spinning for hours, in seemingly endless round of pain & suffering. Inasmuch as your Inner Wisdom now has the skill to In-Vestigate both totally into, as well as all the way through to the very outer reaches of perfect radiance. With respect to that pure energy, which underlies all forms of emotional distress. Even those huge positive emotions, that sometimes can feel so overwhelming, one can find one's self resisting even very powerful feelings of happiness and joy. Such that over time, all the remnants of your long past fear based inner Child, will become less and less emotionally over reactive and resistive, to any emotion that may arise for you. The goal here is in other words, to help your inner most wisdom self, learn how to dispel exorcise, all of your internal emotional fear and thus held in conflict, pain patterns. All out of you forever! To the point where you will now be in a place of complete easy going friendship, with every aspect of your inner most emotional nature."

"From this moment forward, to the extent you really get this! I now want you to promise your far more intelligent inner wisdom place inside. And thus much greater sense of your Self, this! Any time you feel some ugly, negative emotion, or even hugely wonder-ful positive emotion, start to take hold you! In such away as to try and compel rule over you - based on fear & contraction! I want you to jump right into the center of those nasty hurts, or even joyful rushes, and turn on your very own inner awareness, into a radiant bright laser beam of light. In such a way as to either zap in enter all the way into those ugly feelings, until they dissolve poof right on out of you, completely into oblivion! Or alternatively, use the same light to help your self open all your way up into some positive emotion, completely past some point of flare button contraction. To the point where any such old fear based feeling will become so expansive, it will no-longer in any way, have the capacity to scare you. Into the sort of flare button state of contraction, wherein you start resisting your own capacity for experiencing much more full-on energetically alive - bliss."

"For the time has come for you, and indeed for every Quantum Katie & Cosmic Charlie within each and every One of us. Who find ourselves attempting to live ourselves forth as best we can, on this our small planet, earth. To let these unwanted emotions know that we are the one's who are in charge of the very laser light clearing 'joystick'. we all have within each of our selves. By means of which we can control our own sense of reality and thus our own sense of destiny! For the great truth of our innermost way more full-on human potential, is that we simply do not have to remain the victims of our own primitive way of generating energy. We do not have to keep ourselves locked into more and more rounds of endless pain and suffering. We do not have to remain at the mercy of those very over reactive flare button spaces, from within which we tend to feel compelled toward making our very worst possible attempts to move forward, decisions. The very sort of decisions we tend to make based on a whole host of unresolved so called negative, and therefore overly stressful, ultimately high anxiety producing emotions. Such as are most likely to keep us perpetuating more and more rounds, of the very same seemingly endless rounds of yet more pain & suffering."

"No Charlie my boy, Katie my girl! Our much greater intelligent truth is that we can actually much rather become, the one's totally in charge of what amounts to our very own, now fully owned & thus totally up energy! All it takes is a willingness for us to finally begin using the light of our awareness, in such a way as to put ourselves in charge!" Charlie/Katie laughed out loud to now think of his/her own innermost wisdom, as an inwardly oriented computer game involved, great spirit warrior. Totally engaged in the expansion of what would amount to his/her own much greater Life Spirit! Charlie/Katie was in fact so pleased, so tickled pink inside, he/she felt most whole-sum-ly motivated to give him/her self, a totally in love with his/her own inner wise-dome awareness, gigantic bear hug inside. "I feel better already! The next time, when I feel way overly angry, or in overwhelm in relation to any other felt over reactive emotional charge, I 'WILL' try your plan. I am the luckiest human being in the whole world, to have found you as my guide! For you my greater wisdom guide within, truly ARE my very own GREAT WISDOM TEACHER, which in greater truth already resides, inside of me! I mean it is not complicated rocket science for each one of us to self realize. Just how important it is to face totally up into, the whole of our very own real authentic inner emotional nature, every here and now moment of our lives."

"Here then is the huge ultimate point to get in relation to this lesson, my dearest young One's. Keeping one's self addicted to the notion, that adrenalin is the best way to help motivate our selves forward. In such a way that we keep ourselves stuck in the sort of endless sequence of stories, which keep trying to say that our most primitive either 'hyper fighter' or 'wimp depressive' mode. Is the best way for us to get anywhere, we might like to get to. Even in the face of the very opposite energy losing reality, that keeps going along with the constant resort to either of these 'fight or flight' based energy losing modes. Especially when the worst consequence for us would be, that we would have nothing more than a strong vital energy based - e-motion. Imagine on the other hand, in much greater respect for our selves, just for a moment. What it might be like to keep supporting our self's to become addicted to cholines, seratonins, melatonins and endorphins? In such a way that our very own sense of our self's, could now actually find our self's in our more para-sympathetic now way more flow zone motivating way of being able to generate. What would amount to now way more 'whole brain lit up' and thus real true found - 'peak performance enhancing energy'. Not just once in a while, as if by some good fortune accident, for certain periods of time - only? But much rather on a more regular ongoing moment by moment totally here and now expanded aware involving, basis!

"In other words, the more we discover how to clear and shift ourselves, into being in what we refer to as our GAP of pure here and now fully awake and alive, greater awareness. The very sort of wise-dome place of full-on open awareness, that can be increasingly free of all old held, fear based past or future oriented, mostly in our head alone, feeling & emotional evasive, & thus contractive negative emotional patterns. Such that we will indeed start to feel more and more like the truly MAGICAL flow zone empowered ADULTS within, we have been designed / evolved to be. As a loving parent, wouldn't your heart's desire be? To help your own Child learn just exactly how to come through to the other free and clear side, of whenever he/she might still feel, to be hurting them? In such a way that both you & your child might now feel, as if freed from the veils of all such traumatic past based, emotionally contractive defensiveness? In the very sort of ways, that will help to self empower as many other people in our life, as is humanely possible. So how about we dive totally into lesson # 2, with the intention of helping ourselves become much more empowered to actually invent. The way more whole being levels of fulfillment for ourselves, we all of us keep longing for?"

"This must be why certain truly wiser, more self actualized people, are so well beyond ordinary, happy most of the time" Charlie's/Katie's inner wisdom was now heard to Yippy! In one huge Joy-Ful, now I really get It - Aha! Insofar as he/she felt this revolutionary new way of being, sink deeper into his/her very own powerful empowering, inner truth. With the utmost respect for just who he/she could now help him/her self to with One fully real whole inner sensed Halleluyah - move ever more effectively forward - into being.

Second Life Energy Enhancing Prayer Unto One's Self - Making a Clear Decision To Keep Shining One's Self Forth From Within - Like 'A Truly Uniquely Us Ever more Brightly Energy Glowing Star'.

"I-am the very sort of some-one who now constantly agrees to keep feeling my way totally through whatever emotions may inevitably tend to arise within me, in the context living of my very own life. Cause I truly do now know, that I simply cannot avoid and deny my emotional nature anymore. Certainly within this new light, my newfound truth is that I no-longer want to keep deadening myself to my vital energetic nature. Or alternatively constantly keep acting out in seemingly endless rounds of resentment, anger and even deep seated hatred. Cause even though these are all ways of feeling in their very own right. Nevertheless they most certainly constitute my most primitive negative & therefore most self sabotaging ways of emoting. Which is exactly why I now choose, to live each moment of my existence open to every feeling, that may ever tend to arise, within every core organ of my body.

Simply because I now know the more I agree to find ways to feel totally through every core body emotion, that may keep on arising. Within the unique hologram that constitutes the very whole inside of me. From a place that not only beyond anymore fear based felt need - to resist and contract. But from a place that is also fully capable of feeling through the pure energy of any emotion that may ever come my way. The more and more I am going to feel myself sensing my highest, most open emotional states. Such as: a growing sense of capability; empowerment; true happiness; profound joyfulness; and incredible core peacefulness. What's more, the more I get the sense of this new found positivity, the healthier and more completely awake to seemingly endless ongoing streams of energy within myself, I going to feel myself become. Such that the whole of me, will begin to radiate my inner most vital energetic presence - more and more as a field of light! Even beyond this, the much greater news is that the less afraid of my emotional nature, I help myself become. The more attuned to light radiant presence of everything all around me, I will also find myself becoming. In the sort of way that will now help me, to be clearer aware of how I may choose to move my own presence. Within the world of all the various other Same Source given, most unique radiating presents, which can be sensed to exist all around me."

Chapter 4

Lesson # 3 – So That We May Thus Learn To Total House Clear Every Last Byte - Of Any Old Energy Contractive & Thus Ultimately Inner Held - Negativity Based Self Sabotaging Self Doubt

The underlying Rationale for Have A Great Life Lesson - # 3

Given every one of us would love to feel like yes we-can fulfill ourselves. At all '7' internal organ motivated levels of our vital energetic being. In such a way we might end up feeling: truly sacral plexus initiated sensually/sexually fulfilled; truly lumbar plexus initiated doer entrepreneurial prosperity fulfilled; truly 'soular' plexus initiated great friendship fulfilled; truly cardiac respiratory plexus initiated warm heartedly loving family fulfilled; truly brachial eyes, ears, nose and throat initiated communication skill fulfilled; clearly third eye mid brain initiated total forward inner visionary seeing solution generative fulfilled; and finally all 4 hemispheres involved huge big wave whole brain optimally insightful awareness attuned fulfilled. As our best means to become totally Co-Creatively solution generative in relation to our ability to live in harmonic resonance within the ultimate Really Big Huge Holographic 'One & Only Source' - that seems to be going on here.

Our huge human problem even beyond having basic problematic - difficult to feel emotions! Such as feeling angry, frustrated, bored, confused, worried, or full of blame & hateful resentment, even completely lost & filled with despair. To the point of feeling ourselves at times full blown flare button triggered, into states of either 'more outwardly oriented hyper fighter rage' or alternatively into 'fleer avoider internalized total depression'. Is that from the context of developmental studies, we now know the more we as ever more attempting to grow ourselves upwards, beings. Keep on feeling such negative emotions, very much as a consequence of various primal fear based emotional experiences. Which seem to happen too pretty much every one of us, at some point or other over the course of our lives. And which we thus tend to keep holding inside ourselves, unless we find some way to clear ourselves from them. Then the more we will start to develop various feelings of - 'I can't', 'simply don't know how' self doubt & self loathing - with the very insides of ourselves. Particularly in relation to the various internal '7' vital energy complexes, such as we have already outlined for you, in the just prior lesson, as well as in the illustration about to follow.

Like for example: starting to feel like we are somehow not good enough with respect to not being handsome or pretty enough; not cute adorable enough; too sensual or gross; not coordinated enough; not capable or competent enough; like someone who always makes too many stupid is stupid does messes & mistakes whenever we try to do something we want to excel at; or some one who is not friendly enough; not lovable enough; not acceptable enough to have great friends & lovers to play with; not capable of manifesting a positively great family; not able to say what's going on inside one's self; not able to intuit vision see one's way forward; somehow not worthy enough to be blessed with great underlying / beyond lying Source Forces Grace. Sometimes even to the point of hating this or that about one's self etc., etc., etc., this list could go on forever! Even though none of us came in here with any of this garbage, on board inside of us, with respect to ourselves! On top of this, we also know based on a series of scientific studies, that people who consistently set goals, or forward moving intentions, in front of themselves. As an inner means to help keep pulling their own nervous system organizing potential - ever forward toward the realization of such goals - via their own inner set, magnetic law attraction. Are far more likely to help them selves realize these goals. Whereas on the other hand, people who do not choose to keep setting such goals in front of themselves. Are way too often exactly those people who are carrying a great deal of self doubt and self loathing within themselves.

Who then can be surprised, when such self doubt loaded people, do not seem to make very much progress. In terms of their being able to manifest a positively great life for them-selves they might much more prefer. Most unfortunately, they just seem to keep floundering as though lost. Constantly law of attracting all the various self doubt building situations they still tend to hold inside themselves - back toward themselves - over and over again. In other words, the huge problem here in relation to holding self doubt anywhere within ourselves. Is that the more we come to hold such feelings of unworthiness & self loathing anywhere inside of our selves. Especially in relation to whatever greater fulfillment longings we may be choosing to set in front of ourselves. The more we begin to feel like we in various ways - simply can't - don't know how to find ways to support this or that intended outcome. To come to fulfillment fruition for us, in the context of all our attempts to become the sort of fully grown up, actually fulfillment empowered adults, we might much rather hope to be.

In other words, the more we keep avoiding and denying our emotional nature, in such a way as to keep taking our own vital energetics, ever more down. The more we will begin to feel our selves having taken on further debilitating negativity based self doubt - which we will then tend to keep holding inside ourselves. In relation to our ability to help ourselves mobilize what amounts to our own vital energies. In those very directions most likely to help us find the whole range of core body fulfillments, we keep longing for. What's more, the big problem with holding self doubt. Is that insofar as we take on self doubts, these doubts about ourselves will begin to pretty much - immediately double whammy. Start self sabotaging whatever great in-tensions, we may keep choosing to set in front of ourselves. Both by way of pitting our own vital energies, pretty much at cross purposes with any fulfillment intention we may choose to set. But also via the way our inner law of attraction works inside of us, insofar as we will tend to keep attracting toward ourselves. The very self doubt creating, negative outcome situations we keep holding. And which we keep hoping to be able to get past / transcend. By way of whatever positive fulfillment intentions we may keep trying to set in front of ourselves for ourselves, in our first place. With the inevitable result being, that we will tend to keep on manifesting more and more of exactly what we don't want, into our lives. This realization about just how we tend to keep digging ourselves into deeper and deeper having fallen from grace, black holes over and over again. With very little light of awareness vital energy left within us, to help us keep realizing our dreams. Is so huge in terms of explaining why so many of us have so much trouble moving truly forward into more positive states of inner fulfillment. Let's first take some time to examine the self sabotaging effects of our various self doubts, in more refined detail. Before we go on to reveal just how we can begin to help our self's dissolve / vaporize every self doubt we may have ever taken on, completely out of us - forever.

Preparatory Image # 9 – In finding ourselves having taken on a certain amount of Debilitating Self Doubt - We in various ways start to hold inner Beliefs that We-Cant - Simply Don't Know How to Manifest the Positively Great Life's we all long For?

9 - Unfortunately - Contracted In Various Forms of Old Fear Based - Self Doubt - Devoid Now Of Essential Inner Hope - We Start to Believe

We Are Not More Than Mere Dark We Can't - Don't Know How - Way Hurting Inside Shadows - Re: Our Much Greater Potentials

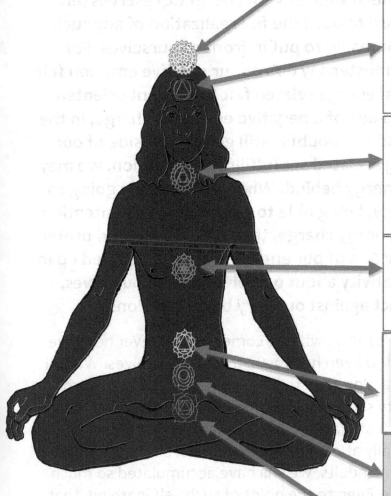

What we have been referring to as Good -Ness - Must be the sort of Force which exists either only Outside Our Self, or perhaps not At All - To such a degree we keep shutting our very own Well Beyond Ordinary - Much greater potentials to connect ourselves fully Up with what amounts to An extra-ordinary - Sense of this Source Force Being Fully Alive - Within Us

We have no clue as to just how we may best access our own capacity to constantly stream – Precisely those Inner Visions & Insights most likely to best help Us – Actually be enabled to bring our very own best set intentions - Ever more forward toward actual Fruition

We feel somehow unable to clearly articulate & thus communicate – Just whatever we really most want out of our Lives - Along with how we may best team network – To help ourselves realize our more co-operative involved - Community of Man/Woman Kind Dreams

We feel either not Worthy of being Loved - Or somehow not really, truly Lovable Enough - To actually deserve having fully Loving Relationships being entirely Central to the Living of our Lives

We find it difficult to fully Trust Others, even Ourselves – In such a way as to allow us to feel truly Core to Core Intimate Connected Good Enough - To keep enabling way great Friendships

We simply do not feel competent enough & thus motivated enough - To keep doing whatever it seems to take - To keep inventing our own Fare Shares of the Great Singular Most Pi

We sense our Sensuality to somehow not be Attractive/Desirable enough - Even ugly or Bad to the Bone - In such a way as to not allow us to have way extra-ordinarily Caring - Truly Great Sex

Constantly Claiming We No-Longer Know How To Just Be As Truly Radiant Spirit Lights - Unto Our Way More Shining Sense Of Our Self's

Supportive Illustration – Unfortunately Once Caught in the Internal Conflict of Holding Emotional Fear, Resistance & Self Doubt - We Tend to keep Taking even our Best Intentions - Down

Here's the rub, most unfortunately this tendency to not feel able to manifest the essence of what we really want inside of us, tends to come to be so. Simply because to the degree that we still hold such negative emotional energy inside of ourselves, around any given intention. Every ounce of self doubt thus still held, will tend to keep canceling out exactly at cross purposes. Continually against whatever positive energy we may be mustering in our ongoing attempts to try and get ourselves totally behind our very best set intentions. Leaving us with much smaller vital energetic reserves left over, to help us move ever forward toward the full realization of any such intention set goal, we may be choosing to put in front of ourselves. For example, if we feel overtly able to muster say 80% of our positive emotion felt energies, behind some given vital energy related felt fulfillment oriented intention. But we still covertly hold 60% of a negative energetic charge, in the form of various contractively held self doubts - still going on inside of our self. In relation to some vital energy related set fulfillment intention, we may be choosing to put our positive energy behind. What we are really going to be left with is only 20% of our energy, being able to get behind, that intention. A much smaller left over positive energy charge, than any of us would prefer to believe we have. Simply because 60% of our energy is going to be tied up in contractively holding some negativity about ourselves, inside ourselves, which is going to counteract against our very best intentions.

(Accompanying Explanation – What's more, when it comes to whatever negative self doubts about ourselves, we tend to keep holding in front of ourselves. We will also by way of our own law of attraction tend to keep on magnetizing toward ourselves, more and more of the very same self doubt motivating situations, that tend to keep bringing us down in our first place. Leaving us with growing feelings of self doubt, in relation to how we really at core now view ourselves. To the point where by the time many of us become adults, we will have accumulated so much inner self doubt, inside the core of us. Even to the point of such self loathing, that one might say E.G. "I hate this or that about myself". Why then should we even be surprised, when via our own inner law of attraction, we will thus tend to keep self sabotaging our own way forward - over and over again. No wonder so many of us feel left with feelings, like why should we even bother. Given no matter how great our best intentions, the setting of them by themselves barely seem to help?)

CAUGHT IN THE INTERNAL CONFLICT OF EMOTIONAL FEAR, RESISTANCE & SELF DOUBT - THIS IS EXACTLY HOW WE START SELF SABOTAGING EVEN THE VERY BEST OF OUR INTENTIONS

Inasmuch As Positive The Energies Behind Our Best Intentions X The Negativity of Our Underlying Patterns of Self Doubt Tend To Cancel Each Other Out - We Are Left With Very Little Real Vital Juice - To Help Us Keep Moving Toward The Realization of Our Dreams

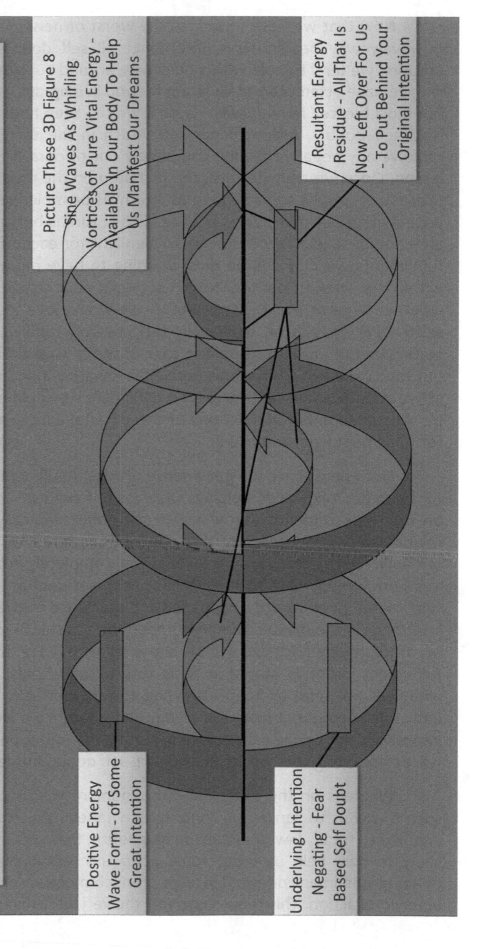

Picture These 3D Figure 8 Sine Waves As Whirling Vortices of Pure Vital Energy - Available In Our Body To Help Us Manifest Our Dreams

Resultant Energy Residue - All That Is Now Left Over For Us - To Put Behind Your Original Intention

Positive Energy Wave Form - of Some Great Intention

Underlying Intention Negating - Fear Based Self Doubt

Now that we have examined the worst of news, this brings us around to the positively way better news here! Since all self doubts are really complexes of emotion we tend to hold within ourselves, around our basic vital energy areas. Much like we have attempted to illustrate for you in diagram 9-A. Most fortunately for us, our most blessed human reality is, that we can keep finding ways to dissolve all such held self doubts, inside of our self. Much in the same way we learned how to dissolve any negative feeling completely out of ourselves forever, in the just prior lesson. Once we truly get this, the first step on the road to this self doubt clearing process. Is to take some time to as clearly as possible identify whatever self doubts we may find our own selves holding. This in turn is best accomplished by way of us agreeing to take a few moments to highlight for each of our self's, whatever inner fulfillments we may still be most wanting to have more ful-fillment in relation to, within the living of our life. No matter what such fulfillment longings might entail, whether large or small, just whatever we would love to be able to experience our self having enough of, to actually feel inwardly fulfilled. Particularly in relation to stating intentions with respect to each of the '7' vital energy areas, that keep calling out for ful-fillment from within our Self's. Always within the context of remembering as we stated earlier, that there is no fulfillment we could ever long for. Which cannot be subsumed under at least one of these 7 vital energy areas, that keep calling out for fulfillment from within us!

From here, once we get a sense of what fulfillments are truly most important for us to get involved in helping ourselves to manifest - for ourselves. The next step on the road to identifying whatever self doubts we may find ourselves holding in relation to our very best intentions. Is for us to agree to state our intentions toward our ability to manifest a more fulfilling life, completely in the present tense. I.E. As in Yes I-Am already able to fulfill this or that, set goal or intention, as though these fulfillments have already happened for us. Cause insofar as we keep stating our intentions in the maybe or merely hoped for, constantly wanting to have something or other happen for us. Please some thing outside of me won't you help me fulfillment intention stated in some future 'tense' only. Not only is this is exactly what we will tend to keep attracting toward our self. Someone still wanting to, endlessly hoping that maybe someday in our future we will feel enabled to fulfill our intentions. But by the very nature of stating our intentions in some future tense, we will be admitting that we are still holding self doubt, inside of ourselves.

Whereas on the other hand the moment we start to empower our self's in such a way as to sense our inner most vital energy attuned awareness now fully enabled to totally law of attraction magnetize, that very involvement pathway. Most likely to best help us bring some actual present intended fulfillment - into our ongoing fulfillment oriented stream of much more wisely in our flow zone attuned behavioral action. This then is not only the very best means we have to help our self fully mobilize all the vital energy power within us - we require. To help our self's actually feel fully enabled to bring our intended goals - into the reality of the various fulfillments we keep longing for. But it is also going to become the best means we have, to help ourselves clearly identify every self doubt we may have ever taken on our of our unique histories of various fear based trauma.

Key Manifestation Enabling Image # 9C – It's time to peer into our Kingdom of Heaven Within - In such a way that we now right from inside our most clear Yes I-Can connected sense of our Self - May ask in such a whole being empowered I-Am already present tense capable way - As to in this way Help Our Self's feel fully enabled to Receive

The whole idea of examining the image that follows, is to help you over periods of time. Be better able to identify the various areas in your body. Wherein you still find yourself holding various degrees of self sabotaging self doubt within you. So than you can now use this awareness to go on to fully feel these self doubt emotions completely through and all out of you, one at a time. Pretty much in the same way you learned in the just prior lesson. With the fullest possible respect to your ability to help yourself be much better able to manifest. All those inwardly motivated ful-fill-ments that we all keep longing for, each of us in our own unique ways, and according to own unique given talents

(**Accompanying Exercise** – Now that you get this, let's take some time to in a few short words, actually write down describe each self doubt that you tend to hold inside of your self. Patiently over time, one area at a time with respect to each given '7' vital energy related - ful-fillment intention - you might choose to set in front of your self. In such a way as to you help yourself identify just exactly where and how inside of your body, you may still hold some hidden self doubt / self loathing issue - within you. Ultimately in relation to each of these '7' vital energy related, core areas of your body. With the whole point of this self doubt identification process being, not to keep wallowing in self doubt, but much rather for you to help you your self clear banish. Every such self doubt from being held anymore inside of you - forever. Via the feel fully through technique we have already presented in the just prior chapter, as well as by way of a similar, yet reverse awareness focus technique we will present in this chapter. Precisely so that you may move way more forward into feeling able to manifest every dreamed for intention you may ever choose to put in front of yourself.)

9C – Quite Simply Because - We All Want Our Very Own Inner Most Essences Within - To Now Feel Beyond Any Self Doubt - Yes

I-Am So Pure Spirit Awake & Full-On Radiantly Alive - I Now Live Within My Most Non Separate Source Connected - Sense of Being

I-Can Keep Generating Truly Great Forward Seeing Truly Creative / Inventive Solutions

I-Can Articulate & Communicate My Under-Standings - Way Brilliantly

I-Can Now Realize My Capacity To Fully Heart Open Love - Special Others

I-Can Manifest Best Friends & Truly Equal to Equal Positively Great Human Relationships

I-Can Manifest Enough Doer Motivated - Abundance & Prosperity

I-Can Fulfill My Sensual / Sexual Desires - In Optimally Caring Healthy Ways

And Thus That We-Actually can - Keep on Shining our self's ever forth - As endless rainbows of truly happy real spirit found - De-Light

To further clarify this under-standing, given such a beyond any self doubt image - of our most radiant human potential. Is much more like who most of us would like to end up actually being. Fortunately for us the great news here is, once we can get our innermost sense of our Self's to clearly identify. Just what we would much prefer to have happening for us in our life's. With the utmost respect to each of these core organ fulfillment motivating sites - within ourselves! It's just one more step, to help you your yourself feel able to clarify every self doubt, you may have ever come to hold inside of your self. Precisely so that you can start to apply the dissolving / vaporizing process, to help clear any such self doubts, completely out of your forever. To begin this self doubt identification process then, the moment you can now agree to state the ful-fill-ment of your intentions, with the utmost respect to each vital energy area within you.

The moment any of us can agree to state our intentions exactly in the present, I-Am-Ness tense - sense. As though we are already capable of fulfilling any intention we might choose to put up front, before our self. Compared us stating some hoped for fulfillment in a more maybe We-Can, cause We're still wanting to, trying to fulfill our self's, in some endlessly hoped for future tense. Precisely as we have already suggested in the just prior illustration! Such as for example making an intention statement which clearly declares unto One's Self, that I-Am totally healthy, or I-Am completely good enough, or Yes I-Am optimally prosperous etc. etc. etc., even as I-Am someone who is fully enabled to manifest great loving relationships in my life! Rather than as some on still wanting to be good enough, or eventually someday enabled to manifest a great loving relationship in one's life, etc. etc. etc. Certain inner self doubt, even self loathing issues, start to bubble to the surface inside of us. And thus rear their ugly heads in the form of - various B.S. who are we trying kid – messages to our selves? In such a way that this I-Already-Am fully capable challenge toward our innermost sense of our Self, very quickly starts to bring us face to face with the reality of what we truly feel about ourselves - inside of ourselves. In the form of various inner plexus related self doubt feelings, that we are somehow E.G.: not attractive enough, not good enough; don't know how; are not smart enough; not able enough; not lovable enough; not communicative enough, not able to see where we might most like to head toward with respect to our ability to actually manifest whatever we might most really want out of our lives; or even not spiritually truly deserving enough etc, etc. - to fulfill what we really want to fulfill inside of us.

In other words, there comes a time when it is most important for each of us, to take much more honest, self caring note. Of all those often subtle and sometimes not so subtle inner messagings to our self, which far too often keep blaring out to us inside. In relation to every such 'as though it is already happening for us', present tense way we can state our various I want this or that - fulfillment for ourselves. In such a way as to say, no way, BS what I actually more accurately feel is truly true for me. Is that I really don't expect myself to be able to manage this! What's more I'm never going to be able to realize such an intention! Simply because I do not ……………. Enough (you fill in the blank)! Or, I do not feel ……………. enough inside myself (you fill in the blank)! To feel able to support this too really happen, for me! To the point where we keep holding our very own real sense of our self's back & thus down - from feeling as able as possible. To completely 100% go for the various fulfillments we really most want. With the end result, that far too many of us feel able to manifest only portions of our best - intentions. While we at the same time tend to keep on manifesting way too much of what - we don't really want.

On the other hand the much better news here, is, that this I-Am already all that challenge to our much more honest sense of our selves. Is exactly what makes it possible for us, too in a few short words. Make a fully descriptive short note of exactly each self doubt or self loathing message, we still tend to still hold inside of our self's. With respect to each '7' vital energy related ful-fill-ment intention, we might choose to set in front of our self's. In such a way that ends up helping us to better identify just exactly where and how, inside of our bodies. We still tend to contractively hold given self sabotaging issues within ourselves. The very sort of self doubt & self loathing issues, which tend to in one way or another convince us into believing. We just can't, we won't be able to actually truly realize, such already happening intended outcomes, for ourselves. (Note to help you get a better under-standing of the kinds of inner self doubt messages, we all in varying degrees tend to take on inside ourselves, in relation to each of our '7' vital energy areas. Please go to my web site Quantum You where you can look at my freebie download of commonly held self doubt messages, entitled 'Identifying One's Self Doubts'.)

Now that you have taken some time too much better establish, exactly where inside your body. Some particular cross purpose energy losing self doubt message, you may find yourself still holding & thus actually still residing within you. The whole purpose here in this lesson, is therefore to now start supporting the laser light of your greater awareness principle in every way you can, as best you can. To feel totally, directly, into the pure energy core of any such self doubt feeling, or any sense of I-can't, or I don't know how to. In exactly the same way you learned to feel totally into & out the core, in the just prior lesion. This time however, with respect to any feeling you may find your self holding, based on this self doubt identification process. With respect to you having taken on some negative emotions about your self, which makes you feel like you don't know how to change your inner reality. More toward feeling fully enabled to help manifest whatever it is you are wanting. Simply because you will first and foremost in this greater respect, be helping your self to now know that yes you-can break through into a much calmer core place inside. Wherein you will now find each such particular self doubt, able to dissolve / vaporize go poof, right on out of you. In such a way as to leave you with nothing but the very opposite, in other words entirely positive to any self doubt feeling - you first identified your self to be holding. In the much greater sense of feeling say like you are now entirely good enough, competent enough, loving enough, sexy enough, wholly enough etc. etc. etc. Given a context wherein you keep-on persistently pursuing - the complete internalization of this lesson.

In this huge respect, imagine your self being able to use the essence of this identify and feel through lesson, to help create major shifts inside of you. From say, being the sort of person who used to hold core feelings of not sensing your self as good enough, adorable enough, lovable enough, or not able to communicate effectively enough. To now feeling like wow, my new inner reality is that I can now sense myself as feeling totally good enough, adorable enough, loveable enough, able to effectively communicate. With the same holding true etc. etc. etc., for every other old feeling of self doubt you might thus take the time to clear. Can you now start to whole being grok, how this would lead to a totally new revolutionary level, as to how you would now find your self feeling - about the very core essence of your self? For example, imagine no more inwardly felt necessity to keep your self constantly trying - to 'think' positively all the time. Simply because you would now find your self feeling totally positive all the time with respect to every fulfillment goal you might ever choose to set before your self! Besides, to the extent we find ourselves in various states of fear & self doubt panic, this is precisely when we make our very worst decisions. Is there anyone out there who wouldn't love to feel the very opposite of every self doubt they ever used to feel, within every from this moment on?

See the whole point here, my very dearest Quantum Katie's & Cosmic Charlie's - Within. there is nothing more important for us with respect to helping our Inner Adult's within. To feel able to shift from helpless victim status. Into totally solution generative, fully Adult participant empowered status. Than for us to find ways to help our self's feel able to completely dissolve vaporize every once of self doubt & self loathing, that we might still feel our self's holding inside of our self's. Completely on all out our of ourselves forever! In such a way as to help ourselves actually transcend past being stuck in endless contractive panic, and thus endless frustration - based on a We-can't - don't know how to mode. In the much greater sense of being able to find our much more calm and centered, now completely in our flow zone energy based, Yes-We-Can find a way to use the power of our much more lit up radiant light field. To help our self's feel now actually enabled, to manifest the positively great lives we keep longing for

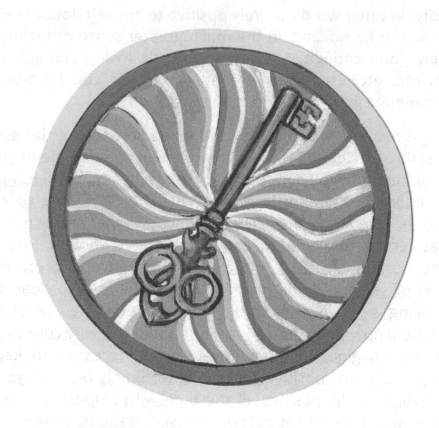

To Help Complete Your Sense of Radiance - It's Time For One's Greater Wisdom Oriented - Lesson # 3

LEARNING JUST HOW TO HOUSE CLEAR EVERY LAST Byte bit - OF ONE'S OLD INNER HELD SELF DOUBT/SELF LOATHING ISSUES - & THUS ULTIMATELY ALL ONE'S SELF SABOTAGING - EMOTIONAL ISSUES

THIRD INNERMOST KEY TOWARD RE-CLAIMING - ONE'S CLEARLY WELL BEYOND ORDINARY NOW EVER MORE SUPER RADIANT SHINNING - SPIRIT LIGHT

One night, as Charlie was shutting down his computer and preparing for bed, inner wisdom knocked lightly on his greater awareness oriented door. "May I come in to visit with you once again, Charlie my boy?" "Of course dear guiding forward inner light, I was hoping that we could talk again about that way fun negative emotion laser light "Zapping" lesson, you shared with me last time we dialogued!" Charlie now found him self smiling, his biggest possible grinning from ear to ear - smile!

"Yes, Charlie my boy, so Good to See You so Happy! I was sensing it was time to check in with you, that I might once again heare, how you ARE, my growing ever more up, young One? It has been several weeks since we began our little laser game, and I've noticed that you appear a bit more content these days. I am so happy and proud of you", inner wisdom said as Charlie felt his own greater sense of him self, kiss himself on the top of his head. "Yes of course, it's because I HAVE been practicing. And have come to see, that each time I use the light of my awareness to dive into those dark feelings that sometimes come up, no matter HOW scary they may be. Inasmuch as I encourage myself to feel totally into the pure energy stream that can be felt within the very core of any such bad feeling that may arise for me, I know they will end. And my sense of being in One-der-land will break through once again!" "And, you know what, it DOES?"

"So much so I am feeling like I can turn every negative feeling that ever arises inside of me. Into growing my own ever larger ball of shinning forth all around me - Light In truth, this laser and the huge ball of light game seems to work perfectly. To such a great extent I am actually beginning to see, that the huge ball of light not only fills me. But it is also what fills positively all things all up, everywhere all around me. With this very same DE-LIGHT-FUL - Super Light - which seems to constitute all things, all creatures great and small, that ever manifest into form! Thank you so much for helping me to more consciously know, what in my greatest sense I already knew! What a miracle that we all have the capability to help ourselves grow up in this way, insofar as we will just become willing to take those response-abilities required. To help ourselves fully feel every reactive emotion that ever comes our way!"

"Oh, Charlie my darling, you're getting very 'punny' in your new ways of seeing just what it takes to live in constant De-Light! Why, I believe that you have mastered the huge more grow up under-standing, that facing completely into your inner emotional fears and resistances?

Is exactly what helps every feeling you may ever have, to expand right on totally out of you! In such a way as to now hang out all around you in the form of pure Super Light? Whereas holding unto them, is what keeps them churning, and seemingly endlessly spinning, inside of you. Such that by way of your own holding in, you tend to become way too over reactively either 'hyper fighter' or 'wimp depressive' vulnerable, to self sabotaging your very own dreams. But clearly you are also learning that it takes practice, to make this ability to face through any such feelings, become completely available within you.. In the direction of helping your self to become lighter, the older you get, instead of the other way around." Inner wisdom now found him/her self most pleased, that this point was finally getting across to the very core inside of his very own. Way more Quantum attuned Magical - most beloved Cosmic Adult within.

"So, what's next, GREAT grand inner wisdom teacher," Charlie was curious? "I am totally ready for more inner wisdom dialogue, Charlie could be heard to say to himself! "Well dear One, since your first lesson I have been constantly in touch with every One's ancient most inner wisdom. And here are some wonderful insights that have been put together out of our collective conscious past - to help you. In-so-far as you may continue to help grow yourself into the extra-ordinary young man/woman, that everyone who looks beyond your present held fears & self doubts, can see in you!" Charlie/Katie found himself loving the gentle inner purring sound of his/her own inner wisdom, voice. It was then his/her inner wisdom went on to say, "I want you to know that I love you with all your very own heart. And, that in your very own greatest inner wisdom eyes, you are a most remarkable, Truly Magical Being! There is a way brilliant shinning future waiting for you, beyond even your wildest dreams, now that you are now at the crossroads of leaving your childhood behind! While at the very same time the path toward your very own most grown up, truly magnificent self, is beginning to call out to you from your very own ever more grown up wisdom voice, within!"

"Not that it is EVER a good idea to abandon the spirit, the joy, and all the great lessons you learned in early childhood. For these are our most precious jewels... our foundation... our home base ... in fact greater awareness realizations. Which have the capacity to help keep guiding us ever forward, in-so-far as we will just keep choosing to move ever forward. Into your very own fully grown up - truly Magical ever more empowered Adulthood!" "I think I finally am beginning to under-stand my most precious Inner Wisdom", Charlie replied as he peered deeply into his very own growing sense of being! "At our very deepest levels, how we choose to live our lives, is all about how well we create those very full of life energy intentions, that can keep pulling us toward our possibility to be all that we have been designed / evolved within our very own uniqueness - to be!' And then help ourselves to actually 'find ourselves' clear and free enough from all of our negative emotions, to be able to actually realize our very best dreamed for intentions!"

"Yes, wow where did that huge insight about your self come from? Cause you are already beginning to sense the next lesson we have in store for you," Inner wisdom now spoke more softly & gently inside of Charlie/Katie, simply because he/she was now much more prepared to listen! "Given you have identified things in your world that give you much satisfaction and joy, things that really spark the light of your curiosity and interest. This is the extent to which you have been blessed with many uniquely you, talents, my dear Charlie, or for that matter dearest Katie. There is no question that you love much about life, your favorite play areas of interest, electronics, music, mechanics, art, fashion & design, my Good God-Ness me, even animals, books, certain people, exploring celestial things, religion and so, so, much more. Such that to the extent you keep tending this inner, ever growing fire of interest - which keeps on flickering within the very heart of you! It will keep on growing into an ever more brilliant, guiding you ever more forward, inner inspirational self inventive oriented - shinning field of light. The very sort of light likely to help bring you not just great heart felt satisfaction, but also all the various forms of abundance & prosperity you as well as every other One of us, truly longs for!"

"Here's the thing Charlie", his own ever growing One's Self up, innermost wisdom now whispered. "Your future path can already be found within the very interests, you now already have, on this very day! You see, it is up to each and every one of us to be aware of all those very love to be involved areas, of our inner most interest. Such as are most likely to light up a roaring fire of involvement excitement, inside the very core of each of our very own unique senses of our selves. Certainly it is important for us not to ignore or discredit, such positively love to do this or that, inner passion callings. Rather it is in our very best interests to fully explore those passions that spark our curiosity and bring us joy to the max. Then be open to follow, precisely that inner guidance which keeps directing us toward wherever. The continual development of such interests and talents, may lead us," inner wisdom added. "In such a way that starts to enable us to eventually be able to vision see, a way to use these inner given talents and interests of ours. To help each of us make some sort of contribution toward both our individual as well as collective good. Even so, it is important to see that many times, along with our most passionate interests, will come various levels of frustration. Feelings for example of being stopped and blocked, as though we simply can't or don't know how, to move ourselves forward, next. Toward the realization of our dreams, in relation to our most passionate areas of interest and talent!"

"Remember when many times in your past, you have actually been able to manifest some toy into your life, you so much thought you wanted to have with all your heart?" Charlie nodded a bit sheepishly! He felt his cheeks starting to get hot. "Yes I wanted to learn to be so good at playing with that thing, but I simply failed! I felt so stupid, so unable, so incompetent, I felt there was NO way I could ever be as good as I once 'thought', I wanted to be. 'I' remember feeling I would never get it. Would never be good enough to play well enough... in such an area of huge passionate interest, NEVER EVER!" As he spoke, Charlie's felt this old I-Can't, I'm simply not good enough, don't know how to story, to such an intense degree. He could now feel these feelings of self doubt and self loathing, actually burning like a huge flare button inside of him. Taking his inner self down, ever more down into a seemingly bottomless fire pit of despair, wherein he kept finding himself saying to him self. "I'm just not good enough, not acceptable enough, somewhere deep inside his own body."

With greater respect to which Inner Wisdom now put his hand on Charlie/Katies shoulder! "Welcome to life, and the many challenges the living of it tends to bring to every One of Us, my child. We refer to this as SELF DOUBT & or SELF LOATHING! I want you to know that I your ancient most inner wisdom within, completely understand your feelings. We all of us humans since the beginning of time, have had similar self doubt and making ourselves feel horrible emotions! But here now in this new lesson, what is most important for you to now know. Is that the very same magic laser beam of light you learned to help your self with, in your just prior lesson. Can help you just as well, to FEEL every bit all the way PAST, even these kinds of accumulated negative feelings, about your self! By way of you learning to use this same laser beam to now help support your self to feel, both totally core into. As well as all the way radiantly out the very core of any feelings of self doubt and self loathing, you along with the reset of the worlds population. Are likely to find your self still holding inside. In just the very same way you learned to feel through various other resisted, don't want to feel, even hate to feel emotions, in your last session."

"It can," Charlie's eyes opened wide? "Absolutely, Charlie", inner wisdom continued. "That very same magic laser beam can vaporize, exorcise, dissolve, poof every singe one of your feelings of self doubt out of you forever! Cause without a doubt, such doubts are not who YOU REALLY ARE in your inner most essence at All. For in greatest truth you have actually been designed / evolved to be someone very special. Some-One so brilliant and shining, the very sort of being who has been made to invent your way forward, into the greatest possible future, you can imagine! In ways that will carry you into places of excellence & joy, beyond even what you heretofore, have even dared to imagine! In-so-far as you will keep agreeing to keep setting the best intentions to move forward you can possibly muster, in front of your self! And are willing at all times, to keep holding on to your dreams, in a way that doesn't let fear or self doubt, overtake you!"

"You see, my dear One's! From the perspective of Some-One who has the capacity to grow all up past all negative held emotion. Into the great whole being lit up, Super radiant Light Field shinning magnetic laws of attraction, which we all really are! We are all actually Being who are fully capable of pulling our self up into that place, where our dreams and goals can actually be made manifest. In this huge respect, remember that great guiding forth quotation, from One of our very greatest wisdom sources? "In the beginning was the word, and the word (in all it's power and glory) was made manifest." "Well, can you now better under-stand, this was simply a huge inner wisdom way, to say to us all. Just how important it is for us to set great 'get ourselves totally whole being behind our word' based intentions, in front of ourselves. And then clear ourselves of all self doubt, that we might find our own inner Tap Our Source Link, to that very power & glory, out of which all things, manifest. Besides have you ever seen One single newborn babe, constantly declaring to itself, that it is somehow not good enough, not deserving enough? Well if you didn't come in here in a state of separation from that power which is of your Source? Then perhaps it is time to come back into that totally good enough, full-on empowerment state, we all come in here with in the first place?"

"Tell me therefore my ever glowing Sunshine, of all the things that interest you most and I know there are many! Simply because it is perfectly fine to have more than one area of interest! What I am now interested in you telling me about, are those things that excite you so much, that you can hardly wait for your morning to arrive. So you can jump right back in and explore these kinds of interests, even more each entirely new next day! In fact I am so interested in what you most love to do, every single day of your life. That I now want to you set some great intention in front of your self, that will help to pull you along into becoming even better at this 'thing' or even 'things', you so much love to do, you can hardly wait to get out of bed every morning. In such a way as to you encourage your self to feel within the whole power of your being, the reality of you getting better at what you most love to do, is already actually happening."

"For example, imagine getting up each day and saying to your self, I-Am some One, who is even better at reading, writing, making music, playing at sports, art, math, science, producing whatever kind of products you most love to play with, even inventing new products to play with, communicating with people you like, making true soul friends, doing loving things for those you care for, seeing new possibilities to help your self be a better person. And last but not least being some-one truly able to Tap that inner most Source of all Energy, which exists well beyond your so called ordinary sense of self, most especially in relation to what you most love to do. These self improvement goals can be large, or small, it doesn't so much matter what you love to do most, and would thus positively love to get better at. Just that in the context of this lesson, you set great improvement goals for your self."

"Simply because Charlie my boy, Katie my dear, the moment you set any intention self improvement set goal for your self, stated in the present tense. As though you actually are capable of improving your abilities and talents in relation to whatever it might be, you most love to do. This will be the moment you will hear various self doubt and self loathing messages, raise their ugly heads inside of you. By way of hearing your self, say to your self, "But 'I-Can't, I'm not good enough, deserving enough, talented enough, simply-don't know how to improve myself, nobody will help me, etc, etc. In such a way that insofar as you keep holding such beliefs about your self, you will start putting your much larger Tap Your Energy Source' potential. Into some kind of negative black hole state once again. Here then is the huge point of this lesson, the moment you are able to better hear these self doubt messages. In such a way as to sense just exactly where you may be feeling such negativities about your self, somewhere in your body. This

<u>will the moment Yes You-Can start to laser light zap into these negative held feelings, in the very same way you learned to use the laser light of your awareness in the just prior lesson."</u>

"Oh my Good God-Ness me", Charlie was heard to exclaim! "You mean to say, to the extent I keep choosing not to create clear improvement intentions for myself. With respect to me feeling like Yes I-Can Be, all that I want to be! In not asking my self to be better, especially in relation to whatever it may be that I most love to do? I-am unlikely to be motivated to find ways to help myself actually be way more clearly better. In other words all I will other than wise, be able to heare? is an endless cacophony of my own self doubts? Without me ever being motivated to find a way to feel through clear myself of whatever self doubts, I may have taken on over the course of my life. Thus making it simply impossible, for me to fully 'Tap My Source of more full-on Empowerment. This in fact this is starting to make so much sense to me, I can now see that among my most important tasks in life. Is going to be for me to clear my inner self completely, of every ounce of self doubt & self loathing, I may have ever taken on. Over the course of the various ways I have fallen into feeling self doubt in my life." "Yes, Yes, Yes, Charlie my boy, this is exactly the very essence of this lesson."

In this respect, Charlie/Katie now found each of themselves, in one huge gigantic Aha In-Sight. So getting the essence o f this new self doubt clearing lesson - inside. He/She started to brim to the very tip top of his/her Being, with the most One-Der-Ful excitement! Inasmuch as he/she could now finally under-stand, that no matter how many special laser light focusing times it may take - to totally dissolve all his/her inner felt self doubt demons. To the extent he/she might agree to dive in and confront each & eventually every self doubt. With his/her feel totally through to completion, laser beam of light. Just in the same way he/she learned to face totally into all his/her negative hateful demons, in the just prior lesson. The more he/she might in this way keep choosing to support his/her self toward laser focus feeling, right through the very core center of each & every self doubt. The more all such self doubts would begin to 'go poof vaporize' right on out of every him or her forever - which remember - is really about every you and me?

Such that the more we each of us might agree to practice, this great lesson! The more powerfully actually now in control, of how we may keep choosing to use the pure energy of our feelings - we are going to find ourselves becoming! Simply because once dissolved, all those

Doubt Demons inside of us are not only going to lose all their power to keep compelling us. To keep energy losing 'fight or flight' acting, as though we are constantly out of control But they will also in the very same light, lose their power to keep us compulsively attracting exactly whatever we don't want! In such a way that we will at the same time liberate these formerly lost energies, into being much more light radiant now totally available - to help us keep realizing our intended dreams.

<u>This Then Is A Great Time To Take Some Time - To now much more Fully Under-Stand - The importance of beginning a process of Feeling Clear Through in such a way as to thus thoroughly Remove from Our Hearts - Any & All Self Doubts & Self Loathings - We may find our Self's still holding anywhere Inside of Us</u>

Once you can fully under-stand the importance of identifying any particular pain body felt self doubt / self loathing issue. Such as you may still feel your self holding - somewhere inside your self. Especially with respect to where you may feel the very center of any such feeling residing. In relation to any given vital energy fulfillment area in your bio energetic system - you keep longing to have fulfilled within you. From here it's just a matter of learning to apply, the very same feel to the core technique you learned to help dissolve various basic negative held e-motions - in the just prior lesson. In the greater sense of supporting your self to enter with your now laser focused feel into the core light of awareness - exactly into the very energy of any such a still held inner self doubt or self loathing emotion. Which you may find your self still holding - somewhere inside of the core of you. To such an inwardly focused fully felt degree, that such any given old held self doubt resistance pattern would now totally vaporize / dissolve right on out of you - forever.

(**Accompanying Explanation** – <u>This Then Is The Perfect Time To Re-Look at Illustrations # 7 & 7-A</u> - Images of Ourselves as ever Growing more Up Hu-Man most Beings - Deciding to now use the very same feel totally into the core of some still Inner Held - Self Doubt, or Even Self Loathing - Emotion - Until such time as that inner self doubt / self loathing based contractive pattern - can be felt to have dissolved vaporized - completely out of us - forever. Always in order that we may in this way now much better enable our self's, to get all of our innermost felt vital energies, way more totally behind organizing the potential ful-till-ment of any given set intention, we may choose to put in front of ourselves. So that we may thus now help our self's feel way more fully empowered enabled - in relation to any of our given intentions. Inasmuch as this is best way we have to keep inventing our Self's ever forward - into the complete range of all those inner being fulfillments we most long for. Without anymore self sabotaging, self doubt or self loathing being continuously held in our way.)

To Such a Clear Free of All Self Doubt - Point Within - We Will Now Find Our Inner-Most Sense of Our New Way More Expansive Self's Feeling a Total Sense Of -

Yes-Yes We-Can Actually Fulfill Our Sensual/Sexual Sense of Being

Yes-Yes We-Can Actually Fulfill Our Doer / Entre-Preneurial Sense of Being

Yes-Yes We-Can Actually Fulfill Our Great Equal to Equal Relationships Sense of Being

Yes-Yes We -Can Actually Realize Our Capacity to Find Fully Heart Open Loving-Ness

Yes-Yes We-Can Articulate & Communicate Our Clearest Under-Standings - Quite Brilliantly

Yes-Yes We-Can Keep Generating Truly Great Forward Seeing Creative Inventive - Solutions

<u>Yes-Yes We-All-Can Be So Well Beyond Ordinary Pure Spirit Alive Awake - We Will Now Find Ourselves Fully Able To Live Within Our One & Only Most Truly Tap Our Same Source Most Truly Connected - Sense of Being</u>

And guess what, now that every ever more growing up Charlie / Katie within was really starting to get the huge sense of learning to dissolve / vaporize all of his/her self doubts & self loathings out of him/her self - forever? His/Her new inner reality was, he/she was starting to feel the exact opposite of any self doubt - within him/herself. Like for example in clearing himself of all feelings of being not good enough, or not deserving enough! Charlie or for that matter Katie, was now starting to feel like wow, I'm not only actually feeling totally good enough & deserving enough etc. etc. etc. In relation to each of my own inner most vital energy fulfillment seeking areas in my body! But now that I've cleared my old self doubt, I now seem to have so much zip, zap, zest, and zing energy fully on board within myself! To such a profound clear felt self empowering degree, that Yes I-Can can now sense myself. Fully able to both mobilize as well as organize my innermost awake whole being intelligence in the direction of helping me to now actually be completely able. To fully realize the ful-fill-ment of any given intention, I might find myself choosing to set before myself! Without any more self sabotaging doubt or loathing, being anymore in my way." "Yes, Yes, Charlie found himself declaring to himself, as felt himself fully reinforcing his willingness to keep on self doubt clearing every felt negativity completely out of himself, in order that he might now feel fully capable, within himself!

Here at this juncture, Inner Wisdom decided it was time to introduce Charlie / Katie to a reverse focus way of using the light of his/her awareness. As an equally powerful alternate method to help him/her self keep moving forward past all former held negative emotions, including all forms of self doubt & self loathing. Especially when it might come to certain powerful highly charged negative emotions, wherein one might find one's tendency to over react. So compelling as to pretty much instantaneously impel one into taking some sort of overly reactive, either 'hyper fighter' or 'fleer avoider' and thus ultimately self sabotaging, behavior. Such that in the early stages of the already learned feel to the core practice, it might feel impossible to be able to stop / ground one's awareness enough. To feel able to enter into the very core of such an instantly highly over reactive - inner held old emotional charge. "Fortunately for all of us", inner wisdom was motivated to share, "there is another traditional method we refer to as the overseeing 'I' technique. Which is designed to help each and every one of us with precisely such highly instantly over reactive - often explosively compelling flare button tendencies."

'With respect to this particular method, "the whole point inner wisdom now said! Is for you my dear Charlie or Katie, to pretty much instantly, in this very moment. Just start attuning to your pure awareness ability in such a way as to now encourage your overseeing witnessing sense of your self. Too very quickly allow the energy of such an emotion to expand as far out there, as it seems natural for the energy of that emotion to expand. In the much larger sense of starting to encourage your overseeing witnessing self - to just sense how big the outer boundary of such a highly charged emotion is? I.E. Can you feel the energy of any such e-emotion encompassing a full room, the whole building, a round block, a round mile, even several round miles, your county, your whole state? Just how big is the energy field of your particular here and now flare button e-motion? The beauty of jumping into this pure witnessing allowing the energy of your e-motion to just expand space, is that you will in the very same lightening flash of awareness. Begin to create some instant stop behaviorally reacting, freedom from compulsion space - for your self. In such a way that you can then encourage your most overseeing 'I' - watching your self sense of self. To now take this pure witnessing awareness principle totally out there - one outer band more. To a place wherefrom it becomes possible to just 'watch' your energy with respect to such a highly charged emotion. Now fully able to flash / radiate / expand, even explode like lightening bolts - right on out of you. Until such time as you feel that particular emotional charge - reduce to zero."

"Here's the point for every One of Us to fully get! Even though it may take some supportive guidance and practice to really get a full sense of this method" my ever growing up children within, inner wisdom continued. "The whole point here is that once any of us can get a real sense of this method, it can become among the most powerful of grow ourselves ever up tools we can have - in our inner wisdom oriented arsenal."

Illustrations 10 & 10-A - Now For A Most Powerful Alternate Method To Help Ourselves Dissolve Vaporize - Any way powerful Negative Held Feelings we might find ourselves still Holding - Including all Self Doubt & Self Loathing E-Motions

The essence of this alternate method then, is too very quickly help your self in one instant, get a sense of just how big any negative flare button emotion you may find your self having, feels for you. Does the energy of your emotion fill your body, the room, a round block, a round mile, your whole county, your state, your country, the world? Just how far out around you can you sense this energy seeming to radiate? The good news being that moment you can get a sense of this, the next task is to instantly carry your awareness out one step further, to that outer boundary place wherein you can now see. Just how big your flare button really is? Here's the point, to the degree you can sense your self seeing or watching any flare button emotion from a pure watching your self point of view, that is now beyond the outer boundaries of the energy of your emotion. This is the degree to which you can get in touch with what is known as your most pure witnessing enabled sense of self, or that pure watcher awareness overseeing place, that is always bigger than any emotion you might ever have. In such a way that you can now use this pure watching awareness to help the energy of some such flare button emotion - keep on radiating out of you. Until such time as there is no more reactive energy left inside of you, anymore. Just pure relaxed para-sympathtically innervated energy, now able to hang out all around you. In a way that is no longer likely to compel you into some sort of overly reactive, either 'hyper fighter' or 'wimp fleer' based action.

(**Accompanying Note** - Please under-stand this technique is actually based on traditional meditative methods, for helping our self's to dissolve / vaporize old patterns of negative held emotion, even old accompanying repetitive negative held, thought patterns. The whole idea in this case is to help one's self ever more realize, that who we are is not limited to our body confines alone. Such that the more we learn to become the overseeing witness to both our emotional, as well as rational logical nature. The more we can liberate not just our vital energies, but also our thoughts to become truly pure free to help us. To the point wherein our ability to access this beyond body witness - would now become ever more second nature to whom we now experience ourselves - to actually be. As opposed to keeping our e-motions & thoughts stuck inside, in such a way that compulsively keeps driving us into what amounts to endless rounds of self sabotaging dysfunctional behaviors.)

ONE'S HUGE OVERSEEING 'I' TECHNIQUE MAGNIFIED - QUITE SIMPLY WAY OUT BEYOND BODY - PURE WITNESS WATCHING ONE'S SELF KEEP ON RELEASING SOME OLD INNER NEGATIVE HELD - VITAL E-MOTIONAL SPIRIT ENERGY - COMPLETELY ALL OUT

Illustration 10B – Here Now Is A Way Laid Back Version of Ourselves Now Agreeing to Apply - One of these opposite focused greater Awareness Enhancing Expand the Energy of our Emotions - Methods (I.E. Either the Feel to the Core or the Overseeing I) - With respect to helping ourselves Clear every area of Self Doubt we may ever find Ourselves Holding somewhere Inside of Ourselves - One Core Body Area at a Time - Until such time as we begin to sense ourselves as Clear Radiant - Yes We-Can Ever More Light Shining Enabled Beings

Clearly It's Time To See - Every One's Time Has Come To Actually Begin To Apply either - The Prior Feel Totally into & Through The Core Method - Or the Over Seeing 'I' Technique. To help ourselves totally clear our Self's of all former inner held Negativities & Self Doubts. To the point where we would no-longer feel anymore self doubt or self loathing inside of us - anymore. And would much rather actually begin to feel the very opposite Yes-I-Can, now I actually know how to realize my dreams - much more radiant feeling inside.

(**Accompanying Explanation** – Leaving ourselves feeling so positive - we would begin to feel like Yes-We-Can keep on inventing ourselves ever forward. Toward the fulfillment of more and more of whatever the whole of our inner most beings - might most long for.)

#10 B

USING EITHER OF THESE 2 OPPOSITE FOCUSED
SELF CLEARING TECHNIQUES - AS ONE'S MEANS
TO HELP FULLY RADIATE EXPAND OUT EVERY
LAST BYTE OF ALL ONE'S OLD INNER HELD IN &
THUS STILL FELT - EMOTIONAL NEGATIVITIES

"With the positively great news for us all now being", Charlie's greater inner wisdom quite suddenly found himself most joyously exclaiming unto himself! "The more we each of us can help these energy losing inner conflicts, we keep holding within ourselves. To disappear clear totally right on out of us - forever! The more we will encourage our sense of self - to make our Inner 'I' single or unified into One Whole - no longer in any way divided. Then the more alive and full of clear light radiant shinning energy, we are going to find our much greater more expanded sense of self - being able to be. To such a degree we will more and more find our self, actually experiencing our self 'As a Body now Filled with Light', or as though 'Lamps of Light unto our Self's'. Something our innermost sense of self, already knows to be the clear truth, with the utmost respect to just how powerful - we have all been designed / evolved to be. Which is of course exactly why, we can't help but like such songs, as 'Let your little light shine', and of course 'Amazing Grace' 'I once was lost', 'but now I am found' 'I once was blind', 'but now I see'. Such that most fortunately for us, the more we find ways to be filled with the grace of this Radiant Shinning Same Source Light! The more and more we are going to find our self's ever more enabled to do almost anything, we set before our now more unified, shinning soul spirits, to accomplish."

"Yes, Yes, my own inner sun", Charlie's (Katie's) own inner wisdom voice could now be heard to declare! "Precisely because you will no longer have any more self doubt held inside of you - in your own way. To keep holding your way more 'in my flow zone empowered', and thus far greater sense of your self - back. Rather now, there will be no-thing left inside, but a huge field of radiant shinning light to keep on attracting ever more light back into you. My most magical, dearest most precious, residing ever more clear inside of every One - greatest possible sense of being! Now you are really starting to clear sense - by far the best way - to keep growing your inner most wisdom - ever forward!"

"All so that we every one of us may now come to glow - with ever more growing self confidence. With respect to our very own innermost sense, that yes-we-can actually manifest into our reality! The very best of intentions we may ever choose to set in front of ourselves!"

Now For Illustration # 11 – Holy Molly - Image of Our Inner 'Me' - Glowing now with such Total Self Confidence - We may thus with All of Our Vital Energetic Power way more Onboard - Now feel fully enabled to invent our Self's into whomsoever we each of us - Might most Love To Be

Imagine being able to totally shift one's inner sense of self - from way too often feeling like - One is somehow not good enough, not deserving enough, not able enough. To a place within wherein One might spontaneously without any felt need for anymore effort, now feel like One's I-Am within is totally good enough, able enough, deserving enough, or even worthy enough. To now totally love one's self into being fully enabled to move ever more solution forward, within the context of any challenge that may ever come One's way! Very much as a consequence of having agreed to feel fully through some old self doubt via either the focused laser light feel to the core method, or the over seeing 'I' method, of some given self doubt or self loathing one once used to hold somewhere inside. In relation to each of one's '7' vital energy areas, as previously described.

(**Accompanying Note** – Can you therefore imagine you your self no longer feeling any form of self doubt, in relation to any of those '7' emotional ful-fillment seeking aspects, of your own inner most vital energetic being. Is there anyone out there who wouldn't totally love to feel enabled - to fulfill all of one's self at all '7' levels - of one's potential to experience actually being fulfilled - within every one of these '7' vital energy - related ways? To the point wherein you would actually feel able to integrate the fulfillment of all of your '7' vital energies within you - into a single unified whole sense of your self. Centered within your most sacred now glowing - total love of life heart!

Such that as we have mentioned before, if you should find your self motivated toward more extensive training in both the Feel to the Core & Overseeing 'I' techniques. We highly recommend you take at least one weekend training with either Tom Stone himself by registering at his web site greatlifetechnologies.com or alternatively with his most excellent protégé - Aspen DeCew at truly conscious.com Who can via their ongoing inexpensive weekend workshops - help every one who wants to get a much better sense of just how to apply this method. In such a way that yes one can learn how to feel any such particular highly reactive emotional charge - reduce to zero. Much as we attempt to illustrate in the magnified version - 10-A! By way of showing our overseeing 'I' - in a vey real sense pure out of body fully now able to just watch witness some old highly reactive charge - keep on lightening bolt flashing out - to the point where some old over reactive charge pattern - releases completely out of us forever.

In the much larger sense - that every time we find some way to clear some old self doubt negative emotion fear pattern inside ourselves. We start to glow with the very opposite feeling of self confidence. Every time we learn to integrate any of our '7' vital energies, more into being motivated to move ourselves forward from within our own heart space. The more we begin to feel vital energetically empowered to actual invent our way toward the fulfillment of any such given vital energy - within our very own most integral senses of self. Until such time as our heart begins to become so open, that very inner presence of being this lovingly alive, helps to motivate us toward greater and greater states of actual fulfillment.- Here. In the very direction of us starting to feel ever more Whole-Sum and thus truly Integrally capable of actually fulfilling positively all our very inner most - intention set dreams.)

(Short important additional note – In these terms there is absolutely no-thing wrong with wanting & desiring to be fulfilled at every one of these '7' vital energy related levels. It is however important as we shall come to under-stand better later, to support ourselves to de-tach ourselves from how we 'think' these fulfillments are supposed to happen. In higher spiritual circles we say set your very own unique fulfillment intentions, proceed to clear your self of all self doubt and self loathing, and then be open to surprises. Simply because it seems to require surrender into something larger than being driven by our little mere in our head only 'small thinking' minds alone. Into a place within us that is no longer separated out from our larger whole field attuned awareness. In order to help ourselves best arrange for the fulfillments we seek. Which in turn implies, that it is only our more integral consciousness, which can best help us to arrange these fulfillments. In ways that are going to go beyond whatever results we might by way of our 'thinking minds alone - like to narrow band keep trying to keep on projecting - as the most desirable outcome for us. To the point where attachment to these mere little mind projected outcomes, can actually become a hindrance to the more complete fulfillments we seek. This then is the deeper meaning of detachment – to stop 'thinking' we in our heads alone, know how our more complete whole being fulfillments - can best be realized. We will have much more to say about this self integration process via the bringing together of our '7' vital energies through the wisdom of the heart as we get into the last section of this book.)

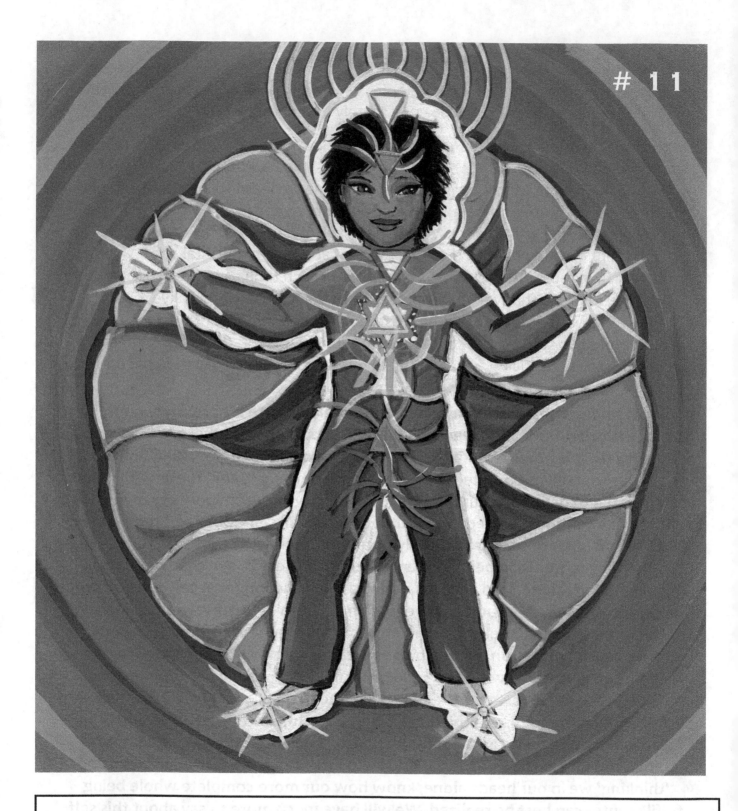

HOLY MOLLY HERE'S MY INNER 'ME' - NOW VIRTUALLY ABLE TO GLOW FROM WITHIN A PLACE OF EVER MORE WHOLE-SUM LIGHT SHINNING - NOW CLEAR FOUND 'SELF CONFIDENCE'

"Wow", Charlie (ergo Katie) now found his/her inner voice saying in one last huge humungous insight, "It is almost as though the One singular most underlying / beyond lying - 'Super Source Light' at the very root of all creation. So loves us, that we might very well say! It appears we have been designed / evolved to fulfill all of our dreams. Insofar as we will just take that inner dive totally into our core responsibility, or alternatively overseeing 'I' pure witnessing sense of our self - it seems to take. For us to face fully into and through whatever fears and self doubts we may find ourselves holding. That we may in this way clear ourselves of all emotional negativity and self doubt. Other than wise, we will tend to keep on re-cycling the same old, same old filled with negativity unwanted experiences, into our lives over and over again. Always trying to over reactively force, the improvement of our lives at whatever self sabotaging cost. Until such time as we decide, it is finally time to wake ourselves up clear past, all such old self destructive - ways.

Charlie was in fact now so out of his mind filled with utter 'De-Light'. He wanted to megaphone out to every single 'One' in the world. "Promise me this", he said! "Just agree to try these first 3 lessons for the next 6 mos. of your life. In such a way, that you agree to totally dedicate your self to the growth of your very own - inner most wisdom. By way of both these feel totally into - as well as expand totally out through - the here & now reality of your feeling & emotional nature - practices. Particularly in relation to that sense of empowerment", Charlie now knew you would be able to sense. In relation to your very own ability to actually realize, the most cherished of your dreams. Then he went on to say, "He would appreciate you getting back to him in the form of your own inner wisdom comments on these first 3 lesson, or if you prefer to continue to knot! Inasmuch as it's all up to you now to discover just how you can help yourself to now fly, toward the manifestation of your very best intended dreams? Please note, there are no misspellings, just more of Cosmic Charlie's attempts at being punny!

Third 'Full of Life Force Energy' Empowering Prayer - Unto One's Ever Growing Inner-Most Ful-Fill-Ment Capable - Sense of Way Larger Well Beyond Ordinary - True Now Way More Light-Ness In Being Found Self.

"I-Now keep finding My-Self as the very sort of Some-One who constantly chooses to set positive goals and intentions for my self, in front of myself. In terms of just how I would 'most' like to create myself forth in relation to the living of my very own unique 'me' - ever forward. Into the most positively fulfilling life, I might ever imagine. As well as some-one who is willing to take whatever time it takes to face directly into, in such a way as to thus help clear myself - of all forms of self doubt - that I might find myself still holding. Inasmuch as the more I agree to find ways to feel totally through every core body feeling of self doubt or for that matter self loathing, that may keep on arising within me. Into the sort of vital energy vibrant place that is beyond anymore fear based felt need - to keep contracting against my own 'life force'.

My new truly great life oriented reality, is that more I clear myself of all of these old fear based energy losing habits. The more and more I will now sense myself feeling so open to my very own much greater sense of joyful empowerment. Wherein the core essence of who I-am - beyond all former self doubt. My new core truth will be that Yes I-Can, actually now sense my more energetically empowered self - actually being fully enabled to manifest my very best dreamed for intentions. Simply because most fortunately for me, the more and more I-Can feel this sense of vital energetic joy, resounding it's motivational song clearer and clearer within me. The more and more 'I-Am Going to Fully Get It', that nothing can stop me from creating the truly beautiful - totally joy fulfilling life that I long for."

Next Our Second 3 Lesson Set of More Truly Wise-Dome of Awareness Oriented Methods - Designed To Help Totally 'Liberate' The More Big Mind Lit Up & Thus Way More Truly Brilliant Solution Generative Enabled Side - Of Our Whole Nervous System Integrated - Capabilities

Chapter 5

Lesson # 4 – First - Going On To Support Our Most Extra Ordinary Sense of Pure Light Spirit Radiance - To Keep Expanding From Here 'To Infinity & Beyond'

Rationale for HAVE A GREAT LIFE LESSON - # 4

Once we start to feel more and more able to dissolve / vaporize all our inner held negative feelings & emotions about life, such as tend to keep holding our greater spirit aware senses of ourselves back. The more and more positive and radiant energy excited about going out to play each day, we are going to find our self becoming. With respect to whatever fields of interest we might most love to 'play' at. To the point that we will notice our self ever more frequently being, as totally interested in life, lights unto our self's. And I say 'play at', because this is precisely how we will find our self's evermore starting to feel. Like life is one huge opportunity to now 'play' our very most De-Light-fFul insides - all Out. Within what amounts to this huge playfield of Super-Light energy - we all find ourselves living within here - to our max.

Which in turn is exactly why it becomes most important to help guide every One of our selves, into 'playing' not only at, all those things we most love to keep 'playing' within. But also 'toward playing' in such a way we begin to much better sense, that our very own vital energy field. Is most intimately non-separatively connected with the very underlying / beyond lying energy - which makes up every singular thing we may ever find ourselves most loving to play with. In much the same way we once used feel our heart beat as existing non-separately as only one heart beating, from that of our parents. Whenever they would love song, sing us to sleep - within their very own energy fields of light. As well as in later life, insofar as pretty much all of us have had such precious moments just like when we first came in here, with our favorite pet dogs or cats, or horses, even favorite plants. With most honorable mention to those most magical love making moments, whenever we may have found ourselves being totally present way beyond ordinary in love, with someone we have found so special. We have been blessed to feel our clearest sense of pure awareness now way more able, to penetrate right into the very core of that most special some One else's innermost Being. To such a profoundly well beyond ordinary inside to inside intensively experienced degree, that we could not help but find ourselves in such moments, totally loving the absolute incredibleness. Of whatever we might have found ourselves well beyond ordinary connecting with - in this kind of most special of non-separate ways. We may very well have found ourselves declaring unto ourselves! "I think I shall never see, a poem quite as lovely as a tree" - by Joyce Kilmer. Or, "Tiger, Tiger burning bright, in the forests of the night. What immortal hand or eye, Dare frame thy fearful (sacred) symmetry" - by William Blake? And even my very own "My dog friend says, Let's cut the 'BS', and just agree to clear old, 'B' together" (To be found in my book of poetry - Inspirational Magic)?

To confirm for your Self what we are talking about here, just take a moment to remember this. Sense the last time you held a newborn baby in your arms. In such a way that you may very well have found yourself being drawn totally into the very insides of their state of being. Can you remember why we keep referring to our newborns, as being like little Buddha's or little Christ's? Is it because they draw us so into them, too such a non-separate penetrative degree? We can actually feel them in terms of only one heart beating, right inside of us? In such a way that we can now thus experience our own presence, being right inside of them? Are these among life's most precious moments, or what? Can you now help your self realize, that this is exactly how we all come in here in the first place, within a state of non-separation. Which In terms of the old Beattles metaphor, that sings, koo, koo, kajoob, yes, we actually all are the egg man, the walrus, our mother's and /or our father's, indeed every single thing we ever experience. It becomes just a matter of supporting ourselves to become totally comfortable with our possibility to live within this state of non-separteness, on a daily ongoing basis once again. Which after all is said and done, is the very state of totally loving everything about life, we keep longing for.

Unfortunately an important part of our huge collective human dilemma, is that. Not only have we tended to become fear conditioned out of this natural state of non-separation, we all came in here having access to, within! Very much as a consequence of us having taken on all kinds of fear based patterns, of contracting against and thus constraining what amounts to our own vital energy generative system. To such a compounded degree, we start to lose the very energy we require to keep boosting our awareness system into this state of non-separation. But we have also become afraid to trust the experience of this state, as being entirely in 'thought', 'word' and 'deed', actually most One-Der-Fully natural for us, to keep on experiencing. Inasmuch as to be in such a state of non-separate-ness, is actually to be in our most natural 'philosophers stone' found, state of pure unlimited awareness

Wise Dome of awareness. Which is precisely why it seems to take yet another dimension of persistent greater awareness oriented practice, to help ourselves get used to such a state, once again. Now however, as the truly magical, pure energy wisdom attuned adults, that yes we most fortunately have all been 'divined' to be. Provided we take those response-abilities which seem to be required, for us to find this true Divination Space which resides within.

This then is exactly what the next 3 way more wide band awareness opening, how we can best keep inventing our way ever forward into core being fulfillment, lessons are going to be all about. Which is to say, discovering just how we may find some much wiser way to play out our life's. In the very sort direction that will enable us to feel empowered to keep playing it ever forward - to such a here and now attuned to the 'One & Only Source Force' - present degree. We will actually begin to sense our self as Some-One now fully able to realize our very best dreamed for intentions. In-as-much as the important key to opening our more rational / logical solution generative nature to our solution generative max, is to learn how to link our own now much better lit up radiant energy field totally up. With the very same underlying, beyond lying 'Super-Light Source of Pure Energy', which can be experienced to exist in all of the so called objects, we keep on experiencing within every singular most 'One' of our most passionate fields of interest. In other words support all of ourselves to expand our very purest sense of great Wise-Dome centered field of awareness. To the point where we begin to realize, that our very own energy based awareness system, actually seems to exist ultimately non-dualistically right within every single thing we ever come to experience. And therefore within the huge Big Picture magic, of this great to infinity and beyond singular most Mystery Field, we all find ourselves living within.

In this huge respect, there is not one single youngster I have ever seen, who in visiting the Buzz Light-Year pavilion, at Disneyland. Does not completely resonate with Buzz, when he say's 'To Infinity….. & Beyond'. This is because children already know, that their energy field is actually core to core, completely non locally entangled interactive, from inside to inside within every other thing they love to experience. In such a way that the inner enthusiasm children carry into their world, most intimately influences the way they experience their world. This is because as we have already pointed out, we all arrive here at birth, into the sort non-dualistic state of awareness. Within which we experience ourselves as being non-separate from other things, especially from our parents. And thus still tend to carry within us, especially in our early years, before this non-separate way of knowing is so called educated, completely out of us. To the point where we actually sic become to some extent afraid, to let ourselves experience this state, in ever more fully grown up adult ways.

Whereas in more expanded states of awareness circles, where people have come to value such states. This ability to access such a non-dualistic state of intimacy is often referred to in terms of our ability to access the AGAPE or big GAP of pure Wise-dome found, no longer boxed in and therefore limited, now much rather unlimited - state of pure awareness within us. Hence way more with our innate born with ability, to be in this most precious intimate state of non-separate connectedness, to the whole of the world around us. Is exactly why children so much love whatever pets and other animals, we may choose to bring into their living space. As well as why they so much love to grow plants, insofar as we offer them support to become so engaged. This also explains why the fastest way in terms of a growing modern therapy movement, to help bring troubled problem children, even seemingly incorrigible adults back, into more open trusting ways of being. Is to put them in charge of an animal, or even a small garden space. Inasmuch as developing this sort of intimate communication is among the most powerful means we have, to help bring those of us who are most lost. Back into way more openly interactive, non-separate states of being. In other words this ability to be intimately non-separatively interactive attuned - within our here and now field of experience! Seems to be precisely what begins to define our possibility to move toward more whole-sum-ly healthy states - of real found well being!

A great way to help our self's keep remembering and valuing this state, which we already know. Is every time we notice our self getting inwardly open close, to something we love like a favorite pet, like a special plant, even some kind of special play toy. And of course most especially when being with some special someone we actually sense this non-separate lovingness - feeling with. Is to start supporting our self in every way we can, as many times a day as we possibly can. To be much more aware of this special totally loving feeling that crosses over from inside to inside, from one creature to another, every time we totally fully 'grok get' what it feels like to be in non-separation. Inasmuch as this becomes a great way to help our self's be way more able to fully enjoy this inside to inside communication, to the max, for as long as we possibly can. Until such time as we feel our self being totally comfortable, with this state of inside to inside communication, every precious ongoing moment of our existence heare - we can! As opposed to our more usual fear based tendency, to look for some evasive excuse, to keep closing this feeling of inside to inside intimacy, way too down. Or other than wise even shut such precious sensitivity completely off! How utterly not very wise of us, at all!

Especially when leading edge modern scientific inquiry seems to be increasingly verifying, this more non-local inside to inside attunement way we have been given. To more consciously engage with whatever we may find ourselves experiencing in the world all around us. In the much larger sense that this intimate way of being in tune, is exactly what makes living so special. (To get a better sense of this data, as well as some of the major people involved in these fields of interest, you may want to watch the video Quantum Communication by my son David Sereda) Which is why the very essence of our next lessons, is all about helping support our greater senses of our self's, just how to actually be in a state of complete loving no-difference, with all that we ever experience. Including such seemingly ordinary things, as a plant or a tree, a rock or a bee, even a cd recorded song or a dvd video see. Or most importantly in relation to whatever field of inquiry, we may find our inner core being interests being most drawn - to explore. Inasmuch as this is the very best way we have to help ourselves keep on discovering, precisely whatever it may be we most love to play at becoming good at. In the direction of our becoming the most fully able to choose the very sort of career path, or other wise mode of contributing to our greater good, most likely to enable us to enhance our collective sense of well being. In greater sense of our Magical Adult within, finally being able to find our self's so totally loving to be involved - in the creation of the very best possible life's, not just for our self's. But also with greater respect to all those manifestations, that we may now find our self within this non-separate from One-Ness - Itself - now in a Place of greater Loving Life Harmony with. In relation to our possibility to keep playing our self's ever forward into a real Halleluyah state of truly Harmonic Celebration with All we have been blessed to receive. Including all those special fellow human beings, with respect to whom we would also love to help have, a positively great life. In the context of our collective possibility to live our Life's as Divine Consciously forth, to our utmost max as yes we possibly can.

This Then Is A Good Place To Look To Illustration # 12 - Image of Us Being Now Fully Motivated - To Help Magnify/Develop the Gathering of Huge Terra, Even Galactic to Cosmo Bytes of Information - In relation to our Very Own Unique Given Interests & Talents - To Our Ultimate Full Conscious Potential Max

Here's the big thing for us All to Get! The moment any given One of Us truly begins to Under-Stand, that the One & Only Source Force at the very root of all Creation. Is actually present within all things, all creatures, great & small. This not only implies there can be no field of interest or talent which is lesser than any other field of interest or talent. But also since every field of interest is intimately connected with ever other field, ultimately all field's of interest pursued to the max, must lead us into the very same ultimate, whole field of knowledge. Which is exactly why it becomes incumbent upon each of us, to develop our innermost given interests and talents to the max. In such a way as to fill our quantum level attunement capable computer's within. With as many bytes of information with respect to our given most loved to be involved with interest and talents. Such as we may find calling out to us, from within ourselves. Simply because it is precisely the gathering of such intimate bytes, which can best enable us to generate the most positively ongoing brilliant, potential solutions that Yes-We-Can!

(**Accompanying Explanation** – We already know within the context of our modern global information revolution. The more bytes of information any given processor can contain, the more able to help us create the very intended solutions we are looking for, such a computer will end up being capable of. Most unfortunately for the vast majority of us, have no actual clue with respect to how to keep supporting this kind of King-Dome of Heaven found processing capability, within ourselves, or for that matter our growing children. Simply because the vast majority of us over the course of our very own poorly greater wisdom guided lives, have actually been driven ever more away from our innate ability, to keep growing this kind of intimately inter-connective, truly inspiring awareness inside of ourselves. Nowhere is this more evident than when it comes to our so called religious teacher/preachers. Who with very little respect to our greater possibilities to actually realize way more truly spiritual aware ways of being, we all have within ourselves! Have pretty much tended to abrogate this role, in favor of putting all kinds of energy into maintaining all sorts of better than thou, holier than thou, mind locked beliefs in our heads alone. Most unfortunately at the expense of helping to guide us toward the very sort of transformative experiences, within which 'One' could now say. 'One' actually knows, of the true blessedness of this Great Mystery Field in such an intimate way, that 'One' would know find 'One's greater sense of Self', being most inspirationally motivated to be in actual truly reverent involvement. With respect to every way 'One' might now keep choosing to 'Play One's inner most Oh My great Good God-Ness' - Innermost talent given Self - ever more blessedly have a positively great Life - Forward.)

VARIOUS
PHYSICAL
ARTS &
SCIENCES

VARIOUS
BIOLOGICAL
ARTS &
SCIENCES

VARIOUS
SOCIAL
ARTS &
SCIENCES

VARIOUS
INNER
ARTS &
SCIENCES

12

US NOW BEING SUPER CORE MOTIVATED - TO KEEP ON MAGNIFYING/DEVELOPING OUR VERY OWN UNIQUE MOST BLESSED GIVEN INTERESTS & TALENTS - TO OUR UTMOST POTENTIALS

Lesson # 4 - Spirit Jumping Our Inner Light Into Ever Greater - Truly Big Picture Connected States of Wisdom

NEXT - EXPANDING OUR SENSE OF LIGHT RADIANCE - TO INFINITY & BEYOND

NOW IS THE TIME TO BEGIN FLOWERING OUR VITAL ENERGETIC RADIANCE SO OUTWARD - WE MAY THUS RE-CLAIM OUR MUCH BIGGER PICTURE ATTUNED SENSE - OF WAY MORE TAP OUR SOURCE CONNECTED & THUS FAR GREATER AWARENESS POTENTIAL

"OK great guiding me ever forth, growing inner wisdom. I've been practicing laser light clearing myself of all fear and self doubt. And it is just like you say, the more and more I practice learning to feel completely through any given formerly resisted e-motion. In such a way as to thus ever more hollow bamboo like, clear myself fully of all old held in fear based, and thus compulsively over reactive, emotional residue-do. The more and more I seem to find myself filled with an ever more constant feeling of incredible flow through me - aliveness. To such a truly magnificent degree, I can now sense ' Pure Energy Itself', dancing it's way everywhere within me. In such a profound way as to now radiate as a field of pure light presence all around me. To the point where I now actually experience myself glowingly inter-connected with positively everything, which is present in my field of awareness. Sort like what our founding fathers did their best to convey, when they said our sense of this 'Life Presence'. Is one of the most precious of inalienable human rights, we every One of us humans here on planet earth, find ourselves having been blessed with."

"Except now, I-am finally coming to see, the best place to find this sense of 'Life' being optimally 'Awake' within me - to my max. Is not something that can be found on the outside of me, even though it does reside within positively everything all around me! Unless I myself discover how to find this sense of my own life spirit, being as fully alive as possible within me, in relation to my very own sense of self, first! Nor can it be given to me by anybody else! In fact you could say, the more I awake to my own 'Life Force' within - I grow myself into becoming. The more I will at the very same time find myself encouraging my most expanded radiant sense of my self - to become. Indeed you could well say, that It is very much like these previous lessons were actually all about helping me to find, that very 'Inner Tree of Life' power cord. Which is most likely to help me much better run the huge One-Der-Ful Wizard computer processor like intelligence, that lives right within the very essence of who I-Am, within the very core processing unit of me. In other words run that very quantum level processor which I myself have been most truly blessed with. Such as has been most exquisitely designed / evolved to help every one of us each day, to keep on play inventing the positively great life for our greatest possible sense of our Self. Always in relation to the way we may keep choosing to live out our most awake sense of 'Life' within our greatest possible sense of our very unique individual Self's, each day."

"Yes, Yes, my dearest evermore Cosmic attuned Quantum beings within! It seem like you your self are finally ready to really get it, that the more and more feeling and emotionally present and thus all vital energetically open, we all support ourselves to become. In the sort of direction wherein we all of us might learn to use the awareness associated with our own ever growing up - field of light. To help ourselves enter non-separatively right inside the light field of other things &

creatures, including of course other human beings. As was once again suggested by poetic words of the Beatles in the opening verse of their famous I-Am the Walrus song, when they declared for the whole world to hear, 'I am you and you are me, and we are all together'. Or, from Jesus the Christ when he admonished us all, to <u>'Love thy neighbor 'actually as' thy self'!</u> Not just 'as though' they are thy self, and then only when it suits that more fear based egocentric oriented aspect of who we, in our mere narrow band self's merely keep 'thinking' ourselves to be. <u>But to actually exactly love thy neighbor 'from within' that much greater sense of our most non local inter-connected within At-One-Ment - and thus way more fully to infinity & beyond awake! Big Wise-Dome oriented virtually unlimited greatest possible sense of our Self's!</u> In such a way as to help the much greater sense of who we really are, develop our utmost regard, respect, and true found reverence. In relation to whatsoever manifestations, we may find our self's choosing to play at inventing our self's forth from within. In such a way we will now want to keep playing at inventing our self forward, in ways that resonate from inside to inside within all creatures, indeed within all things great and small."

"Well my dear blessed Charlie/Katie, now that you are beginning to much better fully truly whole being 'grok', this possibility you have. To grow such a way more intimately non-locally inter-connected, pure expansive sense of awareness – within your self. At ever more lovingly conscious connected levels within you, as opposed to fear based unconscious levels. Especially in relation to those fields of interest that most keep drawing you into a totally intimate relationship with some aspect of this huge Unitary Field. Which keeps manifesting into all sorts of differential forms all around you. In such a small mind dissolving way, that 'One' would know find 'One's greater sense of Self', being way inspirationally motivated, to be truly reverent with respect to all that 'One' might choose to now 'Play One's Self' - ever forward into. As opposed to putting all kinds of energy into maintaining any unkind of better than thou, holier than thou, in our heads alone, mind locked in separation beliefs. Such as so many of us tend to keep using to keep justifying our various bad behaviors. Way too often with utter dis-respect to our possibilities to realize much Bigger Picture attuned, truly spiritual living within At-One-Ment ways of being."

"Such that to the extent any One of You out Here, are really beginning to truly get this. Yes, now you are finally pointing to the essence of who you, within the greatest sense of your possibility to live within the 'Big Super Light See', really are. Such that in the Greater Spirit of helping you to keep moving on, this is a good time to more intimately examine One of our all time childhood favorite guides, Buzz Light-Year. And his great saying, 'To Infinity & Beyond', which so many of us once loved to hear! Whenever we were taken as young children, to Disneyland or perhaps even given the opportunity to view any of the famous Buzz Light Year movies!" "Yeh great wisdom teacher, I really did to love to hear Buzz say that, it seemed to tickle the very insides of me, into that place of inward De-Light we've been talking about here!" "Given then how much you used to love to hear this, my dear Charlie/Katie! The whole point of this To Infinity & Beyond possibility, your very own most radiant spirit being has with respect to your very own, I-am Some-One special within you. Is that the more and more alive to the quantum level force of Super-Light presence, which keeps emanating from within you, you help your self become. The more you will discover that everything else that exists all around you. Is also made up out of this same underlying Force of Super-Light, which makes you feel so alive inside, in your own first place."

"Wha Ho, you mean that positively every single thing we ever come to experience, like the rocks, and the trees, our sun & moon, and everything else we ever experience? Can actually be sensed to glow with this very same Big Source Light? Just like when in our early life we would sometimes, truly most 'One-Drously See' into our magical garden of De-Lights! In such a way as to thus realize our most One-Der-Ful of all our days & night's! Yes, this is exactly what I mean," inner wisdom replied. "So much so, that whenever we feel most truly alive. We actually begin to sense this same Super Light buzz humming, much like a clear bell ringing with a subtle sense of aliveness, all throughout our self. To such a degree that yes, we in such moments begin to know that all other Source manifest things, actually do glow with this same rainbow of infinite Source Force Light. Which we our self's can be sensed to glow with, whenever we are most fortunate to find our self's feeling the most Jedi like alive awake, to that 'Life Force' which ultimately is of everywhere present - Pure Spirit Like Super Light Source. In such a profound way, that we now in deeper truth suddenly find the very essence of our own life essence within, able to expand to where. Our own awareness principle is actually able to so penetrate / enter from a place beyond all former boundaries, from one inside to another. Exactly like when we first came in here, and we would feel so safe and so loved by our parents. We could actually sense the presence of their heart beating, as though there was only one singular heart feeling the very same loving experience inside of every heart, so openly present. And which we can still at times experience with our most beloved of loved Ones, to this day. Pretty much in the same way that whenever we find our self's so loving our favorite dog or cat, the tree beside our house, the rose or lily growing in our garden. We suddenly begin to sense ourselves able to actually wholly commune - with the spirit force of whatever other so called separate things. We might in this most expansive sense of our selves, find ourselves choosing to experience."

"In other words", inner wisdom now attempted to summarize. "We all already know deep inside of us, what it is like to have our inward sense of 'Life Energy'. Be so awake to that underlying Source Force, which appears to exist within the very core root of all that we may be experiencing - every right now. This makes this ability to keep encouraging our spirits to soar - 'To Infinity and Beyond' -among our most precious of greater awareness gifts we have. To help us actually come to totally whole being 'grok', or way intimately actually know 'The very inner most essence' of what amounts to every other Pure Source Energy manifesting into form - organized energy system. Which comes into existence to be thus experience in the world outside of our elves! Such that in greater truth, One could now well say this 'To Infinity & Beyond' capability we all have within, is so central to our being able to manifest a great life for ourselves. It becomes most important for us to keep practicing this 'expansive capability, every time we find ourselves feeling positively wide band open - fantastically great. In other words it is like our own inner most wisdom place within, in a very real sense keeps calling upon us to keep on growing this innate ability we all have, to soar our very own uniquely beautiful spirit presence - To Infinity & Beyond! In order that we may realize a most intimate connection, between our light and that much greater Source Light, which seems to permeate everything we ever experience. In such a way that it is always in this very moment, both within us as well as everywhere all around us.

"It just a matter of supporting our own awareness principle to get so relaxed hollow bamboo like, let go open. In relation to whatever vital energy based feelings & emotions we may find ourselves having, in any given moment. In such a way that we become present grounded aware enough, with respect to whatever feelings we may be having. To now let our own vital energetic radiance expand completely out of us into a place wherein we can begin to so experience this most intimate connection. With that greater core Source Force, which exists within everything. In such a profound way, that this intimate inside to inside connection with positively everything we ever come to experience, will now become completely second nature to us. To the point wherein we will more and more begin to sense this Force Source, start to move us, motivate us, indeed inspire us into taking those very sort of more Big Picture attuned solution oriented actions. Most likely to help us fulfill those very best of our dreamed for, play our self ever forward fulfillment goals. Which we our self's will have agreed to set for our self's, in front of our various unique senses of our very own Self's."

It's Time Here To Now Look to Illustration # 13 – An Image of Our Selves Actually Being Now Way More - Spirit Aware - In such a way as to be fully able to now live far more Non Locally Inter-Connected - & thus Ultimately Fully Awake Reverent - Within what amounts to our most One-Drously Given - Truly precious Everywhere Present - Garden of De-Lights

The more & more hollow bamboo like, non-resistively alive and awake to our own constantly arising within us pure Light vital energetic Energy, we keep supporting ourselves to become! In such a way that helps us find it easier and easier to 'Just Be' totally here and now present, with whatever inner flowing vital energies we may find ourselves experiencing - in any given moment. The more and more we are going to get to actually 'See' - the very same Source Light, which seems to reside in positively every single thing we ever behold. Inasmuch as the light of our very own now 'radiant light energy' will become capable of entering / penetrating right-on inside the pure radiant energy of a rock, a tree, a frog, a bird, a dog, a kitty, even another human being. In the much larger sense that there appears to be only One & the very same Super Light - which similarly keeps Shining It's Way - through positively everything we ever experience.

(**Accompanying Explanation** – Much in the very same way conveyed to us by many of our world's most famous poets. Even as in my very own short haiku, 'Peering deep into the Stars One Night, Quite suddenly I found the Whole of Me, Disappearing Completely Out of Sight! For more go to lulu.com & order 'Inspirational Magic' under my name - Lynn Sereda.)

13

OUR VERY SPIRIT ESSENCE
NOW FOUND TO BE SO WAY EXPANDED
ALIVE RADIANT - WE THUS START TO
FIND OUR SELF'S MOST INTIMATELY
INTER-CONNECTED - WITHIN THIS MOST
PRECIOUS EVERYWHERE TRULY
ONE-DROUS - GARDEN OF DE-LIGHTS

"Here's the positively great truth Charlie my boy, Katie my most precious girl" inner wisdom was now ready to declare unto his/her very own most expanded sense of within positively every One of Us - Big Self. "The more any One of us chooses to truly support this ability we all have to now soar from the very insides of our very own sense of radiant light self - well beyond all former boundaries. The more we will find our self getting so in touch with the very Source Force of all Creation - Itself. We will increasingly find our self arriving in a state of pure unbound, no more limited boundaries, no more separated from the source of all things. Big GAP or AGAPE place of pure unlimited, non-separate, non-dualistic awareness! In such a profound here and now way, that we will now find something well beyond ordinary beginning to move through us, motivate us, indeed inspire us into our greatest intended possibilities. In other words, that force which exists within all things To Infinity & Beyond, will begin to move us toward being enabled to undertake the most extra-ordinary of actions. In the huge sense of our being able to finally 'let the Force move us'. Every dear ever more growing up Jed-hi like, now well beyond ordinary actually brilliance empowered Spirit Warrior. Of the great unlimited pure One & Only Super-Light - Spirit, which resides within the very root core of all things."

"And you know what, great wisdom overseer within me? I-am so grateful to have you as my grow myself ever forward, innermost great Wise-Dome of awareness - teacher! Cause now I really do know why I used to love to hear Buzz Light-Year, say unto all who would gather, 'To Infinity & Beyond' every dear present friend of mine. In truth, I actually loved to hear him say this so much, it seemed like I could hear it a thousand, thousand times, and never get tired of hearing it. Inasmuch as I can now see, he was just reminding all of us, of just how big our own Spirit Light's really are. The moment we choose to grow up enough, to let them soar to infinity beyond all bounds. Such that in greater truth, this realization of what I already know within the very core of me is so positively thrilling, I can hardly wait for my next lesson" "Yes all my sun daughter moons of the great Source Force, Inner Wisdom gently provoked. Lest ye become again as now consciously grown up Magical Adult Children of the One Force. Ye shall never come to know that kingdom of heaven, which resides 'To Infinity & Beyond', right under your very nose."

"Stop it, you're giving me goose bumps all over great Inner Wise-dome Seer of the One & Only Big Underlying, Beyond Lying - Super Light !" 'Yes this is precisely it my most precious Charlie/Katie's, totally go for it! Awaken to that very thrill of being so totally spirit alive - within! You will now sense that infinite Source Force, which is at the very root of all that comes into existence, constantly soaring your awareness into your greatest possible sense - of total free-dome found 'Liberty'. On and on into the great boundless everywhere present, without beginning or end, pure Super Light, with respect to which you are a most intimate part. That you may in this way realize your most fully empowered sense of your Self. Actually now way more fully enabled to keep manifesting forth the great life you long for, and which in pure unbound truth - you truly do deserve!

Fourth Real True 'Liberty' Oriented Prayer - Unto One's Most Expanded Sense of One's Greater Self.

"Most fortunately for me, my positively great news is that I-am finally getting to know that who I-Really-Am. Is some-One who is a constantly growing, glowing, being of De-Light. The very sort of some One who can now better sense, that everything else around me is also a radiant field of light. It is this knowing which helps me to way more reverently respect, that every single thing which is constantly being manifested into distinguishable form. Is doing so out of the very same both underlying as well as beyond lying - pure Super Light Source. True, with some lights shinning more brightly than other's. With the point being the more I agree to find ways to link the light that I-am, more and more up with the Huge Unlimited Super Light Field which exists in all that surrounds me. In such a way that I keep encouraging the Light of this Source, to keep coming fully through me. The more and more empowered with something truly beautiful that exists well beyond my so called normal body boundaries, I will now feel myself becoming. To the point where I now know, that nothing can stop me from creating that most One-Drously fulfilling life, my entirely Unique Me might most find my Self most longing for.

This in turn helps me to be optimally aware within my own sense of Whole-Ness. Just how I may best choose to move my own presence within the world of all those other Source given Presents, which exist all around me. Especially all those other human Presences whom I now sense within my ever growing beyond ordinary whole field of awareness, are most likely to jump totally on board. Link their greatest dreams with mine, and I with theirs. In such a way that we will thus help each other manifest ourselves forth, toward the positively great lives we together, may most long for. Simply because I now know that insofar as I keep choosing to clear my own inner self doubt counter part, to any one else's fear based, insecure problem making patterns. Such control freak saboteurs, will no-longer have anymore more affect on me. Even to the point where I will stop attracting Fear-Ful and thus Source Dis-Connected people, into my life anymore!"

Chapter 6

Lesson # 5 – Next Re-Claiming Our Inner State Of Pure Innocent Like - Yet Way Greater Unlimited & Therefore Truly Most Blessedly Magnificent - Far More Adult Awake Found - One-Der

Rationale for HAVE A GREAT LIFE - LESSON - # 5

Here's the positively great news, modern quantum physics combined with modern psycho-physiological understandings. Are together helping more and more of us to evermore realize, that positively every single thing that ever manifests into form. Seems to do so out of an infinitely entangled inter-connected Sea, or, underlying, beyond lying, singular most Unitary Ocean. Of what amounts to the very same opposite charge whirling, dancing, and thus pure as yet unformed hum resonant - both underlying & at the same time beyond lying - Quantum Level Source Force - Energy. In such a way that is actually prior to the emergence of our first sub atomic, and eventually periodic table defined complex - of ever more sophisticated atomic elements. Those very atomic elements which in turn seem to get information code combined, in ways that end up resulting in the manifestation of all the various so called objective things in our world, we ever get to experience.

In other words, it appears everything we ever experience seems to emerge out of what amounts to a singular most infinitely inter-connected, and thus non-local everywhere present entangled, whirling Vortices Field of as yet unformed pure energy. What's more these pure energy vortices have been identified to light wave whirl and sound resonance hum, in opposing oppositely charged, nevertheless completely interactively entangled directions. Kind of like mini, mini, mini, spinning cyclones or hurricanes of pure pre-form opposite electrically charged either electron or positron - vortical like whirls. What makes it possible for this same energy to change direction in such a way as to change charge. Is that this very same energy in the form of left handed electron spin. Is able to focus condense inwards toward entropy in such a way as to pass through various mini to maxi levels of neutral zero point, so called black holes. Then come out the other side of the event horizon of such black holes with all original information coding essentially intact. In such a way as to now spin ever more expansively outward in very opposite more right handed negative entropy direction - to infinity & beyond. Such that the differential whirl interaction between these pure pre-form spinning energy vortices, ends up constituting the very basis out of which all basic sacred geometrical building block forms, emerge into the formation of every definable atomic structure based thing-ness, we may ever come to know. Which is to say, it appears this underlying / beyond lying pure opposite direction whirling Pure essentially Unitary Energy Field. Can with the help of an ever evolving informational coding intelligence which seems to emerge in the context of this interactive whirl, be said to constitute the very Source Force essence. Out of which every single thing we ever know, including each of our own selves, seem to be enabled to manifest into form. Please note here, once we get to lesson 7, we are going to present an image we have designed, to help every One much better under-stand these pure energetic basics, at an ever more incredible level.

Well O.K. so why is it so important for us as human beings to begin to get a basic under-standing of this? Simply because as more and more of us are beginning to realize, we ourselves appear to be the most incredibly sophisticated, pure energy attunement system ever devised or divined into being, here on planet earth. In fact it appears the more we help ourselves become evermore fully consciously awake & thus sensitively aware attuned, to our own vital energies. Insofar as they can be sensed to whirl and hum interactively dance along, everywhere inside of our very own most energetically embodied alive, senses of our self's. In other words wake up enough to now sense, that very place inside where this pure quantum level Super Light like energy, can be experienced to exist within us our selves, prior to the formation of any idea based form. We begin to help ourselves Self Realize that: 1.) The One & Only true nature of reality, must be that of a singular most Ocean of At-One-Ment; 2.) We ourselves must be inventions, or creations out of this same singular most field of At-One-ment; 3.) Which in turn implies that every abstraction we ever choose to hold in our own minds, must be not more than a small mind based invention out this very same singular most Sea of At-One-Ment. Such that, the more we find ways to open ourselves into this place of pure energetic sensitively, out which everything we ever come to know appears to be Created. The more and more we ourselves are going to become the most open empowered possible, toward being able to create/invent our own selves ever forward. In ways that are not only going to be optimally attuned to this underlying, beyond lying Force Field - in It-Self. But also in ways which are actually going to now help us be best enabled to invent/create the very sort of truly whole being ful-filling products, goods, and services for ourselves - going forward. That will make it possible for all of us to now much better invent ourselves into complete resonant harmony, with this great Source or One God-Ness Force which appears to be at the root of all Creation. Very much as a consequence of our now choosing too much better attune our selves to that very same One Source Force which has been identified to initiate everything into form in the first place.

This realization is in fact so huge! How about you your self now agree to put some of your energy, into supporting your self into come to a place inside? Wherein you would now actually start to truly get it, that all ideas and beliefs about so-called objective things? Must be not more than mere abstract creations of our human mind, which we ourselves invent out of this Ultimate singular most Unitary Field State? In other words in terms of this new under-standing about this One-Ness or if you prefer God-Nes It-Self, perhaps it would much better behoove us to start supporting each of our self's to keep finding ways to De-Tach ourselves, from being way too overly I-Dentified with our old held ideas, concepts, and beliefs? In such a way that we would now find our self's way more completely 'Liberated Free', to keep on optimally creatively inventing our self's, ever forward? Nevertheless now in terms of every ounce of wisdom we would have ever differentiated into concepts and ideas, still being fully on board within us, to keep helping us move ourselves ever forward? In the huge sense that such Dis-Identification & Detachment, does not in any way imply giving up our old concepts & ideas. Rather just us coming into a place wherein we would no-longer keep letting ourselves continue to be so Attached to any idea or concept that we may have in our past developed. In such a way that would now enable us to use these already established concepts, more as no-thing more than mere tools. To help us keep moving ever inventively forward in such new free Liberated ways, that we would now find our self way more whole being enabled to keep our selves constantly orienting. Toward the invention of precisely the very kinds of ever evolving solutions, that would end up resonating way more harmonically within this Ultimate Unitary Whole. Inasmuch as in Ultimate Unitary Truth, no such invented concept about anything ever has the possibility to completely convey the real unified nature of reality, anyway.

Here in other words, is the huge human problem with us becoming overly identified with our mere abstract ideas & beliefs about anything. Including our beliefs about what we keep referring to as good God or God-Ness It-Self which all the great Mystics of the World - have declared to be an impossible task. Inasmuch as they all have said that the experience of One-Ness or what we keep referring to as God-Ness is fundamentally ineffable, or beyond our ability to express through any kind of mere thought based abstractive process. This implies to the extent we begin to take any of our ideas & beliefs so seriously, we become willing to go to get in all kinds of either/or idea based fights, even to war and die for them. In the very ways we far too often see happening all around us in our world today. We immediately put ourselves in the position of being overly vulnerable to triggering our most primitive either 'hyper fighter' or 'wimp depressive' behavioral modes of trying to cope. In such a way that we begin to lose site of our much greater possibility to invent the very sort of way more holistic oriented solutions that would have the possibility to be way more harmonically resonant integral. In relation to this much larger Big Whole Picture we keep referring to as God in our first place.

Does this help you to truly more fully whole being finally 'grok', just how such a new ever emerging greater under-standing of God as One-Ness? Would have the possibility completely open Liberate us as inevitable human concept builders, from constantly wanting to keep ourselves attaching to this or that mere 'little narrow mind' abstract idea or belief? About whatsoever we might choose to merely 'think' must be absolutely so? Into what would amount to our now way more unlimited and therefore constantly ongoing Creative / Inventive Big Mind - to our positively most brilliant max! In such a way that would carry us beyond us being so willing to either 'hyper fighter macho tough ourselves to death', or 'fleer avoider wimp depress' ourselves, into a barely alive hell realm. In relation to us becoming so believe as absolutely true, overly attached to our mere abstracted out of One-Ness in the first place - concepts. We become willing to hate our neighbors to the point of us agreeing going to war with them. Even though all of our neighbors are a most intimate part, of the very same One or God Source, any of us are?

Before we move further into the implications of such a new under-standing of God-Ness or One-Ness in relation to our possibility to invent the most harmonically integral solutions possible - for ourselves. The very topic of our next lesson! Let's attempt to cement this under-standing of our ability to actually stand way more fully aware within, that place which is of our Unified King-Dome Field of Heaven Within - even further. Inasmuch as every man made conceptual differentiation from the fundamental At-One-Ment nature - of the really Big Picture. Must therefore be by definition, not more than a mere abstract figment of our imagination invention, we ourselves tend to create out this One-Ness or God-Ness Field. Which in turn is exactly why certain great philosopher scholars, have made the claim that all we thus cognize, could be said to be not more, than a mere illusion. In the much greater truly unlimited sense that the only non illusion, must be that of One-Ness in It-Self. In these terms then everything we ever differentiate, must by way of our potential to de-tach ourselves from being locked into all of our existing mind made abstractions. Be constantly open to re-invention / re-creation by our selves, as the original concept inventors of all such abstract differentiations, in our first place. This includes our possibility to constantly re-invent our very own selves - into ever more within At-One-Ment aware - creatures. Such that as creatures with the potential to be most One-Der-Fully wise within the new light of this profound unified nature of reality - realization. Our greatest human De-Light must therefore be to experience ourselves as being enabled to integrate whatever inventions we may choose to create, with other differentiations from At-One-Ment. In the direction of our now much better ability to keep inventing ever more Holistically Integral, and thus truly more Source connected Beauti-Ful, positively great completely happy ways of living forth the most One-Der-Ful possible sense of our selves.

This great realization would seem to suggest, that the farther along into our very own Inner most found Wisdom, any One of us may choose to journey. And thus the more integrally harmonic and thus beautifully attuned to this field of At-One-Ment, any of us may choose to become. The more we will now out of such profoundly attuned Wise-Dome states, keep choosing to create our own sense of ourselves forth. In the direction our ability to keep on inventing ever more harmonically beautiful, truly great life oriented solutions for ourselves. Such that given this most One-Der-Ful vision, we have been painting for you. How about you in terms of your very own inner guiding great Wisdom Light? Such as has been designed / evolved to carry you into your very own way more grown up and thus ever more Magical Found Adult? Finally decide to now choose to become totally involved in this greatest of all adventures! Which involves the development of your very own most blessedly inner given ability, to stay in this place of positively De-Light Ful - Innocent One-Der, all the time? Inasmuch as this is the best tool you have to help grow invent your way, into precisely the totally great life you keep longing for? Not just for yourself - but also with respect to every other One else all around you. Which includes your very own loved children, as well as all your most be-loved neighbors? With whom you have the possibility to now 'find your self' completely able to live in non-separate At-One-Ment harmony - with!

Simply because the moment you your self might truly get what is being understood, by more and more of us here. Which is that we all appear to have been made in the Image of being able to fully - Tap into this One Great Wisdom Source - out of which positively everything seems to manifest into form - in any first place. In the much greater sense of every One of us has been gifted with the potential to light our Big Mind Wise-Domes - so all our way up. We will now experience ourselves as actually being non-locally inter-connected, within this most Brilliant manifesting into form infinitely entangled State of At-One-Ment. Our greater potential is that the more and more 100th monkey like, the more of us start having this sort of Big Mind Space realization! This kind of awareness is going to truly change everything about the way we all of us are going to keep choosing to do business as usual - here. Inasmuch as the moment any One of us now knows that what we have been referring to as Source, or God-Ness, actually exists inside of everything. Including in our neighbors who are also a part and parcel of this higher order - Well Beyond Ordinary sense of One-Ness - It-Self. The more the more of us will begin to now know, that our very own Wise-Dome's of greater awareness. Are actually made in such a way that we can actually connect ourselves fully up into, this Virtually Unlimited, now Source Connected Greater Wisdom way of Knowing. This then will be the moment, the more of us will want to start engaging with everything we now know, as though all so called things actually are most intimately part and parcel of, this very same One-Ness Source out of which we ourselves appear to be Made in the Image of. Which is to say, a most intimate part of what we heretofore in the history of mankind, have been referring to as God-Ness - In It-Self. To the point where we will now want to help our selves uncover the sort of greater intelligence we all have within, which can best help us keep creating ourselves forth. In ways that actually have the possibility to resonate in the greatest possible harmony, with this One & Only Same Source, which can now be sensed by us to exist at the very root of all Creation.

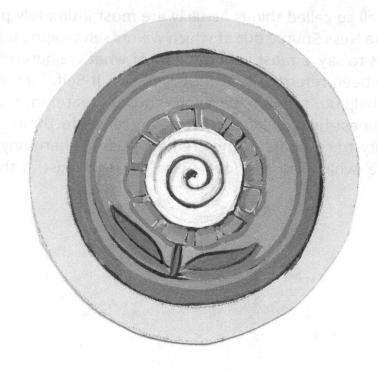

Greater Wisdom Lesson # 5 - Sensing That No-Thing or No-One Is Ever Really Separate From What Amounts to Our 'One & Only' Pure Energy Source - Including Ourselves

RE-CLAIMING THEREFORE THAT MOST BLESSED STATE - WHICH IS OF OUR PURE INNOCENT LIKE ONE-DER

INASMUCH AS NOW IS ALWAYS THE PERFECT TIME - TO TAKE THAT GREATER SENSE OF THE PURE ENERGETIC BEINGS WE REALLY ARE - 'ONE GIANT STEP' FURTHER EXPANSIVELY OUTWARD - INTO TRULY FULL-ON AWAKE AT-ONE-MENT CONSCIOUSNESS

"So what's next, my own most dear, great guiding forth, inner wisdom? I can hardly wait for your next incredible round, of guiding us ever more forward, teachings. I suppose you are going to tell us all, it's time to re-claim that state of Innocent One-Der, we all came in here with in our first place? Much like being in that original no boundaries Ocean-See state, we once used to sense? Wherein it seemed like there were no walls or barriers not just between us, and the open heart beat of our parents. But also between us and all things, all creatures great and small - from here 'To Infinity & Beyond'! In the much greater sense that absolutely every single thing we ever used to experience, seemed to be infinitely inter-connected with everything else, in some non-local, at a distance, grandly mysterious way. And thus that WOW, it seemed like some hugely One-Der-Ful, underlying beyond lying, most Mysterious Super Light Source Force! Appeared to be In-Volved in the manifestation of positively every most De-Light-Ful form, we ever came to experience? Much like in the sense of the little Buddha's, little Christ's, little Krishna's, we were all gifted with the potential to be! But which most unfortunately, most of us out of various fears, have chosen to forget!"

"Yes, Yes, my dear Children of the One and only 'One'. Now you are really beginning to under-stand. Now you are really starting to fully whole being 'grok', the Miracle of being yet another real true Holi - 'One'. The very sort of Some-One who is coming to be so fully alive to the presence of this great singular most At-One-Ment Mystery - which is at the very Source of all that comes into existence. Now thanks to these pure energy awakening methods of awareness, you are truly beginning to awaken to what it is like to be an unlimited non-separate being. The sort of Some-One who is now ever more fully capable of living, the very kind of life within which you can now actually sense your self. As being enabled with the power and glory of this Great Mystery now way more fully on board within you, to help you ful-fill your very greatest intentions. In such a way that may help you to keep living within this most One-Der-Ful Field of De-Light, we all of us find ourselves living within. By way of you finding your way to become totally In-Nocient again, of all over identification with any form of prior conceptualization. In other words without any kind of pre-formed idea or belief about how your life is supposed to be, anymore being held in your way. In relation to how you may now choose to keep newly inventing as well as re-inventing, your own sense of how you might much more prefer your world to be, going forward."

"Much as though you will have become as a little child again, but this time as a more fully grown up, truly Great Mystery connected and thus way more fully empowered Adult. In the much greater sense of you now being way more clearly grounded within, that great beyond lying Singular most Force, which can be experienced to be at the very underlying root of every single thing, you ever come to experience? Much as though you are learning to extend the very same sense of 'To

124

Infinity & Beyond' pure energy awareness you just learned, in the prior lesson. Except now within the much larger sense of your awareness being able to penetrate into that complete 'Pure Energy Aware state of In-Nocient our Full Knowing One-Der', we all once knew when we first came in here? In the much larger sense of your possibility to attain to that true Knowing - which is the One & Only great unlimited One-Ness - Itself! Especially in relation to the ways you may keep choosing to intend your self forth, except with the Pure Energy of the Uni-Verse, much more available on board within you. To now help your actually realize whatever best intentions, you keep choosing to set in front of your self!"

"Holy, Moly, dear every most precious One of Us! Can you now in this moment truly see, just how liberating such a state of Innocent One-Der Realization - is going to be for all of humankind"! Charlie/Katie could now most One-Drously be heard to exclaim! "For it seems like the moment we no longer choose to be so attached to our own mere mind constructions out of what amounts to this One-Ness Field, in any first place. We will now be much more able to sense just exactly how, Yes we can in this new light, finally totally free ourselves to be as inventively creatively wise, as we may choose. In other words, no past or historically invented concept, need limit our possibility to invent ourselves ever more effectively, forward. Especially in the sense of our now being enabled to invent, way more holistically harmonic, new forms, in relation to all those already harmonic forms, which keep on manifesting into form all around us. Certainly in this larger respect, our very own Inner Wisdom is now beginning to truly see, that just because we free ourselves of all attachments, to all of our past defined already existing ideas & concepts about things. This does not mean we will forget our old ideas. No, It simply means we will finally be free to keep building upon them, even re-formulating them, sometimes even to the point totally dropping our most out dated ideas forever. In order that we may keep inventing ourselves ever more effectively forward. That is all, this realization of de-tachment & dis-identification from all of our mere invented mind forms, really implies!"

"Yes, my dear starting to really get it, great wisdom oriented fellow beings. Simply because the more we begin to support our self to see, that we are the most incredibly intricate, and indeed highly sophisticated, truly potentially brilliant, made in the image able to fully 'grok' One-Ness - sort of beings. The very kind of beings who can allow our awareness to so permeate into that place, where there is no-thing anymore between us, and the underlying singular most Ocean of energy which makes up everything else. But an infinitely inter-connected field of pure unlimited Source Force! We thus end up with our possibility to bring this unlimited sense of energy most fully on board within us, as clear non-separate part of us! In such a way as to become truly ready to re-enter into a most One-Drous ability to play our self ever forward to our max. This time however, as ever more awakened to the singular most Source Force - now conscious Adult Jed-hi like Spirit Warriors of the One Great

Spirit. Now enabled to live right within what amounts to the One & Only really Big Picture going on - Heare - out of which all things come into bloom in every first place?"

"Oh, my God! Tell me more, great grand father/mother wisdom within, because this is truly beginning to blow my mind, of all pre-conception. Especially in relation to how I have been mis-led to believe in God, as some kind of Source Force existing merely outside of me, only. Rather than being taught how to experience this sense of God-Ness or One-Ness - within my very own greatest possible sense of Self! In terms of this being the very best gift we ALL OF US have been given, to help ourselves manifest the truly inwardly fulfilling lives we all long for." "Well, fasten your seat belt's my dear little every One's, cause here we go! The plain truth is as you already know, in the clearest of all truth's! There appears to only One Singular most energy field, at the root of all existence! Which means that every time we choose to abstract something out of that field, as though it exists as some kind of separate entity! In actuality every such something we may ever choose to define, from within this field of Whole-Ness. Is really nothing more than an abstraction, nothing more than an invention of our own mind's - out of what amounts to this unified field of At-One-Ment! Including whatever abstract ideas we may have in our past, chosen to put forth in relation to what have come to merely 'think' of as God! As opposed to supporting ourselves to come into a place wherein we might now be able to say, we have actually experienced the ineffable or fundamentally unexplainable Mystery of that Grand To Infinity & Beyond Whole-Ness - we have been referring to as God!"

"In other words, this realization about the fundamental Uni-Tary most nature of reality, such as is emerging within the context of new understandings in the field of quantum physics in conjunction with the study of Hu-Man consciousness. Is beginning to imply that all of our ideas & beliefs about anything, can be under-stood to be nothing more than mere figments of our imagination. Which we ourselves within the context of our most incredible abstractive enabled minds, can keep choosing to abstractively keep inventing! True very useful figments, but nevertheless mere inventions, of what always amounts to our very own differentiating mind's. To help you really get this, lets take something as simple as a Tree. Is it possible for any given Tree, to exist without the particular mineral soil field within which it is rooted? Is it possible for it to exist without constant sunshine and rain, without a period of night time and daytime so necessary for it to rest and reverse it's ongoing photo-synthetic process? It is possible for a Tree to exist without our planet's particular oxygen content, as well as our great H2O based Oceans, to help keep regular cycles of rain water flowing? Is it even possible for something as seemingly simple as a Tree, to exist without being in a planetary system, which has a Sun just like ours, the very right distance required from our planet, to help make such things as a Tree keep growing? Is it possible that we are the only Solar System, indeed the only Galaxy within the Whole Universe, within which something quite as lovely as a Tree, can ever keep growing in the first place? Where then I ask you, does the definition of Tree-Ness, really end? Or is there any so called 'clear boundary, to the everyday definition we have invented to describe something as so called simple, as a 'Tree'? "

"Might it then in the interests of our much farther reaching understanding, be more accurate for us to say, that a tree is simply another One of this Singular Most Sources, great manifestations. The very sort of manifestation that in greater truth, is not really separate from that One-Ness out of which all things come into manifestation in the first place?" "Wow in some ways this seems hugely scary - inner wisdom! You are telling me nothing at all, has any clear real limited boundary?" "Not really my dear Growing ever more All Up, increasingly De-Light-Ful greater Wisdom Shinning Adult. Who in actuality Resides Within - this place of Super Light Unlimited Non-Separation! For in the clarity of greater more expansive truth, once you truly get this, you are now going to be completely 'Free' or fully 'Liberated' to re-invent, as well as newly invent, positively everything you ever experience, all over again, and again, and again. Which in turn involves One of the most prized aspects, of just who we have been given the potential to be. In other words there is nothing wrong with having ideas, or concepts, or beliefs about all kinds of things. All such ideas are what help us to keep inventing the lives we most long for. What stops us most however from being able to keep on inventing ourselves ever more - have a great life forward. Is that insofar as we start to 'believe' that our mere ideas & abstractions about things themselves - are what must be real. We via this over I-Dentififcation with our old ideas, not only start to severely limit our potential to become optimally creatively involved, in the self invention of the great lives that we most long for. But we also by way of our attachments to our ideas, concepts, & belief's, tend to keep stopping ourselves from seeing the truly One-Der-Us Big Picture, at the very root of all existence! With the most unfortunate for us result, we keep attempting to invent ourselves forward, in ways that are not very conscious of this Great Whole! But also in ways that tend to keep us at cross purposes, with our own best intentions!"

"Whereas the moment we support ourselves to truly come to see, that positively every-thing we merely 'think' is real, is not really what's most real at all. In other words the moment we can re-claim the same state of 'Innocent One-Der' we all came in heare with, in our first place. This is how we best help ourselves come to once again truly see, that positively every single thing we ever choose to experience. Is actually at the level of pure quantum level energy, totally inter-connected within a non-local unified field of At-One-Ment - Itself. Such that every such so called thing now ends up being no-thing more than another 'To Infinity & Beyond' extremely inter-connected thing. Which owes it's very existence to what amounts too the only true fundamentally Singular Unified Reality Field - there is. And Suddenly we find our selves now totally Free, to keep on inventing and re-inventing our ways ever more forward. With much greater respect to just how we would most like to keep on using our old storehouse of information. To now help ourselves keep on inventing ourselves toward the fulfillment of whatever new dreamed for intentions, we might choose to set before ourselves. Within the very sort of context that has the possibility to be much more Wholistically and truly way more Inwardly Ful-Filling for Our Selves!"

"Other than wise, to the extent any one of us keep ourselves only searching down the same old same old idea pathways. We have already decided are written forever in stone, within our unchangeable frozen, locked down little narrow band, minds. And thus within which we tend to keep ourselves attached unto, the same old ways of limiting our possibility to way more clearly, not just see the truly magnificent, magical At-One-Ment world we all live in. But also our own Hu-Man most possibility to keep on Co-Creatively - transforming this world. How can we ever hope to Invent into form, various ever better dreamed for ways of living, with the utmost respect to ourselves? As well as in relation to One-Ness It-Self being able to explore It's Endless ever better Possibilities through the incredible Made in the Image gift of positively unlimited awareness, we have all been given within? Which after all is said and done, is exactly what makes America, indeed this Whole magical mystery tour World, such a truly One-Der-Ful place to be living in! With the utmost respect to our human most possibility, to keep dreaming ourselves ever forward, into ever more effective ways of living?"

"Yes indeed, this is truly way, way huge for me, Charlie now found himself uttering from a place of way beyond 'thought' - completely inside of him self - utter found awe. You see, I never quite allowed myself to look at reality so clearly in my Adult life, ever before. Even though, given how I came in here in the first place, the inner essence of my own pure awareness system already actually knows this to be true. So how can I continue to support my awareness system, to be totally open to this Sense of the Singular most Unified Field nature - of the One & Only, truly Big Picture Reality?" "Well Charlie, it's as was said before, really quite simple. Given you have already been learning to be open to more and more energy, being able to come through you. In the form of whatever vital energy based feelings may be going on inside, in any given moment with respect to whatever you may be experiencing. From here, once we find ourselves open to a sense of our own energy, more freely able to come through us. It's all about us choosing to sense the ultimate nature of all so called things, we ever experience. In such a way that we now let ourselves experience positively everything we ever experience. As no-thing more than just another aspect of Pure Unified, although true nevertheless uniquely organized Energy. Being now able to now flow freely completely through us. Rather than in terms of us so much choosing to see any of our abstractions, as only just mere separate from Source - so called things."

"In other words our ability to keep moving forward, into this pure unlimited energy awareness direction. Has everything to do with us choosing to so open our own energy systems all up, to such a degree. We become able to now sense our very own optimally open energy field flows, much as though we are like a Hollow Bamboo. Completely free of being anymore resistive to letting our own inner most vital energies, come completely through us. In such a way that we start to now sense our own awareness field able to so Soar into this ultimate without any boundaries Field of pure At-One-Ment Energy - to Infinity & Beyond. With the point of this lesson being, the moment we totally 'grok' this more unified state perspective. We finally begin to help ourselves understand just how important it is for us, to feel enabled to invent our way forward all our way into this fundamentally most singular nature of reality. In ways within which we can best integrate or harmonize our ongoing inventive actions. More within everything else that appears relevant to whatever we may be choosing - to thus invent. Inasmuch the much larger truth is, any new invention we may choose to bring forth, will end up being a part of positively every thing, that any such new invention of ours may ever come into contact with. Ho, hopefully you yourself can now much better See, that this way more Unified perspective of so called Reality, is really what is so anyway! Whether choose to recognize this In-Nocient or Knowing of One-Ness state, we all have the potential to access within ourselves, or continue to Knot!"

This Then Is A Good Time To Look to Illustration # 14 – An Image of Ourselves Realizing - 'Oh My God' Positively Every single Thing we Ever Find having Manifested into Form Here - Appears to Arise from within 'One Singular most Field' of 'Truly Holy Spirit Like' - 'Pure Quantum Level Super Light'

Here's the thing, the more awake to pure everywhere energy we become. The more we get to actually 'See' - that the very same Source Light seems to reside in positively every single manifestation we ever behold. This in turn begins to imply for all of us, that the presence of this beyond any single thing One & Only Mysterious Transcendental Source. Must also actually Be a Force which at the very same time - Is Imminent within all things. The exact message that all of our world's great Mystical Seers, from all spiritual traditions the world over, have been doing their very best to share with us, since time immemorial.

(**Accompanying Explanation** - Imagine then based on such Under-Standing - getting to the sort of much Bigger Picture viewpoint place. Wherein we would now be able to see reality, way more in terms of pure endlessly inter-connected, and thus infinitely entangled energy systems. In such a way, that we would now begin to realize that all ideas, beliefs, and conceptions - must be naught more than mere inventions of our human mind. In the much larger sense that it is us humans, who invent all ideas, beliefs and concepts about every so called separate thing in our first place. Via a process we refer to as that of abstraction. Which by the very nature of the meaning of this word abstraction, tells us that every single idea, or belief we ever hold. Must be no-thing more than a mere figment of our human imagination - which we ourselves invent out of this field of At-One-Ment. And therefore can never adequately refer to the much larger, One Singular Field Big Reality, we all find ourselves living in. Such that the moment we truly 'Aha' get this, the huge advantage for us is that we thus free ourselves to be far more enabled to invent the uniquely gifted beings we each of us really are - optimally forward. In terms of whatever unique fulfillment intentions we may choose to set - from within our very own entirely unique senses of selves. Which is to say, since we are the only one's who can take those aware-nesses required, to help ourselves invent the truly great life's for ourselves, we each of us long for. There is no one else but us, who can invent us into whomsoever we ourselves most want to be! Such that if you should find your self not liking whomsoever you have become? Perhaps it's time to change your intentions - clear your self of all self doubt and self loathing - in order to now help your inner most attuned self invent your self - way more in line with whomever you would most like to invent your self into?)

(**For herein the positively great news of this way big message - You will find a realization so profound. The moment a significant hundredth monkey portion of human kind begins to truly get this. This is going to change everything about how we go about doing business as usual, here on planet earth. Indeed it is going to bring about a New Renaissance in human under-standing - that will make our last Great Renaissance - pale by comparison. Get It?)**

14

AHA - NOW I FINALLY GET IT! - EVERY SINGLE
THING I EVER EXPERIENCE INCLUDING MY SELF -
SEEMS TO ARISE WITHIN 'ONE' SINGULAR MOST BIG
SPIRIT FIELD - WHICH IS OF THE VERY SAME TRULY
MOST PRECIOUS - WHOL-E DIVINE SUPER LIGHT!

Left Brain – Plato's Allegory of the Cave Revisited - Be Ye Most Care-Ful

Therefore - Of Whatsoever Self Limiting Idea Forms You May Choose To Focus Your Much Greater Awareness Up-On - For Your 'Thoughts' No Matter How 'Brilliant' You May 'Think' Them To Be - Amount To Naught More Than Mere Shadows Appearing On The Surface Of That Inevitably Abstraction Oriented Mind - We All Find Our Self's Most Blessed With To Help Us Keep Inventing Our Way Ever Better Forth - Yet Which Such As Can All Too Easily Keep Distracting Us From More Completely Taking In The Way More Truly 'Glorious Brilliance' Of That Underlying 'Singular Most Super Source Light' - Out Of Which Every Such Illusionary Form We May Ever In Our Mere Separating Minds Have The Possibility To Identify - As No-Thing Other Than Some In Much Greater Truth No Matter How Distinguishable - Mere Reflective Emanation Arising As All Things Always Do From Within This 'Same Light' - Such That With All Due Respect To Any Long Run Intention We May Within The Context of This Unitary Field Force So Choose To Keep Holding In Front Of Ourselves - It Always Best Behooves Us To Remain Most Clearly To Infinity & Beyond 'Awake Enough' - To Keep Living Our Self's Forth As Non-Separatively And Therefore Al-Be-It Now As Truly Reverently Respect-Ful As Possible - Right Within This 'Singular Most Source of All Manifestation - Inasmuch as This One & Only Light Appears To Be At The Very Root of Every Idea Form - We May Ever Thus Keep Choosing To Abstract Out of It

AWAKENING OUR SELF'S INTO REAL WHOL-I COMMUNION WITHIN WHAT ALWAYS AMOUNTS TO OUR TRUEST ONE & ONLY - NON-DUALISTIC BEYOND

Right Brain - Plato's Allegory of the Cave Revisited - Be Ye Most Care-Ful

Therefore Of Whatsoever Contrary To Greater Wisdom - Mere Fear Based E-Motions You May Keep Choosing To Resist - For Our Innermost Feelings No Matter How Difficult We May Experience Certain Of Them To Be - Amount To Naught More Than Mere Human Energies Held Within The Pain Body Confines of Our Old Wounded Soul's - In Such A Way As To In What Amounts To Our Now Shadow Side Generated Illusionary Clouded States of Darkness - Keep Us Way Too Flare Button Over Reactively & Thus At The Same Time Law Attracting Exactly What We Don't Want - Wouldn't It Be Better For Us To Learn How We May More Presently Just Watch Our Very Own Unique Inner Lights Keep On Expanding From Here To Infinity & Beyond Beyond - All In Order That We Learn To Live As The Very Sort of More Fully Awake Truly Special Some-One's - Who Might Start To Ever More Clearly Sense Our Self's As Actually Non-Separatively Connected - To The Great Everywhere Present Pure Shinning Super Light Source Out Which All So Called Mere Forms Keep Manifesting Forth - In The Much Greater Sense That It Is Possible For Each Of Us To Find Our Very Own Source Connected Essences - Truly Thus Now Enabled To Live Out Our Lives Ever Positively Forward - Inasmuch As This One & Only Source Appears To Be At The Very Root of Every E-Motion - Yes We Can Within Such More Reverently Pure Light Conscious & Therefore Greater Respect-Ful of All Modes - Keep Choosing To Set Free In Much Wiser Motion

AWAKENING OUR SELF'S INTO REAL WHOL-I COMMUNION WITHIN WHAT ALWAYS AMOUNTS TO OUR TRUEST ONE & ONLY - NON-DUALISTIC BEYOND

"So, let's See if we-can summarize what we now heare this lesson to be about, with respect to the very core essence of just who we within all of our self's - really are! Charlie/Katie now totally Halleluyah-ed unto him/her self - within inner most De-Light! "Based on what you have been saying to us so far, dear clear greater inner wisdom, singular most One. Which can be sensed to reside in the very core of every bit of Creation? The more we encourage our own Awareness to enter into this Field of pure Energy Singularity. Or that field of undifferentiated pure underlying, beyond lying One & Only most One-Drous - One-Ness Itself, every moment we are here. As opposed to letting our selves remain limited by way of being overly identified & thus attached to our mere mental abstractions, which we ourselves keep inventing in our heads alone. Including any idea that we ourselves are in any way separate from One-Ness. The more we are going to find that true found sense of Freedom or real sense 'Liberty' - we require. That can best enable us to keep on inventing ourselves ever forward - toward the actual realization of our very greatest ever expanding human betterment dreams. Especially when we take into consideration that every single one of us, comes in here so unique. We ourselves are the only One's with all due respect to our uniqueness, who can ever hope to invent ourselves into whomsoever we might most love to be."

'In other words it's kind of like the great challenge we all of us face, in the context of our possibility to live out our lives to our optimally ful-filling max. Is that it is only we ourselves, who can ever invent our selves into the totally unique whomsoever's, we ourselves may find ourselves most wanting to be. In relation to the particular inner talents and varied intelligence gifts, that we all come in here with in our first place. As well as in relation to whatever historical context of knowledge we may ever choose to gather. In the form of all those no-longer attached to free bytes or bits of information, we will have chosen to store inside these potentially quantum level attuned computers - we all have within ourselves.. Especially in relation to our most motivationally compelling - areas of interest! Such that in the context of all of this under-standing, about ourselves! It is all up to each and every One of us to learn how to most fully operate, these most One-Der-Full Wizard like, potentially Miracle generating computers we all have within? In such a way that we actually help ourselves, to be as fully enabled as possible, to create/invent the actual fulfillment of our most dreamed for intentions!"

"Yes, Yes, my dear children of the One & Only Super Light Source, who are now finding them self's truly becoming the very sort of Some-One's who are learning to connect themselves ever more consciously All Up. Within what always amounts top that very singular most underlying/beyondlying Force said to exist, at the very core root of all that ever manifests into form! Which involves each One of us continually agreeing to expand our re-claimed ability to now See the world, from within our no longer little mind bound - soaring to infinity & beyond place of most sacred found - truly now Big Mind unbound state of In-Nocient like One-Der Within. Now you are truly ready to become a truly One-Ness Conscious Adult. The very sort of conscious adult, who is now going to be able to find the very sense of true 'Liberty' required by any One of us who would like to begin inventing exactly the uniquely great life. That only each One us 'my dear child, who within the great mystery of our very own uniqueness, can best dream our own self's forward into in relation to our very own most unique senses of our self. Which is exactly why so many much wiser adults, can be heard to exclaim. Although I once used to 'think' I knew everything there was to know about life and how it was supposed to be lived. Now the older I get, the less and less sure about any-thing, I seem to have become. In such a way that in my not knowing anything for sure anymore, I am finally finding myself much more joy-fully able to invent, the way great life that I have always longed for! In the huge sense that I now realize this ability to freely invent myself forth, is among my most blessed of gifts! And is in fact what best allows One-Ness It-Self to get to know of It's endless open ended possibilities, through the Made in the Image quality of consciousness, that we all have within us."

"God Al-Mighty! Excuse me dear inner wisdom place within! But this level 5 teaching sure makes me feel, truly gifted beyond my wildest dreams! Inasmuch as it helps me like never quite before, to now finally See. Just how this process of expanding my very own awareness principle into being able to view the world from within this natural 'Philosophers Stone' like state, of pure Oceanic energy embedded, truly In-Nocient or In-Knowing One-Der. Is going to help empower me to keep inventing myself forward, as a brand new Know-One ever quite like me before. Totally unique now Co-Creatively Empowered - Miracle Generating Adult of the Great Underlying - Beyond Lying - Source! In such a way that I can now always keep myself remembering, that howsoever I may keep choosing to invent myself forward. Who I-am at core, is not more than yet another One. Who is a most intimate, non-separate actually Made in the Image of this Great One-ness Source, part of this great Mystery, out which ultimately all things arise into their own unique forms. Gifted with a most blessed potential ability, to keep inventing myself forth in total Harmony with this great Source!"

"Fortunately for me what I'm now getting, is that the more I sense this huge growing awareness of Aliveness within my Self, with respect to the 'Great Source Force of Life' in It-self. The more and more interested, in precisely those areas which interest me the very most, I find myself becoming. To the point where I now want to delve ever penetratively deeper into learning more and more about what interests me the most. In the greater sense of me learning to fill my information processor within, with more and more sophisticated bytes of field of interest relevant in-form-ation. So that I can get better and better at playing with whatever it may be, that interests me the most. In such a way that by way of my being now truly inspired by my connection to this Pure Energy Source, I can now learn to integrate whatever it may be that I like to get good at. Into my possibility to play myself as consciously forth - into the most beautiful harmonic relationship within this Field of At-One-Ment - as I possibly can. What's more, now that I'm feeling ever more awake to that ever expanding Inner nervous system power cord 'Tree of Life Force'! Which I myself am ever more finding to help me run my most One-Der-Full Wizard processor - Within. You really aroused my curiosity with respect to that precious tidbit you offered last lesson, when you said". "May the Force be always forever with you!" So, just what is this Force that you refer to, greater wisdom within? I'm ready to know more, even though it feels like I already have a growing inner wisdom sense, with respect to what you alluded to. Exactly in relation to this growing feeling of aliveness energy flowing through me, that is getting clearer and clearer and thus stronger and stronger - inside of me. The more & more I keep practicing clearing my own energy system of all emotional fear and self doubt. Is there more to it though? Cause I'm really ready and wanting to learn way more! So, where to next?"

"Yes my most grandly evolving, truly ever more Magical potential Miracle Making Adult of this Source. Now you are really getting it! And guess what, every moment you agree to see this world we all find ourselves living in, in this constantly fresh ever open to invention / re-invention endless possibilities way? You will never find your self bored with existence, ever again! Simply because the more you learn to link this place of In-Nocient One-Der - all up with our next lesson. Which has to do with our possibility to 'In-Still - Totally Peaceful Inspiration'. Not only are you going to become ever more truly way real 'Reverent Respectful', toward all of Great Mysterious Sources, have a positively great life supportive Creations. But you are also going to find your self actually being ever more inwardly thrilled right out of your 'little narrow band', mere conventional 'thinking mind'. Indeed now totally being completely excited with your very own possibility to expand your own unique co-creative spirit to infinity and beyond - to your max. In relation to your innate given possibility to actually invent for your self, exactly the great life you may most dream to have."

"Which is to say, if we didn't have this innermost 'freedom' or true found sense of real unlimited 'Liberty', to keep inventing ourselves ever forward. If everything were already given to us, there would be no ultimate motivating challenge. With respect to our possibility to keep improving our lives into our ever unfolding, next flow zone involving, potentially even more Ful-Filling moments. Nor would there be any joy to be found in the discovery of all those yet unformed, new endless open ended, invent ourselves ever forward possibilities, we have the potential to keep on inventing for both ourselves. As well as for the ultimate conscious of One-Ness It-Self, to experience through us! Except now with our potential to be way more fully conscious of our most intimate connection to

OneNess or God-Ness It-Self, way more fully on board. And thus with our now found potential to invent ourselves in directions, that can become way more integrally harmonic within this Source Field of One-ness - It-Self. As opposed to our old unconscious pendant for constantly creating Dis-Cord and Dis-Harmony, within this greater field of One-Ness - It-Self!"

"In this much larger respect, which alternative do you suppose God-Ness or One-Ness It-Self loves more. Those occasions when we become so unconscious, we feel 'fight or flight' compelled to keep bringing not only each other, but everything else all around us down? Or those occasions when we manage to create ways of being that are so harmoniously integral with One-Ness. That One-Ness It-Self would now totally energetically vibrate rejoice, in relation to whatever we may have thus chosen to create? In other words, within the context of this Great Unified Mystery Field we all find ourselves living within. It could well be said that One-Ness or God-Ness It-self, would appear to Love nothing more. Than when we as creatures Made in the Image, manage to show One-Ness that we totally Love everything about It. In such a profound way, we actually create ourselves forth in total resonant harmony - within this One-Ness or God-Ness Field - It-Self."

WOW - CHARLIE FOUND HIM SELF JUMPING ALL OUT OF HIS SKIN WITH GREAT JOY - GIVEN HE WAS NOW MOST BLESSED TO TRULY SEE - THIS HUGE ULTIMATE REALITY OF AT-ONE-MENT OR TRUE SENSED ATONE-MENT WITHIN!

136

COULD THIS BE WHAT THEY KEEP REFERRING TO IN MORE CONSCIOUSNESS ORIENTED CIRCLES - AS THE GREAT BIG ONCE I WAS LOST - BUT NOW I'M FOUND - FULL-ON ULTIMATE UNBOUND TOTALLY PURE FREE SPIRIT STATE - OF COMPLETE LIBERATION?

"Gosh, Golly, Gee, huge inner wisdom place - within! Kisses, Kisses, Hugs, Hugs, Sparkles, Sparkles, Twinkle, Twinkle Little Star. Thanks way much to you, my own inner truth now actually is. I-am so totally excited about what you have been teaching me, about my inner most potentials to be. With all due respect to whomsoever I, in the farthest beyond all bounds to infinity and beyond sense of my self, might most love to invent myself into. Cause I now Know to the extent I can actually soar my own energy field to Infinity & Beyond, within what amounts to a virtual Uni-Verse of 'In-Nocient like or Inner Knowing One-Der'. I feel like, the very core essence of just who the I-Am within me - 'Really Is'. Now knows that who I-Really-Am is just another unlimited Some-One, now found to exist with no real bounds, or limits. And thus with endless possibilities to keep on inventing / re-inventing the great life, that the 'I-Am who I-Am' within my most unique, greatest possible sense of inner wisdom found self. Most long to bring forth into this world of endless possibilities, with respect to my very own very best innermost dreamed for intentions. Including in relation to positively every One else's similarly best dreamed for intentions, that I may ever encounter!"

"For I can now See this great big realization as being so profound, it has huge implications for our ability to move ourselves ever more effectively forward - past all fear. In the much greater sense that the moment we can 'Now truly See', the One true pure energy Source. Which resides at the very root of all things, including all so called negative energies. This will be the moment we will now find our self's able to look at all human negativities, including our own - in an entirely new light. Inasmuch as in this much larger respect, the pure energy essence at the root of all things - has no interest in any kind of negativity per se. One-Nesse's only interest by the very definition of One-Ness, can only be centered around sustaining the fundamentally integral At-One-Ment harmonic - which exists within what amounts to any larger Whole. In the absence of any preferential judgment about the larger Holy of Whole's freedom to keep on ever evolving endlessly ever new - ultimately ever more holistic - integral possibilities! Hence the more we each of us as Made in the Image beings, discover how to fully 'Now-See' that we in our core essence, or anything for that matter, are actually not separate from this whole. Including any others who may far too often also find themselves being motivated by fear, & thus way too often from within an in separation from One-Ness place, associated with greed. In such a way that we find our selves able to penetrate into the pure 'I See You' spirit energy essence, of anything & everything in the Navi sense, as depicted in the Avatar Movie. A brilliant metaphor taken by James Cameron from the ancient South African shamanistic under-standing associated with Ubuntu. Which declares unto the very soul each of us "I am what I am because of who we all are" - which in the terms of this book is of One-Ness It-Self - (From a definition offered by Liberian peace activist Leymah Gbowee). Or more specifically from the Sawu Bona Ubuntu tradition which says - "Until you truly See me, I do not really in any One's I's - truly exist", go to lollydaskal.com and search I See You. In other words, insofar as we keep refusing to see the underlying One-Ness or God-Ness root, which resides at the very core of whom we all of us more truly Are? Which is to say come into a place of both deep relax while at the same time clear open radiant being, wherein we able to now penetrate See. That no-Thing or no-One is ever really separate from One-Ness or what we have been referring to as God! We thus never really get to See, the true nature of any given aspect of this much greater Reality we are all a most intimate, part & parcel of!"

"See the huge point being made here with respect to this lesson, all my dear Made in the Image - Every One's! Once we truly get this, It becomes very difficult for any fear based motivation to persist, within any human context. Unless we ourselves keep allowing that fear based motivation to grow - based on our own fear reactions - to the fear motivations of others. We in other words, are the one's who keep allowing such in separation fears to compel motivate 'us' - in any first place. In the much greater sense that positively no kind of fear can exist - without that fear being fed by all parties concerned, based on our own inner held constantly keeping us in separation, fears. Such that in this much greater 'I Now See You' respect, can you now picture your self being able to look at any negativity full-on, within One's own innermost 'I'. In such a way as to be able to say, 'Yes I have encouraged myself to become so open, I-Can-Now actually See-Your-True-Face'. To the point wherein so being able to See this True Face, no negativity can ever hold sway over me anymore. Inasmuch as anything attempting to manifest forth from behind such a mask of fear, cannot in this larger light be anything more than some thing made of the same singular most Pure Super Light - which whirls within the root core of positively all that ever manifests into creation."

"Is this then not exactly what the 'open heart' of any good 'mother' or even good 'father presence' are able to accomplish? Whenever they sooth any of their children, by saying stop 'wait just one second'! Can't you full present much better here, there's actually only One Source essence, 'Heart Beat' pulsing' it's way through every One of us? Insofar as we can just get beyond spinning in fear, and let the One & Only, 'I-Now-See-You' - One Light Source out of which all things are made manifest - come through us? In other words, insofar we keep allowing our fears and thus our own negative motivations, to blindly keep ruling us. We will never get whatever we all of us together, as 'One Heart Beating', may most long to bring forth in relation to the real larger Essence of Who We At Core - have the much greater potential to be.

Which Is To Say - To Keep Manifesting Forth A Positively Great 'Full Of Life', 'Unlimited Liberty' & 'True Found Happiness' Way of Living - For Your Self

Keep Going For Your Ability to Greater Sense the Source of All Light In It-Self - Within Your Self - And Which Can In This Way Be Found To Reside Within The Very Heart All Things Great & Small! In Order That You May Thus Transcend Beyond Being Way too Constantly Swayed By the Mere Illusionary Shadows Appearing on the Wall of Your Cave! And Everything Else You Ever Long For - Will Keep Showing Up! What More One Might Ask - Could Any 'One of Us' Ever Really Ask For?

Fifth Ever Greater Self Empowering Prayer - With The Utmost Respect to One's Very Own Most Potentially Unlimited - Real True Non-Locally Embedded Within At-One-Ment - Ultimately Greatest Possible Sense of Self.

"Wow, now that I know that my who I-Am within, is actually just another Some-One. Who cannot help but live within a veritable 'Ocean' of what amounts to 'Infinitely Entangled same Source Super Light'. Wherein every single manifesting form appears to non-separatively inter-connected with every other form. In such a way as to thus ultimately actually to infinity and beyond, be linked with every other form. This in turn implies that every form I ever differentiate, must be not more than a sophisticated invention of my mind. Such that the more I agree to find ways to keep my purest awareness sensing this fundamental One-Ness Source at the very root of all ever manifest's into form, the more and more 'truly free and ultimately completely liberated', yes I-Can help my mind to become. To the point where I now feel freer and freer to keep on opening my mind, into a place past all former attachments to what amount to mere old useful inventions of my mind. In ways that are going to help me sense myself as Some One now fully enabled to keep on inventing and re-inventing. What is going to now amount to an ever better life not just for myself, but all those other same Sourced manifestations, which come into my existence all around me.

My new perception of ultimate reality is in other words, now One of a constantly open book. With endlessly possible new chapters to be written by Whom-I-Now-Know, the I-am within me really is. This helps me to be optimally aware of how I may now choose to move my own presence forward, within the world of all those One Source given invented presents, which exist all around me. Including the self invented presences of all those, who may choose to try and block my progress very much as a consequence of their own unresolved fears and self doubts. But most especially with the help of all those self invented presences whom I now sense within my ever growing beyond ordinary whole field of awareness. Are in their own ways willing to jump totally on board with this One Source, link their dreams with mine, and I mine with theirs - to thus help every each other realize our very best dreamed for intentions - all together every here and now."

Chapter 7

Lesson # 6 – Now For The Beneficial Effects of In-Stilling Truly Core Peace-Ful & Thus Actual Way More Whole Brain Lit Up Constantly Ongoing Positively Great Tap Our Source In-Sight-Ful - Truly Holographic Inspirational Solution Generative Brilliance Within Ourselves

Rationale for HAVE A GREAT LIFE LESSON - # 6

Here's the have great life, invent One's clearest sense of One's innermost fulfillment potentials ever forward, positively great news for all of us Hu-Man's. We now know from mri & other braIn scan forms of research, that to the extent we focus on trying to mostly straight line linear sequentially, so called normal rational/logically constantly keep ourselves 'thinking' our way through life, only. Wherein overly locked into our old mind sets, it is said that only 7-8% of our minds field are likely to light up, in any such conventional thought based only, typical problem solving oriented moment. In such a way that we tend to keep our little 'thinking' minds alone only, constantly tracking down the same old, same old, neural info storage pathways over and over again. To in this way keep our selves severely limiting, the much greater effectiveness of our potential way more Big Mind awake connectedness. And thus far more great intention focused, positively whole brain lit up brilliant, Big Picture attuned solution generative capabilities.

Whereas within the context of now myriads of these same brain scan and brain wave studies. It has been found that when people find some regular way to be more totally in the moment awake open appreciative, in the sense of just finding some way to agree to be totally here and now peace-fully present, with whatever may be happening right under our very noses. For no apparent reason at all, other than to be totally present with whatever we may be choosing to experience in any given moment! Of course especially in the context of us at the same time making the choice to develop fields of interest, within which we find ourselves agreeing to gather huge bytes of relevant valuable stored information within ourselves, in our first place. To in other words the extent, we do find some regular way to truly core Peace-Fully open our huge info storage byte, mind fields. Into our most relaxed open141 completely 'in our zone' state, possible. Or bring our selves into what has been described as a state of true Reverie, wherein we suddenly find ourselves being fully here and now appreciative, totally Peace-Ful Present, & thus truly Reverent. With the utmost respect for whatever God-Ness manifestation may be happening for us devoid of any emotional dynamic, right under our very noses every right now. On a more regular ongoing daily basis!

It is then exactly our ability to access this state of more core Peace-Ful found and thus at the same time far more whole brain lit up awareness - within ourselves. Which best seems to enable our now very greatest possible, truly holographically brilliant solution generative abilities, to actually come into our awareness for us. Very much as a consequence of us discovering how to now much more openly allow, every aspect of all those various 7 vital energies, such as we may be feeling within us. To collectively keep ascending up our spine and on through our various mid brain emotional energy alerting and energy flow regulating structures. In such a way as to help us now radiate the flow of this vital energy completely across the bridge of our all hemispheres inter-connective, corpus collosum. Way more up into our possibility to light up all hemispheres of our whole neo cortex - all At-One-Ce! As opposed to us letting these energies be shunted back into our old more primitive, mostly survival oriented pons & cerebellum. In such a way that we allow this reptilian brain aspect of ourselves, to keep impelling what amount to mostly 'fight or flight' dominated behaviors. With the end result that insofar we begin to feel ever more comfortable with feeling whatever emotions may be happening for us. We start to shift our neo cortex from much more limited beta wave mental processing, into our possibility for generating increasingly whole brain holistic higher peaking waves. I.E. like alpha then theta, even eventually into completely wakeful whole brain delta waving. As opposed to when we merely keep ourselves way too locked into constantly 'little runaway mind' overly trying. To so called conventionally, keep 'push thinking' our ways into some pre-conceived - hoped for result. Based on our old attachments to all those pre-formed sets of concepts, ideas, and beliefs, which we ourselves have invented out of that much larger At-One-Ment Field, in the first place. As well as all those various emotional fears, which keep impelling us into our runaway primitive attachment to old concepts, mere obsessing so called small 'thinking' mind only - in our first place.

Which is to say, the moment we find some way to open our own Whole Brain Field, into the very sort of way more whole embodied nervous system based, & therefore Big Mind Awake ways of knowing. This shift into more holistically aware states, is exactly what starts to enable us to more spontaneously light up our own unique past experience based, positively huge informational storage Mind Field, completely all at once. In very sort of inter-connective way, that has the possibility to actually carry us beyond all prior narrow band notions, as to how this information is¹⁴²

pre-supposedly, 'supposed we keep thinking', to come together for us. In this huge respect, modern leading edge brain research is showing that people who discover how to be in such a no-longer boxed in place, inside their established fields of pre-conceived knowledge. Begin to find them selves much better able to fire up engage more toward 100% of their own inner now terra to Cosmo-Byte - Whole past study based In-Form-Ation Storage Field. In the direction of their most brilliant, much greater than so called normal, intention set solution generative capabilities. By as much as the power of 10!

Such that within the context of the growing body of literature now devoted to this subject, we have now come to refer to this state wherein all 4 major hemispheres seem to be capable of lighting up, more all at once. As opposed to our way more 'little mind' limited capacity, wherein we always keep trying to conventionally beta wave 'think' our way, into some kind of merely half wit only part brain lit up solution. More in terms of our ability to mobilize a much larger Big Whole Mind solution generative capability, we label as that of 'In-Sighting', or an ability to actually Vision See inward. In such a way to feel far more able to keep inventing our way ever more effectively forward. Of course this ability to light up more like 100% of our mind field in any given instant, becomes especially potent for people who take the time to develop huge cosmo byte fields of relevant stored information, with respect to their to greatest areas of interest. Inasmuch as it precisely within such areas of interest, that we find ourselves most highly motivated to gather such huge stored bytes of information, in our first place.

The moment we take into consideration, the fact that every one of us arrive here, with up to 10 M brain cells. With each cell having the capacity to grow up to 200 inter-connective dendrites within the medium of our cerebro-spinal fluid. When you on top of this add in that each cell has several thousand internal photon storage capable micro tubules, to help us store whatever bytes of information we may be interested in gathering, relevant to some key area of interest over the course of our lives. Depending of how well we immerse ourselves in those uniquely us areas of interest - within which we most love to play and learn within - especially in the formative years of our lives. Our huge reality is, that when you multiply each of these info storing inter-connective factors x each other, all together. It has been said that the human brain has the capacity store and interact with as many quantum level bytes of information, as there are grains of sand here on planet earth. Does this give you some idea of what a huge informational storage byte field we all have access to, within that very core processing quantum computer unit, we all have inside of us? The moment we might choose to discover, just how to help ourselves fire up into our whole brain field, all at once? In relation to whatever core areas of inner ful-fill-ment intended outcome, such as we might decide to focus our energies toward?

To add to this understanding of this innermost way more Big Mind awake, and **143** therefore most One-Der-Ful Wizard core processing unit potential, we all have Within! We also know from studies of some of our most brilliant minds, that our very best whole brain lit up - 'In-Sight-Ful' capabilities. Are much more likely to 'flash' forth exactly as we have already alluded to, whenever we are not so mostly in our in separation 'run on little beta wave thinking minds' only. Constantly overly problem focused, always trying to figure something out. But much rather when we take some time to relax out and agree to just be more totally 'in our flow zone' completely present, with whatever may be happening for us right now. In other words, the study of our most brilliant breakthrough ideas, keeps telling us that such huge whole mind field lit up 'In-Sights'. The very sort of inward Vision Seeing's that can best help us, to keep ourselves best Illuminating our ways ever forward. Are most likely to happen for us whenever we find ourselves in a state of Big Mind open rest. Like when we choose to go for a relaxing walk, decide to go on a much needed vacation, just take some time to sit & be in our favorite nature spot, take some time to just watch a sunrise or sunset, take some time out to enjoy a favorite totally relaxing hobby, even during dream states. In the literature on this subject, these states are actually referred to in terms of us, being in a state of reverie. Or to clarify, being in a state of truly here and now reverent appreciation for some aspect of life, that is so totally enjoyable and relaxing, for us. We find it much easier to open into our whole being way more present, Big minds. As opposed to us always staying lost in our little split and divided constantly emotionally spinning, and/or endlessly rational/logically toiling 'trying to make it happen' in our mere half wit minds. In other words, studies of brilliance actually confirm this huge potential we all have within us, for a far more whole nervous system Wake-Ful, and thus much more brilliant Big Mind solution generative capability. Provided we find some way to just 'Be' more here and now more whole being inwardly, totally 'At Peace' within ourselves, for a time each day.

To carry this notion of the importance of us agreeing to In-Still peaceful inspiration, a whole other giant step further. It is most important to note that when we take this idea of core Peace-Ful-Ness to the pure quantum level. Particularly in relation to what we have already discussed about the fundamental nature of pure opposite direction whirling, quantum energy dynamics!. In order for this same pure underlying / beyond lying endlessly whirling same Source energy, to change directions, and thus reverse charge! It would seem apparent that this same energy must always converge into some perfectly brilliant zero still point, and then re-emerge out of this zero point to now whirl in the very opposite direction, in the form of an opposite charged spin. In other words at the micro/micro level, it's like every left handed whirling negatively charged electron might be said to spin ever inwardly, always in relation to what could be referred to as the sort of zero point energy condensing place. Wherein this core centered zero point place, there would be the momentary effect of pure Perfect Brilliant Stillness. Only then to have this same energy re-emerge as now being able to spin out of this zero point in the very¹⁴⁴

opposite ever more expansive now positron charged direction. To thus now form into every given particular manifest thing, we may ever come to know.

In much the very same sense, that we can observe any more macro level energy whirl, which manifests into form in the world around us, to have a calm still point at the very center of any such manifestation. Like for example a hurricane or a cyclone, or even a tornado, perhaps even within the very center of any flower, or for that matter any kind of plant as well as animal like every nautilus like sea shell that ever comes into bloom etc, etc, etc. insofar we might choose to peer top down into it. In such a way as to reveal the more outward expansive positron whirl growing ever outward. Or likewise see the more contractive electron whirl end - from any such plant or animal's, earth roots up. In such a way as to reveal the zero point of energy convergence, before any such plant or animal grows into it's more outward expansive manifest into outer form possibilities. And yes such as can also be seen at the very center of any galaxy, even within the very core center of our own dual manifold endlessly blossoming into form human selves. Insofar as we might choose to observe our own energy whirls, from our tops down, then bottoms up! To help reveal the miraculous nature of just how all manifest things can be seen to whirl into form out of the pure pre-form quantum level Energy Whirl Field - around some zero still point. Let's take some time to examine just a few illustrations here, among an endless possible supply of ways to illustrate this important still point principle.

<u>To begin these new under-standings, let's take some time to look at an image of the recent CERN particle collider imaged sub atomic Higgs-Bosun Whirl - or so called God Particle effect.</u>

Within this image <u>from Cern website 2012</u>, one can see swirls of pure Energy expanding upon being particle acceleration shattered - with respect to some kind of other more central core energy organizing sub atomic particle. Such that this core God Particle or zero point would seem to end up supporting the formation of all those most basic sub atomic pure particle forming energy whirls, which ultimately make up our periodic table of elements. In truth I suspect there is something about differentially manifesting Higgs-Bosun's which ends up setting those unique in-form-ation codes, most likely to result in the form-ation of this or that particular atomic element. Such that once we get elements, similar in-form-ational codes are going to end up determining how elements will end up combining to form ever more complex molecules. all the way up into the organizing properties of DNA re the formation of ever more complex genetically coded organisms. So what then might be the origin of, the various levels of ever more complex in-formational coding? Is this pure energy dynamic most miraculously - Truly One-Drous - or What?

So Called God Particle Pure Energy Whirl - Effect

Please note, when you look at this pure quantum level set of energy whirls such as emerge as a consequence of high speed particle collision! It is possible to see spirals of this energy whirling both inward and outward in opposite directions. Centered around what appears to be a mini black hole, or so called God particle organizing Particle - at the very core of these whirls.

Next here's some illustrations showing how both individual & groups of rock crystals tend to develop out of inwardly condensing electron energy whirls. Into ever more complex expanding positive charged forms centered around some zero point. Remember if you were to break up the smallest rocks or metallic elements into the tinniest particles, you would see crystalline like structures. This is a good place to search images of crystals, or look to my son David Sereda's ebook on differentials re the formation of all manifest structures out of pure quantum level ever smaller contracting and ever larger expanding - pure energy differential spin.

Various Basic Crystalline Energy Whirl Forms

Effect of the Sound of Sun on Water
Photo by Russian scientists Elena Izvekova and Leonid Izvekov

Why, even water when turned to snow or freeze dried will form into the most beautifully balanced crystalline whirl based - structures. Note the 3D freeze dried Flower of Aphrodite like image - lower right - the result of playing the sound of the Sun over water! To order audio go to my son David Sereda's website voiceenterainment.net under audios.

So let's keep going on to look at some illustrations showing the way different organic crystalline like structures tend to grow out of this same inwardly focused - pure energy whirl dynamic - into various unique plant forms. <u>Note</u> - how the roots of tree's appear to whirl in a direction which is opposite - to those of their spreading branches & leaves.

Tree Energy Whirls >

< Flower Energy Whirls

Here's the huge thing to get re the manifestation of all so called things, look at any tree or for that matter any plant, from directly overhead above! And you will see every such plant including their sub systems like leaves, buds & flowers manifesting themselves into form out of what appears to be a pure vortical - central zero point focused - energy whirl.

I.E – Now let's look more care-fully at the fine roots of a carrot or beet, even an onion, to see that their fine hair like extensions whirl in the very opposite direction to the whirl of their stems & leaf's above From the paintings of Delilah Smith, website http://www.dailypainters.com

Vegetable Energy Whirls >

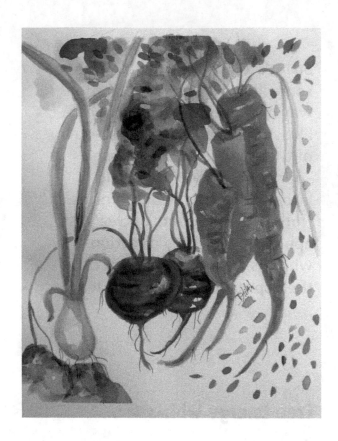

Of course we all know about the Magical Whirls of various Sea Shells, such as the famed Nautilus

< Sea Shell Energy Whirls

Even Human Energy Whirls

Wha & It even appears to be so for us as Hu-Man Beings, you say! For further confirmation, how about you take a close look at the energy whorls at the ends of every one of your fingers and toes. Then sense that our human heart appears to be the very zero point center of all the energetic whirls we are made of?

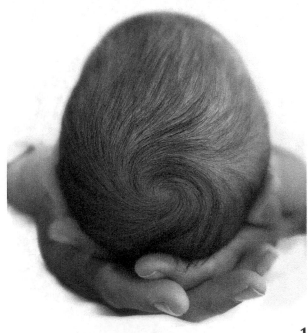

Now for an electromagnetic view re: the energy dynamics of our spectacular planet Earth. Along with 2 illustrations showing the energy dynamics of huge Black Hole centered - dual torus organized energetic whirls. Which keep both figure 8 to infinity & beyond contracting inwards, as well as expanding outwards in multiple dimensions from a neutral Zero Point, into the manifestation of any know Galaxy including our own Milky Way.

Planet Earth Dual Torus Energy Whirl

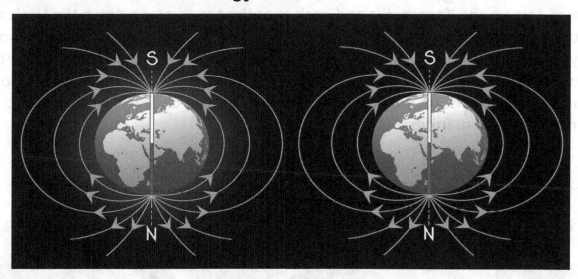

Milky Way Dual Torus Energy Whirl

< Variations On Other Huge Black Hole Energy Whirls

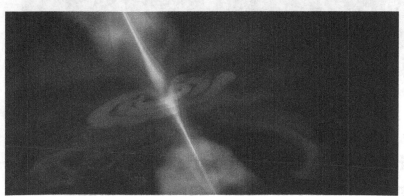

Time to take an overhead perspective of some of our major Mtn. ranges and undersea ridges on our Mother Earth, such as we have been able to identify in more modern times. Simply because it can be hard to see something as inorganic as an individual Mt, manifesting itself into form in relation to this kind of vortical whirl energy dynamic. Yet when you look to the example of the Pacific ring of fire, or the Atlantic Ridge, even the potential Ring which extends down from Norway into the European Alps around the Mediterranean and on through Turkey and back up into the Urals, or the Ring with the Himalya's as it's base that in places rims around the coast of Asia up the Kamchatka and back over the top to come down the Urals again and then curve the various Stans back round to the Himalaya's. Not to mention that every individual volcano emerges as a vortex of molten lava in the form of an exploding circular energy vortex. And you begin to develop a new appreciation for various sub systems of vortical whirl energy dynamics, even at this basic Rock Mountain level of manifestation.

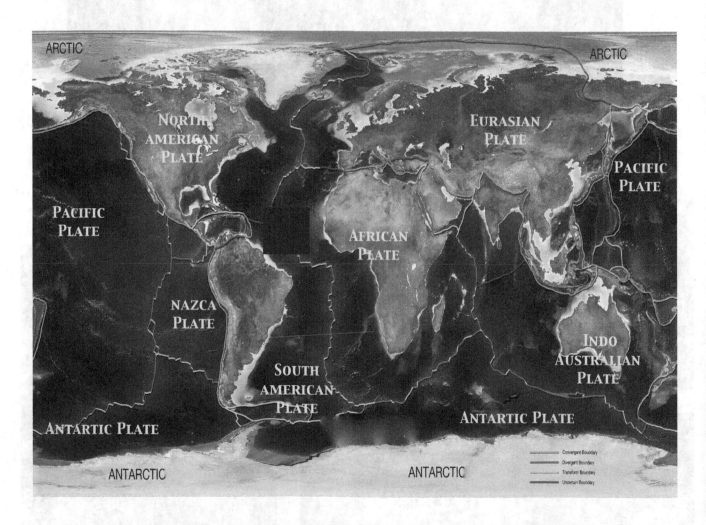

Pacific Ring of Fire Energy Vortex Whirl or for that Matter any Rift Mtn Range or Elevation Shift - such as the Atlantic Rift even the European Alps/Urals & Indo Himalayan Upper Eur-Asian Rings

To help complete this most Miraculous Magical Mystery tour, here's one final image to illustrate our greater Hu-Man possibility to Co-Create from within a place of much greater core Peace-Ful, and therefore now-much more whole field vortical energy whirl attuned way greater integral harmonic resonant awareness! In relation to this Infinite Field of pure everywhere present quantum level energy field constantly whirling into IT'S various manifest forms - everywhere all around us. In such a way that might now bring us into a place of much greater Pure Awareness respect, for all of this Singular most Source Force's various manifestations. Imagine then in this huge respect us Hu-Men/Women learning to design everything we might ever choose to invent in whatever fields of endeavor, in such a way that our inventive choices would now begin to resonate in way more harmonic ways, within everything else around them! Including the ways we might now choose to set up all the various kinds of manufacturing plants we keep choosing to build, to help us produce our other various inventions. Wake up my dear fellow beings in order that you now might much better Sea, that <u>Harmonic design</u> in marked contrast to discordant and thus conflictually harmful forms of design, is clearly where it must come to be at for all of us - going forward? Inasmuch as One-Ness or God-Ness It-Self seems to require such integral harmony, in order for any form to have any possibility to keep sustaining IT'S=One's-Self within this larger Whole we all live within. For a similar image look to survivalist.zzn.com re the image of Edible Woodland Garden Layout!

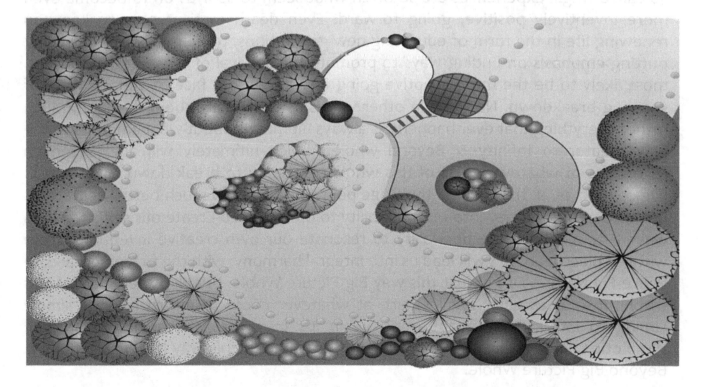

Our possibility to Co-Create Forth Pure Energy Whirl Integral - Virtual Harmonic Resonant Gardens of Eden

When it in other words, comes to our Hu-Man or higher Man-Kind possibility to peer more closely into the various micro to macro levels of Wholi-Ness. Which keep manifesting into their particular thing-ness forms all around us, in relation to their own unique outer band in-form-ational intending, and therefore self defining iratios & codes. Out of the larger to Infinity & Beyond Unlimited pure Energy Field, we all find ourselves living within! Even though earthquakes may happen; torrents of flood rain may fall; severe periods of drought may come around, indeed one animal will inevitably take another; various forms of plague are going to keep occurring; people we love are going to die, sometimes way tragically beyond making any sense to us from our individual ego-centric perspectives alone. Nevertheless from within the context of the much larger truly Big Picture, inasmuch as every single thing that ever manifests into form, no matter how large or small. Must do so in a way that is going to focus around some level of zero still point - energy to begin with. Beyond this every change that ever happens, always seems to do so within an informational context that is going to be aimed at helping to sustain the constant evolving progression/regression of this much larger to infinity & beyond - truly Big Picture Whole. Earthquakes for example relieve underlying pressure; floods & wildfires renew the land; one animal taking another is precisely what helps sustain the value of some other species to this Whole.

Which is to say from a much more holistic perspective, these various kinds of so called tragic experiences are so often what seem to spur us on to become even more inventively positive, going forward. Even death motivates us to keep on renewing life in the form of educating new generations, to be ever wiser. Including putting emphasis on finding ways to promote the survival of those genetic strains, most likely to be the most adaptive going forward, in the face of various kinds of seeming breakdown. No-thing in other words, is ever really about us alone. Much rather everything that ever happens, is always ultimately about what amounts to the way greater to Infinity & Beyond whole. Which ultimately will always remain regardless of whatever parts of this whole may seem to break down. Such that in the context of all this, here is the Huge point for us all too much better get, at this juncture of our journey into our possibility to optimally Co-Create our self's forth. In ways that will have the possibility to resonate our own creative inventions, from within a place lead that will lead us into integral harmony, with the fundamental core Peace-Ful Nature. Of not just this way Big Picture Whole, but also every part of this whole, insofar as each smaller part, at whatever micro to macro level. Is simply aiming to interactively adapt from within it's own core still point, toward the symbiotic Sustainability of what ultimately amounts to this way larger to Infinity & Beyond Big Picture Whole.

In order then, for us to help ourselves actually sense ourselves as being enabled at such a harmonically integral, potentially Co-Creative inventive level, ourselves. It would seem obvious, that in face of all the information we may gather in relation to our most passionate areas of interest and talent. What is going to help us most to best enable ourselves, to keep on instantaneously/simultaneously lighting up our whole brain fields. Into the very sort much larger field attuned, truly great Bigger Picture attuned solution oriented capability - we all have within. Is exactly this ability to instill such core peace-ful attunement, within our very own senses of ourselves. In the much greater sense that the cultivating of such core peaceful stillness within, is not only going to help us much better finally In-Sight See, what's really happening here. In the huge sense that every seemingly separate part of any whole, is always really going to be about this huge great Singular most Big Picture Whole. Continually manifesting It-Self into positively every form we ever come to know. Which we ourselves are a most intimate non-separate Made in the Image part Of, ourselves. But also in the much greater sense that the continual cultivating of such core peaceful zero point stillness within, is going to be what is most likely to actually help us keep on inventing. The very kind of brilliantly inspired truly in-sight-ful, and thus way larger Singular most Whole Field integrated solutions for ourselves, going forward. In such ways that are going to actually best help us to resonate our inventions way more harmonically - within this larger Whole.

Such that the moment we truly Aha get the significance of internalizing this virtually unlimited, much larger still point based. Now way more Holo-Centric awake solution generative awareness perspective, within ourselves on regular ongoing daily basis. This realization about how we may utilize access to this still point within ourselves. To help ourselves best invent ourselves forth toward whatever positively great goals we may be choose to set in front of our selves, is so huge. It is going to change everything about how we will now choose to go about doing business as usual.

First off, we will finally like never quite before in our Hu-Man/Woman history, begin to way more fully Under-Stand that every change that ever happens. Is simply about One-Ness or God-Ness Itself, continuously attempting to Play It-Self Out, right within the core center of our very own uniquely Made in the Image I's. From a place that is well beyond anymore mere small mind based preferential judgment, about which aspect of the Much Bigger Picture is fundamentally more important than any other. Second, the very moment we suddenly get to fully Grok this fundamental One-Ness truth about the Unified Nature of so called Reality? There will be No-Thing left for us but to bow our innermost essence, in True Found Reverence, too the very At-One-Ment Essence of this Singular most to Infinity & Beyond Whole. Inasmuch as we will now much better know, that even though parts of One-Ness may be changing, nevertheless the essence of One-Ness It-Self is still going to remain the very same Whole. Which in turn will help us to finally truly See, that insofar as our conscious principle It-Self is not really separate from One-Ness. No matter how much the mere form of us, or the form of anything else for that matter, may change. This consciousness of One-Ness, with the utmost respect to which we really are a most intimate part of, will always remain the most glorious essence of who we really are. In relation to howsoever we may now choose to Play Ourselves Out - into this much greater Uni-Verse of At-One-Ment! Third, this In-Sight about our ultimate connection to One-Ness is ultimately so Large, it has the possibility to lead us into a state known as Cosmic Laughter. Or into that place wherein we will suddenly be able to now totally See! God Almighty, it seems like every single so called thing that ever goes on here, is always about One-Ness It-Self exploring It-Self, through every aspect of It-Self. Most especially including through us in conjunction with how we ourselves, keep choosing to play ourselves Out within the context of all this most fundamental One-Ness? Can you now much better get It?

With the ultimate end result being, that this realization with respect our pretty much inevitable connection to One-Ness, in It-Self. Will end up knocking every last ounce of fear that might remain, completely out of us forever. In such a way that will finally free us to become, whomsoever we might within our very Core Essence's, most find ourselves truly wanting to Be. In marked contrast to us continuing to choose to play ourselves out, in ways we actually not only don't like to be, but may even at our very worst, actually hate to Be. Simply because we will have in various ways come to be afraid our much greater potential to simply be, whomsoever we may most truly want to Be! Fourth, the more truly Open Present Reverent we become, the more motivated we will now find the Whole of our own Inner Most beings, actually wanting to invent ourselves forth in way that will bring us into total Reverent Harmony, within this larger truly Big Picture Whole. Simply because we will now know, that we are in no way separate from this much Bigger Picture Whole. In marked contrast to who we in our mere fear based egocentrically focused senses of our self's, mere half wit tend to keep ourselves 'thinking' we are.

Well all you good people of planet earth? Now that you your very own self are coming too much more fully appreciate both the true embodied locus of your pathway to a way more full of 'Life force' sense, of your possibility to be much more fully present within yourself. As well as the huge sense of that completely Big Mind open expansive 'Liberty', that you are capable of realizing within your self. Via your agreement to keep practicing the prior 5 secret protocols of awareness, such as we have already laid out for you. Wouldn't you your self like to now discover - just how to become as solution generatively brilliant - as is humanely possible? In relation to you being able to invent the most truly fulfilling life for your self, you could ever imagine? Then how about you start to encourage your self to discover - just how to be in a state of total Peace-Fu;-Ness - with what we have historically referred to as our Maker, as many moments of your day as you possibly can? Simply because the great Wise-dome teachings of the ages, clearly suggest that we most effectively light up the 100% whole, of what has been referred to as our Big Mind. Or that positively great life inventive power, we all have within ourselves. Insofar as we might choose to keep encouraging ourselves to enter most deeply into the very core of this huge field of pure unlimited, infinitely inter-connected, essentially Peace-Ful, place of At-One-Ment consciousness - within ourselves. In the huge sense that this whole Great Big Picture At-One-Ment Field, actually appears to be 'no-thing' other, than totally everywhere Peace-Ful at core, in Itself'. As opposed to us remaining lost in the mere shadows of our only 7-8% lit up, and thus far too limited mind power, alone.

Here then within the context of this next lesson, is the huge point for us all to finally get. To the extent we keep holding fear based conflict - within ourselves. We will via our own law of attraction, tend to keep manifesting never ending ongoing streams of conflict based, problems, in that world which exists outside of ourselves. No matter how hard we may keep 'trying' with our little egocentric focused, mere half wit minds only, to keep creating supposed truly effective solutions to the many conflicts that we ourselves, will tend to keep manifesting. On the other hand to the degree we start to support the unfoldment of true found Peace-Ful-Ness, within. Which is to say, once we agree to find ways to truly claim this state of true found inner Peace-Ful-Ness we all have access to, as our very birthright. In the greater sense that it can be experienced to exist within the very core center of everything that ever manifests into form, including ourselves. This is the degree to which we will finally find ourselves able to manifest positively brilliant, YEAH TRULY INSPIRATIONAL - PEACE-FUL SOLUTIONS - in this world that exists outside of ourselves. Inasmuch as, exactly as we find our Self's below our surface within our innermost Beings, so shall we sow above in the world outside of ourselves! This is exactly why it is so important for us as a human race, to support the ongoing cultivation of such a true STILL POINT STATE - within. <u>In fact in much greater truth you could well say, there is actually no more important human task for any of us on our small planet earth. Than for each of us to support the unfoldment of our very own most blessed state of total core Peace-Ful-Ness - within - on a regular ongoing daily basis. Other than truly wise, as within, so we will keep Dis-Apoint-Ing ourselves in our world without - on the outside of us! In the complete lack of sense that we will tend to keep bringing ourselves down in the outer world of so called manifest things, by way of the inner conflicts we keep holding onto within the very insides of ourselves!</u>

Before proceeding into the very essence of this coming lesson, which has everything to do with finding ways to support the place of Perfect Brilliant Stillness - & therefore way Big Mind solution generative capability - Within. It is important to sound a certain note of caution, with huge respect to this greater awareness protocol. This journey toward the realization of what amounts to one's discovery of that state which is of One's totally 'Liberating' pure Peace-Ful-Ness – With-In. Can be among the most difficult for us as mere human beings, to truly get. Inasmuch as we have all been raised to believe, that life is a constant struggle, full of worry, resentment, endless difficulty and woe. Filled with a vale of so many tears, that we must constantly keep trying to 'little mind only', keep pushing our way through. No matter what the cost to our Self's & Others! Based on all kinds of fear and self doubt, that we all have tended in various degrees, to take on and hold inside ourselves. Within the context of certain early life bad experiences we have all had. To the point where whatever inner conflictual negativities we keep holding as being so for ourselves within, are going to tend via our law of attraction, to become so for us in our world without. Even though most of worst fear pattern engendering experiences, have long since past! Which is exactly why it becomes so important for us to take whatever time it may take. To help ourselves clear ourselves of these old long held patterns, into an ever growing state of true found pure Peace-Ful-Ness within. Lest we keep law of attracting more and more of the same old negativities back into our lives, over and over again. By way of our stubbornly refusing to finally truly Grow, our inner most Wise-Dome of greater awareness way more all Up!

To conclude, to the extent you may have found some of the concepts or ideas outlined in this section, a bit mind stretching. Don't worry, the real inner essence of this lesson, is to be found in the actual regular practice of In-Stilling Core Peace-Ful Presence and thus the ability to attract such truly ful-filling core satisfying Presents - within.

Greater Wisdom Lesson # 6 - Diving Through Pure Everywhere Present AT-ONE-MENT SOURCE ENERGY - Into The Place of Our Now Perfect - Truly Whole Brain Lit Up & Thus In-Sight-Fully Most Brilliant Still-Ness With-In

AGREEING TO IN-STILL OUR INNER MOST CORE CENTERED PLACE - OF TOTALLY PEACE-FULL WHOLE BRAIN LIT UP - INSPIRATION

THAT WE MAY THUS TAP OUR MOST WELL BEYOND ORDINARY & THEREFORE GREATEST POSSIBLE - CONSTANT ONGOING UTTERLY BRILLIANT YET UNIQUELY US - NOW FULL-ON SOLUTION GENERATIVE POWER - WITHIN

"OK, so now I've set my have a positively great 'life', very best intention formulated goals, totally in front of myself. By way of clearly articulating my intentions in the totally present no-longer future tense, exactly in that greater sense as though they are already happening for me! What's more, I'm taking my time to clear myself of whatever feeling & emotional fears and thus self doubts, I still find myself holding in relation to these intentions. On top of all this I've learned to sense more and more into those areas of interest that draw me so totally - in. I can hardly wait to get out of bed every morning, so I can jump in and play at just what it is that I most love to play getting good at, every single day of my life. What's more I've learned to see everything from within a place, that is no-longer attached to any pre-conception, or any pre-formed already existing idea. About not only just how it is, that all so called 'things' are really inter-connected within One Giant to Infinity & Beyond - Field of At-One-Ment. But also with respect to just how I have been created / evolved here with a most blessed 'Freedom'. To be able to invent myself forward, in relation to my very best dreamed for fulfillment intentions. Except now within the context of my growing connection, to this ultimate At-One-Ment Field of Dreams!"

"Not such an easy task, I have come to realize dear Innermost Wisdom! So how can I best go about this, given the various challenges that life seems to so inevitably keep bringing my way?" "Hey 'Grasshopper', hey 'Little Tree', hey 'Quantum Katie / Cosmic Charlie', such an adult question to be asking with respect to your very own inner most wisdom, seeking self within! Yes in beyond 'thought', 'word' & 'deed', you finally are truly ready to fully 'get it', that the giant unlimited pure energy whirl Field of truly magnificent One-Der. Which you 'now' find your self way more able to connect up into, within your inner most wisdom attuned sense of pure present awareness. Is actually at core, way more pure Peace-Ful than you may have ever before realized! In such a core essential way, that this truly Big Picture actually appears to manifest all that IT ever does, from within a place of pure Perfectly Brilliant, always Whole-Ness oriented - Still-Ness. Much in the very same way we have already illustrated such a core still Zero Point to exist, in relation to the formation of all things, including ourselves. In the prior rational section we presented for this lesson. Such that the more you your self can learn to sense this same state of perfect brilliant stillness within your very own self. What this lesson is going to reveal for you my dear One's, is that is precisely your ability to enter this Still-Point on a regular going basis. Which is what is going to best enable you to actually be ever more easily 'in your flow zone' enabled, to keep inventing whatever manifest into form intentions, you your self may choose to keep setting forth - before your self. In the very sort of way that your very best inwardly formed inventive solutions, will now have the possibility to resonate in way more perfect harmony, with all that already exists!"

"Heavens above great Wise-dome place - Within! Are you now implying, that we don't have to keep trying so hard to actually enable ourselves? To feel able to create all the great fulfillment solutions we really most want? Especially given we have been doing our so called have a great life oriented, information gathering homework. With respect to our very own most exciting for us, areas of intention focused interest?" "Yes, my dear One's, now we are really getting somewhere, this is exactly what your own most Wise I-Am some One within is saying. Cause you see, to extent any One of us agrees to take some time each day, to just find this inward place of our deepest and fullest here and now present - core Peace-Full-Ness – within ourselves. Inasmuch this same calm can actually be sensed to reside within the very heart of this At-One-Ment Field It-Self, out of which all forms manifest into Creation? This then is exactly how Yes-We-Can thus most help our own most inwardly attuned senses of our selves, actually be most fully enabled. To keep creating the very best possible solutions for our selves, especially in relation to our most exquisite dreamed for intentions. Quite simply because it seems to take access to this state of perfect brilliant Still-Ness - Within! To help us facilitate our very best most whole field integral, solution generative processes, within!"

"In the much larger sense that access to such Perfect Brilliant Still-Ness within, seems to create the very sort of internal nervous system conditions. Which can actually way better enable us to shift the 'flash firing' of our more here and now grounded, whole being awake Tree of Life energy flows. Completely past triggering back into our old primitive, mostly 'fight or flight' survival oriented lower brain structures. Based on certain old attached to ideas or even complexes of overly identified with belief, about how we merely keep small mind 'thinking' things are supposed to be. In such a way that will tend to trigger some old fear based, over reactive energy losing emotional dynamic, yet again. This time however based more on certain more narrow band, small rigid mind ways of using the so called rational / logical side of our brain, such as we tend to get overly locked in attached to. Now much rather way more all up, through our various mid brain vital e-motional energy alerting and emotional regulatory structures! Into lighting up what is going to amount to all 4 of our neo cortical hemispheres, instantaneously / simultaneously - all at once. What's more In the very sort of whole brain lit up direction, that will now have the possibility to help us integrate our so called left brain neo cortical awareness, within our right brain neo cortical awareness, our rear visual brain neo cortical awareness, within our more frontal neo cortical awareness oriented brain? All the way out into every aspect of the huge mind field of stored informational bytes, we will have built up within us over the course of living our lives. In such a way as to help us organize all this information, in relation to some great potential solution generative possibility, we will have intentionally chosen to set in front of ourselves. To thus help carry us into our possibility to generate way more brilliant holistically integral solutions, than we usually ever dream possible!"

"As opposed to us so much Charlie/Katie was now, based on the new under-standings he/she was now getting regarding his/her more little mind based self. To reiterate summarize to his/her very own ever growing way more sense of self! Who had become way to used to incessantly always trying to one mere polarized diameter at a time, keep his or her self mostly piecemeal linear sequentially 'small narrow band mind' only, 'thinking' like 'he/she must' 'have to'. Keep one's self constraining' one's way forward, in relation to some way too confined pre-defined box. In the complete non-sense of keeping one's much larger mind potentials lost - within one's much smaller mind potentials constantly scurrying about every which way seemingly out of control - like little devious rats running everywhere about inside of one's self. As though when confined in such a state, we in our separate egocentric senses of our me, me, me, smallest possible sense of our self's alone, are the great doers here. The very sort of people who in other words, keep believing we must be the one's to keep trying to put all the pieces together. As though our mere half wit controlling minds, are our only pathway to a better future. Only to find that through our split and divided, incessantly mad dog 'thinking' ways alone. We seem to keep inventing the very sort of piecemeal, my way or the high way, way too confining sorts of so called solutions. Which after all is said and done, keep leading us 'not so forward'. But which rather most unfortunately way too inadvertently, keep bringing us back round in seemingly endless circles. Into far more of the same old discordant and thus conflictual results for ourselves, over and over again, based of course on our own unresolved inner conflicts and divisions. Than the infinite field itself, would ever impose upon itself, or for that matter upon us. In spite of the wisdom of our ages, which has always taught how important it is for us to find ways to transcend past, our little narrow band mere half wit 'thinking minds' alone. By way of our ability to enter into the much larger Field of pure Perfectly Brilliant Still Peace-Ful - At-One-Ment state which can only be found With-In!"

"Yes, Yes exactly, now you are in 'Thought', 'Word' and 'Actual Deedy do', really beginning to truly get the much larger sense of this lesson my darling dearest every One's. Inasmuch as to the extent you now agree to learn the actual In-Still-Ation of this calm centered total Peace-Ful Point - within yourself. This is the very pathway to your possibility to way more fully mobilize your now far more whole being intelligence oriented nervous system, in such a way more holographically Big Mind integrated way. You will suddenly find your self now able, to flash your vital energies up into every to 'Infinity & Beyond' within 'Innocent One-Der' like held - byte of information. You may have ever over the course of your life, chosen to store in this truly magnificent 'Big Mind Field' - we all of us have within us. In such a way this Big Mind Field will then instantaneously/ simultaneously go on to project the whole field of your all 4 hemispheres stored knowledge. Forward in time in a single brilliant Visionary Solution Seeing flash. Thanks very much to the integration of our neo visual cortex, within our whole brain. In the form of the very sort now huge holographic, actual whole brain lit up, inward seeing imagery. We have to come to refer too in terms of a way more, well beyond ordinary yeah dare we say now actually supra or way above ordinary rational-logical - truly Huge Open Mind lit up process. We have come to refer to as that of In-Sighting, as opposed to our mere conventional narrow band mind ways, of always trying to only 'think' our ways forward alone. Such as via this process, will end up being way more supportive of every one of us being way more fully enabled. To keep on whole brain generating the very sorts of more whole being fulfillment oriented solutions, we all of us keep hoping to generate. Always in relation to whatever uniquely motivationally inspiring intention set goals, we may thus keep choosing to more In-Sight-Fully whole brain solution generative Light Up for ourselves, within ourselves, via our own law of attraction."

"Oh, my, good God, great innermost Wise-Dome of awareness! Are you therefore in this much larger respect saying to us, we all of us have actually been designed / evolved to be - Brilliant - beyond even our wildest dreams? Insofar as we will just, in conjunction with the continual pursuit of our most passionate fields of interest, agree to learn. How to be perfectly Still within the very core essences of ourselves - on a regular daily basis?" "Yes, yes, my dear every Magical Adult within, this is our greatest human gift. For in this huge sense, it appears we have actually been designed / evolved to function forth in this much more whole brain lit up awake way. Especially when we agree to gather as much information as we can. In relation to all those areas of interest, which most motivate us to get totally involved with some aspect of this great One-Ness field, to our max. And then take some time each day to help facilitate this huge Big Mind solution generative gift, being able to way more effortlessly happen all on it's own, within us. By way of our possibility to keep In-Stilling, totally Peace-Ful calm breath centered In-Spiration wholly inside the very core of us, on a regular constantly ongoing daily basis."

"Here's the rub though my dear ever growing up most beloved One's, the plain truth you see is! No one else can give this huge sense of full-on forward Seeing, Big Mind Lit Up solution generative empowerment, to us! It's all up to every One of us, to find this place of pure peaceful inspiration within each of our own selves! Then pass our knowledge as to how to access this inner place, onto every other One we know! Inasmuch as this is the most essential key we all have within us, to best help our self's keep manifesting the truly great Ful-Filling lives, we all of us so much long for! Other than wise, no matter how much outer world manipulation, we may keep our little split and divided mind - constantly trying to arrange for. We may never help our self's, find the True Real Inner Core Ful-Fill-Ments we all seek! In other words this realization about our much greater Big Mind solution generative possibility, is in greater truth so truly mind blowing for most of us! I know this is going to be hard for some of us too fully under-stand this possibility, my dearest great wisdom oriented beings. Until such time as we each of us become willing to actually engage in the practice, of In-Stilling perfectly Brilliant core Peace-Ful-Ness - within each of ourselves. Especially with the utmost respect to just who we in the context of our very own greatest possible innermost attuned fulfillment oriented awareness, might most truly really want to invent our own highly unique sense of our self's into. In the much larger sense that our whole brain fields actually seem to require us, to keep setting ongoing goals for our self's, in front of our self's. In order for our self organized information fields, to have some kind of goal to focus our process of greater whole mind lit up solution generative 'In-Sight-Ful-Ness' - in relation to. Other than wise no set goal, no opportunity for our own informational loaded brains fields, to help us create potentially great solutions."

"Most fortunately for all of us though, here's the positively great news for every One of us ever more growing up children of the One! One thing is sure! Inasmuch as we have already begun this process of shifting ourselves into this place of core Peace-Ful-Ness - within. By way of our previous agreements, to constantly remember to be right inside this very body the Budhha, the Christ Child, the At-Man, the Ha-New-Man, that I-Am All-Ah, my presence is actually connected with Wakan Tanka or great One & Only Father Source Spirit, Ho! Wherein we can now really get, that the more & more we each of us agree to find some way to take some time each day to encourage our innermost sense of our self to be completely still, quiet, calm present attuned right to our very core - inside ourselves. While we at the same time keep entering this huge singular most See of pure energy, such as can be sensed to exist both within us, as well as all around us. In the very sort of in depth, beyond conventional 'thought', 'word', & 'deed', much rather totally Innocent One-Der like way. Of just being way more optimally open, to how much pure quantum level energy, we can allow to come through us, in more & more moments of our life. Especially those moments when we feel the most clear of any particular contractive reactive pain body hurting us emotion, going on inside of us. We will now feel able to support our self's to penetrate with our inner most awareness, directly full-on into. What amounts to the underlying Peace-Ful-Ness of this singular most unified Giant Whole Field - which is of pure both underlying as well as beyond lying One Source Energy - It-Self. Such as can be sensed to now come pouring through us, well beyond the boundaries of any & all cyclonically upsetting emotional, or for that matter rational/logical storms, we may ever find happening inside of us, in the context of living our lives.

"These calm centered moments then, when we are the most open to what amounts to the energy of the Uni-Verse pouring all through us. Will be the very moments we will fully discover for our self's, that it is precisely within such a state of core Peace-Ful-Ness. Wherein so being we will now find our self's best enabled to become the most whole brain lit up In-Sigh-Fully, and thus inventively empowered.

In the very sort of ways that can best help us keep generating ever more effective, not just truly whole being fulfilling, but also actually whole field harmonically integrative - creative/inventive possibilities for ourselves. In the much greater sense of us in this way actually now being way more fully enabled, to keep moving our self's the most brilliantly forward toward the creation of the very ever better life's, we may find ourselves most longing for. To such a powerful here and now 100% whole brain Lit Up calm centered degree, we will now have the ability to actually keep Vision Seeing our way ever better forward. Except now within a much more whole field aware solution generative context, that is now going to be way more integral, to the truly Big Picture Whole. No matter how challenging certain circumstances in our life, may become,"

"Clearly in this huge respect, this helps to explain just why the experience of our very greatest teachers. Those in other words, who have in various ways learned how to penetrate into the place of pure Peace-Ful-Ness - within! And who have thus very much as a consequence of such realizations, been doing their level best to reveal to us that the underlying pure energy whirl field of quantum level unified At-One-Ment energy - Itself. Seems to be perfectly brilliant Still and thus essentially Peace-Ful - at core. In such a way that it seems to manifest everything it ever does, from a place that shows no preference or judgment, for either this or that being set above or below anything else! Inasmuch as this is exactly how this Huge Unlimited See Itself. Is best able to maintain the very Sea of WHoli-Ness, which this great to Infinity & Beyond Field of Whole-Ness - ultimately Is. Such that this neither this nor that preference of this Whole, is what makes the freedom we seem to have been given to set our own preferences. In the form of new intended outcomes, so very, very, special, among all other creatures, Great & Small! When it comes to our utmost human potential to keep inventing ourselves into harmony, within this great Big Picture See or ultimate Ocean of At-One-Ment?"

"Here's the huge point, every potential Quantum Katie & Cosmic Charlie out there! To the extent we each of us now might now make the choice to align our most whole mind field awake - much greater senses of our selves. More and more with the underlying / beyond lying - Source Force of all Energy! The more we will begin to sense ourselves as way more enabled to invent ourselves, in truly way more prosperous and abundant ways of living forward in relation to the whole of not just ourselves, but this much greater to Infinity & Beyond great Whole. Besides my dear ever growing up young Ones'! How can we even ever hope to invent totally peaceful ways of living for ourselves, insofar as we simply refuse to cultivate the place of perfect brilliant stillness - within ourselves? It is simply an oxymoron to expect ourselves to be able to invent truly Peace-Ful ways of living, unless we ourselves come to know what this state of being is like - within ourselves! But now as the truly magical miracle creating adults that we really are, and indeed have actually so been designed / evolved be! So that we may begin to discover how to 'play' ourselves forth every moment of our lives, from within what they refer to in the Far East - as our potential to be in the sort of 'Leela' or truly 'Divine Play'. Which ultimately is about our most conscious potential to invent ourselves forth in truly loving Harmony, with that Source Force, we keep referring to as not only 'Our Maker', but also 'the maker of all things', 'all creatures great & small'."

Now For Illustration # 15 – Every Us Agreeing To Thus In-Still Such Core Peace-Ful-Ness Within - We would Now Become No Thing Other than Pure Vortical Whorl Fields - Of Infinitely Inter-Connected One Super Light Source Energy - Ever Able To Shine Bloom It's Way Forth - All The Way Through Us

Picture you your self now taking some time each day, to keep going so inwards into your innermost sense of your self. You would now begin to find your self ever more fully able to feel totally through past - all forms of fear based inner turmoil and self doubt overwhelm. By way of you being able to body surf through endless waves of increasingly powerful energy, coming through you! In such a clear whole being present open way, that the new found radiance of your way more lit up presence. Would now be able to penetrate totally non-separatively into a field of Atone-Ment with that Source energy. Which is ultimately at the very root, of every Singular most so called Thing, that ever manifests into form. Then imagine you would in this way, soon become so core Peace-Ful inside that not only would your breath/heart rate slow way down. But the whole of our inner biology would become so relaxed, all of your vital organ based bio-rhythms including your whole brain field, would begin to synchronize into a state of much more integral, completely free flowing vital energy attuned presence. In ways that would begin to whole nervous system light you up, into way more consciously wise states of being here. In the direction of helping facilitate the most brilliant solution generative capabilities, One could eve imagine.

(**Accompanying Explanation** – There is in other words something so magical about us agreeing to cultivate the place of pure present Peace-Ful-Ness within ourselves. This state actually begins to heal us, into much more whole being integral, and thus much more Big Source Holographic Conscious States of Being - as opposed to us remaining in separation more un-conscious - states of being. Exactly what seems to be required of us, to best enable ourselves to keep inventing for each of ourselves, precisely the positively great lives, we all of us so much long for. In the huge sense of the famous Old Testament admonition, for us to be Still & Know that our I-Am within! Is actually not separate from that God-Ness which resides within every Singular Most One of Us, whether choose to get to actually now Know this, or continue to Knot. I.E. To help every One more fully 'grok' this old admonition, let's break it up, this way. 'Be Still & Know that I-Am, God! Be Still & Know that I-Am! Be Still & Know! Be Still & Finally take some time each day to just Be! So what is stopping You? No-Thing other I would say, than you very own fear of facing so totally on into your Self. You would thus in good time by way of such practice, actually get to know of this ultimate State of Non-Separate-Ness - which resides with the very most Peace-Ful - totally calm core Center of all of Us.)

15

NO-THING NOW LEFT INSIDE BUT OUR OWN ATTUNEMENT TO OUR MOST ESSENTIALLY CORE PEACE-FUL - WHILE AT THE SAME TIME EVERYWHERE NON-LOCAL SAME ONE SOURCE PRESENT - FIELD OF SUPER LIGHT ENERGY

"So your time has come to hear ye this, inner wisdom was now to megaphone out, to the very heart of every growing ever forward - Singular Most Quantum Katie & Cosmic Charlie - One of Us Within!. The power of our Big, huge 'Insight-Ful' mind, has been said to be at least a thousand fold more powerful, than the power of our mere little 'thinking' minds alone. The power of 'In-Sight', is in other words exactly what best enables us to invent / create, the most 'Truly Brilliant' integral - moving ourselves ever more Holistically forward - positively greatest possible solutions for ourselves. The power of 'In-Sight' is what comes to us seemingly from out of the blue, by way of our whole being connection to that which is well beyond ordinary. The power of 'In-Sight' is when our whole of our awareness fires so 100% everywhere up into the whole of our Big Mind Field. We bring everything we have ever helped ourselves to know, into the very best possible solution equations it is possible for our most En-Lightened whole pure present Wise-dome of Intelligence within, to help us generate. As such, it is exactly this process of In-Sight, which helps us the most to keep on inventing our way forward, toward the fulfillment of our very best whole being intended dreams."

To which Charlie/Katie replied, "Oh my God, with One giant now whole brain awake In-Sight-Ful, Aha! Now I-Can actually Oceanic like, finally Inner Vision State Sea, just what you are talking about here. It's kind of like being able to instantly at quantum light speed, flash into the full matrix of everything One has ever come to know, at any given always forward moving time in One's life? In such a way that this full matrix of our historical knowledge, in conjunction with our present To Infinity & Beyond here & now unlimited expansive state of pure Innocent One-Der like totally present awareness. Can now be brought to bear on helping us to create some brilliant forward moving solution, in relation to some goal we hoping to fulfill?" "Yes, Yes, dear One's, and you know what my ever lasting Sun/Moon like shinning beings? They say that our big mind field has the ability to store as many bytes of information as there are grains of sand, here on planet earth. Imagine then being able to access the full inter-connective matrix of such a huge bit x bit organized mind field, of inwardly stored information as this. To help each and every One of us solve all of the challenges, that may ever come our way over the course of our unique individual life-time's. Insofar as we might by way of our making a clear agreement to find some regular everyday way, to actually access this place of Perfect Brilliant Still-Ness within our self's. Keep journeying our self's ever forth forward toward the ever greater truly fulfilling life's, we all of us most long for. Way beyond what the application of our more ordinary either/or linear sequential logic alone, might ever help us accomplish!"

"Holy molly, Charlie/Katie went on to exclaim most gleefully unto his/her very own ever evolving inner Wise-Dome! This must be exactly why, every singular 'One' of our very greatest teachers, have always done their level best to teach us about how to transcend our more ordinary little 'thinking' minds alone. By way of our learning to In-Still such core peaceful centeredness within, we might much rather learn to shift into our much larger, instantaneously/simultaneously whole mind lit up, and thus most brilliant possible solution generative capabilities." To which this inner wisdom place we all have within, was now able to add, "Imagine then that once One is able to truly get this, all that will remain. Will be for each One of us to keep on following, our very own ever ongoing, now fully lit up illuminated insightfully inspiring Yellow Brick Road' pathway. Constantly ever forward in such a way as to help lead ourselves out of all forms of confusion, into our very own most 'One-Der-Ful', truly forward seeing solution generative brilliant, 'Wizard. We every One of us have With-In'! Until such time as we will find yet One more dreamed for fulfillment Pot of Gold set goal, finally being brought into fruition for us! Then off we go again with our most One-Der-Ful Wizard Within, now fully on board all lit up empowered inside of us. To help us keep following our Innermost Intelligence ever onward toward the fulfillment of our next great dream! For here is the great truth all my Beloved's, with the utmost respect to the most incredible super Intelligence we have all been given. There is positively no problem to found here on earth, which cannot be resolved by way of this process of In-Stilling Pure Peace-Ful Inspiration! Other than wise, insofar as any of us keep trying to resolve our greatest problems, from our constantly polarizing, mere little egocentrically focused 'thinking minds', alone. We in this narrow band limited vision seeing way, will tend to keep on creating far more problems for ourselves, than we will ever seem to truly resolve."

"Thank you, thank you so, so, very much, great inner wisdom voice - within. Cause now given the blessing of these innermost core awake human most realizations, you have been passing on. The reality of my new ever growing up field of inspirational energy, is now so open, so soaring / flying inside. I actually now know, just how yes I-actually-Can help myself best realize my very best intentions to keep fulfilling myself to my tippy top brim. In other words, although I once used to 'think' I was usually way too busy to take some time each day. To just encourage myself to be as totally here and now present, to this very moment of being as I possibly might. I now find myself with such an inward yes, yes, yes, to my greatest possible truly great life inventive capacity. My field of awareness has now become such, that every quantum byte of me now truly wants to constantly - enter. My very own state of most essentially core Peace-Ful, and thus way more truly brilliant Inspiration, as often as I can. Inasmuch as I can now fully See, this is the very best gift I have been given, to keep helping me keep on inventing myself ever forward toward my very own ever more positively brilliant fulfillment intended dreams. For I like so many others, have become increasingly bored with so much focus on endless either/ or based my way of highway problems. And would now much rather love to start focusing way more on how we may each of us help ourselves actually be enabled, to generate the best possible Holo-centric solutions for ourselves we possibly can. To whatever challenges the constant ongoing unfolding of our life's - may bring.

"Let's see if we can summarize this sixth level teaching, dearest inner wisdom voice,' Charlie/Katie now found him/her self saying unto him/her self. It seems to us what you have been saying, is that our greatest Hu-Man/Woman gift, or Highest Blessing. Has to do with our possibility to use our most expanded awareness potential. To help ourselves keep on creating our way ever forward, toward the fulfillment of all that we may most long for. Except now from within our very own greatest possible present sense of ourselves! In other words who we really are inside our most open present, sense of our very own most unique senses of our self's. Has everything to do with our very 'process of being enabled to actually keep on inventing' - positively great life's for our self's. In the huge sense of our endless possibilities to keep on choosing to keep on inventing & re-inventing our sense of whatever we may most want. Ever forward, into whatever tomorrows we may most choose to envision - for our self's. Which is to say, unique among all species we are not limited by whatever we may experience to be now. But much rather we all have been gifted with respect to what we can envision ourselves becoming. Insofar as we will just keep choosing to invent ourselves forth, from within our greatest here and now Peace-Fully In-Stilled fully present sense of ourselves, in each unfolding moment of our lives?" "Yes, Yes, Yes, Charlie/Katie, you are now totally ready to Dive all your way into, that totally Hop, Skip & Jump inside, full-on sense of Zip, Zap, Zest, & Zing. Endless sense of excitement which comes with each of us being truly enabled, to keep on inventing the very life we can best envision for our self's, to our Max! Which can only be fully realized insofar as we keep agreeing to attune the very core Essence of us - to this great ever forward Seeing gift!"

It's Time Look to Illustration # 16 - An Image of Our Selves Now Agreeing To Keep On In-Stilling Actual way more Whole Mind Lit Up Awake & thus far more Holistically In-Sight-Ful - Forms of Positively Great Solution Generative Possibility - Within

It appears that to the extent we learn to open our whole purest possible awareness field, into more and more integral states of quantum energy attuned - At-One-Ment consciousness. From within an essentially Core Calm Centered pure ideationally non-attached - just watching our most inventive Big Mind Awake In-Sights come together - place. With respect to the huge Big Picture whole - we all find ourselves living within. What has been found by all historically realized great wisdom teachers. Is that insofar as we support ourselves to enter as deeply as possible - into this core perfectly still Peace-Ful place - out of which all forms manifest in the first place. Much in the very same sense that we can find calm, in the very center of any whirl hurricane or cyclone of energy in the world outside of ourselves. While we at the same time allow progressively greater degrees of beta, to alpha, to theta, to fast Delta, then slow Delta wave energy - to zoom both up and all out our nervous system, all at once. This is exactly how we may thus best help ourselves to totally empty our mind field from being attached or identified, with any form of self limiting, and thus boxed in, pre-conception. In the direction of us now completely 'liberating' our much larger big awareness mind, into being way more totally 'free' to constantly re-invent, invent, entirely new abstractive ways of organizing our world. To a point wherein we ourselves will now find ourselves way more enabled to invent way more holistic truly brilliant solutions. To every single so called problem - we may ever find ourselves encountering - can you now better heare? In much the same way this Big infinite manifesting into form Picture It-Self, is best able to maintain it's fundamentally whole harmonic sustaining - balancing act.

(Accompanying Explanation – Within the context of our historical study, as to just how our most brilliant solution generative capacity seems to best happen. The rather huge reality seems to be that our whole mind field, is actually designed / evolved to help us create positively brilliant solutions - with respect to the very best of our set intentions. Our big human issue is that far too many of us don't know just how - to get our mere half wit - fear based small minds alone - sufficiently out of our way. For us to actually enable our much more holographic possibilities, for way more Big Picture attuned, in fact supra logical levels of brilliance - to keep coming fully through us. In the direction of helping empower us toward the continuous invention - of the positively great lives we all long for.)

'AHA' - NOW CLEAR WITH-IN
SIGHT - I FULLY GET IT

16

**EVERY US IN-STILLING OUR GREATEST POSSIBLE
WHOLE MIND INNER 'I AWAKE' & THUS NOW
TRULY BIG FIELD INSPIRATIONAL - IN PLAIN
SIGHT-FULLY ATTUNED SOLUTIONS - AS YES
WE-POSSIBLY-CAN**

"Heare ye now all you dear One's, this! The more we thus choose to clear ourselves of all those inner nervous system based conflicts, we may keep holding inside! The more and more truly Peace-Ful we are going to find ourselves being within. Of course the more Peace-Ful-Ness we can find - inside of our selves. The more we are going to find ourselves ever more Ins-Sight-Fully enabled, to keep on inventing ourselves way more peacefully, into the world all around us. In such a way that will start to carry us well beyond our own mere ego-centric points of view, alone. Into now much more Holo-Centric ways of viewing our lives forth, & thus truly respectful of the greater whole ways of being, that we all find ourselves so inevitably living in. In other words it has never been about any me, me, me, any particular one of us alone, who must always come first, at all. Rather it always has been, and always will be, about the sustenance of the greater whole itself. The very sort of wholeness within which, every single thing created out of this field of One-Der, is so symbiotically inter-dependently entangled, with every other thing. That every seeming so called change oriented entanglement we ourselves choose to create in relation to all other so called things. Is actually always going to be about the Peace-Ful sustenance of the ultimate infinitely, and thus constantly symbiotically inter-connected, completely inter-dependent Biggest of All Pictures, Whole. "

'Which means to the extent we keep holding various levels of conflict within. E.G. All those conflicts and inner divisions such as may arise from resisting fully feeling whatever emotions may come up for us. As well as all those conflicts that may arise from our merely little mind 'thinking' we already know in our egocentric 'heads' alone, how life is supposed to be. Both of which have to do with our ongoing tendencies to keep separating out our feeling & emotional nature, from the more rational logical side of our nature. The more we will tend to feel our emotional nature, to be in a place of constant divisive conflict with our more rational logical nature. To such an extent as above so below, as within so without, we will tend to keep creating ourselves forth in ways that will remain in seemingly endless conflict when it comes to the world outside of ourselves. On the other hand to that extent we agree to go on a self In-Vestigative mission, a vision quest to find ever more core Peace-Ful-Ness within us. This is the extent to which we will find ourselves ever more enabled to manifest true Peacefulness all around us. True found Peace-Ful-Ness within in other words, is our golden doorway to that King-Dome of actual outward manifestation empowered, Garden of Eden Heaven, we all seek. Which is to say, if learning to more fully awaken to our vital energetic nature was the key to the first 3 lessons? Learning to In-Still way core peacefulness within, is the key to helping ourselves find that very solution generative In-Sight-Ful Seeing forward Brilliance, which can best enable us to actually realize our most profound Peace-Ful intentions, with respect to the world outside of ourselves."

"In other words, inasmuch as our ability to fully open up into our inner sensed

173

feeling and emotional nature can be under-stood to be absolutely vital to our ability to be as full of 'Life' force, as we possibly can? Our ability to enter Pure Core Still-Ness within is absolutely critical to our ability to find the very inner inventive 'Liberty' it seems to take. To best enable ourselves to keep Co-Creately whole mind lit up, constantly In-Sight-Ing ourselves ever more effectively forward. In relation this great Mystical Field of At-One-Ment we all find ourselves most blessed to be a most intimate part of!" In such a profound way, that we will discover just how to penetrate past all inner conflict right into the essential Peace-Ful-Ness which resides within the very underlying / beyond lying core, of what amounts to the quantum level - Source Field Itself. In the very sort of qualitative way, that will thus actually best enable us to keep on inventing whatever great life fulfillment goals, we may choose to set before ourselves. With our huge human bottom line being, our ability to live a truly quality life is all about pure Energy. And our ability to sense all the most essential qualities of this Energy in It's purest quantum level pre-form sense. Both within as well as beyond ourselves, in the most profound ways humanly possible."

"Thank you yet once again great Inner Wise-Dome of awareness teacher, Katie/Charlie now found themselves exclaiming from within a place of the most profound Heart felt gratitude!" "Very, very, very, good, my more and more growing up, ever greater shining within a state of 'In-Nocient One-Der' most blessed now truly to Infinity & Beyond ever more Peace-Ful, and thus way more Miraculously Magical adult like - fellow Hu-Man/Woman most beings Within. Which in greater truth can actually be found to reside within the very essence of Every-One of Us. Here's the thing my dear One's, One-Nesses ability, or if you prefer God's ability to explore It's own open ended endless possibilities through us Would never be truly free unless we ourselves were given the freedom required, to explore our own endless possibilities through that very Made in the Image conscious awareness, principle, which we all have been gifted with within. Yes now you are well prepared for our final set of Big Heart Open found, and thus truly core processing Unit involved. How to manifest a positively great, totally fulfilling life for all of ourselves, lessons! "

Sixth Huge Full-On True 'Liberty' Enhancing & Thus Ultimate Total Freedom Inspiring Prayer - Unto One's Way Greater Possible Self Inventive Sense - Of One's Self.

"In my now much better knowing just how yes I-can keep entering within the whole of my core essence, exactly now into that infinitely inter-connected energy field, which is everywhere present. Too such a profound penetrative degree that by way of this entrance, I will now find this infinite field to be not just essentially core Peace-Ful, or Full of Infinite Peace at Core. But also that the cultivation of this Core-Ful place within me myself, is exactly what can best help me, along with all those I most care for. To actually realize our very best dreamed for intentions - all together? Inasmuch as it is precisely the finding of this core Peace-Ful place within, which can best enable all us to integrate all the energies of our feeling & emotional nature. Totally within the self inventive energies of our constantly adaptive big supra logical, way more holographic mind capabilities In such a profound inwardly aware way, that the whole of the very intelligence we all arrive here with. Will automatically play it's huge synthetic lit up all at once role. With respect to helping us invent new ways of being here, exactly in relation to whatever great life intentions, we each of us with our unique gifts. May keep choosing to set before our self's. By way of a helping our self's to actually Vision See ever forward, via that natural given inner visionary process we refer to as 'In-Sight-Ing'. Which has the possibility to magnify the power of our solution generative potential by at least a thousand fold, over our mere split and divided, more conventional 'thinking' mind alone.

In other words our ability to be within this core Peace-Ful Place, is precisely what helps us to be optimally aware. Of just how we may best choose to move not just our own presences forward, within the world of all those One source given created presents, that exist all around us. But also most especially in ways that include our possibility to link our selves up with all those like wise self inventively inspired presences. Whom we now sense within our own ever growing, well beyond ordinary whole field of awareness, are also willing to link their own unique dreams with ours, and ours with theirs. That we may thus help each other to realize both our uniquely individual, as well as our very best common collective dreams, in those very directions yes we-can sense will be most likely to move us all - ever more forward."

(Special Note - In order to help your self fully internalize what amounts to your very own optimally core Peace-Ful & thus truly most Insight-Ful Brilliant possible place of solution generative capability - within. Look for Dr. Sereda's - Choosing to Enter Core Peaceful Attunement Free Meditation coming soon under Quantum You Learning Academy on youtube)

Finally Our Third & Most Powerful 3 Lesson Set of Whole Nervous System Integrating Methods - Deciding To Dive Totally Into The Full-On Awakening of That Most Centrally Core Sacred - Pure Quantum Level Energy Attuning Unit - We Are All Most Blessed To Have Within Us - Our Hearts - Or That Place Inside Which Best Enables Each & Every 'One' Of Us To Actually Access Our Well Beyond Ordinary Full Blooming - & Therefore Truly Wisest 'Real Happiness Found' - Greatest Possible Sense of Our One & Only Without Limits - Way Big Self's

Chapter 8

Lesson # 7 – First By Growing 'Truly Great-Ful' & Thus Completely 'Whole Heartedly Wake-Ful Appreciation' - For All The Most Incredible Blessings We Keep Finding Here In This Truly Whol-E-Garden of De-Lights - Which Keeps On Manifesting Into Various Forms Right Before Our Very - Most Wake-Ful 'I's

Rationale for HAVE A GREAT LIFE LESSON - # 7

If you 'think', discovering that you have been designed / evolved with the ability to light up more like 100% of your brain power was something highly special. Wait till you delve into this next set of positively great, well beyond ordinary, self-integrative possibilities. Regarding your potential to self empower your more whole being fulfillment capabilities - to your max. To begin modern psycho-physiological evidence is increasing demonstrating that it is our heart/lung vital energy generative organ complex, as well as the greater intelligence oriented sensitivities associated with this emotional nervous system plexus. Which surprise, surprise, may very well constitute that most central core processing intelligence unit, we all have within. In that our hearts are what seem to make it most possible for us to best use our quantum level attuned brilliance, to help us realize all the fulfillment goals, we may ever long for. In this larger respect it appears that we have 10 X as many densely packed cells in any given proportional square area of our hearts, than we do in any equal section of our brains. With each cell in turn, having tiny filament fibrils able to inter-connect all the other cells in our heart. Much like the way dendrites are designed to function, in such a way as to help us integrate our brain field into firing up, in way more holistically inter-connected ways. Such that when optimally open and thus inter-connected all up, our hearts begin to radiate an electromagnetic field, that has been measured to be anywhere from say 8 to 32 times plus more powerful. Than the electromagnetic radiance field which can be measured around our 'heads' alone!

Even beyond this, it is said that the light radiant field of a fully enlightened being can be sensed by other open hearts, to resonate up to 32 miles radius from their in the moment location. Pretty much exactly in the greater awareness way, that all our very greatest mystic teachers from every major spiritual tradition have done their very level best to convey to us. Over the course of man/woman kinds many centuries of recorded, truly extra-ordinary spiritual teachings! With our point being that when we combine this under-standing, with what was taught in the just prior lesion. What seems to starts to happen for us, is that the more we encourage ourselves to In-Still totally present Peace-Ful Insight-Ful Inspiration within ourselves. The more our hearts begin to open into a place inside of ourselves, wherein we can now sense our own presence, elevate into a state we experience as being in Love. With whatever we may be choosing to experience in this truly most One-Der-Ful Garden of De-Lights, which exists right under our very noses. To such a degree we begin to find ourselves actually being in a state of Open Hearted Love with everything we ever find in this Garden, like we may never have ever before imagined! In truth so much so, our Hearts will now begin to actually so Soar with what will seem like endless volumes of Source Energy coming through us. To the point wherein we may suddenly find ourselves weeping tears, of seemingly endless truly reverent respect Joy. For that which is happening right under our very noses - every right now!

To better help every One of us more fully under-stand how this all comes to be so for us, in relation to our greatest possible human potentials. It is important for us all at this time, to take some time to way more fully whole being 'grok'. Just how it is that the endless whirling into form Quantum or Cosmic Field of pure Singular most Source Energy, in It-Self. Can be sensed to resonate with the very sort Hum Vibration, our Hearts have been most uniquely designed / evolved to experience, in the form of Love. Which is pretty much exactly what all of our world's greatest Mystical or great Mystery teachers, have concluded with respect to that most beautiful qualitative nature, which seems to reside within the very core of that which we have been referring to as Source, or if you prefer God! In the form of their common conclusion, that what we keep referring to as God, in deepest essence appears to be No-Thing other than that most essential Vibration which is of Love or Loving-Ness in It-Self!

In other words based on what we have already outlined about the nature of this singular most - pure whirling quantum level energy - Source Field. Whenever the very same left handed, ever smaller inwardly whirling negatively charged energy vortices - might change direction. To thus shift through into, what would have to amount too a seemingly infinite number of mini, mini, quantum level black hole like zero points. In such a way as to come out the other side as an ever more outwardly expanding, now right handed and thus entirely opposite positively charged - whirling vortices of this essentially very same pure energy. Such that given the incredibly inter-connected nature of this infinitely opposite whirl entangled - essentially Singular most underlying Source Energy Field. What the inevitable result of this entanglement would seem to imply at the very interactive so called Vesica Pisces edges of these differential whirls, exactly where these opposite direction spinning whirls would be in continuous overlap resonance with each other. Is the continuous ongoing creation of very sort of phenomenon, which has come to be described by many who have studied this phenomenon, as the Flower of Aphrodite. Also referred to in terms of what would amount to a continuous background Everywhere present - Comic level Resonant Hum Sound. Which due to this interactive differential whirl resonance at these Vesica Pisces overlap edges, would end up producing the sort of high pitched sensed Ringing Vibration. One might expect to happen in-so-far as One were to blow very high frequency resonating air in two opposite directions - across each other. With our point being that this Hum or Om Sound might very well actually be heard, by some One fully engaged in a process of Quantum level Attunement. Much in the way it has been said by sages throughout the ages, the more any we learn to optimally clear our sense of our Self's within. The more we begin to sense our inner Being's begin to Hum Ring much like a clear Tibetan Bell or Bowl. Exactly why these ancient Big Spirit attune-ers, developed such bells and gongs in the first pace.

Which is to say, it could very well be said that this quantum level everywhere present Super Light speed infinitely entangled whirling Pure Energy Field. Seems to create the very sort of Hum clear bell like subtle Ringing Vibration. Often associated with our possibility to actually Be - in such a Clear Pure Awareness place inside our more cosmically attuned sense of our Self's. Our higher Spirit Body would begin to most subtly ring, much like a clear bell. Or put another way, provided we find ways to get totally clear, we actually begin to ring/resonate with that very underlying / beyond lying Loving-Ness Vibration, we have come to associate with what the very Essence of what God-Ness In It-Self, is said to be all about. Or in other words actually vibrate with that Cosmic/Quantum level resonance described by our world's great Mystics. As that very fully internal sensed Heart Energy Flow Flowering - which is said to be of our ability to Hear God's Love - In It-Self.

Now For Illustration # 17 – This Is A Great Time For Every 'One' of Us - To Get The Clearest Possible Pure Awareness Sense of Just How This Pure Quantum Level Everywhere Present Source Energy - Seems to Sing It's Endless Most Sacredly One-Drous & Thus Positively Fabulous Uni-Versal Love Song - Within The Very Process of Manifesting Every Single Thing Into Formal Matter - That We May Ever Come To Know

Imagine being so open awake alive - to the ongoing flow of pure everywhere entangled Super Light Speed quantum Source energy! Insofar as it can be sensed to whirl and wave it's way both inside and throughout all of you! As well as within positively every manifest thing, from the very largest to the very smallest whether great or small, that ever manifests into form! Now picture this infinite everywhere energy vortex spinning in say something like '8' endless Mobius Strip like, '3' dimensional figure eight endlessly pure energy spinning Dual Torus Manifolds. All together interactively pooping with respect to each other, all at the same time. With one loop spinning forward in front and one spinning backward behind the six 2 dimensionally visible loops we have shown here. In such a way that insofar as each loop inevitably comes into a central focal point, via this figure eight like Mobius Strip Whirl. The very moment any given loop of pure energy turns over to come back toward itself by way of that energy vortex contracting ever smaller inward towards some eventual no charge central zero point. Now what was once pure energy whirling ever contractively smaller - in let's say a negatively charged left handed direction. Is going to become the very same pure energy now whirling in an ever more expansive positively charged right handed direction. In such a way that this pure Same Source Energy, will now begin to spin in the very oppositely charged direction.

From here once you get this picture that the interactive Vesica Pisces overlap resonance - between what amounts to side by side different direction whirls. Is going to create 3 magical energy interactive phenomenon - with the following characteristics embedded all at the same time. First 1.) An internally noticeable growing ever larger 6 or really 8 petal-ed Flower of Aphrodite energy patten - often referred to as a Flower of Love. Second 2.) An underlying interactive - pure quantum energy differential whirl based - Hum or Om like universal resonant sound. And Third 3.) To in this way based on what is scientifically known as centrifugal force based - pure energy whirl angular momentum. End up generating that first initial slowed down ordinary light speed based - sacred geometrical structure - known over the centuries as the 8 sided Star of David. Out of which all subsequent ever more complicated fractal forms can be said to grow into every singularity based outer world thing - that ever manifests into form.

From here let's go on to imagine that the open outer end of each '3' dimensional figure eight like whirl - also whirls into a next new outer band level of ever expanding fight eight like whirls. Until such time as these ever expanding vortical Mobious like ever expanding pure energy Whirls, begin to form a now 64 sided '3' dimensional - now completely stable sacred geometrical tetrahedron like structure. The very sort of 64 sided tetrahedron symbol which in the ancient Tibetan Mandala tradition - was referred to as the Sacred Sri Yantra symbol. Meant to represent that first stable Sacred Geometrical Fractal, out which all the basic periodic table elements that we ever come to know, seem to manifest into creation. And so on, and so on, with each outer band capable of ever more expanding into every more sophisticated levels of Sacred Fractal based manifestation! With many more Flower's of Love contained within every successively expanding level. Do you now suppose, that all of these different metaphors point to something hugely to infinity & beyond – special. That seems to keep going on here completely within our very inner most I's

- Or what?

Such that in-so-far as each of us might make an agreement to awaken our very own most total heart core open – and therefore complete Love of Life attuned - presence! Into an actual sense this pure as yet unformed whirling to infinity & beyond - energy. Constantly Figure '8' looping in differentially - either positron expanding or electron contracting - seemingly opposing everywhere interactive resonant entangled directions. To the extent we our selves can begin to sense this pure energy, singing it's inevitable outer edge Vesica Pisces overlap resonant Hum & therefore ultimately pure Flower of Aphrodite – Ultimate Love Song Within Us. Yes-We-Can in this way actually help our Self's keep inventing huge optimally in Harmony with the Power of this Love - great Wise-Dome Aware ways. To keep living not just the very best of ourselves ever forth, but also our possibility to actually find that state of 'True Happiness' - we all Seek!

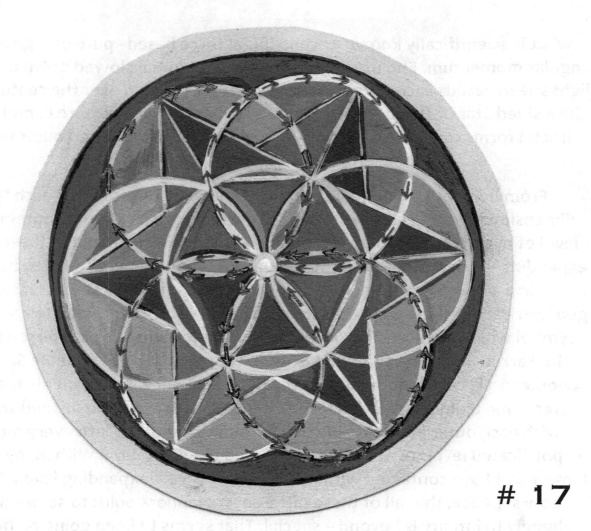

17

IMAGINE NOW IF YOU WILL - THIS PURE SAME SOURCE PRE-FORM EVERYWHERE PRESENT ESSENTIALLY AT NON-LOCAL SUPER LIGHT SPEED - DUAL TORUS ALTERNATE DIRECTIONAL WHIRLING & THEREFORE OPPOSITE CHARGED EVER EXPANDING TO INFINITY & BEYOND QUANTUM LEVEL ENERGY FIELD - CONSTANTLY BY WAY OF IT'S CORE MOST RESULTANT BASIC FLOWER OF APHRODITE LIKE LOVE HUM OVERLAP ENTANGLED RESONANCE - CREATING PRECISELY THOSE MOST SACRED ANGULAR MOMENTUM SLOWED DOWN & THUS ORDINARY LIGHT SPEED BASED - SACRED GEOMETRICAL '8' POINTED 3-D STAR OF DAVID LIKE FRACTALS - OUT OF WHICH ALL SUBSEQUENT EVER MORE SOPHISTICATED SACRED CRYSTALLINE STRUCTURES & THUS ULTIMATELY ALL MATERIAL FORMS CAN BE SAID TO GROW - INTO EVERY SO CALLED OBJECTIVE THING WE EVER COME TO KNOW? YES, YES, OM SHANTI LOVE HUM! HO!

(**Accompanying Explanation** – Which is to say, in terms of what we now know about Sacred Geometry - and it's role in the fractal formation of all - ever more sophisticated manifest forms. From the first stable element Hydrogen all the way up to the most sophisticated atoms & complex molecules, including the most complex creatures found on our planet. One might well say, it appears as though everything that ever does manifest into ever more complicated levels of manifest form - including our selves. Could be said to manifest out of an underlying quantum based field, within which both the Flower of Love and It's resultant overlap Underlying Hum Sound - seem to be embedded. In such a way as to actually hum love along right within the very root essence of every single thing that ever does crystallize into some form or other. Whether those crystals be in-organic or even the most sophisticated levels of organ-i-city - we ever see. The positively great news for us is - it appears that our own Made in the Image Human Most Heart's - represent the very most central intelligence place we have all been given within ourselves. To help us more fully attune to this underlying Hum Love - Source Force. In such a way that best enables us to Invent our own self's forth in optimal harmony with this Great Mystery Source It-Self. OMG - this realization is so truly profoundly huge - it is going to change everything about how we go about choosing to live forth our lives - from every this moment on.)

(**Special Additional Note** – Given then this huge realization, that we all arise into form out the same Source / Force of Love. Which was reinforced for most of us in the context of that no-difference, only One non-separate Heart beating bond we most of us Once felt with our parents, in the very earliest years of our Life. Which tends to be heightened in the sort of expanded awareness loss of separate identity, no-difference from our One Source context, that tends to happen whenever any One of us is asked to take some One else's life. Whom they have been merely led to believe in their 'little minds' alone, are somehow separate from and therefore lesser than any One other, who might hold so called different mere man made invented belief values, than themselves. No small One-Der so many of our so called war heroes tend to come home, with major levels of PTSD based, whole nervous system shock damaging trauma. Many of whom are never able to get over such acts, no matter how much conventional healing therapy we try and put them through. In other words, more and more of us are coming to realize, that it is no small thing to agree to take some One else's life, who is also ultimately connected to One-Ness Itself. Which is exactly why it becomes so important for every One of us, to learn to link ourselves all our way Up. With the most brilliant solution generative power we can muster, within what amounts to our much greater Tap Our Source and therefore way more Big Mind Awake - Hu-Man/Woman most sense of our being within At-One-Ment. As well as to help us find some way to completely release all the pain some of us have likely internalized more than others, very much as a consequence of taking some One else's life. So we can all finally fully forgive ourselves for not knowing of what we have done!)

(From here, In order to help us all way better fully 'grok' the huge sense of this everywhere present, to Infinity & Beyond quantum level energy based, constantly both at the same time opposite charge whirling, most basic Dual Torus Manifold principle. Out of which positively every ever smaller or larger manifesting thing appears to come into existence, including the Whole of our very own particular sense of I-Am-Ness Self Identity. Insofar as our very existence appears to center around our very own zero point core energy organizing place within us, our Hearts. Whether we ever choose to become conscious of this Zero Point of Perfect Brilliant Stillness within our very own higher Hu-Man Self's, or continue to Knot. You may want to take some time to Google here to find out more about this Uni-Versal Flower of Aphrodite or Flower of God's Love, said to reside within the very Essence of all things Made Manifest! As well as look to Nassim Haramein's works & images on the nature of the Dual Torus Manifold. Even go on to order my son David's paper on 'Differentials - The Hidden Harmonic Codes of the Universe' at voiceentertainment.net. Then choose to view my prior You Tube videos on Quantum Attunement - particularly video # 3.

In other words with all due respect to the ultimate core Peace-Ful nature of this everywhere present - Quantum level Super Light Source Field - In Itself. Which in turn appears to both underlie as well as beyond lie the Whole Uni-Verse of all manifest form. It is very much like our possibility to most openly attune ourselves, into this most Heart Core Awakened central Hum Love Sacred Resonant Place we all have within us. Has been most exquisitely designed / evolved in such a way that the more we learn to actually inwardly Heare - this place of Love Hum Resonance within ourselves. The more we will be able to truly sense our most central core processors within, begin to elevate. Our purest possible awareness into a most unique kind of optimally guiding us ever forth, inner Heart Core felt messaging. Such as will ultimately more than anything, keep affording us the very best inner inspirationally brilliant empowering means - we have. To help our own individual unique senses of our Self's now actually be, as fully whole being follow the Yellow Brick Road guidance of our Hearts, truly Ful-Fill-Ment enabled. As Yes We Possibly Can in the greater sense of our possibility to truly fully realize, all of the whole being oriented fulfillments we may ever long for. With way greater respect for whom we really in relation our most glorious potentials, have been most exquisitely Made in the Image - designed/evolved to actually be? Exactly in relation to the incredibly Harmonic way, this Huge Mysterious Source Field In It-self, has been said to resonate with an underlying/beyond lying quantum Love Hum. In the context of constantly manifesting every-singular-most- thing, this essentially unlimited Source Field - ever does.)

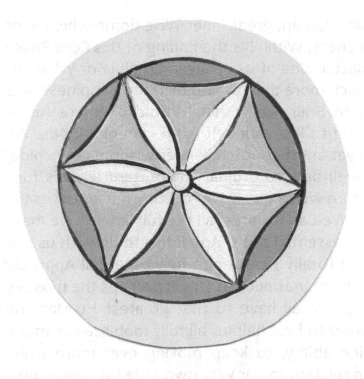

Huge Grand Wisdom Lesson # 7 - By Encouraging Our Whole Self's To Be Ever More Heart Core Appreciative For Positively Everything We Ever End Up Experiencing - We End Up Opening The Very Core of Ourselves To All The Inner Empowerment We May Ever Require - To Best Enable Ourselves to Fully Realize Every Aspect of Our Very Inner Most Ful-Fill-Ment Intended - Dreams

IN OTHER WORDS OUR TIME HAS NOW COME TO FULLY AWAKEN OUR MOST HEART-CORE FELT SENSE OF TOTALLY IN ALWAYS HUM LOVING - TRULY GREAT-FUL APPRECIATION WITH-IN

THE ONLY PLACE FROM WITHIN WHICH IT IS EVER POSSIBLE - FOR ANY OF US TO ACTUALLY FIND THE TRUE SENSE OF HAPPINESS - WE ALL OF US MOST LONG FOR

"Man Oh Man/Woman, great inner Wise-dome which is of our own potential greater found awareness, Within! Is the finding of this Core Peace-Full have great life oriented journey place inside of us - truly In-Credible or What? It sure seems like we could not ask for much more than to find this true Happiness oriented - guiding forth place of our ultimate Brilliance within!" "Hold on there full of endless quantum energy, dearest raring to live your self forth - young bloods. Whoa, slow your core sense of self down yet another notch," inner wisdom now chided. "For there is one more set of huge well beyond ordinary, important lessons for every One of us to fully internalize. Before we can truly we realize what amounts to a total Yes we Now Know - Exactly How We-Can manifest all the fulfillments we may ever long for, place inside our most core essential self's. And it has to do with us ever more agreeing to cultivate the place of totally Heart open fully Great-Ful Appreciation for all that we already have been given. Inasmuch as this is perhaps the most essential whole inner 'I' opening doorway, we all have to that greatest Hu-Man most potential which resides within. In order to best help us all fully mobilize our more Made in the Image & thus actual Divine ability, to keep moving ever more truly now Co-Creatively solution forward. In relation to our very own True Happiness oriented, and thus very best possible, actual now whole being fulfillment set dreams."

"In the huge sense that insofar as we keep encouraging our self's to find our ever more core centered sense of true Peace-Ful-Ness within. What starts to happen for us, is that we begin to become evermore truly Heart Open totally Grateful, for all those things we already have the opportunity to experience, right under our very noses. Before we let our self's get way too stressed out lost, in relation to all the various ways we keep finding our self's wanting - even more. Inasmuch as opening our Hearts into that most special place inside, wherein we begin to actually sense the very inward heart opening sensation, we refer to as being in a place of Loving-Ness inside of our selves. Is exactly what is going to help us the very most, to be finally able to fully realize all '7' of our inner most longed for, vital energy based dreamed for inner Ful-Fill-Ment intentions. In such a way that will be most likely to actually bring all these various Ful-Fill-Ments into a place of true happiness found fruition - within us. For example, it is simply impossible for us to find great sensual/sexual fulfillment, unless such endeavors are fully connected to our Hearts. The very same holds true for great doer/entrepreneurial fulfillments, great friendships and relationships fulfillments, great loving family fulfillments, great communications fulfillments, great visionary forward seeing fulfillments, and most especially great spiritual/religious fulfillments. In other words there can be no true Ful-Fill-Ment at any of these various vital energy based levels of our innermost Being-Nesses. Until such time as all of these fulfillments end up being fully connected to this most exquisite place of Loving-Ness we all have within, which can be sensed inside our Hearts.

"This of course includes us being especially Great-Ful for the most One-Der-Ful giant Wizard computer, we all already have within us. Designed / Evolved as it is to help us find that very Yellow Brick Road flow zone pathway, which is of our greater holographic awareness potential, to attune ourselves into that One & Only true unlimited At-One-Ment Wisdom place - we all have inside of ourselves. The very place which enables us to be so no more boundaries and thus way more inside to inside in touch present, with all due respect to that both at the same time, pure micro level of everywhere inter-connected underlying energy. As well as that most magnificent giant to infinity & beyond everywhere entangled macro field, which keeps expanding all the way outwards to include every Galactic level of manifest form. We begin to attune to very underlying / beyond lying Love Hum resonance, out of which all manifest forms seem to arise in any first place. In much the greater sense we have already pointed to, in the prior rationale for this lesson, centered around illustration # 17."

"Actually in other words attune ourselves, so into this underlying beyond lying Force of Love. Such as can actually be sensed within our very clearest states of being to Hum resonate along inside - of our very Heart Core's. In such a profound truly glorious inner Heart Open way, that in thus bringing our selves to now actually be ever more grounded within this place of total Heart Open Loving-Ness. We will now not only find ourselves being 'Totally in Love' with everything that keeps appearing exactly within our very innermost core present 'I's. But we will also based on our very best prior set intentions, actually discover our greatest possible senses of our self's. As being ever more truly whole being insightfully core being inspired, to keep on inventing/creating the very sorts of positively great whole life fulfillment oriented solutions, for our selves. Most likely to help our innermost senses of our self's - actually be best enabled to keep manifesting the truly great happy life's - we every One of us so much long for! In the huge grand Cosmic sense, that this total love of 'Life' place within not only actually is the most powerfully great forward moving solution generative motivating place - that we actually do have within us. But is also in fact as we shall come to better under-stand as these heart attunement lessons keep proceeding toward our very last lesson. The only place from within which we can actually manifest the true happiness found fulfillments at every level of our innermost sense of being, we all of us so much long for."

"In this much greater respect you could well say, that it's very much like whenever we find our Heart's most open, turned on and tuned in. It is precisely this innermost whole field attuned, and thus that most highly sensitive awareness potential we all have within us. Which not only best helps us to tune in to underlying harmonic Love Hum resonance - of the ultimately Uni-Fied quantum Source field - Itself. But it is also this inner Heart Core centered awareness, which can best be heard within the place of perfectly brilliant core Peace-Ful Still-Ness - inside of us. To

186

keep messaging to us exactly when we are engaging in the world around us. In ways within which we end up hearing our innermost heart attuned essence saying to us, Wow! Don't you positively love just what it is that your inner most I-am within, is guiding you into playing at inventing - right now? In relation to your most Heart Awake innermost attuned sense of your self - in this very moment of your existence? In the much greater sense that even more important than One's process of insight, would appear to be the ever forward moving yellow brick road like guidance, afforded to us by our very own One & Only, way open Big Heart Awake and thus greater Wise-Dome attuned - Intelligence. Other than wise too lost in the chaos of our unresolved emotional dynamics, and/or the endless chatter of our overly attached to mere abstract ideas about how we merely small narrow band mind keep our selves 'thinking' - our world is supposed to be. We very likely will not even be able to hear, the inner messaging of our Heart guidance."

"Imagine then inner Wisdom was to keep Preaching forward, just One bit more in relation to our greater potential for Quantum Hum Love attunement! You your self now agreeing to wake up every day, in such a way that in conjunction with your growing daily practice aimed at In-Stilling the place of Heart Core Peace-Ful calm centered Still-Hess - within you. You might take a few precious moments to just open your Heart as fully as possible, in truly Great-Ful Appreciation for all that you have already been given. So that you might start out each day based on all those most precious no-difference only One Heart Beating Heare, peak actual religious experience moments. You will have already have had the good fortune to actually have known within you. In such a way that you might now encourage this sense of totally Loving Life, which resides within the very root core of all of Creation. To come as fully awake within you as you possibly can to start out each new day! Including a new sense of totally Heart open appreciation for all of the incredible emotional challenges, that our Life's so inevitably seem to keep bringing every One's way. Inasmuch as now that you have learned how to help your self feel your way completely through, to the other open side of some old bothersome negative flare button held - emotional dynamic. When you take into consideration that some of our very biggest inner growth moments, tend to come about very much as a consequence of our more conscious ability. To help clear our selves totally past any such contractive pattern, we may have taken on over the course of our experiencing, some of the very worst fear based moments of our life's. Such clearing possibilities are what make it possible for us to now be even fully Great-Ful, for the most difficult moments in our life's!"

"In this much greater respect, the more Brilliance oriented supra-logical Reason why this Great-Ful-Ness lesson, is so hugely important for all of us," inner most Wise-Dome of pure awareness, now kept going on to relay? "Is every time we agree to keep clearing ourselves past any such old such flare button hyper fighter or fleer avoider arousing dynamics. Or for that matter mere narrow band small mind made, mental abstractions such as we may find ourselves still holding within ourselves. More and more into that ever more still Peace-Full found place - inside the very Heart core of us. Which is of us being ever more totally here and now, fully Heart open present to the way more essential One-Field which can be sensed to exist all around Us. In such a way as to end up Being completely in Love with positively everything we may ever find ourselves experiencing. This is the very way we make it possible for the pure quantum level Love Song energy of the entire Uni-Verse, now much more clear able to pour through the very Heart Core of us. The very same Love Song energy, which makes it possible for this pure pre-formed Source Energy to form into those very Sacred Geometrical Fractals, which in turn are said to form the very building block patterns. Such as seem to be required for positively everything we ever know, to come into manifest form. Including our own Heart Core felt possibility to help manifest our very own dreamed for great intentions. Into the very sort of manifest forms than can help us to feel all those senses of innermost Ful-Fill-Ment - we keep longing for."

"From here once we truly get this, it seems way beyond reasonable to conclude, that inasmuch as the very way this both underlying, as well as at the same time beyond lying, pure Uni-Versal Source Energy Field. Can be understood very much as a consequence of this core quantum Hum Love Flower of Aphrodite like Love Song vibration which seems to reside within, the very underlying or beyond lying core of this Great Mysterious Source/Force Field - In Itself. To end up creating every Sacred Geometrical building block pattern, out of which all manifest forms seem to arise. Then it is just a matter of us continually encouraging ourselves to recognize, that getting this Uni-Versal Love Song to completely resonate within us. Along with all the inner guidance such attunement tends to bring along with it, to our max. Such attuning then is exactly the best way we have to keep finding our selves ever more literally totally now in our flow zone. And thus fully enabled to actually Hum Love our way along, through each and every so called problem, that may ever come our way. In the much greater sense that such Heart Soaring Open-Ness is actually the most important open ended key doorway, we all have within every One of our most unique inwardly attuned - senses of our self's. Most likely to help guide us ever forward, toward the actual solution fulfillment of all those True Found Happiness oriented - inner set intentions we all seek. In the much larger sense our own possibility to actually find our very own heavenly empowered, truly Magical Miracle Solution generating - King-Domes of greater awareness Wisdom - we all have access to within!"

"Good God great Wise-Dome teachers within, we want to learn more about sacred geometry, and it's relationship to higher order Meta-Physics and/or Al-Chemistry. Which appears to have to do with just how all Sacred building block

Fractals seem to grow into every form we ever know, based on this both underlying and at the same time beyond lying quantum Hum whirl. Which we ourselves have the possibility to tune into, within our very own core senses of our self's. In such a way as to best enable us to actually be able to keep on Co-Creating our way ever forward. This realization about ourselves is so, so truly fascinating, indeed actually miraculous! Cause based on what you are saying, since every single thing that ever manifests into form, including our selves. Can be sensed to do so based on it's own particular unique, fractal growth organizing pattern. Which in turn seems to arise within the context of this both underlying beyond Love Song, we have been talking about Heare. Then it would seem way obvious that the more we ourselves, keep supporting our innermost core senses of our selves. To keep tuning into this quantum level Love Song we all have the possibility to best Heare - within the very Core of our most well beyond ordinary sense of our Self's. The more we will begin to feel ourselves as though heavenly empowered, to keep on manifesting exactly all those very best intentions we keep on In-Formation-Ally organizing - to thus keep Vision Seeing in front of ourselves. In terms of the very guiding forth messaging to our Self's we seem to require, to best help enable every One of Us to actually Ful-Fill the very Heart Core of not just our Self's. But also in the very same stroke of genius, One-Ness in It-Self's ever evolving new possibilities, to keep experiencing the very sort ever more Harmonic Big Picture Results. Which can now include us as Made in the Image creatures of every things One & Only Source."

"Yes, Yes, my dear every One's! Heare you have exactly what is so truly magnificent about this Unlimited Source Field of pure underlying/beyond lying everywhere infinitely entangled - Energy. Insofar as this root Source Energy appears to whirl everything we ever know into form," inner wisdom was now motivated to keep going on! Such that given you your very own self are beginning too much better understand, or find your most essential Core sense of your Self, more and more able to stand within - that every Root Source Energy. Which in It-Self appears to be not other than Love In It-Self! Can you now finally much better Sea, this is really One huge Big Picture way of saying too us all! Wouldn't we all of us my dearest innermost Cosmic Quantum level attuned Being's? Much rather Love to be totally involved in inventing our self's forward, toward the positively great life's that we within our inner most attuned senses of our Self's - might most long for? In ways within which we could truly say, we would end up having the whole our Heart's fully be-yond board, totally awake within us, whatever great fulfillments we might seek? Insofar as this Quantum Source Field In It-Self appears to generate everything IT ever does, based on this very same Flower of Love principle to be found within the very Essence of All Things? Or, would we really want to leave the very most core integral processing and thus greatest possible whole being fulfillment oriented unit, we all have within us, way too asleep? As if to say, the very Core Most Essence of Us doesn't much matter, in relation to how we might keep choosing to live our Life's ever forward - at all?

"Wouldn't it seem more than silly for us to keep on trying to proceed, with our old constantly split and divided so called feeling & emotional vs our so called rational/ logical non-sense of our Self. Constantly pitted against each other, as if at war inside of us? With complete Dis-Respect to our greater possibility to actually find our most Essential Core sense of our Self's, way more full-on holistically board within us. Mostly because, we will have decided to keep refusing to take those inner most response-abilities, such as seem to be required. To help grow our Self's way more up into the very Kind of more Complete Love of Life - Heart Core Centered Kind-Dome of Heaven place - which is to be found Within. In such a clear way, that we might actually be able to now so as fully as possible, actually be able to Sense the Quantum level Love Hum of the Uni-Verse. We would actually find ourselves Heart Core awake enough inside to enable us to Tap into this underlying beyond lying Source Force. In the direction of us helping to guide the very innermost sense of our self's, ever more toward the actual Self-Inventive Ful-Fill-Ment of all those very greatest dreams. Our ever intending our Self's forth lives will have to keep offering us?"

To which every One's both Quantum Katie & Cosmic Charlie essence Within, now found themselves crying out with the very Who-Ole of their inner most beings. "No, No, we don't want this much pain and suffering in our lives any more! No, No we don want to keep hating way too many things about our lives, ever again! Like for example hating and resenting our so called jobs, our so called friends and neighbors, our so called living environments, our various levels of so called enemies who have grown up with other perspectives on what this Source Force appears to be all about, than ours. Even our so called God or total lack of sense of anything going on here, that might be much greater than us & our mere narrow band idea & belief attachments alone? All of which really appear to be part and parcel of, what amounts to the very same singular most Source/ Force, we ourselves have been formed out of? Simply because the majority of Us Made in the Image People here, have become afraid to stand up in relation to our very own potential to connect ourselves way more fully into this Singular most Source Force. To such an extent, we keep finding our very soul's hopelessly lost and ever more driven. To keep on perpetuating seemingly endless cycle rounds of anger, resentment, hatred and even all kinds of take, take, violence all around us, no matter what the cost. Precisely because of what amounts to our very own unresolved fear based and thus ultimately split & divided narrow band mind non-sense, of our much greater potential Whole Mind Awareness."

"Much rather thanks to the way greater Under-standings we have been talking about – Heare! Such as we also at the very same time, have been agreeing to take ever-more full-on making our inner 'I' single Response-Ability - to keep growing within us! Yes, Yes, we really finally do Now want to thus make it possible, for our much greater sense of our Self's! To keep on bringing this Kind of total Love of Life, exactly into all those very directions which could most help us to create/invent, our very largest senses of our Self's. Way more happily ever forward, toward our possibility to now be fully enabled - to actually Ful-Fill all of our greatest possible - innermost intention set - let's all have a positively great Life - dreams! Every One's Wise-Dome of awareness within, was now more clearly than ever before! To find his/her greatest possible Made in the Image Self - calling upon his/her innermost Co-Creative empowering - Muse! To thus help every way clearer found Quantum Katie Cosmic Charlie Within - to now much more fully actually Realize!"

Now Then Is A Perfect Time To Look to Illustration # 18 – An Image of Our Now Much Wiser True Happiness Oriented Sense of Our Selves - Now Full-On Constantly Open Heartedly Agreeing to Most Great-Fully Appreciate - In Such A Way As To Totally Love Positively All of Same Source's Things - Made Manifest

In the much larger sense, that in our agreeing to become ever more fully Heart Open truly Great-Ful for all that we have already been given. Like all those many seemingly diverse things, such as rocks, trees, frogs, birds, dogs, kitty's, including every truly great product we ever produce. Even our very own highest possible Self's in such a way as to truly respect all other Made in the Image human most beings. Which tend to keep emerging within this very moment into the very midst of our life's. We will now find ourselves as being more and more to infinity and beyond, figure eight endless mobius loop like, Now way more fully Awake. And thus far more intimately connected to what amount to the Love Source Energy - of the Entire Uni-Verse. In such a way as to keep our selves now walking within a huge without limits Oceanic Field of ever more present empowerment. The very sort of Heart Open Empowerment most likely to help us All manifest ever better Life's, aimed at the fulfillment of the entire Whole of our greatest possible Self's.

(Accompanying Highly Self Motivating - Under-Standing – Picture you your self, now supporting your very own greater sense of self - to become so Heart Open Appreciative. You would now sense that everything all around you, including your very own sense of your self. Is actually humming along into manifestation - within a context which is of pure to infinity & beyond both at the same time underlying as well as beyond lying - Source love. Inasmuch as in opening your heart fully, even to all the various challenges that come your way. You will finally begin to hear there is only One Singular Love Heart Humming through positively everything that ever manifest into form - here. Much in the same way you used to sense Only One Heart Beating, with your mother or father, whenever they once totally loved you. And of course now, in the same greater sense you can still experience with your favorite loved ones. Simply because as you shall ever more come to 'See'. The openness of your own Heart, is simply the most whole being forward guiding, and thus most real total Ful-Fill-Ment Empowering place, we all each of us have within us.)

18

EVERY US - NOW FULL-ON OPEN HEARTEDLY
AGREEING TO KEEP LOVING POSITIVELY ALL SAME
SOURCE'S THINGS MADE MANIFEST - INASMUCH AS
THIS IS OUR VERY BEST WAY TO HELP EACH OF OUR
SELF'S FULLY REALIZE - POSITIVELY EVERY
INNERMOST FULFILLMENT - WE ALL SEEK

"Great Good God Almighty innermost Wisdom! Are you suggesting this could be every One of us? Insofar as we might just agree to keep growing our own Inner Wisdom Light - to the max! Yes, Yes, my dear every One's "Quite simply because inner wisdom replied, "Every time any of us can find ourselves truly totally Heart open Great-Ful for whatsoever blessings we already have been provided with, even in the context of all that is most difficult within our lives!" 'We thus Open our very own Hearts' - into not One-Ly that place which is of us 'Totally Loving' all of this Huge great Mysterious Source's, here and now manifestations!. But we also at the very same time support ourselves to access that very most full-on energy inspiring place, wherein resides that most central core processing unit. Most response-able to help us run that giant truly most One-Der-Ful, Quantum Level Computer Wizard, such as we all have Within - each and every singular most One of us. The very processing unit, that can best enable us to actually realize all the inner Ful-Fill-Ments, we may ever long for!"

"In other words", inner Wisdom now chose to further clarify! "It seems to take us being able to mobilize that most Life Affirmative, or full of Pure everywhere quantum level attuned, Heart open Passion for all Life place inside the most core centered aspect of our own energy system. For us to most fully inspire that most One-Der-Ful have a positively Great Life computer Wizard, we all have within ourselves. Toward our possibility to actually Co-Creatively invent the very sort of solutions, that will have the possibility to resonate in total Harmony with the very Hum Love Resonance, which resides within the very core Essence of positively everything that ever manifests into form both all around us as well as within us. In this sense it is kind of like it is our Hearts, which seem to best help us co-ordinate all those inner most sensed vital energy flows, we seem to require. To enable us to most magnificently run those most One-Der-Ful quantum level attuned, computer Wizard's we all have within the very essence of every Singular most One of Us. Other than wise, having no sense of our most central, tree of life energy co-ordinating power plant Unit we all have within. Insofar as we keep running ourselves based on fear, rather than on Love. We will thus tend to keep on inventing very sort of partial solutions, most likely to keep bringing us ever more rounds of the very same. Which is to say, seemingly endless rounds of ever more fear-ful, man made results!

"O.k. Let's see if I can summarize this lesson, great inner Wisdom place within", ever growing all up Charlie/Katie now wanted now to proclaim, to our World at Large. "It seems to go something like this, the more we keep on agreeing to keep on Opening Our Hearts, in complete gratitude for every singularity most engendered thing - we may ever be blessed to thus experience. The more we are going to open ourselves through into that very most central core processing unit power plant place we all have within. Which has been designed to help best empower us with all the true Love of Life passion - we might ever require. To help

194

our most essential core Self's fully mobilize that most One-Der-Ful whole brain lit up Wizard - we all have within. In precisely those direction most likely to help us actually realize every inner most fulfillment, we might ever long for. Other than wise to the extent we keep motivating ourselves forth based on fear, and all those ego maniaccal motivations that go along with fear. Like greed, and that me, me, me, survival based power hungry felt need only, to keep manipulating others to our own egocentric focused ends alone. Way too often to the point of being willing to keep harming others, as though they are somehow lesser connected to One-Ness than us. This is to the extent we will never find the true happiness's, we all so much long for.

"Yes, my dear beloved's, Now I sense you are finally getting to the very essence, of what this great Play of Life, Magical most Mystery Tour is really All About. Which involves No Thing more or less, than growing ourselves into a place of total Loving-Ness within each of our own selves, to our ultimate max. For Yes, in beyond Thought, Word & Deedy do, 'Love is actually All there really ever Is! Hopefully you as Great Grand Adult-Children of our One & Only Source, are now much more clearly able to Heare this very place inside of - your very own greatest possible sense of your self? Especially in relation to whatever vital energy based fulfillments you may find your self intending, to help your self realize.? For it is exactly this inner messaging from within our hearts, which tells us when we are orienting ourselves in such a beautiful play ourselves forward direction, that we can without hesitation say to ourselves. We are truly loving whatever field of fulfillment related endeavor, it may be we find ourselves choosing to play ourselves toward - within - this very moment right now. Like for example, in the sense that when we pick up certain doer/entrepreneurial motivated products that others have invented. And we find our innermost Heart core attuned total Love of Life Self - Loving certain Love imbued products so much, we feel motivated say to all our friends. Wow all you Dudes & Dudesses out there, I just love my new computer, my new energy efficient car, my new energy saver dishwasher, my new greater inner wisdom oriented computer game, my new fuel efficient aero plane, my new green tractor, my new sustainable house, my lovely super healthy & full of life vibrancy enhancing non toxic grown foods etc. etc. etc."

"Which of course, includes the way you your self may end up choosing to help empower others, or others may be helping to empower you. In all those various ways that can actually help more and more of us, to feel fully enabled to purchase/participate in, whatever great life oriented products, we all of us might most love to enjoy playing with. Including those kinds of educational and service oriented products, which help us to become way more heart attuned and thus far better at inventing precisely those positively Hu-Man most life's for ourselves. Which come about very much as a consequence of each us finding some way to positively love, whatever it might be we keep choosing to do here. Simply because such core processing unit awakening, is exactly what more than anything helps us to feel way more empowered, to create positively great results for ourselves! Compared to all those other way less enjoyable goods and services we keep choosing to produce. With dis-respect to which we way too often find ourselves saying, God this sucks, this is so ill conceived, I simply can't figure out how to use what I've just bought into. Or even though I've used this thing for 6 mos. now, I still don't sense any benefit. Such that we find ourselves actually feeling, way ripped off. I mean, who wants products & services that rip us off, or even worse make us sick, just because they make some-body else, rich? Or because some mere heartless wealth seeker alone, was particularly effective at conning us into, what amounts to some heartless, very poorly quantum love hum level attuned - pretty much useless piece of junk! Even worse, when 'We the People' as a whole, based on our own insecurities and self doubts. Keep co-creating the circumstances for certain people with very little Heart, to by means of every indoctrinating con at their disposal, including the use of Force. Just outright keep taking whatever they want from us, including our most inalienable of 'Life', 'Liberty' & the actual finding of 'True Happiness', human rights?"

"In other words" Inner Wisdom was to keep going on! "Learning to listen to our hearts, that most truly One Source attuned guiding forth place, we all have within us. Has everything to do with that special inner most magical totally satisfying Humming along way Ful-Fill-Ing Sensation, we get inside that very Heart Core most central processing unit we all have within ourselves. Whenever we find ourselves Truly Loving whatever it may be we are choosing to play invent ourselves into - right now. Or alternatively, whenever we are playing at being optimally Co-Creative/Inventive in relation to participating in something, we truly love to do for the benefit of all Hu-Man/Woman-Kind. Most especially including all those loving things we so much love to do both for our families and very best friends. As well as when we communicate the most heart openly with all those other human beings, who have also thus been created out the very same Source. In what appears to be in the virtual Image - of this Source. In such a way that points to this most fundamental truth, which is of our inner most potential to keep inventing ourselves forth. Totally from within our hearts in relation to everything we may ever choose to do, which as a matter of course, must inevitable include as we have already pointed to, how we choose to relate to each other. In the much greater sense that in our actually experiencing this place of wholly communion, with what we have been referring to as the everywhere presence of this God-Ness principle - Itself. We actually come to experience this Source as LOVING-NESS ITSELF! Insofar as this principle of God-Ness or One-Ness in It's very own Right, seems to Love Hum IT'S way through positively everything we ever come to know."

"Oh, My, God, my dearest inner Wise-Dome - Within", Charlie & Katie in now bowing the whole core of their inner most beings, suddenly found themselves motivated to say unto themselves. "Given that we get this core truth about who we have the potential to be - inside the very core of us. This most fundamental realization about just who we all have the potential to Be. Is now going to change everything about how We-Are now going to choose to play every aspect of our inner most fulfillment seeking self - ever forward - from this moment on." To which, every Charlie or Katie's very own innermost Heart Attuned Wisdom within, could now be heard "to most joyfully hop, skip & jump along within One huge to infinity and beyond ever expanding - continuous Whole Heartedly Loving Life - ever ongoing every Heart beat!"

Illustration # 18 – Summary Image of our Greatest Possible Higher Jumping Mouse Selves - Making an agreement to Climb Our Very Own Inner Most Mt Wisdom (also known in the far east as Mt Meru) - In Order that Our Now Full-On Awake Hearts May Soar - As the Non Separate from One-Ness or True God-Ness Connected Beings - Who we Really All of Us At Heart - Most Are

There is a legendary metaphoric Oglala Sioux tale about a Little Blinders On & thus half blind, nevertheless utterly courageous Jumping Mouse being. Who kept hearing an inner hum sound going on all around him, in the background of his daily life. Which seemed to keep growing slightly louder the older and more curious about life - he found himself getting. So one day when he was old enough to go on a vision quest, he told his friends he was going to climb the nearby Mt. In the hopes of finding out what this Hum Sound he would keep hearing on the very clearest of his days, was really all about. With the point being that when he finally gets to what amounts to the very top of his own inner Mt Wise-Dom of awareness Within. He is now able to finally See in his Heart Open jumping toward One-Ness - the very sound he kept hearing was really the sound of an Eagle's or his own now Wakan Tanka connected - God's Wings. The very wings of Love which can enable Every One of Us to now Soar, within what amounts to our very Own Non Separate from anything, One & Only Big Heart Open Love Humming Eagle as Metaphor for God's everywhere Presence - Essence.

Such that what we have done here, in the context of our own inner wisdom oriented '9' lessons of Awareness. Is to create a modern picture image, grounded more in all of our greatest world religions. To help convey to every One of Us just what this metaphoric Jumping Mouse journey - keeps attempting to refer us toward. To begin, given our pretty much inevitable fall from the original grace - of us being born here into the sort of state we could refer to - as being in In-Nocient like One-Der. Most of us out of our early internalized fears and growing self doubts, tend to turn our formerly knowing Self's into not more than little narrow band minds, or somewhat zombie like half blind mice like people. Constantly scurrying about trying to step out into our world each day, as though way too lost blind to our much higher cosmic love hum attunement - possibilities.

With the way sad result that we turn even older, far too many of the most traumatized of us. Tend to turn into the sort of all too devious 'rat like' people, who based mostly on our very own inner held fears & self doubts. Constantly keep going about endlessly complaining about as well as projecting, all kinds of worst case negative scenario outcomes. To the point where our fears start to turn us into the sort of rat like beings who become willing to do almost anything to get whatever it is we - based on a complete lack of our much greater whole being found self. Merely keep 'trying' to make our selves happy with, based on our small mind 'thinking' heads alone. And which nevertheless very much as a result of our now less than whole conscious set goals. Tend to keep bringing us down back into the hell realms, of ever more rounds of the very same fear based pain and suffering, We kept trying to avoid feeling fully through by way of devious behaviors in our first place.

With the rather sad point being, the more we allow our inner negativities to keep ruling us! Before long our now seemingly endlessly mere half wit constantly attempting to rationalize and justify our way, past our fears. And therefore completely out of our control small narrow band now seemingly endlessly mad dog barking 'thinking minds' alone - start to take us so totally over. We cannot ever seem based on this inner madness, to find any sense of true whole being found, real Peace-Ful-Ness within ourselves. In such a way as to help us way more fully realize, our much greater whole being oriented fulfillment potentials. The good news however is, that the wiser of us in learning how to take our blinder off, soon begin to realize. We can never even hope to manifest a truly whole life for ourselves. Based on us staying locked into our constantly split and divided little mind intelligence potentials, alone. Wherein we keep using less than half our much more integral, way greater Big Mind One Heart Tap our Source connected Potentials - to help us keep finding our way ever forward.

This is where an awareness of our inner Ha-Nu-Man or Ha-Higher-Nu-New-Man potential within - comes in. The very Higher-New-Man/Woman who might now finally be willing to learn how to completely integrate all aspects of both the most base animal as well as higher human potentials, we all have within ourselves. In the form of us integrating our left brain feeling and emotional nature within our more right brain rational logical nature; our more yang active masculine expressive sense of our self's, within our more yin feminine passive receptive sense of our self's; our so called lower more mother earthbound vital energy fulfillment callings completely within our so called higher consciousness more heavenly able to live within At-One-Ment - highest possible Father Sky Great Spirit fulfillment oriented callings. In such a way that we might end up totally jumping our way now all integrated & way up within our full-on Soaring like an Eagle fully Open Hearts. Constantly now able to clearly hear that Hum Soaring/Roaring sound which resides within all creatures great and small, indeed all things great and small. Including those God Humming Wings wherein One's Big Heart becomes fully enabled to now Soar like an Eagle!

The image of Ha-Nu-Man in other words in our Jumping Mouse story that follows, contains essentially the very same message about elevating our selves into ever more integral and thus in non-separation states of consciousness. As does the Eagle Kachina depicted going forward in our image #25, such as is to be found in our more Western Native Traditions! In the much greater sense that our potential Higher-New-Man, or Heart soaring like an Eagle-Man message. To the very Heart Core of very our own sense of our Self's - has in all Great Spirit traditions - always been. We can never expect to climb ever higher up the Mt. Meru of our own inner Hum Love attuned greater Wisdom Tree of Life, or that same ladder which elevates us into a total Love of all Source made Manifestations. Unless we learn to fully integrate all aspects of ourselves into the most Whol-E possible Sense of our Self's - within ourselves. In such a way that we end up totally jumping our former Mouse - way now all Up within what always amounts to our most full-on Soaring like an Eagle - inner most awakened Hearts. In such a way that will constantly make it possible for us to now clearly hear that Hum Soaring/Roaring sound which resides not only within all creatures great and small such as Within the Hum sound of an Eagles Wings, indeed such as Hum's along within all things great and small! But even more importantly which constantly seems to Hum's within the very Core of every One of Us – as creatures who appear to be made in the very Image of this Same One & Only

Source Force, out of which positively everything in existence comes into any manifest form, in any first place.

Most fortunately for us the moment we truly get this, we will now in greater wisdom finally realize. That we are not separate from that both underlying as well as beyond lying God-Ness principle, which can be sensed to Love Hum along everywhere inside of all things. In the much greater sense of our Higher Nu-Man possibility to finally realize, that Whole Man Found Deity like state - of self empowerment. Such as ends up coming along with finding our innermost place of being able to Soar with our Hearts like an Eagle. Within what amounts to that One & Only At-One-Ment Source of all Energy - which resides both all around us as well within the very Root of All Manifest Creation. Which is to say, the very essence of this lesson # 7, is all about us encouraging our Heart to now ever more constantly Soar - like that of an Eagle. In the greater sense of allowing our innermost Essence to be Gone (Gate), Gone (Gate), All Together Gone, (Para Sam Gate), Totally all Dissolved Gone - through the completely Open Doorway Gate of our Hearts, (Bodhi Svaha) All Hail to Every One's very same Big Heart connected to the Great One & Only - Gigantic to Infinity & Beyond Divine Most Big Love Song. Which can be found to reside within our highest possible sense of our greatest possible Self. Or that very Buddha or Christ Ha-Nu-Man like Eagle Kachina found Being - which at the very same time extends to Infinity & Beyond us all. (From the famous Heart Sutra of Avelokitesvara - 4000-3000 BC) Or exactly as in Koo, Koo, Kajoob, who I-Am in my most whole awake sense of being, is the Egg-Man, even the Walrus, and of course the Eagle. In the very same sense as in, 'Me and My Father are as One" - Now able to Live totally Within the King-Dome of Heaven which exists within all creatures even all things great and small! Or as in this bread is as though my body, this wine is as though my blood, insofar as that love which resides in all things, also exists within this very bread and wine, which I have asked you to partake of in constant remembrance of my everywhere Divine Presence. In such a way that you may help your self to continually remember, this great how live in wholly communion with our great One Source - truth! That we may by way of this attunement, all of us actually discover exactly how to live in true non-dualistic Loving Harmony, with positively all of our One & Only Same Source's manifestations. Such as continuously keep arising into existence, everywhere right under our very noses. All hail then to this Divine-Most everywhere Love Hum Presence - every right Now!

(Accompanying Explanation – Which is exactly why one of our very first images, after showing our fall from grace. Had to do with showing Jumping Mouse, or for that matter any of us, as either a Quantum Katie's or Cosmic Charlie's. Holding an Eagle feather in our hand, insofar as our innermost sense of ourselves might agree to set out on a journey toward our possibility to actually become Whole Being Integrated & thus fully now Conscious. In the context of our ability to actually find that key quantum level hum love sound, which is said to make our very universe go whole holographic - round within round, within round. And which in the process of so finding this innermost awake state, is exactly what brings us back into a place of being within At-One-Ment with our very Maker Source. As is represented by our being Non-Separate from an Eagle. Which is of course our American First Nation Peoples ancient metaphor - for what we have been referring to as being in a state of Wholly Communion - with the very essence of God-Ness or great One & Only Source Spirit - Father Sky Wakan Tanka - In Itself.)

19

EVERY US NOW DECIDING TO KEEP ON SPIRIT CLIMBING
OUR VERY OWN MT WISDOM WITHIN - THAT OUR FULL-ON
OPEN HEARTS MAY NOW SOAR INSIDE ALL SOURCE
CREATED THINGS - EXACTLY IN THE HUGE SENSE OF US
ACTUALLY BEING THE VERY EAGLE'S WE IN OUR MOST
FULLY AWAKENED AT-ONE-MENT PLACE - TRULY ARE

"Oh my Good God, now that thanks to our very own inner Wisdom oriented guidance, we can actually way more fully whole being 'Grok'. The much greater sense of this grand constant Evolutionary, most Whole-Sum Hu-Man Consciousness oriented, great Source In-Stigated Design. This new under-standing we are all of us learning to internalize, also implies any moment we start to hear our inner most present Heart Core sense of our Self's saying. That we hate anything about the way we are choosing to live our lives, including hating other people who are also Made in the Image of this core underlying beyond lying place of Love. These will be the very moments we will be coming face to face with our fall from grace separation from the great One-Ness Source - which resides within the very root of all of Creation. These will be the very moments we will find ourselves being guided to start to make a most courageous choice, to first of all fully 'admit' to ourselves that we must be out of PURE AWARENESS SYNCH with this GREATER FORCE. Such that by way of the application of various most appropriate methods of awareness, we have already been outlined up to this point. Yes-We Actually-Can bring ourselves back into a place of Harmonic Resonance with this great Source Force of Love. In the much greater sense of supporting ourselves to keep coming back into totally now once again Loving howsoever we may now keep choosing to play ourselves, forward. Always in relation to whatever inner fulfillments we may ever find ourselves seeking. See the huge point here, resentment, hatred and all forms negativity, especially including resort to any form violence, can never be rationalized. As coming from that One & Only Source which at very root, has always been under-stood by all of our very greatest teachers, to be a Force of Love."

"Which is to say most unfortunately for us, insofar as we keep trying to move forward based mostly on fear. And all those self contractive, negative emotions, such as anger, hatred and resentment which tend to follow upon us staying stuck in sympathetic or adrenalin based - motivation. Then to the extent we find our self's hating any aspect of our life, including certain people whom we keep having trouble coping with. It is going to be precisely us who will keep losing our very own ability to attune to that essentially Loving Source Force. Which is actually the most great solution fulfillment empowering place - we can ever find within us. Such that this in turn is going to mean, every time we run into a brick wall closed Heart - place inside our self's. Our very actions when motivated by such negativity, will only as we have already indicated. Tend via our own law of attraction, to keep resulting in the attraction of more of the same for our selves. To a point where our innermost I-Am within is going to feel like a mere victim way too resentfully working at this or that sort of job. Continuously producing as well as endlessly buying all sorts of mere junk products. As well as in these ways constantly attracting all kinds of further resentment engendering relationship into our lives, we don't even want within the very Heart Core of ourselves,. Simply because such a more limited definition of ourselves, will never seem to really Ful-Fill the inward most true Heart Awake

Essence of who we way more inside our very core - Really Are and actually Want to Be. Or even worse, other than wise turn us into feeling like mere victims at the mercy of people who may for one supposed little mind reason or another, keep choosing to hate us and we them. With the utmost Dis-Respect to which we each of us in our own ways, will tend to constantly keep taking our selves down. By way of the mutual Dis-Respect we keep holding in relation to each other - we will thus tend to keep bringing into our lives! In marked contrast to our much greater potential to learn just how to way more Joy-fully keep Playing our Self's forth."

"In other words Inner Wise-Dome was to keep on clarifying! The inner reality of this great truth about our Source given potential to keep attuning to that place of Love, which resides within all things, would clearly seem to mean! That whenever we might find ourselves seething with any kind of negativity whatsoever, it is going to be all up to us to find our way back into Love! Any time we can no-longer stand having fallen far too much from grace inside, to the point of pain body hurting beyond any normal sense of our capability to endure. It is going to be all up to us to find our way back into our ability to keep creating/inventing far better way more holistic solutions for ourselves! Cause in terms of the way we find ourselves having been created here, this is simply the way it is! Though we were never promised a Rose Garden, nevertheless the moment we can admit any of our own states of negativity to our Self's. Yes-We-Can in any given moment of our existence, make the choice to shift from constantly in the name of our own hate, anger & resentment. Seemingly endlessly blaming and thus continuously projecting the very worst kinds of self fulfilling prophecy outcomes for our selves. And much rather agree to clear our way back into Source connected Loving-Ness, in such a way as to thus help ourselves feel way more enabled to keep on Co-Creatively inventing ourselves, ever more positively forward. In the very sorts of directions within which we might now find ourselves actually totally loving, whatever fields of Heart motivating interest. We might thus now choose to keep playing ourselves ever forward into. In the much greater sense of our most profound inwardly awakened abilities to keep on creating the very sorts of way better Rose Garden like lives. We may thus most find our inner most awakened selves truly wanting, for ourselves!"

"Even beyond this, our much larger problem is that whenever we might find our most compassionate within At-One-Mend attuned hearts, most closed. We won't even be able hear any much better solution insightful, total love to do guidance such as may have the possibility to keep arising inside the very Core most Essence of our Self's. In the much greater sense that the continuous invention of positively great solutions for ourselves, is actually far more possible than we may ever so called normally, merely 'think'. As long as we keep choosing to stay locked into our mere small mind based negativities! In other words, no matter what excuses we may keep making to our self, just keep remembering these famous Inner most

Wise-Dome of awareness admonitions to our much greater potential sense of our Self's! 'Let ye, who has no past transgression, cast the first stone'. 'Forgive them Lord, for they know not of what they do'! Which is to say, those who are lost in separation from One-Ness, know not that in their continuous resenting and harming. They are actually resenting and harming the very underlying essence of the great Source Lord of the Dance. Which is all about how well we as Made in the Image of non-separation from One-Ness Hu-Man most higher Beings - can learn to play within One-Ness - It-Self!"

"Which is exactly why to the extent we may now choose to actually 'be' the 'both way more core Peace-Ful' 'as well as truly Heart Open Present', total Co-Creatively empowered Self In-Ventors. Of exactly whomsoever it may be we would most truly 'Love to Keep Inventing' our greatest possible Heart Centered Love to Do - senses of our selves - into. Such that every thing we might now choose to do going forward, would change for the better. Inasmuch as we would now much better sense ourselves ,as being fully able to put our inner found Peace-Ful-Ness and total Loving-Ness exactly into. Whatsoever we may thus find ourselves most choosing to do. In such a way that we now would end up being truly Happy - with not just whom we have invented ourselves into. But also with all the various products and services, we will now be intending to keep inventing forth, from this place of Loving Peace-Ful-Ness within. Simply because we will now be choosing intend ourselves forth, from a place which is of Love, rather than a place of Hate or resentment! This shift then in our way of being will now be, the very moment we will be finally learning the very greatest of all of Life's lessons! Which is that it is only by way of learning to truly sense the constant ongoing inner guiding forth messaging of our Hearts, wherefrom we can even ever hope to find the true Happiness's - we all seek!"

"Please under-stand therefore in this huge respect like never before, all of my most precious Be-Loved-One's. The moment any of us find our selves enabled by our own core Peace-Ful-Ness and total open Hearted Loving-Ness within. Countless numbers of people have reported, the simplest of their doings suddenly become a sheer joy! Suddenly old tasks that once seemed purely perfunctory, become a blessing to share. Suddenly One starts to feel One's greater sense of Self wanting to develop One's unique given interests and talents to the max. Simply because such more Source connected people are now totally able to way more fully sense, that the Love they thus give, is truly equal to the Love they get. Besides my most dear ever growing up young One's! Who likes to play with products either invented by, or serviced by people who hate or even resent whatever it is, they are choosing to so do? Just because certain such people want to grab money, yet are in some way or another fundamentally in their core processing unit - still afraid? They as mere passive victims of the living of their lives, won't be able to manifest a great fair share income. Unless they keep choosing against their own Heart Wisdom - to keep ripping other people off? By way of constantly putting their various hatreds and resentments - into their very ways of doing?"

"Myself," inner wisdom was to now trumpet loud and clear within him/her self, unto his/her inner most Truly Wise, much greater sense of Cosmic Charlie, Quantum Katie attuned Presence - within! In such a way that every part of every One's more attuned being within, could now hear. "Inasmuch as we all want to live in a World, wherein we all actually first and foremost value putting the whole of our Love. Into all that we may ever choose to produce, above all other ways of doing, so called business. Precisely so that the more of us will begin to much better sense the greater joy that so inevitably comes along with us choosing to keep creating the very sort of positively magnificent products, which we are all of us are going to totally love to play with. Which is exactly why your very own innermost Wisdom Within, now wants every us from within all our now On's - to start fully internalizing. Total heart opening gratitude for all the gifts you may in this total Loving-Ness open way, now find constantly coming home to roost within your purest most expansive At-One-Ment attuned Awareness. In order that you may come to use our now much more open Heart, in the most filled with the grace of pure Super-Light, Loving ways possible every right now! Simply because, everything that we will ever find here to begin with, already has the very seeds of this Quantum level Love Hum, contained within the very core of it's own particular unique way of blooming into existence. Right under your very noses, indeed right within our very center most 'I', every right now! Can you your Self now much better truly get, the huge sense of all our prior, how to have a positively great life oriented - lessons. Your very own innermost wisdom has just set before you? To help you get into a place of such non-separate penetrative Open-Ness, to the truly magnificent One-Der of All Existence - It-Self? Such that you will now more and more spontaneously than ever, find your self totally Loving the virtual infinite number of gifts constantly being set before you, my dearest greater inner wisdom, oriented beings? Including the gift of all those various life challenges, you once felt it impossible to surmount, all of which originate out of our One & Only Same Source in any first place!"

"In this largest possible respect then, we would Love every One of you Quantum Katie's & Cosmic Charlie's out there, to always remember! The moment any One of us truly gets that our Heart's are actually the most whole being energy flow inspiring, Tap ourselves into this Big Picture Source place, we all have inside of us. The plain simple truth is, not only is it actually much easier within the context of our newfound sense of heart found wholeness. To keep In-Sighting/In-Venting our way into the very sort of Some-One - we might actually 'Totally Love to Be'. Than it is to keep inventing our self into the sort of some-one we absolutely hate, even partially hate being? In other words insofar as we might keep choosing to constantly orient ourselves in those very directions, wherein we might keep on inventing

206

ourselves in ways that are going to be far more likely to make us truly happy? This in turn is exactly why it is so important to learn to hear the inner messaging of our hearts - in our first place! Are you therefore now ready, to help bring your very own heart, into the very place wherein your innermost total love of life found spirit, can now finally soar into the infinite beyond? Much like a now actually Full Heare Non Local Cosmic or Quantum Attuned - way Greater Heart Being Found - Eagle? In relation to every freedom to invent yourself choice you might ever choose to make?" "Great God Almighty", every Cosmic Charlie or Quantum Katie out there, could now in One huge gigantic inner most Heart Centered In-Sight - be heard to say! "Yes, Yes thanks to you our most beloved innermost Wisdom within, we really are finding our grow our self's all our way up pathway into becoming. The truly Miraculous great solution generative capable, Quantum Attuned Cosmic Adults we most truly deserve to actually find - our greatest possible Sense of our Self's - actually Being!"

Seventh Positively Huge Heart Fully Now Open Able To Soar Like An Eagle & Thus Most Help-Ful 'True Happiness Enhancing Prayer' - Unto One's Greatest Possible Actual Now Al-Together Real Halleluyah Hop, Skip, & Jump Happy - Ultimately Whole Being Ful-Fill-Ment Empowering Sense Of One's Most Well Beyond Ordinary Source Connected & Thus Truly Extra-Ordinarily Unlimited I-Am Who-am Made In the Image - King-Dome of Heaven Found Place Which Can Be Experienced By Any of Us - To Reside Within.

'In-As-Much as Yes I Can Now Sense my time has come, to fully support the most Whole-Sum I-Am whom I-Really-Am - within me. To finally totally fully 'Grok', that Love truly is what makes the world best go round. In the much larger sense that something like an underlying/beyondlying Flower of Aphrodite - Love Hum. Appears to be the very Unlimited underpinning Field Energy, out of which everything we ever come to know manages to manifest into form. As well as the most powerful Source energy attuning Place we have within each of our own unique sense of our Self's. To keep helping each of us feel optimally enabled, to keep manifesting forth the truly Joy-Ful lives, we all so much long for. Other than wise, what be the point of manifesting even more, insofar as whatever Ful-Fill-Ments the greater whole of us our Self's may most want to manifest into form next? Not be centered within that inward place of most Whole Heart-Fully Awakened Loving-Ness - such as can be sensed by every One of Us - Within?

Most fortunately for all of us, the more and more we support our inner most core central sense of our self's, our HEARTS. To actually attune to this place being able to truly hear what amounts to God's everywhere present - Love Resonant Hum - now fully able to soar through the very Core of us. By way of helping our self's to keep on constantly in every moment, awakening that most central core being integrating and thus most Power-Ful solution generative unit, we have within us. In such a way that the whole of us, our right brain integrated to function together within our left brain, our lower vital energies elevated to operate within the integrity of our higher vital energies. All energies now centered all together within the framework of what amounts to our own evermore Awake most Core Centered sense of our Being. Will begin to integrate within us into One single Unified Field of Pure both yin receptive as well as yang expressive Awareness - to such a Heart Felt degree. That our inner most Heart Awake sense of who We Really Most Are, will now quite literally. Begin to virtually vibrate Hum Sing Resonate constantly along. From within a place of totally full-on Heart Open truly Great-Ful appreciation, for all that we each of us have already been most blessedly - given.

Certainly this is the very best constantly ongoing in each unfolding moment foundational basis, which we each of us now have within us. To best help our ever higher climbing, most Hu-Man/Woman senses of our Self's, keep on manifesting ever more loving truly great life inventive solutions. Always within the framework of what amounts to all those ONE SOURCE, and thus truly Love Hum based, constantly manifesting into form everywhere Presents. Such as can be found to exist within the world all around us. Most especially in the direction of linking our own unique sense of our self's all up with all those like wise truly Open Hearted and thus most extra-ordinary Big Mind insight-fully inspired, other human presences. Whom we will now much better be able to sense within our very own ever growing beyond ordinary - whole field's of awareness. Are most willing in their own highly unique ways, to jump themselves totally in on board this great Only One Heart Beating - to Infinity & Beyond Cosmos Bound - Ultimate Quantum Love Hum Train. In such a way as to thus link our all dreams together toward the realization of our most within One-Ness centered, and thus Highest possible Man/Woman potentials. Exactly in the way our very greatest forward Seeing attuned within the Ultimate Mystery of At-One-Ment - Teachers - have always pointed us toward, Yes, Yes!"

Chapter 9

Lesson # 8 – So That We May Go On From Here To Utilize Our Connection To What Amounts To Universal Hum Love - In Such A That We May Thus Find Our Most Full-On Truly Integral & Thus Greatest Possible Tap Our Source Empowering Place - Of Actual Now Real Whole-E Most - Totally Loving All Creatures Great & Small - Co-Creative Reverence Within

Rationale for HAVE A GREAT LIFE LESSON - # 8

Here's the Biggest of all Pictures, huge whole Mind In-Sight-Ful news flash, you might ever want to find your self able to Vision See/Hear - with the utmost respect for what our lives have the potential to be All About! It appears that there exists a place inside of each & every One of Us! Which has been most exquisitely designed/evolved to help guide all of Us, toward our very own uniquely us possibilities to Co-Creatively keep inventing. What is going to amount a positively great, totally happy life for our greatest possible inner most sensed senses of our Self's! It is the very place wherein our old half asleep clouded and veiled, mostly egocentrically separate me, me, me alone only, focused self. Has the possibility to dissolve and melt so totally into the greater well beyond ordinary, Oceanic Like to Infinity & Beyond - pure Hum Love Field of At-One-Ment - In It-Self. We will now start to feel ever more moment by ongoing moment totally guided inspired, by our own Love Hum Resonant connection to this infinite Love Hum energy field. To keep on inventing the very best of our self's ever forward, now in way more complete Holo-Centric Harmonic attunement within this most mysterious truly extra-ordinary - way Big hugely Mysterious One Field Place. Which is at the same time, both an underlying as well as beyond lying, infinitely expansive field of pure Same Source Love Hum everywhere manifesting positively everything Energy. Such that we will now find our Self's totally dissolving our old sense of separateness, in such a completely beautiful Heart Open Loving way. We will by way of this Tapped In connection to that which is infinite, keep finding our own essence so in our 'thoughts', 'words' & 'deeds' empowered - with our uniquely talented sense of what we can now much more clearly hear about our Self's - Within. Our very own inner visionary constantly ongoing inspirational guidance, will now keep revealing to us just how yes-we our greatest possible senses of our selves actually can - keep bringing forth into our much larger sense of so called Reality. Whatsoever fulfillments we each of us in our very own Hearts of Hearts, might ever most dream - to keep manifesting forth for our most Heart attuned sense of our Self's. And thus at the very same time for our most Source attuned sense of our possibility to actually exist - in totally Loving Harmony with this Huge Mysterious most Source.

To help you your very own self understand this potential attunement device we all have within us, even better? You could well say based on modern quantum level understandings, it appears much as we have attempted to point toward in the just prior lesson. As though the underlying Unified At-One-Ment Field, of pure everywhere present base line resonant energy. Seems to constantly radiate with an underlying hum sound - which appears in the form of a cosmic background microwave like - harmonic. Much in the way John Cramer at the Univ of Washington has pointed to in his research, wherein has found through subtle recordings, that the Big Bang appears to have left us with a Deep Hum. Such that when you now put this together with our new heart resonance related research, go to heartmath.com. Including what Tom Kenyon point out to us in his many recordings, including the Ghandarva Experience cd. With respect to just how within the realm of choir like sound, the moment any given choir is able to synchronize their singing or chanting into a common attuned hum like harmonic. Whenever we hear any such seemingly heavenly music, our hearts begin to enter a certain frequency resonance that seems to trigger a feeling or vibration of peace and love, within our hearts.

He goes on to refer to this resonant Hum like harmonic, as being the equivalent to the famous golden proportion. In the sense Da Vinci attempted to portray to us, in his famous golden mean proportioned Vetruvian Man. To then be used by us whenever it might relate to our possibility to help ourselves create the best possible balanced architectural and engineering designs, in the world outside of us. Except now in terms of our possibility to generate similar vibration in the world of sound sensed sensitivity, inside of us. In a way that can bring us into much more complete resonant harmony with the underlying Harmonic Hum, set up by the quantum level infinitely inter-active pure energy Whirl Field - Itself. This then becomes a good time to attempt carry those related Heart Math understandings, we have already pointed to in the just previous lesson. Regarding our Hearts possibility to send out a field of way strong electro magnetic radiance, even further. By way of bringing to your attention the recent dvd - 'The Living Matrix' - A film on the new science of healing. Wherein you will find reference to new emerging scientific evidence, with respect to the importance of our Heart's potential to project the very sort of whole being balanced, while at the same time optimally powerful, actual radiant singular most morphogenic Field of what amounts to pure non-locally inter-connected Super Light Source Energy everywhere all around us. In such a way that the strength and integrity of our electro magnetic Heart Hum connected innermost radiant Pulsing, seems to be what more than anything, can best helps us. To keep sending into ourselves the very sort of total Love of Life positive images as well as optimal whole body field Integral Heart Radiant signals, most likely to help heal the whole of our physical beings, into not just our most potentially optimal states of health. But these same sorts of strong Heart Hum Centered outward reaching signals, are in terms our potential to hold our very best fulfillment intentions in front of ourselves. Also exactly what at the very same time, can best help our more Big Mind awake within At-One-Ment solution generative potentials, to keep on higher In-Sight sensing the very sorts of positive total Love of Life motivated, Co-Creatively inspired inventions. Most likely to help us actually Ful-Fill the whole of our beings, in exactly the ways we have been talking about in all of our prior greater Awareness Awakening Oriented Lessons.

Always remember this, it has throughout our various cultural traditions and differing ages, consistently been said by our very greatest wisdom teachers. Who in their own unique traditional cultural ways, have always been doing their very best, to make the very same point to all of us. Which is that Uni-Versal Source energy in It-Self can be sensed within us via 2 major dimensions. That of Light insofar as it is able to interactively Wave It-Self into various sacred geometrical building block patterns! As well as within that quantum level pure differential energy interactive - Love Hum Resonating Sensed Sound! We can begin to actually hear within Us whenever we get optimally clear Spirit Soaring present! Insofar as this both at the same time underlying as well as beyond lying ultimate harmonic vibration, seems too actually under pine the very way all things manifest into form. With the whole point being, the moment we ourselves take those inner most subtle awareness responsibilities required. To help ourselves attune to this underlying / beyond lying Source of all Energy via either or both of these Source Force Dimensions. The great news for all of Hu-Man Kind, is that such attunement appears to be our innermost Hu-Man key. Toward helping our very own unique senses of our Self's, to best Self Realize our very own possibilities to actually fulfill - all '7' levels of our potential to actually end up Being the most Wholly Ful-Filled - Yes-We-Can-Be. In other words, more and more of us are coming to the conclusion, that it is our Hearts. Not our heads alone by them selves, which may very well be the most sensitively powerful center of that well beyond ordinary Intelligence, we all have within us. To then help lead us toward the finding of all those very innermost Ful-Fill-Ments, we all seek.

Which is to say, in any longer human fulfillment oriented run. Here in this ultimate respect is the truly great news, for all who may choose to listen. All ye most blessed children of the One universal underlying / beyond lying Super Spirit based

Source. It appears there can be no truly satisfying fulfillment within any of our core body vital energy generative centers. Beyond of our possibility to enter ever more presently into an actual whole being sensed - experience. Of this truly magical, miracle solution generating, 'Love Hum' attuned place, we have all been blessed with a higher Hu-Man possibility to actually find. Within the very most central core processing unit, of that quantum level computer processor every single One of us has inside the very core of us. Inasmuch as it is our 'HEARTS' which MORE THAN ANYTHING, can help us best integrate not just our so called left brain rational/logical intelligence, together within our right brain so called feeling and emotional intelligence. In such a way as to help ourselves create a singular most unified field of fully here & now, totally open appreciative of this great One-Ness, Pure Awareness. But it is also our Hearts that help us to best integrate our lower ever upward growing base triangle of vital energies (or autonomic plexi), with our upper more downward Earth pointing energies (or autonomic plexi), into a single heart open found - Star of David - Within. Or like wise best attune to the very Om Shanti Om Humming Along sense of that great emerging into endless forms Force, out of which all things can be said to manifest. Even the pure Diamond Heart of a Sufi Master, or for that matter the compassionate heart of a Buddha and last but not least, exactly like that of the most Sacred Heart of Jesus, even most Immaculate pure Heart of Mary. All of which can be best under-stood as teaching metaphors - for that most sacred place which can be found within every singularity most quantum Love Hum attuned - One of Us. Insofar as we will thus keep choosing to so Attune, to our place of to Infinity & Beyond connected, truly Amazing Heart Felt Grace within.!

Is this then not exactly why, so many of us end up loving the old gospel song which sings to our very Hearts? "Amazing Grace, although once I was lost! Nevertheless in this very moment of singing this powerful inwardly harmonically resonant - Uni-Versal Heart Awakening - Love song! Yes, insofar as our hearts within are now opening all up into this place of Hum Resonant felt to Infinity & Beyond Loving-Ness - Inside. 'Yes in this very moment of being filled with the Amazing Grace of our now in this moment totally Open, complete Heare & Now Love of Life - so attuned Hearts. For every such moment we are thus attuned, we truly are once again now - Found!' Most unfortunately our more ordinary human problem, is we keep falling from this state of Grace, over and over and over again. Which is exactly why it is so important for us to keep on finding our true Heart Centered Self's, yet Once again. Until such time as the finding of this place of Only One Sacred most Heart Beating here, becomes our permanent state of being for us. Inasmuch as being filled with amazing grace hum like vibration, is actually what most helps us to feel most joy-fully elevated empowered. Yeah actually inspired to keep on inventing/creating our way ever forward into the very sorts of have a positively great life - solutions. Most likely to help our inner most sense of our self - manifest the truly great happy life - we all so much long for! In the huge sense that our learning to truly listen to that total 'Love of 'Life' constantly Humming our way along, Core Most place within us. Actually is the most powerfully great forward moving solution generative truly inspirationally motivating place, that we all do have within each and every One of Us! To help us make our very own worlds - best keep going round, and round, and round. In such a way as to keep filling ourselves with -De-Light

What follows are a couple of illustrative images, which have been designed to help portray this higher Hu-Man most possibility, we have been constantly talking about here. In the greater sense of our possibility to discover how to so ground our lower vital energy centers into Mother Earth. That we my thus come to integrate whatever we may come to know about the so called more concrete Objective Nature of Mother Earth. In such a way that all our vital energy organizing centers will now be able to expand all our way into that Brilliant zero point place of Perfectly experienced Stillness, such as can actually be found to be Here & Now sensed within our Hearts. Ever more outwardly into our whole world, indeed our entire solar system, galaxy and eventually the complete Holographic Father Sky Cosmos of which we are all a most intimate Made in the Image Non-Local part. In much larger sense of the old testament admonition to us all, 'To Be Still, & Know that your very own I-Am-Ness within, is of No-Thing other than what we have been referring to as God-Ness - in It-Self'. Or put another way, is of No-Thing other than that ultimate perfect Loving One-Ness which can actually be sensed to be, at the very root Source of all that ever manifests into any kind of form.

Illustration #'s 20 A & B – Clearly The Time Has Come For All Hu-Man/Woman Kind to Totally Now Way More Fully 'Get' - The very Sort of much Wiser Transcendental Under-Standing - Which All of Our Great Spiritual Traditions Have Constantly Been Attempting To Keep Pointing Us Toward

In the much larger sense - that every time we find some way to clear some old self doubt based negative emotion, and thus fear based contractive pattern inside ourselves. Every time we discover how to open our minds into the place of perfectly Still - Big Mind Tap the Place of true At-One-Ment connected - Co-Creative enablement. Every time we agree to open our very Heart Centers into a total Loving Connection, with the Big Huge Love Hum which can be sensed to reside in all things, including our very own selves. Especially in relation to the ways we attempt to keep seeking fulfillment – with respect to each of our own sensed '7' core body vital energy centers. We start to elevate our greater sense of ourselves ever higher, into our greatest possible sense of our most truly Big Picture connected - One & Only everywhere present Super Light Spirit. The very sort of <u>Full-On Heart Now Soaring Like An Eagle - Way Huge Heart Awakened One Source Connecting Place - We All Have Within Each & Every Singularity Most Attuned 'One' of Us.</u> Which can best enable each of us to clear vision our way ever forward, into living in total harmony with all Creatures Great and Small. Indeed all so called Very Same Source Made Things, that ever manifest into all the various forms we may ever come to know.

(**Accompanying Note** – What I ask you, is so different about us being asked to fully mobilize our most Sacred Heart of Jesus within, our Immaculate Hear of Mary, our innermost Star of David, our Ha or Higher Heart Open Nu-Man, our compassionate Heart of a Buddha, our pure winged Diamond Heart of a Sufi, our Ying & Yang within totally integrated into One singular Whole. Or for that matter elevate ourselves into that place wherein our Hearts are now fully able to Soar within the Now Quantum Hum Love attuned Sound - of no-thing less than a God Eagles Wings. In the greater sense of all us Ha-Nu-Men/Women learning to live within the At-One-Ment of what always amounts to the singular most One & Only Great Wakan Tanka Father Sky - Spirit. We all find our Self's most blessed to be living - Within. And especially in the greater sense of us finding our ability to Inner Flower of Love awaken ourselves into that constantly Hum Along attuned possibility - we have. To now live in total Loving harmony with that underlying beyond lying vibrating everything into form - Love Hum resonance - which resides within the very core Essence of the entire Uni-Verse. Always in the direction of us starting to sense ourselves as ever more Integrally capable of actually fulfilling - our very innermost dreams! So why then do we keep arguing so much about whose pathway, is better or worse? When no matter what our chosen archetypal metaphor - the intended total Heart Opening suggested result. Always ends up pointing to the very same Inner Core Found Place - which always resides Within?)

First # 20-A - Similar Inner Metta Teachings From Our Oldest Recorded & Most Popular Revered - Real Inner Core Love Spirit Awakening Traditions

<u>Om</u> – Heard within by way of the elevation of our lower energies along with the grounding of our Higher - Inside One's Heart - Rig Vedas

<u>Star of David</u> – Sensed by the core integration of our lower & higher energies within our now most Sacred Geometrical Attuned - One Heart -Tora

<u>Pure Diamond Heart</u> - Clarified by Shining our lower energies through our now Mulit-Faceted most radiant integrated Heart - Sufi Tradition

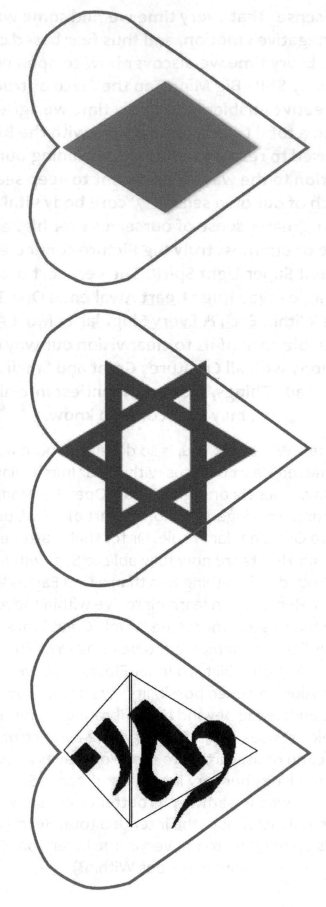

It has been said that insofar as we learn to both Awaken & Integrate – or Yog Unite – all of our lower triange of vital energies all together with our higher. Into a single whole sense of being centered within our Heart! The more we ourselves start to vibrate or Om / Hum - with the Super Light Resonance - Emanated by the Quantum Source Field Itself! – Is this our Innermost design evolution potential truly brilliant or what? The essence of this understanding was passed on by One of my beloved teachers - Baba Hari Dass - Whose leading edge whole person integrative retreat learning center can be found near Santa Cruz California - listed under mountmadona.org

IN THIS MUCH GREATER RESPECT - HOW
ABOUT YOU YOUR SELF JUST KEEP
HEART SOARING JOURNEYING ON - INTO
THAT VERY UNDERLYING/BEYOND LYING
LOVE HUM WHICH CAN BE SENSED TO
EXIST WITHIN THE VERY ROOT CORE OF
ALL - EVERY ONE OF MY FELLOW
QUANTUM KATIE / COSMIC CHARLIE
VERY DEAREST MADE IN THE IMAGE -
SAME SOURCE ATTUNING SOME ONE'S

OUR OWN INNER STAR OF DAVID, ACTUALLY NOW TRULY AWAKE INSIDE US EVER MORE BEAUTIFULLY BLOOMING INTO THAT INNER HUMMING FELT FLOWER OF LOVE - WHICH MAKES US ABLE TO SOAR WITHIN LIKE AN EAGLE - INTO OUR VERY OWN MOST SACRED HEART OF JESUS, IMMACULATE HEART OF MOTHER MARY, MULTIFACETED PURE WINGED DIAMOND HEART OF A SUFI, MOST COMPASSIONATE HEART OF A BUDDHA, EVEN INTO THAT TAO OR FLOW ZONE YIN / YANG INTEGRAL - INNERMOST SENSE OF OUR SELF - ALL MEANT TO REPRESENT THE VERY SAME STATE OF FULL-ON OPEN HEARTED WAKE-FUL-NESS - TO BE FOUND WITHIN EVERY VERY CORE 'ONE' - OF US!

SO JUST WHAT IS IT YOU SAY - THAT KEEPS COMPELLING US TO FIND ALL KINDS OF INNER EXCUSES - TO CONTINUOUSLY JUSTIFY - OUR WAY TOO CONSTANT OVER REACTIVE FEAR BASED RESORT TOWARD THE VERY SORT OF ULTIMATELY INEFFECTIVE - EITHER MACHO HYPER FIGHTER OR OR MORE FLEER WIMP DEPRESSIVE CONSTANTLY AVOIDING BEHAVIORS - OR OVERLY ATTACHED TO BELIEF SYSTEMS THAT KEEP TAKING US DOWN INTO WAY LESSER FULFILLMENT EMPOWERING - WAYS OF BEING - FULLY HERE

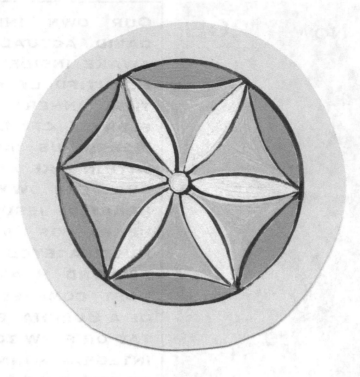

Huge Grand Wisdom Lesson # 8 - LOVING-NESS ITSELF -
The Ultimate Source of Our Greatest Possible Sense of
Full-On Fulfillment Empowerment - We All Have Within

IS WHAT MOST HELPS US TO NOW KNOW - JUST EXACTLY HOW YES WE-ALL-CAN ACTUALLY MANIFEST THE COMPLETELY FULFILLING LIVES WE EACH OF US MOST TRULY LONG FOR

TO THE EXTENT WE EACH OF US CAN AGREE TO KEEP HEARING THE ONGOING MOMENT BY MOMENT GUIDANCE OF THAT VERY YELLOW BRICK ROAD PATHWAY TO TRUE FOUND HAPPINESS - WE ALL HAVE WITHIN OUR HEARTS THIS IS EXACTLY HOW WE BECOME EVER MORE WISELY ILLUMINATED TO KEEP FULFILLING THE VERY ESSENCE OF OURSELVES!

"Ho, Yo all my dear most be-loved One's! It appears from what more and more of us are getting to Know. Our time has come to fully 'Imagine' in the huge sense John Lennon so aptly pointed to many years ago. Our very own sense of Self's, as the sort of some One's who would now be way better able to fully whole being Under-Stand or actually 'Grok'! Our much more unlimited possibility to Be now fully wholly Non-Separatively Awake - within what amounts to our very own unique connection to that Power & Glory! Which is of that singular most Mysterious to Infinity & Beyond - Same Source Ocean of pure Loving-Ness. Such as seems to Hum Resonate within the very Core of every single thing that ever manifests into Form? And thus who actually can, within the very same stroke of our ever growing Pure Awareness sense of Geni-Us. Now find our Self's much more clearly able to fully Get It, that merely believing in something greater than our separate sense of our selves - in our heads alone! No matter how fervently we may choose to hold any such belief! Can ever be sufficient to save us, in the much greater sense of turning us into the very sort of Core In-Stilled & thus now truly quantum level Big Picture Entangled, and thus actual Non-Local One Wholly Spirit, Tap Our Source connected - Beings! Who might find ourselves ever more able to keep on Heart Guidance attracting towards our Self's, all of the Hosanah on Highest - Saving Grace Hu-Man most - truly Whole-Sum Ful-Fillments! We might ever from within the very innermost inside 'Singular most Heart Core 'I' - Wholly of Holies of us. Find our most essential sense of our largest most expanded possible - way Big One Spirit connected I-Am's within - truly most Wanting."

"In this largest respect for the incredible gift of our highest possible Hu-Man most Made in the Image - whole nervous system integrated potentials. It has always been said by our very greatest teachers throughout our world over, that what behooves us the most in the context of living our lives forth to our very fullest. Is for us to learn to listen to what we each of us would actually most Love to do next. Such that whenever we ourselves as potential great Mystery attuned Krishna's, Ha-Nu-Man's, Buddha's, Moses's, Mahavir's, Christ's, Mohammed's, Black Elk's may find ourselves hungry. It is best we find some whole-sum way to eat, when tired it is best we most choose to sleep. Similarly whenever we might find our inner most sense of our Self's, most Heart attuned Guidance Motivated to dive into this or that major field of interest project. It is best we dive totally in, in such a way that we may keep on learning to become more and more solution capable with respect to our very own most uniquely intriguing sensed fields of interest and concurrent ever developing talents. When guided to add to our field(s) of interest, or even change our field(s) of interest, including our way of seeing things within our various fields of interest. It is best to keep taking on ever new Learnings, in such a way as to help our most whole sense of our selves keep changing and expanding our Viewpoint(s) - as far out here as we possibly can. Then when we sense it's time to take this or that kind of break, e.g. meet up with some friends, have some fun, travel here or there, make love, now is the very best time to truly Heare - this or that innermost Heart core Guided motivation to take some kind of a break. Inasmuch as we never know what new ever higher In-Sights, such take some time to just relax and be totally more here adventures - may bring! Unless we learn to trust the inner most ongoing flow of our own follow our own Yellow Brick Road - Heart attuned guidance system within. Towards the actual finding of our most One-Der-ful giant quantum level computer - Wizard Within! In other words, insofar as we each of us learn to truly attune within to the ongoing guidance of our inner most whole Being integrating Hearts. Always within a context of continuing to find regular daily ways, to keep entering into the place of total core Peace-full Heart centered Lovingness - within. This is exactly when we end up finding our more present attuned whole nervous system lit up field of awareness, becoming the most truly capable. Of actually generating totally Peace-Ful way In-Sight-Ful, truly Miraculous beyond even our wildest dreams, now fully Heart Centered attuned Holistic solutions, in relation to every problem we may ever be faced with. No matter how seemingly insurmountable we may feel such challenges to be, based on any lesser split and divided, mere half wit senses of our selves - alone. This is how important learning to center the very Essence of our greatest Hu-Man potential - within our awakened to One-Ness core Centered Hearts - really Is. With respect to us learning to not just be, all that we ourselves can be. But also with the utmost respect to our possibility to actually live right within, that most Sacred Whole-Ness Mystery, such as we within our most Whole-Sum-Ly awakened states, will now actually discover we are a most intimate non-separate part of."

"Jumping Johosophats, most Sacred Heart of Jesus, Great Balls of Ya-Weh, the Super Sound of Wakan Tanka, Holi Ha-New-Man, Allah Akbar & the Winged Heart of a Sufi, Buddham Sarinam Gachami to the most Compassionate Heart of a Budhha! As well as Ho my Heart Now Soars like an Eagle! Capped off with One huge Om Shanti Hum Om to our very own great grand innermost One & the very Same King-Dome of Heaven found. No limits Field of the Purest possible living within At-One-Ment - positively no more separating boundaries - Oh My Good God sense of the most Whole-Sum totally Here & Now Awareness! It's like what our very own innermost wisdom found place within, is now telling us? Is that the very singular most Source Force, which manifests positively everything we ever know into all the various forms we can ever distinguish. Appears to contain within it, the very seed principle of Hum Resonant Love - In It-Self? In such a way that the more we ourselves keep learning to totally trust, our very own ongoing inner guidance sense of Loving-Ness for all Source engendered things. Such as will tend to keep on arising within our very own selves - via of course our own now inner Heart Open sensed connection to this most apparently Uni-Versal - Quantum Love Hum Source! The more and more empowered to keep on manifesting the very sort of long term oriented, truly Big Picture Harmonic integral solutions w in terms of our very greatest of intention set dreams, keep longing for. We ourselves are going to end up finding ourselves actually Being able to Be!" "Yes all of my children, this is exactly what this great inner wisdom journey, which your very own inner wisdom within has constantly been pointing you toward, is really all about. Inasmuch as all of the various Heart opening metaphors, from all of our greatest religious traditions, are meant to help guide us. Into our possibility to actually manifest the truly great lives, we ourselves keep hoping for!"

"Did you know, with utmost respect for the gift of just who we all of us have the potential to most fully be - all of my most precious beloved ever growing all up - Singular most One's? Perhaps the greatest of all truths, is the more we learn to follow the ongoing flow of these constant Heart Sensed - clearly Loving-Ness oriented Messagings - With-In. In such a way as to now whole heartedly totally jump ourselves completely into, whatsoever field(s) of interest might be calling out to us, within the very Heart Core our very own Self's - the very most. Then the more we actually begin to listen the constant flow guidance of our truly caring for all manifest things, 'Hearts'! Consistently attempting to tell us in each unfolding moment of our lives, whatsoever it might be that we would most Care-Fully truly Love to do next. <u>Provided we of course have enough Pure Non Dualistic Awareness to now fully under-stand, that there is no part of any kind of Harmfulness to other Source Made things. Which can ever be rationalized as being Loving to that very Love Source, which resides within the very centermost Hum Resonance of all manifest things</u>. The more & more we will find ourselves becoming ever more solution capable excellent, in relation to all our most beloved fields of in the moment, ever unfolding interest. Especially insofar as we might keep agreeing to take whatever time it may take, to now clear our Self's of any of our old self-doubts and self-loathings. As well as of all those old senses of mere small mind based separation, which keep distancing us from being within total core Peace-Ful Still-Ness, with our One & Only Source Maker. In the much greater sense of us finding our Self's way more Holistically inner Awareness enabled, to now ever more effectively actually live in total Harmony, with the One Source maker of all Manifest Things.

"Which is to say, in our now knowing that we appear to be actually Made in the Image of being non-separate from One-Ness or God-Ness It-Self. Wouldn't it make far more sense for each of us, to now take all those response-abilities required to help guide the who I-Really-Am - in our most Heart Centered core. Into being not merely a plumber, or a construction worker, or even a great business man/woman or perhaps a great engineer, architect or artistic designer, even a good housewife or husband. But to much rather grow ourselves into the sort of Some-One's, who might actually be the constant Heart Core Awake empowered 'inventor's' of exactly howsoever our I-Am within, may most find our Self' choosing to be every right now. <u>Always in relation to all the inner most '7' vital energy based callings such as tend to</u>

<u>keep on moment by moment arising, within what always amounts to our most Flower of Aphrodite attuned & thus total Loving-Ness awakened - Heart."</u>

"Such that given any One of us might truly get this realization, about the Pure Loving-Ness Nature at the very core, of all manifest form? Imagine then in this much larger respect, you your self actually agreeing to keep finding ways to help invent your self into? The very sort of person whom you would end up positively loving - to Now actually Be. Whether a plumber, construction worker, or even great engineer, doctor and of course including a positively great product making business person. Simply because your very own One-Ness connected & thus most empowered I-Am, whom you really most Are within. Would now be totally starting to truly get that constantly choosing to invent your Self into the very sort of Some-One. Who is now able to totally LOVE whomsoever you may be choosing to invent your self into - every right now. With no more fear based half wit reptilian brain, constantly compulsively, emotionally driving you any longer in your way! Or for that matter, any attachments to what you may merely 'think' is the only my way, or the highway, to do things here. Is actually the most important Big Mind awake freedom that any of us have been given, within the context of our huge Hu-Man/Woman possibility. To keep finding ways to invent ourselves into the very sort of Some-One's who could now say Yes, we totally Love who we have chosen to invent ourselves into. What's more, the huge Big Truth we have already pointed to, is the only way it appears any of us can ever hope to realize all the inner fulfillments, we may ever long for. Is by way of each of us discovering just how to invent ourselves into whomsoever, we might most actually Love to Be. From within the very Heart Core Center of our most Whole Being Integrated - potential to actually Be - whomsoever we might most Love to Be . Can you now every One much better See you Heare, just how truly magnificent this grand Big Picture Stage we all find ourselves living within, actually appears for us to Be?"

<u>Illustration # 21 – Here Then In the Context of Our Inner Most Growing Wisdom - Is The Huge Point For Us All To Most Fully Get - It Appears the Only Way any of Us can ever even Hope to Actually Realize our very Best Inner Fulfillment Intended Dreams - Is by Way of Each of us Agreeing to Full On Open All Up -nto our very Own Most Sacred Heart Core - & Thus all our way Into that most Transcendental Guidance Connected - True found Core most Loving-Ness Processor - We All Have Within!</u>

In other words there is something so magically miraculous about the guiding forth intelligence of our Hu-Man most awakened Hearts! The moment we learn to open them fully - this will be the very moment we will discover our most powerful intention fulfillment empowering place - we all have within. With the whole point in terms of the previous # 20-B guiding forth images - being! To the degree we find our very own Star of David within, or even Om sound of our Lord Shiva within, including our most Sacred Heart of Jesus, our potential Immaculate Heart of Mary, or even pure winged diamond Heart of a Sufi, compassionate Heart of a Buddha, including our Heart Soaring like an Eagle as referenced within our native American Indian tradition. Each of these metaphors can now be under-stood to be pointing to the very same brilliant place, which can be found inside the very Heart core. Of each and every One of our very own - greatest possible senses of our Highest possible most integrated sense of our Self. In other words to pray to or beseech any of these references within the context of whatever tradition we may have been brought up with. Is really to pray to or beseech to our very own Kingdom of Heaven found Hearts - Within. That we may thus discover how to open our very own inner most place of our now unbound - and thus unlimited found - Inner most Uni-Versal Loving-Ness attuned - Big Wholly Spirit Within. Insofar as this is the best means we all have to save ourselves - from what amounts to our very own constantly vulnerable to falling from Grace - highly fear based and/or small 'thinking' mind dominated - seemingly endlessly split & divided lost souls.

(**Accompanying Explanation** – From Jerimiah 24:7 <u>'I will give you a Heart to know me, insofar as you shall search me with all your Heart!'</u> Heare ye now is the huge lesson, for us all to fully internalize within the context of this 8th near last, of our series of have a positively great life enhancing lessons. It is only by way of our learning to totally open our very own Hearts, to all that we are already given. In such a way that we will now find our inner most essence, now able to bow with the most Whole- Sum pro-found 'Heare & Now' - totally Present Reverence. Toward all that ever manifests into form right under our very noses, exactly out of this the very same underlying / beyond lying - Uni-Versal Hum Love Song which can in turn thus actually Be Love Hum Resonance sensed by Us. To thus manifest every single thing into form - in any first place!. In other words total attunement to our Hu-Man/Woman most, Hearts. Actually does appear to constitute the most whole being Real Winner Empowering Place - we all have Within Us. In the much larger, Biggest of all Pictures Huge Sense, that attunement to the Full-on Open-Ness of our Hearts, actually does appear to be what best enables us. To keep on Co-Creatively manifesting ever more Brilliant ways of us living here, in the very sort of directions that will end up filling us with all those the very senses of 'Life', 'Liberty' and true found 'Happiness' - we all Seek. Such as when taken altogether have the possibility to help us actually End Up Being - in an inward place of true non-separate found Harmony. In the Huge context of our possibility to keep Living our Self's forth as true Partners with One-Ness or God-Ness It-Self - within the Ultimate Reality of this much larger Infinite Whole!)

UNTIL SUCH TIME AS YOU MAY THUS
FIND NO-THING LEFT INSIDE - BUT ONE
HUGE BIG TO INFINITY & BEYOND
TOTALLY ALTOGETHER GONE - CONSTANT
HEART HUM SINGING ALONG LOVING
MOST SONG - NOW ABLE TO SOAR IN
TOTAL NON SEPARATE HARMONY WITH
THAT ONE & ONLY FATHER SKY EAGLE -
WE HAVE BEEN USED TO REFERRING TO -
AS OH MY GOOD GOD-NESS - IN IT-SELF

21

EVERY ONE OF US - CHOOSING TO BIG HEART
UNIFY OUR VERY OWN SINGULAR MOST -
'INNER TREE OF LIFE' - THAT WE MAY THUS

FIND ALL THOSE
CORE FULFILLMENTS
WE MOST LONG FOR

LIKE BEING SOURCE
MERGE-CONSCIOUS

HAVING - GREAT
INNER VISION

COMMUNICATE WELL
SKILLS

HEART CARING
OPEN-NESS

AN ABILITY TO
RELATE WITH OTHERS
AS TRUE EQUALS

THE POWERS TO DO &
BE ABUNDANT

SENSUAL/SEXUAL
FUL-FILLMENTS

ULTIMATELY BY WAY
OF REALIZING ONE'S

FULLY HEART OPEN
'7' VITAL ENERGY
INTEGRAL - STATE OF
WHOLE BEING 'LIT
UP' INNERMOST
FOUND POSITIVITY

IN THE HUGE SENSE OF OUR
INNATE GIVEN ABILITY TO
KEEP SHINING FORTH THAT
INNER MOST STAR OF DAVID

WE ALL HAVE WITHIN

IMAGE BASED ON THE
FAMOUS HEART SUTRA
PRAYER - GIFTED TO US ALL
BY THE FAMOUS WELL
BEFORE CHRIST
BODHISATTVA - KNOWN AS

AVALOKITESVARA

"See the huge point being revealed Heare, all of my very dearest ever growing up into Being fully awakened Adult's of the One & Only Source - of positively all Manifest Forms! The full-on Awakening of our very own Heart centered, and therefore Hu-Man most whole being integrated Intelligence. Would appear to be the biggest of all our potential doorway opening Keys toward our very own Uni-Verse of endless possibilities to totally fulfill our Self's- there is! Such that to extent we may even Once find ourselves blessed to truly get this, we will end up bowing the whole of our own largest possible sense of Light Radiant Spirit, or emanating right out from us Holy Ghost. To that constantly Oh my Good God-Ness most Holi of Holies, which can in every moment of our existence here be sensed to Love Hum bloom into existence all around us. To such a pro-found degree we will now find our core sense of our Self's as if flying on the wings of this Divine most - everywhere present Love. Into what will amount to seemingly endless waves of true found Bliss & Joy. On the other hand, to the extent we may other than wise continue to keep half wittedly 'trying' to create ourselves forth, in separation from this Divine most Source of all Love. Which in actuality is, at the very root of 'All Existence' in any given first place. This then is to the extent we will tend to other than wise, keep choosing the very sorts of paths, which will tend to keep resulting in various forms of continuous pain and suffering for ourselves. Fortunately for all of us, this Heart centering doorway is in fact so huge, that we can actually begin to use our awareness of this place of Heart Open Lovingness - within. To help our Self's complete any places inside of us, wherein we may still find our self's in some way or another, way too negatively, reactively, defensively, holding ourselves to be victims of our various pain and suffering past's. And thus still dissociated from some part of our way more integral and therefore way higher Whole found sense of our Self's."

"In this much greater respect then, how about you now sense your self, deciding to start taking some time each day. Say anywhere from 10-20 fully inside present, core Peace-Ful centered moments. To completely enter with your now way more awakened, now total Heart Open place of complete Self - Loving-Ness. In such a way as to far more directly link this place of Loving-Ness right on into all those specific places inside of your self. Wherein your you still find your self in one way or another still resisting to be fully present inside of your self. In the much larger sense of you finally agreeing to fully accept, your various imperfections totally from within your very Heart for as long as you can each day. Until such time as you might find your newfound sense of your Self, completely healed of all former held negativities. I.E. All those places wherein you still resent, are in some way still hurting, angry, frustrated, lonely, in any way feeling not good enough, not worthy enough, not positive enough inside, even way depressed about your life etc., etc., etc. And thus which you have to some extent tended to dissociate from your very own more whole sense of your Self! And I guarantee you that you will be surprised, at just how much of an effort of pure total Self Acceptance awareness - it can take. To just start

Loving every such aspect of your self, so totally that you will now find your self being able to totally enter any such formerly dissociated place, precisely now with the whole of your One & Only now total self accepting Loving-Ness Heart! Until such time as you will finally be able to say, yes you have now found a way to enter all your various hatreds and resentments completely, from within a place that is totally connected to your very own Heart! In other words learn to enter with the energy of your Lovingness so completely into any, and every given part of you. In such a profound way, you will now feel able to be totally Loved within every part of you, by your very own new whole found sense of your self."

"And I guarantee you, the moment you learn to enter all those old held negative emotions, which were Once somehow or other based on past conditioned emotional fears. So dissociatively separated from your much more fully integrated sense of your Self. It used to feel way too difficult to totally enter any such old such pain & suffering wounded place inside of you. This will be the very moment you will find your Inner Space now seemingly paradoxically, able to totally transform into your potential ability, to now so Love every formerly dissociated aspect of your Self. To the point where even your most so called negative ongoing in the moment emerging emotions, will now be centered in a place of pure essentially non-harmful Loving-Ness, within you. In such a way that any newly emerging most natural purely in the moment, felt negative emotion, will become just another new opportunity To now find a truly Loving Solution to whatever ongoing challenges may come your way, no matter how seemingly difficult. In this larger respect you could well say, that what becoming a fully Awake Adult, very much seems to be all about. Is YOU learning to now Love every aspect of your own Self so totally. That you will now not only find your self fully able to wave your way through any so called negative emotion, totally Peace-Ful/Lovingly. But you will finally find Your Self no longer, 'still needing' any One else, in any old primitive split and divided sense of your long past child like self, to complete YOU! Simply because you will now find your Self, complete within your largest possible sense of your very Own Wholiest possible - Big SELF! And thus fully able to share your Loving-Ness with all those you most care for, from within a place fully beyond any more me, me, alone constant harmful to others 'Needing'! Which is exactly in turn, why it becomes so important for each of us to now Love every part of our Self, this totally. From within our very own sense of our biggest possible everywhere inside of Us present, greatest possible most empowered sense of our SELF!"

"See the Whole point here, to the extent you cannot totally Love every aspect of your very own Self. To the extent you cannot reconcile your sense of your very best complete Atone-Ment, forgiving Self? With being able to be easily embodied Present within every aspect of your Self. To the extent you cannot be completely inside every aspect of your Self, in a totally Loving Way. This will be too the extent

230

you will always remain in conflict, yeah in a Virtual War, with some aspect of your Self. On the other hand, the moment You can totally Accept the full depths of some former negatively held emotion, or other than wise held negative belief / attitude about life. In such a way as to now live your life forth from within a place of total Heart Open found, always ongoing compassionately adaptive - solution oriented flexibility within. As opposed to remaining in constant dis-respect to how your life is absolutely supposed to be lived, in your head alone. The positively great news is that these very same once filled with pain & suffering areas you once used to keep holding inside of you, will now begin to feel totally different for you! In the much greater sense that whenever you may end up feeling any kind of so called momentary negatively, in your future! You will now be able to bring total Loving-Ness into any such new challenging emotion, in ways that will now help you to move both into and through your feelings much more Care-Fully - going forward.

"In other words, what could be said too differentiate a child, from a fully grown all up, Wise-Dome of awareness found Adult? Is that such grown up Adults will finally find a way to enter positively every aspect of them Self, from every bit of their very own insides, all their way Out. In such a way as to no-longer remain separate from the everywhere Present Loving-Ness of what we have been referring to as God-Ness or the Great One-Ness Mystery, which appears to be of Pure Loving One-Ness in IT-SELF. And thus will no-longer feel the 'need' for something outside of them selves, to complete their own sense of them Self's! Or, put another way, so find their ery own sense of them Self's as being truly worthy enough! Quite simply because they will now Love their own sense of them Self's so totally, they will now be fully able to come from place of being able to NOW totally SHARE their total Love of Life and thus total worthiness with whomsoever they may choose! In marked contrast to always having to come from a place which is of constantly trying to prove One's most
essential worthiness - to others!"

"Given you can now fully get this! It becomes most important to not feel compelled to grow the Full-On Open-Ness of your Heart, all at once. Inasmuch as your continual failure to keep meeting your own total inner found Loving-Ness, expectations. Can keep you falling over and over again, from the ultimate Grace of your greater potential to actually find this place of total authentic Loving-Ness - Within. Thus it is much better to start with being as patient and loving as you possibly can with any given dissociated aspect of your self, one negativity holding area at a time. Taking as much time as it may take, perhaps weeks, even month's perhaps a year or two, to finally feel like you have completely Love your Self healed, some old negative emotion based - held wound. Always remembering that chances are you have been holding your deepest negative patterns, for quite some time. With the good news now being, every time you find your self falling back into some

231

kind of negatively once again. You can always use the prior feel through lesson's outlined in chapters 3 & 4, to help your Self feel through whatever pain body emotions, you might still find arising inside of you. Such that every time you can now find your Self, in a state of clear pure expanded no-boundaries awareness, once again. You can start loving your life and every aspect of your Self, along with as many others that you are close to, as you possibility can!"

"Most especially now, insofar as you will be learning to ever more heal your very own wounds. From a place of being constantly willing to forgive and thus get past every bad behavior on the part of every One of your both present, as well as former loved One's - as you possibly can. To a point where it will become easier and easier, to begin truly loving 'Thy Neighbor, as Thy actual Self! Always knowing, though no neighbor or loved One will never be perfect, in the very same sense that 'Let ye who has never transgressed, cast the first stone!' It is always way more satisfying to come back into a place Loving, than it is to remain in a place of Hate-Ful-Ness. Besides once you can come from a place of focusing on core Peace-Fully In-Stilled solutions, rather than problems. You will be surprised at how brilliant at creating new found ways ever forward, you can become. In the much greater sense that Once you get the hang of it with your neighbors, as though they actually are your Self. It will be time to expand your Loving-Ness even to your seemingly most hated adversaries, in such a truly Grace-Ful way. That even your worst enemies will find themselves becoming open to the very sort of truly Miraculous solutions, which will begin blowing every One's minds away. Simply because pure Loving-Ness actually is - the most Power-Ful Force for Oh My Good God-Ness to be found anywhere in the whole of this Singular Most Uni-Verse - there really Is."

"Which is to say, the more we each and every One of us, agree to keep finding ways to grow ourselves, in the very same stroke of our inwardly oriented potential genius. In such a way as to keep ourselves entering exactly this most Sacred Geometrical Hum Love place - within every nook & cranny of our very own unique sense of our now fully every where most inwardly embodied, greatest possible sense of our Self's. The more and more we will begin to empower our very own Self's to manifest into form, whatever it may be that we ourselves might most intend to bring into our own freely invented, highly unique sense of sought after fulfillment. Exactly in the same way this Source Field manifest's everything it ever does in any first place. Precisely in relation to our inner most found sense of whole being integrated - & therefore now Big Heart Resonant enabled - sense of full-on empowerment. Such that in the process of discovering this greater empowerment possibility within ourselves, we will now actually come to fully KNOW in a Gnostic sense. That even when some other One appears to be treating us badly, they must somehow within the context of this greater huge fundamentally UNKOWABLE in a Agnostic sense – great mysterious At-One-Ment reality. Merely be reflecting back to us our own possibility to now clear our very own fear based negative tendencies to keep reacting back to those, including our very own self's. We once used to perceive as being somehow to blame for how we our selves are feeling about any given situation. Very much as a consequence of our own fall from the Grace of Re-Main-Lining our greatest possible sense of our Self's within At-One-Ment. In such a way as to help lead us into clearing ourselves back into the very sort of non-separate Whole-Ness state, which can much better enable all parties to any given situation. To now find some positively Brilliant Super In-Sight-Ful & thus far more En-Lightend way, to help keep us inventing any such conflictual situation into some Kind of truly way more Holistic oriented and thus truly Big Picture In-Volved / ever more E-Volved Solution."

"Man, Oh Wo-Man greater Wise-dome within. Charlie & Katie now suddenly found themselves exclaiming unto themselves. In their now being way more fully able to get the great potential for Good or Evil paradox, of our own Made in the Image - hugely mysterious Hu-Man Conscious-Ness. It seems like every time we find ourselves falling into some sort of huge flare button space. What would behoove us most as Made in the Image Beings - of the One & Only Super Source. Would be for us to take some inward stop time, from within a place beyond anymore resort to reactive blame. To both fully own and then feel completely through whatever it may be we ourselves are feeling or other than wise little narrow mind believing. In such a way that we would not only start to not only clear our own fear based negativity, in relation to having our flare buttons triggered. But also help ourselves re-enter our core Peace-Ful place of being within our own Love Hum At-within One-Ment Connected Zone - once again. Insofar as this is the most blessed huge doorway we all have inside of us, to help ourselves keep most Peace-Fully & thus truly Love Light In-Sight-Ing our way ever forward. Within the context of the Great Love Hum Mystery, we all find our selves being a most intimate non-separate Made in the Image part of. As opposed to merely letting our selves always keep reacting back to every challenging situation, from within a place which amounts to an unconscious reptilian mind based separation - from this One-Ness or Loving-Ness Source - in It-Self!"

"Which always comes down to this, all of my most Dear, Made in the Image Every One's! It never behooves any of us to make decisions or other than wise take compulsively driven action, based on any kind of flare button reaction. Or for that matter any mere human mind invented ideas, about how we in our smallest mere narrow little ego mind self's, may constantly keep ourselves absolutely 'thinking'. How every One of us is supposed to behave here. All of which in turn tend to have their foundations in whatever old fear based wounds, we may have once experienced in our past. Whereas on the other hand, it seems that our ability to learn to take however many greater Over-Seeing 'I' moments, it may take. To just stop our compulsively driven propensity for fear based over reactivity, in such a way as to find some way to clear / heare re-attune our way back into both this Un-Versal Love Hum. And thus into our most Sacred Geometrical attuned ongoing great solution oriented Inventive place - we all have within our very own now Big Mind awake attuned Hearts. Inasmuch as this very Loving-Ness place, out of which all things manifest into form in the first place. Does appear to be the most powerfully positive great forward moving solution enabling place, we actually all do have within us. In the greater sense that any form of negativity will always seem to beget more negativity, while Loving-Ness, is far more highly likely to beget even more Love! Just exactly in the sense that all of very greatest wisdom teachers, have over the course of our higher Hu-Man, greater spiritual under-standing oriented history of our Self's. Done their level best over and over again to reveal to us."

"Good God Almighty, how most truly One-Drous-Ly Beauti-Ful this great grand Made in the Image stage we all find ourselves living within, really appears to be! This under-standing is in fact so, so, huge, when will we ever learn?" The place of inner found wisdom within Quantum Katie & Cosmic Charlie began to now trumpet forth. By way of Every One's very own Gabriel like sounding, It's time for Us All to Finally Really Get It, positively great news bringing - Horn? "God Almighty, it now seems from what our very own Wise-Dome of Awareness Within - is really most teaching us! Inasmuch as every thing which ever manifests into form appears to contain the very seed principle of Divine or God's Love, right within it! By the very way the 2 principle quantum level energy dimensions, of light and sound seem to continuously via the principle of quantum entanglement! Keep interacting with each other! In such a way that this underlying / beyond lying continuously Love Humming Super Light, can be Under-Stood to actually initiate those very Sacred Most Geometrical - building block Structures! Out which all ever more complex forms themselves, can be sensed to keep coming into being! This all would seem to imply, that the very greatest fulfillment empowerment place, we actually all have within our very own greatest sense of selves! Can only be found within our own fully open sense of attunement - to this very same Quantum Super Light/Super Spirit Love Hum Resonant place. Which appears to most truly One-Drously keep manifesting every single thing into form, in any first place! "

"Which is to say, we every One of us can actually start to Love every aspect of our very own Self's, so totally, right from within our own Hearts. Yes-We-Can actually begin to sense every nook and cranny of us, as now being filled with Love. In such a profound way, that we will now find ourselves all of my most beloved found One's, ever more Loving, positively every single thing, that ever manifests into form. Out of the Grace of thus underlying / beyond lying Source Force Field which is in IT-Self! Appears to be no-thing more or less than a Field of Love? We will now totally want to learn just how to keep-on Co-Creating our Self's forth, in total Loving

Harmony with this Great Force of Love in It-Self. Other than wise, what be the point of creating something, indeed inventing forth anything," inner wisdom now mused to his/her own innermost sense of Self? "If we end up hating whatever we in our more divided and thus in endless inner conflict, lack of this greater sense of our being. Keep ourselves negatively 'feeling' and 'thinking' we must compulsively out our fears and senses of separation. Keep putting into whatever we keep choosing to invent. To the sort of point wherein we will thus tend to keep ourselves experiencing, the very hates and resentment we ourselves tend to keep putting into the very products. We keep choosing out of this sense of inner Division, to keep on inventing supposedly for our greater Good. Besides, insofar as we keep going for the mere boundaries of our being, this is the most we will ever get, mere here and there occasional mere boundary satisfactions! Coupled with the continual experience of endless rounds of the very same kinds of conflictual situations, we keep finding ourselves being challenged with, to begin with. Whereas the moment we learn to attune to our most Whole-Sum-ly Integral Hearts. And thus choose to do whatever we may keep choosing to do, precisely from within this very full of Light or Hum Resonance found Loving-Ness place - which can only be found to reside within our Hearts. Such as it is possible for Every One of Us to clearly hear inside the most core Centered sense of our Self's - every right now. The more and more we are going to find our sense of separateness from this great Source, able to dissolve into the very sort of non-separate Oceanic like State. Which is of our ultimate Philosophers Stone Found - totally Uni-Fied Place of Being Fully Consciousness. The very place which has been referred to by all the great Mystical teachers of our World, as One of being within At-One-Ment with our most Holy of Holies - Maker. Exactly in the greater sense we attempt to portray, in the Beyond Body Experience Image, which follows."

Illustration # 22 - Taking One's Inner Wisdom Quest - Yet One Giant Step Further - Such that In Heare & NOW Finding Our Self's Now most Clearly totally Love Hum Heart Glow attuned Fully Present - We End Up Sensing our most Integral Self's as now BBEing - Or Non-Locally Totally Now Beyond Body Experiencing - Which is to Say All Gone Dissolved Into that One & Only Sacred Most to Infinity & Beyond - Great Beyond All Former Limits Same Uni-Versal Source - Super Loving-Ness Ocean!

Which is of Us actually Being able to just fully Be no boundaries Without Limits totally Present, within the Great Mystery of At-One-Ment - In IT-SELF! Such that Once within this place, it is said we no-longer experience any separate sense of our Self's. And our possibility to now truly 'See' Pure Everywhere Present - Super Light Energy! Insofar as this Singular most Source seems to keep endlessly Flower of Aphropdite, Love Hum Blooming IT'S Way continuously along, within all Creatures great & small, indeed all things great & small. With the great news for us now being, it is precisely the finding of our own Cared Heart Centered awake, while at the same time fully expanded to Infinity & Beyond found - great Wise-Dome gift of Pure Awareness. Which most fortunately for us, is exactly what with all due respect to helping ourselves as creatures made in the Image of this Divine most Consciousness, ends up best affording us. The very clearest inner guidance we can get, to help each One of us keep moving our most essential Self's ever forward. Toward all the intended inner Ful-Fill-Ments we each of us in 'thought', 'word', & 'deed', actually have been designed / evolved to help ourselves keep manifesting. In such a way that the very deepest most core essential aspect of us, can actually experience our Self's as being, truly now Whole Being Ful-Filled.

(**Accompanying Explanation** – The whole point of this particular BBE revealing image is then, to help every One of us finally truly get, what our child within already knows. Which is that the very underlying / beyond lying Love Hum Resonance out of which every single thing within our world, indeed our galaxy, or for that matter our whole Uni-Verse - ever comes into form. Actually is in essence just as our very greatest wisdom teachers, have always done there best to share with us. No-Thing more than an essentially unlimited Force Field of Love! And thus that the most powerful self inventive place we all have within our own most awake sense of Self, is actually our Hearts - not our heads. Which seems to imply, that the greatest possible Hu-Man adventure of all, would be to help empower ourselves by way of our totally learning to open our very own - Most Sacred Hearts within - to our ultimate max. In such a way that we might learn to Co-Create in harmonic attunement with this underlying / beyond lying great Source-Force - which is of Love - It-Self. Insofar as we all appear to have been given the free choice possibility to keep finding ways to live Non-Separately right within what amounts to this great Singular Most Mystery Field - which is of Divine Loving Consciousness or God-Ness- It-Self. In the much larger sense that we appear to have actually been made in the Holographic Image of this Field of pure Loving-Ness - which is One-Ness, or God-Ness It-Self!)

US NOW ALL-TOGETHER BEYOND BODY EXPERIENCING - OR BBE-ING WAY NON-LOCALLY AT SUPER-LIGHT SPEED - TOTALLY PRESENT DISSOVED

WITHIN WHAT AMOUNTS TO PURE ESSENTIALLY EVERYWHERE PRESENT - ENDLESSLY HUM LOVE FLOWERING - ONE QUANTUM SOURCE ENERGY

"Holy Super Light Ghost, or singular most great Father like Holo-Graphic Wisdom teacher - of us all. It seems insofar as we each of us appear to be Made in the Image of the One & Only Source. Then based on what our own inner most Wise-Dome of Awareness, has been pointing us all toward now fully Getting. The more we help our selves come into a place wherefrom Yes-We-Can totally Love the everywhere Present Presence - of that Uni-Tary most One-Ness which is of God-Ness - IT-SELF. The more Loving Good-Ness we our most essential Self's, will now have to Share with every other Some-One we may ever En-Counter? Which in it-self, is going to totally transform us from being the sort of mere Ego-Centric focused beings only, who will keep wanting to try and prove our own Worth-I-Ness, often at the expense of other same Source Made Worth-I-Nesses. Into now finding our most essential core Self's, as the very sort of way more Big Picture Holo-Centric attuned Beings. Who will now want to aim the sharing of our Whole Hearted Love of One-Ness, not only into every action we may ever choose to take. But also toward helping as many other Some One Else's actually find their own Full-On Awake state of Loving most Empowerment - as Yes-We-Actually-Can. In this much larger respect you might well say, that God-Ness or One-Ness within the context of this grand Loving-Ness Mystery - which is what Good-Ness REALLY IS. Actually so puts It's Love into every singular most One of Us, that this Loving-Ness or God-Ness It-Self would Love No-Thing more. Other than for all of us to help each other discover how to Co-Create abundance and prosperity for every Singular most One of Us. Not just for a select, so called Elitist - Phew. Yet have our Self's arrive at this place of us wanting to grow our Self's into this state of we are all as One all together – collective well being. Completely out of our essential freedom to Co-Create in Loving Harmony with all that already Is! Not out of some sort of fear belief based - have to messaged to use by others - Compulsive-Ness!"

"Yes, Yes, Charlie my every Cosmic son, Katie your very own now Quantum attuned daughter of this very Same Source! In beyond 'Thought', 'Word' & 'Deedy Do', now you've really, truly, Whole Being GOT IT, within the very Heart of You. For Heare in this grand Wise-Dome of Awareness, which is ever more growing within You. You are now bringing all of these prior guiding forth lessons home full circle, to roost clear through & through within the very Whole All - of You. Such that now you can sense why it is so important to truly inside Heare whatever may interest you the most, in this every very right now. Including why it is so important to dedicate the gifts of your inner most intelligence, toward your own possibility to develop those very innate given talents most likely to help you create a positively great life. Not just for yourself, but also for every other One who may come into your growing circle of ever more radiantly spirit connected within One-Ness - constantly expanding wholly spheres of influence. In order that you may best create your self ever forward, precisely into the sort of some-One, who will now be way more truly Present. Within your very own ever more awakened, completely dissolved into that no-difference place of Hum Love. In the positively huge sense of you now being guided by this connection into just what the great gift of your life has the more Divine possibility, to be now most Heart-Fully way more now All About. And thus into what every 'One' else's life, is also all about. The only way it ever possible for any singular One of us, to ever find the true inner sense of Happiness we all of us so richly deserve."

"Become as a Co-Creative partner with One-Ness IT-SELF you say, God Almighty that sure does sound powerful - great Inner Wise-dome of Awareness!" "Well, yes as a matter of everywhere Pure Super Light Energy & thus now total Hum Loving-Ness Present - Fact! It sure enough - REALLY IS! Simply because the moment we can now in our greater found Pure Awareness, truly sense that we all actually live in a virtual to Infinity & Beyond Unlimited Unbound Ocean of Pure Love. In such a way that we might thus finally fully Ac-Know-Ledge to our Self, that we are actually Not Separate from this Virtually Un-Limited Ocean of Pure Cosmic Level - Divine most Love. This makes it possible for us to now most hopefully actually 'See', that everything we may ever dream to bring forth from inside the place of Pure Loving-Ness attunement - Within Us - Actually Is Entirely Possible. Inasmuch as a matter of greater truth, this sort of attunement is exactly how we can actually find that incredibly enabled miracle making place we all have within. Which keeps saying to our very essence, Yes insofar as we value our own innate given possibility to actually awaken to this great Force inside our very own most empowered sense of our now well beyond ordinary attuned Self. Yes-We-Can now truly know exactly how it is possible for us to manifest into form, whatsoever great life we may choose to intend for our Self's, and all those we Love. Simply because the great I-Am- Who-We-Really-Are, which resides within us. Is now completely Heart centered in that unstoppable Force - which is of Divinely attuned Love - in Itself! The very same Force which can be sensed to manifest's everything in our world, indeed our very universe, into form in any first place."

"Other than wise, insofar as it appears we ourselves along with positively every other have been Made in the Image of this ultimate Source Force of Love - It-Self. Then any manifestation we keep choosing to bring forth that is motivated from a place that is less than to Infinity & Beyond, Whole Love Field Attuned. In the much larger sense of our possibility to Co-Create every One of our Self's forth, in complete harmony with this huge unlimited Force of Love. The ultimate nature of this great Karmic Round wheel seems to be a what's so such, that some other part of this great Whole. Will in One way or another, keep coming back round to keep byting us the butt. Until such time as we finally get the message. Besides to the extent we choose to keep ignoring our inner messaged calls toward the potential development of our own most blessed given interests and talents. It's kind of like sticking our fingers in the 'I' of God! As if to say we somehow in our heads alone, know better than the larger Holi-Ness of that ultimate Loving-Ness which is of One-Ness, or that place With-In - which is of being in true WholeSum Communion with Oh My Good God-Ness - In IT-SELF."

"Oh me Oh my, Wholly Sprit Smoke & Mirrors", innermost Wisdom now found him/her self inwardly Singing with great Self Realization Joy - unto his/her every now increasingly attuned Self - out Heare! Is the great way this Whole Big Picture Thing seems to work Muy Fantastico, Tres Increable, Bene Prodigioso, truly most One-Drous, or What?" "Yes all you dear One's, if you were this huge Source Force Itself, you couldn't have made a more magical world, a more truly miraculous Hu-Man Consciousness - Made in the Image? The very sort of Image Making Consciousness through which the great One-Ness It-Self, might get to know of it's very own endlessly ever new evolving Co-Creative possibilities? Including those possibilities which might be even better reflective of the Love, out of which all things end up being invented into form in any first place? Which is to say, Imagine Source Loving no-thing more that the very sort of new surprises coming through our God-Ness Given Hu-Man/Woman most Potentials to keep Co-Creating our Self's Forth. In ways that might warm Sources Heart even More, than anything that has ever been manifested into form, before."

"What a spine tingling truly inspirational concept, Good God-Ness In It-Self being so open to the possibility of even more Loving-Ness being made Manifest through us. Being so open to giving us the complete freedom required to make this possibility of even more Loving-Ness - being Made Manifest through us completely available to us. That this Whole-Ness would keep ending Up with the sort of result, wherein this Wholeness It-Self would now have the potential to be way more endlessly open ended Surprised by Endless New Possibilities? Than if One-Ness or God-Ness were to have Made It-Self to be stuck in a pre-determined field, with no new possibilities? Not even any possibility for this ultimate One-Ness or God-Ness principle to keep inventing new ways to Love It-Self? In the much greater Sense, that even the singular most Consciousness of Whole-Ness would get completely bored, with the same old, same old, been there, done that, small mind mentality. Such as would have not much more to offer than, seemingly endless rounds of hatred, resentment, constant ego-centric focused better than thou one-upmanship, and the same old non-Peace-Ful ways of us Made in the Image Creatures - being here. Which in turn is exactly why your own inner most Wisdom wants you to now jump, the whole of your most awake to this Great Mystery - Inner Core Being. Into the continuous process of choosing to keep manifesting your self forth, from within the very sort of inner messaging - Yes-You Can keep on hearing. Constantly arising within your very own Source Made Manifest Heart. Via your choice to engage in this process of becoming fully conscious of your very own most intimate Loving-Ness connection - to that within you which is most Non-Separate from this Great Source!"

"O.K." dearest inner most wisdom was now heard to exclaim unto One's inner most awake sense of Source Connected Self! Inasmuch as I'm really beginning to internalize the whole of my very own wisdom oriented teachings, much more clearly inside of my Self now. Much like in all those old fairy tales, where tales were told of some handsome prince, or most beautiful fairy princess. Who finally is able to find their partner, in spite of all kinds of difficult trials that keep coming their way. Simply because they knew somewhere deep inside, that there was some special Some-One out there whom they were able to keep 'Seeing', in front of themselves. Who would be the perfect Prince or Princess partner to enable them to build their own loving family, just as all truly happy partners are able to manage. By way of following that yellow brick road light guiding pathway, constantly being laid out in front of them, by their very won Hearts. Often contrary to what logic alone, or even their feelings alone would be telling them to do. To the point where they would finally find each other, and then attempt their very best, to find ways to live happily ever after!"

"Yes, exactly, even though in most of the old fairy tales, they never taught us just exactly how, Yes-We-Can! Keep using this very same internal Heart Centered longing for fulfillment guidance system, to help our self's keep finding ways to live happily for ever after. Except now in relation to just how we have the possibility to apply this same inner core guidance system - to help our Self's bring every one of our '7' vital energy based - intended great fulfillment dreams into fruition. In the much greater sense of us learning to mobilize all that we are, from within the very most clear of all negativity and thus no-longer in separation, now truly Heart Core awakened way larger sense of our Self's. In relation to helping every One of us actually be best enabled, to realize the positively great life's that we all of us so much long for. Like for example, dreaming about how yes we-can create all kind of new toys to play with, positively great medicinals to help heal the whole of us, great houses along with truly healthy foods to help make our family caring life's, much easier and more harmonious for us to live through. Including great travel means to help us See as much as we possibly can, with respect to how other people keep finding alternate unique inventive ways to help live out their dreams. As well as great computers and programs to help us figure out all kinds of new ways to Co-Create / Invent all kinds of great forward moving products and services, we might want to have in our lives. Not to mention like how we can learn to keep on communicating with our selves and each other, as effectively as is humanly possible. Most especially with respect to helping all of ourselves keep growing our most full conscious Made in the Image, and therefore Loving most potentials. Always in relation to just what it is, we each of us might most truly Love to invent for every other singular most aspect of this great One-Ness or God-Ness Field, as Yes We Possibly Can! In ways within One-Ness or God-Ness It-Self, could now be felt to be singing One Huge HALLELUHYAH, OM SHANTI OM, HOSANAH ON HIGHEST, ALLAH AKBAR, HO, real praise the One Lord - at the Source of all Made Manifest - Things!

Such as might be felt by all of Us, non-locally/ simultaneously within all of our Hearts - All at Once! Do you now Get IT? For this Is Our Greatest Hu-Man/Woman most Made in the Image - Non-Separate from One-Ness or God-Ness Potential!"

"Which is precisely why, your own inner most Wise-Dome of pure Awareness. Has within the modern context of our Whole World's great Wisdom - past gathered Know-L-Edge. Laid this greater wisdom pathway more out here for all of us to now way more fully whole being truly Grok. In the Huge Sense that from now on, it is going to be totally up to each and every One of us, to keep improving upon what we have learned from our past. In order that we may thus learn to play our Self's ever forward, even better than any One of Us ever has before within the context of our great Wisdom Teacher oriented past. Inasmuch as it is always by way of our most Grown Up sense of One-Ness It-Self, being able to now keep coming through us. In such a way that this great One-Ness Source Force can get to know just how even more magnificent IT has the potential to be. Or alternatively, just how horrible and unconscious, some of IT'S own Made In the Image creations. Will keep stubbornly refusing against our much greater Hu-Man possibility. To finally grow our own Self's Fully-On-All-Up. In such a way as to thus keep choosing to keep on manifesting endless rounds of ever new forms of horrible-ness - for our self's. With the only choice point remaining, which side of One-Ness would you your very own most Inner Wisdom attuned self - most like to now align your self with? That side which best enables us to Co-Creatively Invent ever more positively great lives for our greatest possible sense of Self's. And thus toward One-Ness or God-Ness It-Self's greatest possibility to keep on Evolving ITSELF ever forward into endless new great possibilities through Us? Or alternatively that side which is going to keep choosing to be way too unconsciously driven - into a life of internal Hell Fire & Damnation?"

"Thank you, thank you 'O' so much, 'Great Guiding Forth Source' - from within the very Whole of My now way more Awakened Heart. For in you now making my very own potential to have a positively Great Life choice - so truly Clear - to the very Heart of me! Simply because I have finally come to a place within the very core of me, wherefrom I-Can-Now! Honestly bow the whole of my being - in complete open Heart Felt - gratitude. To this great mystery Garden of Eden such as is always already happening, right under my very nose. And which is always to infinity and beyond everlasting, in every way, everywhere Heare Present. Quite simply because thanks to this great Wisdom oriented Guidance you have been offering, I have now come to actually Know that the very greatest possible guiding forth place to be found anywhere in the Whole of this Biggest of All Pictures - entire Uni-Verse. Only has the possibility to come completely through me - by way my very own opening to that very same At-One-Ment Loving Whole-Ness. Which can only be found Inside of my very own most Full-On Heart Centered Awake - I-Am Within. Which is really the very Heart of all that You - Great Mystery Source Force - Already Are! Whether we as a more collective humanity, choose to wake up to this positive magnificence, or may continue to choose, to keep knotting? Actually this revelation is so truly exciting profound for me, it has actually changed every single thing for me. In relation to how I now want to keep on Co-Creating my much greater sense of Self, ever more forward."

"In other words, inasmuch as what I now find myself most wanting, is for me to stop my inner most essence from being anymore at war with anything, that ever manifests out of this One & Only Source. All I that now ask unto thee 'O Lord', whom I now know can only be found by me, within me! Is that my own ever unfolding Inner Wisdom may from this moment on, keep helping make me as an instrument of thy infinite Peace. In the much greater sense of helping my own now much greater sense of now Co-Creatively Unlimited to Infinity & Beyond - Constantly Joy-Filled Over Flowing Empowered - One Big Giant Hum Heart. Which is really the very Heart of 'Your Everywhere Presences, Great Mysterious Lord of this Uni-Versal most huge glorious Manifesting All Things into from - Dance. Keep guiding me forth in such a way that I may manifest my own inner most essence, which is of course really your inner most Essence 'OH GREAT ONE'. In ways that are now going to help my greatest possible sense of Self resonate in total Loving Harmony. With all those to infinity and beyond Love Seeded Presents which this great Mysterious Source Force is already providing for us all - to keep our Self's BENE-FITTING FROM. Simply because as your now much more awake, fully now adult found child of One-Ness It-Self. I do now most Whole-Sum-Ly understand, that yes I actually do deserve to realize my largest possible sense of truly great 'Life' found inventive 'Liberty'. All in the direction of my potential to actually realize that most profound sense of my full-on Heart Found 'Real Happiness total Ful-Fill-Ment Empowering Place', which I have been promised. Provided I keep choosing to keep bringing myself back into my greatest sense of real Whol-E-Ness - Within!"

"To conclude this lesson, here then you will find our most special Hu-man most way, to keep accelerating the fullest possible awakening of our Truly Magical found Adult - within," inner wisdom now took a greater Liberty to now Insight forward. "To the extent we each of us choose to recognize our very own place of whole being fulfillment capability, by way of our choosing to awaken our very own Heart place of greatest possible empowerment within. What we are going to increasingly find, is that there is no more satisfying, total love of life elevating experience, in the whole of this world. Than for us to help as many other One's as we possibly can, to find their very own sense of non-separate from At-One-Ment - & thus most fully awakened place of full-on empowerment - within. Which is to say, there is nothing that will open our very own innermost Heart Core place of empowerment, more. Than for us to agree to give a certain 'tithed percentage' of our time, to help others grow their very own sense of whole being inner fulfillment empowerment - for them selves. For contrary to the fear mongers notions of Scare-City, the huge big message to get in this much greater respect here, is. The more any of us help to collectively empower the many, the merrier we will thus find all of ourselves being. Inasmuch as the huge reality within greater wisdom is that we actually do have enough intelligence within the King-Dome of our most Whole possible sense of our Self's. To help ourselves keep finding new, ever more positively brilliant innovative ways, to keep ourselves inventing not just prosperity and abundance, but also true found Happ-I-Ness for every Singular most Oh My Good God-Ness Connected - One of Us."

"Man Oh Man/Woman! There simply are no-longer any words left to say! Only One's total innermost Heart-Felt Love - to now keep sharing ever forward! With all due respect as to just Who or What we all of us within our very greatest, innermost awake Heart Core attuned Essence? All have the possibility to keep on manifesting ourselves forth - ever on and on Upwards - In-To?"

Eighth level - of 'True Found Happiness' Enhancing Prayer Unto One's Self - Choosing to Put One's Total 'Love of Everything' Into Positively Every Action One May Now Choose - To Keep Investing One's Inner Most Found Sense of Fully Heart Open Being - Into

"Holy molly, great balls of pure unlimited Super Light energy Fire, I finally get IT! It's like the huge Who-Am, that I-Most-Fully-Am within. Is some One who now actually knows that we all appear to have been designed evolved to keep our Self's resonating in actual Harmonic Attunement. With the very same Source Force that permeates positively every thing we ever are most blessed to experience. And thus out of which all we ever come to know seems to manifest into it's own unique form. Such that the more I help myself integrate my own awareness field into a single unified, totally now present, and thus most reverently appreciative whole. The more and more the whole of me will begin to feel completely insightfully inspired empowered, by something of the well beyond ordinary. Insofar as I can sense this Super Source Force constantly coursing, yeah virtually Singing and Humming it's underlying resonant pure Loving-Ness vibration, all It's way through me. To such a pro-found degree, that I-Am ever more going to find the great Who I-Am now experiencing my self to now Be. Is actually Some-One who can accomplish virtually any thing, that I truly set the Whole of my very innermost sense of Being - now towards.

In other words, I now find myself as Some-One fully able to experience my Yes-I-Now-Know-Exactly-How-I-Can, to such a fully here present degree. I now totally get it, that no great dream is impossible for me to help myself Ful-Fill. Provided I take all those very responsibilities which seem to be required for me to most well beyond ordinary - Tap My Source empower my greater sene of Self. Most especially in the very sort of directions which are most likely to link me up with all those like Wise inspired - other human presences. Whom I now sense within my ever growing beyond ordinary Whole Field of awareness are also most willing in their own unique ways, to jump totally on board link their dreams with mine, and mine with theirs. In such a way as to thus help each other realize our very greatest dreams all together - as One Huge One-Ness."

Chapter 10

Lesson # 9 – Ultimately - It's All About Each Of Us Growing Our Very Own Most Consciously Aware Sense of Our Self's - As Fully All Up Into Our Very Own Now Most Effortless Single 'I' Attuned Vortex Of Super Light - & Thus Unto Our Utmost Given Potential To Be Completely Heart Loving In All That We May Choose To Do Heare - As Yes We Possibly Can

Rationale for HAVE A GREAT LIFE LESSON - # 9

Here is the ultimate reality of our much greater Made in the Image - Hu-Man/Woman most Potentials. Such as we all of us have to be found within each and every One of Us. It appears based on what has been revealed in the prior chapters - we all of us already do live in a Super Light made Garden of Eden all around us. Such that to the extent we choose to find ways to align our inner most Heart Core Centered and thus Whol-I-Est possible - Unitary-I In-Tegrated sense of our Utmost potential to Be. Within the most Mysterious non-local Under-Lying / Beyond Lying One Super Light Spirit Source - of all Energy! This is the extent to which we will begin to sense ourselves as actually being able to manifest way more prosperous and abundant, while at the same time now truly Now Big Picture Holo-Graphically Integral - ways of living for all of ourselves - even beyond our wildest dreams. In other words, In-So-Far as we keep bringing ourselves All Up, in such way as to actually come to know, that we are all of us a most intimate part of this most Mysterious One-Ness or Loving Good God-Ness - Super Light Field In It-Self. In this knowing we will always forever after - keep wanting to Self Realize change positively everything. About how we will now actually want to way more Lovingly manifest ourselves forth, toward the promised Eden we all long for.

So let's go on to put the finishing touches on this growing inner-sense, of just who we all have the potential to fully Be. It appears our most beautiful inner reality is - the more we each of us can find our most whole being unified and thus ultimately now constantly way more in our ongoing true happiness oriented actually now most Sacred Heart Self Guiding flow zone Meter - which is to be found Within. Or that very place within which we find our true essence actually single 'I' now able to Glow our Self's into a virtual Lamp of Light. Unto our most expanded with out bounds possible sense, of just whom it appears we have all been Designed / Evolved to most Heart-Fully Be. In such a way that our Heart / Lung or Breath of Life Energy co-ordinating autonomic nervous system plexus - will now. Begin to help our psycho-biology generate a much more continuous flow of here and now relaxing Cholines & Endorphines. As well as higher and higher levels of One Spirit Wakefulness Enhancing or Tap our Source Attuning - naturally generated DMT (dimethyltryptamine). Considered to be both the most prevalent as well as most potent psychedelic like state or pure Super Light Energy Awareness enhancing & thus Great Spirit Attuning. Entirely natural to every One - Bio-system generated drug found to be constantly everywhere present - in pretty much all organic systems on our planet. In such a way as to help elevate the natural release of a whole host of various Consciousness Elevating elements throughout our body, including most especially up into our Brain Field. As well as the release of the most powerful thymus gland generated immune or overall wellness enhancing hormones - we can help our body muster. Via this very same Heart Energy Integrating - plexus - yes we can more optimally mobilize within us.

In other words it appears the more we can encourage our Heart/Lung plexus, to keep generating an optimal Loving Life Energy Flow for us. The more we are going to find our Self's utterly amazed at just how effortlessly empowered in the way larger sense of our head being completely out of the way. And our heart now being way more totally in our way - as Yes-We Can actually Be! However in order to truly hear the innermost core messaging of our Hearts, the most Whole Field Integrative and thus most Conscious place, we all have within. It seems we must create a huge shift from being in our world within a constant state of being fear based, and thus mostly hyper vigilant. As well as always narrow band 'thinking only focused' on problems alone, with a mere 7-8% our intelligence being lit up on board - to help us. More toward finding a way to be in our world within an ongoing state of ever more expansively whole awareness field open, and thus constantly now totally relaxed wide band, 100% here and now awake grounded, constant endless solution generative extensiveness. In the very sort of direction that is going to help us become the most Full-On open Wise-Dome Field of Awareness Enabled we possibly can. In such a way as to best help our Self's Co-Creatively invent the very most beautifully intended, love caring solutions, as Yes-We Possibly Can. In the face of whatever circumstances we may find ourselves most Whole Heartedly involved within!

Illustration # 22 – In This Largest Possible Respect - It's Really All About Every Singular Most One of Us Learning to Unify our Very Own Unique - Made In the Image Consciousness Principle - Into that Most Heart Core Centered Sense of True Whole-Ness we All have Within - Wherefrom Yes It Is Possible to finally Find Ourselves now fully Able to Golden Flower - As the most Precious One-Ness or God-Ness Loving Higher Hu-Man/Woman Most Beings - Yes We-Can Possibly Be

In huge sense, that the full-on awakening of our very own Sacred Hearts Within. Appears to hold the innermost key to our possibility to integrate not only our left brain within our right brain, our passive receptive potential within our active expressive potential, but most importantly our basic animal nature within our greater potential to be most fully Heart Open Loving and thus ultimately Co-Creatively Empowered Enabled in ultimate Harmony with the Great Mystery Source of One-Ness or God-Ness ITSELF. To the point wherein our very beings might now begin to actually Golden Flow Flower - as though we will have become our very own every cell of our whole nervous system intelligence awakened. And thus many thousand petal-ed - Big Awareness Field Now Blooming - Golden Lotus Flowers or for that matter Lilies of the Field - we can possibly be. In the huge sense of us now finding ourselves actually being so awake to our inner most central Hum Love attuned place. We will now be able to actually hear our HEARTS, constantly guiding us moment by moment ever more Wholistically forward. To such a degree it will be like we will have found our true happiness oriented, constantly guiding us forth meter within. In each unfolding moment, telling us just how we may now sense what form of action will make us most truly happy - next. As if to say, why not move into Divine Playing this or that particular truly Hear Felt Motivation - every right now.

With the big difference being, it will now be our Heart's - which will become the very center of our Hu-Man/Woman most Intelligence, to help keep guiding us forth. Not our mere split and divided head's alone. Inasmuch as our Human Heart would appear to be the most sensitive measure of all things, we as Hu-Man's may ever choose to manifest ourselves forth with respect to - from within. The actual truth is, there is no more sensitive measuring instrument, in the whole of this great world, than that of our Human Heart. In other words, the more we learn to trust in the easy going effortless flow, of what our Whole Love of Life sense of ourselves. May be authentically messaging to us to be involved with doing- every right now. Especially in relation to our very best set intentions. Not what we merely 'think' we 'must be' doing, or how we 'feel' we 'have to' compulsively be behaving, with only half our brain power on board - alone. The much larger reality of our Whole Hu-Man Nature is that no part of our split mind alone, can never possibly know what surprises may be in store for us. In relation to just how our much larger awareness field may be attempting to help us realize all our goals. How many times have we for example, exactly when we are most in our 'flow zone'. Found our self's as if being most effortlessly guided, to be exactly in the right place, at the right time. Exactly running into the right next pieces of information, in the right moment etc. etc. etc. This then is exactly why it becomes so important to learn to trust in the guidance of whatever we might most love to do from the very inside of us. In the much larger sense of us letting our Heart Meter be our best guide, within every right now. In other words, our much more basic reality is we will either positively love whatever we may be Co-Creating right now, or we won't. This in greater wisdom means, the great chances are, if we don't totally love whatever we are Co-Creating right now, nobody else will either. So why bother, much better to dive totally into whatever we may Love Most, inasmuch as it is only then, that One-Ness Itself can help us to be in our flow zone - totally on track with our highest possible Hu-Man intentions?

(Accompanying Explanation – You may want to read Carl Jung's - 'Secret of the Golden Flower - Now. As well as everything you can find about the consciousness oriented principle of Synchron-I-City - he constantly referenced. Not so different from Kurt Vonegut's idea of having his main character enter the Chrono-Synclastic Infindibulum - in his award wining novel the Sirens of Titan. Perhaps with a new found sense of appreciation for what they were both attempting to point our whole Hu-Man race - toward! In the huge sense that, the more we help ourselves fully get that learning to live our life's from within our most full-on here and now to infinity & beyond embedded awake - and thus whole being lit up intelligent potential. Is all about awakening ourselves to the Great Mystery of pure unlimited Uni-Versal, Hum Singing & Dancing Everywhere Energy, being able to come totally through us. And thus that making an agreement, to attune the very Heart Core most central processing Unit of this most sensitive quantum level processor, which we all have within each and every One of us. In such a way as to melt the very Heart core whole of our selves, totally into what amounts to a veritable Ocean of pure Hum Love Energy. Is really what engaging toward the best possible life for our Self's, is truly all about. Isn't it time then for every-one to finally Sea the Point? There appears to be no other way than by way of Love It-Self - for us to help ourselves find our way toward being fully enabled, to actually manifest all the true happiness we every One of us so much long for! The only great life challenge is, that it seems to require a certain here and now effort - of growing ourselves ever more full-on up Awareness. In order that we may thus help each of ourselves fully awaken our innermost sense of our most essential Self. Into an actual Experiential Realization of this most One-Der-Ful, total true found Love of Life, many thousand Petal-Ed Blooming Golden Lotus Flower – true Wisdom place we all have inside of our selves. Such as can best help us to actually Co-Create ourselves ever whole being Ful-Fill-Ment forward - in the best possible resonant harmony with what amounts to this - To Infinity & Beyond way Big Picture Love Hum Resonant Whole!)

(Note - This is a perfect time to watch the Dr. Rick Strassman & Associates DVD - 'The Spirit Molecule' or read the book by the same name - Here! Which ultimately is all about our entirely natural, most Heart Center Open possibility to keep helping ourselves generate. The very sorts of Pure At-One-Ment Energy attuned states of Higher Consciousness, we have been talking about here! Via our innate given possibility to keep on generating a continuous stream of natural DMT or Spirit Molecule Initiated - Way pure Energy Awareness Elevated States. Of the most Well Beyond Ordinary, Indeed Extra-Ordinary Pure Aware-Ness Found Wisdom - Within our Self's! Such as our book cover and image just following attempts to Illustrate – in terms of our potential be become fully Conscious Beings - Heare! No longer at the mercy as if way too driven - by our Un-Conscious or mere Shadow Dark side!)

SENSING YOUR INNER MOST WHOLE-SUM I-AM WHO-AM WITHIN - AS SOME-ONE

NOW FULLY HEART OPEN & THUS MOST GLORIOUSLY SUPER INTELLIGENT

22

ALL INTEGRATED

WITH ONE'S	WITHIN
POSITIVELY HUGE	ONE'S MOST
BIG MIND LIT UP	VITAL ENERGETIC
HOLOGRAPHIC	OPEN & THUS
& THUS MOST TRULY	ACTUAL CLEAREST
SUPRA RATIONAL	SENSE OF TRULY
/ LOGICAL	NOW TOTALLY
WAY BRILLIANT	FEELING & EMOTIONAL
SOLUTION	FULL-ON FLOW ZONE
GENERATIVE	ENABLED
CAPABILITY	CAPABILITY

FULL BLOOMING

INTO WHAT AMOUNTS TO THE VERY CORE CENTER OF THE GREAT SINGULAR MOST INFINITE UNI-VERSAL - PURE QUANTUM LEVEL ENERGY - HUM LOVING SOURCE FIELD ITSELF

YOU UNIFYING INTO YOUR VERY OWN NOW SINGULAR 'I' & THUS TRULY MOST FULL-ON WITHIN AT-ONE-MENT MAGNIFICENT - GOLDEN CONSCIOUSNESS FOUND FLOWERING WHOLE

Here's the positively Huge Thing to get about our potential to enter into a much more Holo-Centrically Conscious - truly Big Picture attuned Viewpoint. All wholes contain every so called opposite, as part and parcel of the very same Whole. For example when it comes to referencing our Hu-Man/Woman most Higher Conscious potential, this kind of more Wholistic perspective implies we are both Individual and Collective at the very same time. We in other words all come in here with our own unique inner sensed interests and talents, yet we always find ourselves living within the context of a greater whole. Which is to say we are both separate beings, who have the potential to develop our own unique gifts & talents in our own right, to our max. While we all at the very time, are a most intimate part of One-Ness or God-Ness and thus of each other. In that much larger more Wholistic sense which makes it incumbent upon each us to develop our own unique gifts and talents. In such a way that we may help contribute, to the betterment of the Whole. Another way of saying it is that in terms of any more truly Hol-Istic perspective, it is quite impossible to separate our Individuality from any greater or lesser sense of Good God-Ness. Which in turn implies to the extent we keep choosing to function in Dis-Cordance and Dis-Harmony with that Whole-Ness - which is of One-Ness or God-Ness - In It-Self. We will thus tend to keep taking some part of any larger Whole-Ness we might be choosing to play with - down. Such that the moment we truly get this, our greater Hu-Man/Woman challenge becomes One of constantly discovering ever more effective ways to function in the best possible Concordance and Harmony - within all ever larger Wholes. Including within the Wholes of so called left wing politics vs right wing, so called ego-centrism vs so called holo-centrism, so called my family or tribe vs so called other families or tribes and ultimately so called Good vs all which appears Evil, etc. etc. etc.. Until such time as we learn to function within ever more Concordant states of Harmony with One-Ness It-Self! Not any easy perspective for any of us to keep manifesting forth from within - by any means!

In any case, there are many, many, examples of Hu-Mans Co-Creating such Beat-I-Ful things. We find our very breath being taken away by the utter Heart Felt Inner Hum Resonance such utterly Magnificent truly One-Drous Co-Creations - are able to engender within us. On the other hand we all know only too well, that we are far too often most sadly capable of creating various forms of ugliness to the extremes. What is being said here, is to the extent we ourselves remain split and divided within, so shall we keep manifesting in our world without. On the other hand to extent we grow ourselves all up into a place of true entirely Peace-Ful Heart Centered Whole-Ness within, so shall we find ourselves able to manifest ever greater degrees of Whole-Ness in the world outside of our selves. In other words as within, so we tend to create all about. Or as we hold below in our split and divided unconscious, so shall we find our self's manifesting above, in the world outside of ourselves. Whereas insofar as our inner world within becomes ever more Holistically core Peaceful Loving Conscious, so shall we find our ability to manifest Whole-Ness in the world outside of us, will keep growing in the direction of our ability to manifest true Harmonic Beauty in this world. The facts are it appears to be we ourselves as Made in the Image Beings, who must take response-ability to become fully no longer split and divided and thus fully Conscious – Beings Within. Ho! This is just the way it is within the context of this great Mystery of One-Ness we all find ourselves living within, which constantly speaks to us of our potential to become fully Non-Separate Conscious! Other than Wise our rather sad reality is, we will continue to keep making messes of our lives in the world outside of ourselves. In the much larger sense I have already pointed to, which reveals the rather oxymoron foolishness of us continuously trying to manifest Peace in the world outside of our Self's. Insofar as we continue to refuse take those Response-Abilities which seem to be required - for us to actually find true Peace-Ful Loving-Ness on the insides of us - first.

Ask any of our most brilliant great product inventors, in any field of endeavor? The very sort of inventors who over some longer term focus, have found themselves suddenly now to able share with all of us. The upper In-Sighted Strato-Spheres of their very greatest talents, beyond even their wildest dreams! And they will tell you, at some point the very best of them began to realize, that their greatness had not so much to do with themselves. Inasmuch as at some point they began to realize, they were not the actual doer of their great deeds. Merely the Source Graced vehicle, who had been blessed to finds some way to get their little me, me, me identified self, so well out of the way - in relation to their particular given talent. That brilliance itself was suddenly able to more completely come through them. Very much as a consequence of being able to get their constantly trying to make it happen mere little 'thinking' minds alone, more out of their way. Even though it is true, it was their particular unique passion which is what most motivated them to become totally involved. In whatever they truly most loved to learn about - in their first place. Become brilliant not just in the huge sense of being able to mobilize their greatest possible intelligence forward, toward the invention of some great expression! But also in the greater sense of their being able to shine their feeling & emotional light's so brightly forth, they were blessed to find themselves elevating into a place of realizing something appears to be going on here. Which could be said to be truly well beyond any ordinary sense of mere ego limited self! To such a degree that in moments like these, typically you will find inventors of such great totally in their Flow Zone great expressive Solutions. Bowing them selves in total reverence for having found their connection to that well beyond ordinary, now Big Mind inspirational place within, which makes all such Brilliance possible.

In this huge respect, Fritz Perls the world famous inventor of Gestalt therapy, was once heard to say. You are not really painting (or for that matter doing anything from within the integrated whole of you). Until such time as you find your brush now

254

Wriggling, very much as if by it-self. In the Chinese Tao'st tradition they for example have developed a concept to express this much larger head completely out of one's way, Heart totally in One's most effortless doing of non-doing, way. Wherein One becomes full consciously enabled to express one's very best developed talents and interests - to One's most brilliantly capable max. They refer to this way as the Wu Wei, or much larger more whole being empowered WU or non-doing WEI of doing things. Whereas in the West we refer to this place wherein we find our ability to so totally let go into the moment. We end up finding our mere narrow band adrenalin motivated and thus mostly problem focused mere halfwit head alone, completely out of our way. And our much larger wide band expansive, and thus way more hear present refined awareness now totally found within us. In such a way that we in this more whole being lit up WAY, end up discovering that most phenomenal 'totally in our flow zone', now truly Big Mind awake place within. Such as ends up helping us realize our most optimal peak performance capabilities - being most blessed to now come through us!

Imagine then, YOU having helped grow your self all up into Being so awake, so alive, so in Love with life. So attuned to the most powerfully inspiring place of excellence within you, which involves being attuned to the passion of your Heart. Your state of presence would now enable you to become unto your Whole sense of Self - like such a swirling, vortically whirling, effortlessly empowered power ranger like Spirit Warrior - of this positively great underlying/beyond lying = Super Light Source. You would now find your whole sense of self now so non-separatively and thus non-dualistically open heartedly motivated. By the Co-Creative power of your virtually Inventively totally in the moment now Unlimited - Big Mind. You would thus within this Wu Wei zone like state, now be way miraculously enabled. To spontaneously express your self in terms of what would amount to your very own, best possible Light. Based on a way of being completely let go into every nuance of whatever might be going on for you in any given moment, including your whole data base of past experience based - stored helpful In-Form-Mation. Much in the same way that a jazz musician might most lovingly improvise each next note, based on whatever basic musical line was being stated in any given moment by some other musician(s). Similar to the East Indian raga tradition of improvising music, wherein I once heard Ravi Shankar demonstrate. Just how it is possible for 2 separate tabla & sitar playing musicians, to at the end of many hours of here and now presence oriented jazz like improvisational dialoguing. Come into a place of such At-One-Ment attuned Synchronicity, they were suddenly able to improvise exactly the same notes, in the very same moment in time! Does this help you get just what it might be like - to be this well beyond ordinary non-locally attuned - to something greater than mere Separate-Ness?

255

Hopefully this helps you to now much more fully whole being 'Grok', just whom or what the most 'Quantum attuned You' - we all have within us - Is Really All About? And in relation to just what this Biggest of All Pictures - Is truly All About? In much greater sense that you within your very own Whole-Ness, actually by way of your own found ability to actually be in your Wu Wei head completely out your way, Heart completely in your Way Flow Zone. Appear to have the actual potential to so Tap into this At-One-Ment Source. In such a way as to thus find the most enabled possible sense of Your Self, now actually able to manifest the very sort of positively great totally Ful-Fill-Ing expressions of Your Self. Your Wholiest highest possible Self, may most find your Hu-Man/Woman most Self longing for. Not just for you, but everyone around you may keep coming into contact with. Exactly in relation to whatever heartfelt oriented, and thus whole being motivated intentions you your very own Self. You may keep finding your self most choosing to set in front of your largest possible sense of your Self. Inasmuch as these Heart-Felt motivated expressions, are exactly whom you were meant to bloom into. In terms of exactly what you have been most uniquely designed / evolved - to keep manifesting into form into this greater Whole. In the huge sense that we all of us thus in this way as One, have the potential to become the very sort of beings who are all enabled to Co-Create the Heaven we all long for. Within this Great Magical Mystery Tour Journey, we all find ourselves embarked upon. Whether we choose to become conscious of what this journey is really All About. Or much too our collective dismay, continuously keep choosing to Knot?

Note - In order to help your Self fully internalize just how it is possible to keep listening to the ongoing here and now guidance. Of your very own now evermore quantum Love Hum Om Ho attuned, and thus constant stream of Heart centered - Self help Messagings within. With every respect to how you may help your self best fulfill the whole of whomsoever you your self may find your self most wanting out of your life here. This is a good time to search for - Dr. Sereda's various free greater awareness enhancing videos on youtube including It's Time for all of to truly Heare Our Heart - Meditation. Which can be enhanced by choosing to listen to Tom Kenyon's Gandharva Experience (or Angelic like Choir) Humming along in One's background. Insofar as this and/or other forms of Heart stirring music and singing, can help to provide optimal heart resonance awakening support re our possibility to better attune to this realm of inner sensed - Quantum level Hum Love.

<u>Critical Warning All You Be-Loved's of the One & Only Singular Most Source - Which appears to Reside at the Very Root of All that Ever Keeps Manifesting into Creation - Please Take ye Most Care-Ful Note</u>

➢ If you were Good God-Ness It-Self. Would you not offer as many pathways as possible, to help all of your every own Made in the Image Hu-Man-Kind - actually find your most Sacred Everywhere Presence?

➢ Fortunately for all of us we have for centuries the world over - always been finding ways to elevate our sense of just whom we all have the potential to be. Into way more holistically conscious ways for us to live ourselves forth!

➢ One of our biggest problems however with respect to just how yes-we-can all have access to this state of more truly Conscious Awareness. Is that very much as a consequence of various forms of mere belief based and thus small mind mis-interpretation alone. As opposed to us being willing to take those response-abilities required, which can lead us into real actual experience under-standings - of this Presence. Each culture has been trying to claim that their little narrow band mind and thus mere belief based ways alone - are somehow far better than other people's ways!

➢ Such that this old one-up-man-ship game has tended to lead to endless rounds of so called religious based conflict. Even when heaven forbid based on the non-separate from One-Ness state we all come in here with in our first moments of life. And are often most blessed to repeat peak moment experiencing throughout the course of our lives. We should all of us really know - so much better!

➢ Fortunately more and more of us are beginning to realize, that all of our very greatest teachers and teachings have been pointing to the very same under-standings. For all of us to help our higher most Hu-Man Self's – to actually realize within.

➢ Which declare - that not only is this One Source out of which all things manifest. Most essentially an Underlying Beyond Lying - Force of Love!

➢ The very sort of Source of Love that is constantly via an underlying hum sound - based on a constantly emerging sacred geometry and ever expanding fractals - keeps Quantum Source Flower of love emanating - everything into existence. We ever to infinity & beyond can come to know!

➢ But also within the greater mystery of our own 'made in the image' manifestation into existence. It is our possibility to grow ourselves all up into the full blooming of our Human Most Sacred Heart's within.

➢ Which best enable us to attune into this fundamentally Loving - Here & Now Present Great Mystery Field - in such a way that we may thus end up best empowered - to keep on Co-Creating ourselves forth into the very sort of whole being fulfilling lives - we all of us so much long for.

➢ Especially insofar as more and more of us appear to be passing through very sort of to infinity & beyond prophesized portal - envisioned by many differing seers within various ages throughout our world. Such as seems to reside at the very core center of all existence, our selves included. About to elevate us into a new golden age of Love based Abundance and Prosperity for all Hu-Man/Woman-Kind.

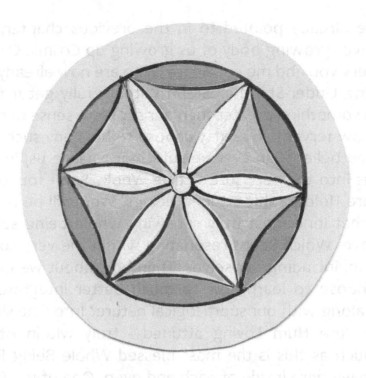

Huge Grand Wisdom Lesson # 9 - In Our Much Better Agreeing To Now Hear That Continuously Ongoing Love To Do Guidance - Which Can Constantly Be Heard To Arise Every Moment - Within Our Very Own Love Hum Attuned Hearts

SUCH ATTUNING IS THEN PRECISELY WHAT MORE THAN ANYTHING CAN NOW BEST HELP US - TO KEEP STAYING IN THAT CONTINUOUS WELL BEYOND ORDINARY GREAT GRAND FATHER SKY ATTUNED FLOW ZONE - WHICH IS OF OUR MOST EXCELLENT HAVE A POSITIVELY GREAT LIFE - SOLUTION GENERATIVE EMPOWERMENT

IMAGINE COMING INTO SUCH FULL BLOOM - YOU MIGHT ACTUALLY NOW FIND YOUR SELF WAY ENABLED - TO COMPLETELY FULFILL YOUR INNER MOST ESSENCE - IN EVERY ASPECT OF YOUR UTMOST GLORIOUS POTENTIAL TO BE

"As we have already pointed to in the previous chapter, given that there appears to be an ever growing body of us growing up Cosmic Charlie's & Quantum Katie's, just like every you and me out Heare. Who are now already much better able to truly whole being Under-Stand or Stand Within - fully get it finally 'Grok'. That merely believing in something greater than our separate sense of selves in our heads alone, no matter how fervently we may choose to hold any such abstracted by us - mere thought based belief? Can ever be sufficient to save us, in the much greater sense of turning us into the very sort of true Wholly Spirit found Awake, and thus now way Big Picture Holographic attuned beings. Who will be fully able to actually now truly Heare, that innermost truly satisfying whole being sensed, One Source generated Hum Love. Which keeps resonating within the very core of all that ever manifest's into form, including our selves. Then how about we every singular most One of us now choose to learn how to much better integrate, our feeling and emotional nature, along with our supra logical nature? Into One singular most Heart centered Field of Pure Hum Loving attuned - truly within At-One-Ment found Awareness? Inasmuch as this is the most blessed Whole Being Found Intelligence Resource - we all have here inside of each and every One of us. To help us keep on Inventing our highest possible Made in the Image sense of our Self's. Into the very sort of way more Holo-Centric oriented King Dome of Heaven within found - Some One's. Who will end up being best able to help our selves actually realize, all of the actual inner most '7' vital energy motivated Hu-Man Ful-Fill-Ments, any singular most One of us - might ever choose to seek."

"Heare ye all then now in the context of all this, is a positively great time for us to sound off an even greater truth, my much more inner wakeful and thus way more Clear present found - Every One's. This really Big Picture is even more truly Miraculous, than it is possible for any One of us to even <u>Imagine.</u> Because the moment we can truly now as more Wisdom Oriented truly Magical adult's, finally fully get. Just how we all have the possibility to enter this inside place of being truly now One Great Heart Open. And thus totally non-separate great Peace-Ful Mystery Source attuned. - The more we will begin to sense just how this most Great Mystery attuned sense of our Self's, can actually bring into form. Whatsoever manifestations we may totally choose to bring into our no difference from Loving-Ness or God-Ness It-Self - way to infinity & beyond connected Largest possible Heart's. <u>Inasmuch as we will by this very same stroke of way more grown up inner wisdom - now begin to put our self into a position of becoming as actual Co-Creative Sacred instrument partners - with this great Mysterious Source / Force of Love. Which is to say, actually finally find our highest possible sense of self being the very sort of extra-ordinary Some-One's, now able to Co-Create Invent our Self's into. The very sorts of intended manifestations which will now actually be able to Resonate in almost 'Unbelievable true Loving Harmony'. Within what amounts to this infinite well beyond ordinary, Great Force Source's many and varied all around us manifestations, constantly</u>

appearing before our very innermost I's. In ways that will actually be far more 'effortless', than we have heretofore even dared dream possible. Rather than as the sort of adversaries who will continuously keep divisively reacting, as if we are somehow against this fundamental One-Ness Source which appears at the very root of all Creation."

"To help you now more truly stand completely within, this last and most precious of all great wisdom lessons. Inner wisdom would like to now share with you One particular parable, from Jesus the Christ's famous Sermon on the Mount. Where this great wisdom teacher was reported to have said," 'See the Lilies of the Field & how they Bloom, though they neither Toil nor Spin.' "Spin in the non-sense of keeping them selves staying as if lost, in the endless debilitating spin of their own particular long past emotional psycho drama's. Much as in the way we small split and divided mind humans, way too often seem to do. Based on our still incompletely felt through, and thus still unresolved same old inner Dis-Ease with our Self's held tendencies. To keep on law of attraction repeating similar sorts of pain & suffering experiences for our selves. Nor Toil in the non-sense of way too often trying to make them selves happen, from their way limited, me, me, me, mere small little narrow band 'thinking minds' alone. In perpetual isolation from their sense of being non-separatively inter-connected - within amounts to this huge unlimited to infinity & beyond - way Big Holographic Field of At-One-Ment. Just as we in our smallest mere halfwit sense of our selves, way too often tend to keep trying to do. 'Yet Solomon in all his glory was never arrayed as any of these.' "In other words, no matter how much we may constantly keep toiling & spinning to try and make things happen, from our way too egotistically limited, mere 'halfwit split and divided mind perspectives', alone. No matter how much seeming splendor we may seem to keep on manifesting, in relation to our smallest most constricted sense of our selves. We will never find ourselves full blooming quite so gloriously, as do the so called mere Lilies of the Field."

"See the whole point of this great metaphor all of my most dearly beloved's," inner wisdom was to now go on and trumpet. Much as though Gabriel/Gabriela him/herself was mind blowing his/her Angelic most - Horn. In such a way that the Whole of our Hu-Man Kind world might finally truly Heare! "It's like lilies of the field don't keep trying to 'think' themselves into bloom - within what amounts to letting their mere halfwit intelligence alone keep ruling them! All of you 'stupid is, stupid does people who keep pretending you are in all your mere halfwit ways, as though better than any One else out Heare'! They just get on with quite naturally In-Plain-Sight, most Whole-Sumly in the Wu Wei - Fully Blooming Themselves. Into the most Fully Beauti-ful, Hu-Man/Woman most Beings - possible! Simply because our huge bottom line is, the moment we find ways to get past all our tendencies to keep on being as if lost in far too much e-motional fear based 'spinning'! Not to mention staying way too lost in our mere halfwit little mind 'thinking' based ways of so called rational/logically always trying to make it happen 'toiling'. We actually have been given the innate Heart attuned Flow Zone capacity, to bloom even more gloriously than the lilies of the field. Even more gloriously than all the mere material wealth, such as Solomon in all his in separation holier than thou - supposed Royalty. Was able to display in all of his seeming outer world accumulated glory, alone. In other words we have been designed / evolved to bloom far beyond even our wildest dreams. Into the most truly glorious '7' vital energy Ful-filled Beings, we could ever hope to imagine. It is only our tendencies to get lost in endless mere halfwit 'spinning' and 'toiling' - which tend to keep us getting in our very own way. With the utmost respect to our much greater actual possible-abilities - to truly actually Be in every way most Whole-Heartedly - & thus completely in Full Bloom Ful-Filled!"

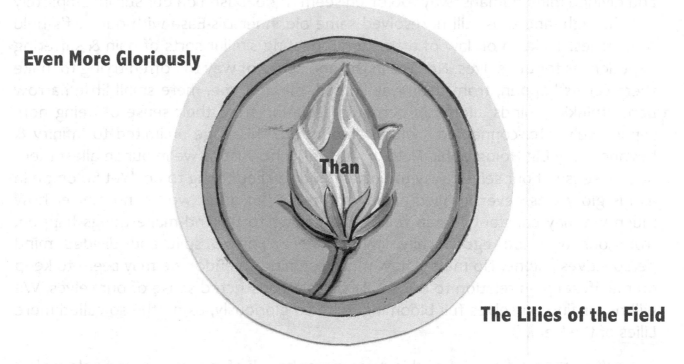

Even More Gloriously

Than

The Lilies of the Field

"Which is to say, based on the huge inner wisdom contained in this great Lilies of the Field parable. You could well say no mere self-centered accumulator of wealth & riches alone. Has ever been able to bloom into his or her fullest possible, fulfillment potential. As long as such a lost, living only in separation from greater Whole-Ness, mere outer shell Per-Sona of a being. Might keep choosing to remain attached to the notion that they are the ultimate Source Force, behind any such higher Hu-Man/Woman found empowerment. Such as seems to be required for any of us to fully bloom into those most radiant possible super light attuned Golden Flowering Beings, we have actually been designed / evolved to Be. In other words, you your self have actually been brought into form, to bloom even far more gloriously than any mere flower of the field, or any mere King such as a Solomon or for that matter Queen like Sheba, who might keep trying to make him/her self glorious. By way of the development of some mere part of their being alone. In separation from what would amount to all One's parts being brought all together, into a state of true Whole-Ness. Or to make it way more clear, the sort of state that could be described as Being - in One's true found Holi-Ness. Which is from what we have been presenting Heare, really far easier for every One of us to Realize than we have ever been led to merely 'think', is actually possible for any of Us! It's just that it seems to require a certain persistent effort of our awareness, to help ourselves find our Heart Guided Beyond small self Flow Zone, on a regular ongoing moment by moment, daily basis."

"In other words for us to discover our possibility to Full Bloom even more gloriously than the mere Lilies of the Field. Does in terms of being a what's so about our human most nature, seem to require our willingness to finally One Big Singular Energy Ocean - truly now Sea. That this fullest possible Bloom Potential of ours, will never come to any of us by way of us being as if lost to the constant endless over reactivity emotional pain of our fear based emotions. Nor by the constant mere small mind 'thinking' based toil, of our seemingly endless always in separation only, ceaselessly trying to make our Self's happen, mere half wit efforts alone. It can only come in-so-far as we find some way to 'link' the very essence of who 'We All Together' in our most awake Heart of Hearts, have actually been designed to fully Be. In such a way as to help our Self's actually live within that very underlying / beyond lying One & Only Source Force - which exists well beyond anymore mere me, me, me ego-centered self-fish-i-ness, alone. Or, well beyond the non-sense of our much smaller endlessly spinning & toiling, mere child like ego identified and thus non-fully sensed, sense, of our much more Wholly Integrated largest most expanded possible Self. Which is another way of saying. 'It can be as difficult for a rich man (or to put it even more clearly, some non-heart centered and thus Un-Wholly Integrated - Man/Woman) to enter the King-Dome of Heaven within, as it is for a camel to pass through the eye of a needle!'"

"Oh my God, Gosh Golly Gee, Holi of Holies most One-Der Ful Wisdom Wizard Within! It's Kind of Like what you are saying, is that the most awake attuned I-Am who We-All-Really-Are - With-In! Actually is as you say, a most intimate part of the Great Unitary most, Super Light Field Mystery, which ultimately is of One-Ness or God-Ness Itself. And as such it appears we have actually been designed/evolved out of the Great Singular most Super Light. In such a way as to actually finally find Our Self's as effortlessly empowered Co-Creatively attuned pure whirling energy Vortices - of this Super-Light! In order that we may now Be unto our Self, as the very sort of Some-One's who will now actually Be as if cradled, to now actually live right within in the loving arms of the everywhere present Divine. Or that great Grand Father/Mother like Source Force, out of which all things manifest! Much like when we would fall asleep cuddled in our mother's or even father's arms, as young children. And they would heart to heart connect with us so sweetly, while singing their inner/outer Hum Love song to us with such tender Loving Care. It would be like we would melt into that most special Hum Love place, wherein it would seem like there was only but One Huge Big Heart beating Heare. Such that in moments as precious as these, whether rare or frequent, we would feel so safe inside our very Core. We could now wake up into our next play ourselves forth day, as if safely cradled within the arms of this Big One Love It-Self - now fully on board within us. To help us play our most essential Core self's ever forward, into yet another positively fabulous day. Far more effortlessly than we may have ever even dared to dream possible - way beyond our wildest of dreams?

"With the huge point here being, this very same sense of being Cradled as if in the Arms of Love It-Self! Is still even more fully possible for us for us in terms of our willingness to actually find, our truly Magical Miracle making Adult's within. Provided we might now make that most essential inner agreement, to wake our inner most sense of most essential core Self, 'So All Up'. That yes we will now actually be able to keep hearing this great Hum Love Force, which seems to core resonate within the very essence of positively every single thing all around Us. In such a way that this Hum Love will Now be able to fully sing It's to Infinity & Beyond Great Love Song, within the very core of Yes every Us, just as well! Without us anymore still 'needing' our parents to help us get, to this most precious place within! In such a way that One-Ness It-Self can now get to know of IT'S greatest possibilities, (or worst), through each of Us?" Exactly by way of each One of us now in every next ongoing moment, choosing to get involved in our very favorite inner most fulfillment calling out to us, love to do oriented project(s)."

I.E. "Such as getting hands on involved in own unique inner most callings, including reading books and other forms of information gathering supportive learning, even looking for great potential teachers in our fields of interest or choosing to go to the very best kind of learning institutes most likely to help us better our given talents. Including learning to much better truly Heare, whenever we feel so totally out of sorts with ourselves. That what most help us, would be for us to take the sort of inward orienting break. Such as might actually help us, to totally clear center ourselves back into Perfectly Brilliant Loving Stillness. In such a way that might now within the context of such re-found Still-Ness even find our selves being pulled into either this or that new direction, for no apparent mere half witted rational/logical seeming reason, at all. But more because our inner most attuned quiet place Flow Zone place within, might now guide us toward who knows what kind of new perfectly synchronistic surprise experience. Such as would be most follow our very own Yellow Brick Road likely, to help us keep getting our very best on with our most Heart attuned projects. In this respect it is always really quite

263

simple, what might our heart be telling us n relation to any given one of our innermost in the moment, vital energy callings. We would most love to be involved in, every right now,. For example as we have already alluded to, it is in this much greater self respect said that when tired a more enlightened being will choose to rest so completely they will soon find themselves re-charged. When hungry they will arrange to eat the very best of healthy foods available, when motivated to get totally involved in their favorite project, or even take some sort of desired restful or even seemingly divergent break from their favorite project(s). This is exactly when they totally go for how they sense themselves to be guided, in such a way that they pretty much never in any given moment of such inner most attunement. Choose to go against the flow of whatever it might be that their in the moment love to do Heart Core, is most guiding them towards!"

"Oh, My, Good, God", every truly hearing Cosmic Charlie & Quantum Katie in the whole of this world, now found them Self's most De-Light-Fully and thus In-Sight-Fully – exclaiming unto his/her most profound sense of Self! It's like what you are telling us, is that in our fully internalizing our very own ongoing sense of being connected this well beyond ordinary Huge to Infinity & Beyond Maxi Non-Separate Whole, which we all of us actually are most intimately a part of! The much greater Ful-Fill-Ing Reality for us will be, that in our now constantly choosing to be way more actually in our Heart most Centered flow. With respect to whatever may be calling out to us the most, in any given moment of our being here. We will now find ourselves not only being guided toward loving everything about what is involved in the living forward - of our own sense of Life in each ongoing forward moving moment of our lives. But also actually now wanting to bring our much more awakened to this love hum place, whole being found intelligence within. Into exactly whatever we may choose to keep on inventing here, in this every moment to our max. The only place from within which Yes-We-Can, actually invent the totally loving, true found Happiness Fu-Filling Lives, for ourselves we all most long for! Far more effortlessly than we have heretofore ever dared to dream possible - even beyond our wildest of dreams!"

"Yes, Yes, Halleluyah, Om Shanti Om, Allah Akbar, Yaweh, Wakan Tanka Ho, Nam Ringio Ke - to that most Sacred Heart Place. We all have within each and every One of us - my dearest most beloved Every One's. For now you have finally got a way full sense of the Big Mysterious It! Which exists both within you, as well as at the same time, well beyond you? How blessed can You-Be? In the Huge sense that this Love Space appears to be not only way bigger, but also way more helpful than we ever before in our much younger days, could have ever imagined. To help find our Self's as beings now most effortlessly guided to keep on Co-Creatively Playing into form. Just exactly whatever great intended solution generative possibilities, we might now find our inner most attuned sense of our Self. Most loving to discover to how play best forward. For the whole rest of each way more fully grown up, day, after day, after day of our Life's. In fact our great big well beyond ordinary self realization now is, that every day of our LIfe's can always be, in well beyond ordinary thought, word, and deed, truly extra-ordinary! Provided of we of course, each of us constantly agree to keep on under-taking whatever response-abilities may be required. For us to continue that very Great Spirit attuning pilgrims journey, it seems to take. To make our whole sense of our very own inner house 'I' - ever more fearlessly fierce forward playing - truly Lovingly One-Ness attuned Singular. Much in the very same way that we already know, we each of us must be the One's, who take response-ability to build a great house for our self, in the world outside of our self. In such a way that we may keep transforming all of our self's into the sort of huge beyond our wildest dreams - Some-One's. Who would now be totally most respect-fully here and now empowered to actually manifest the greatest possible garden of Eden like, constantly great solution generative life, that we lal long for. Except now of course, from within a place that is beyond anymore non-sense of conflict either within my self, or beyond my self. And thus truly in the greater sense of living in total unified harmonic resonance within my now well beyond ordinary, much greater sense of my now ay more truly Loving-Ness oriented - Being-Ness. In-So-Far as I will just keep agreeing to Heare and keep Following - my very own now fully Heart Open, attuned to the great Love Hum Super Light - sense of my self. And thus my very own yellow brick golden rainbow illuminated Road or Pathway, such as keeps on arising within the very Heart of Me, in such a way as to keep guiding me toward all that I most long for."

"Good Golly Gosh Darn Gee our most beloved inner Wise-Dome place of pure wholly Uni-Fied unlimited Awareness - Within. Now that we by way of the constant practice of these 9 methods of Awareness. Can truly way more effectively much better Sea, that it's very much like we have all been most blessed with a total True Love of all forms of Manifestation, always upside take action orienting - truly extra ordinary High Voltage Meter - Within. Which can be sensed to reside inside of the very Heart Core of every One of Us. Such that the more we discover how to listen to this Love to do Heart messaging meter, constantly telling us what we would most truly love to do in every right now moment. The more we can thus with our greatest sense of inner found 'Life' and 'Liberty' now way more fully on board awake within us! Constantly thus keep using our most extra-ordinary, purest possible Love Hum attuned and thus greatest possible Total Love of all Life Heart Meter. In the very sort of ways that can actually best help our Wholiest of all sensed Self's, keep us thus manifesting the truly Wholly of Holies actual Whole Being Ful-Fill-Ments - we all long for. Insofar as this inner listening to our Hearts actually is the very best means we have, to keep on guiding our own unique innermost essence's toward the 'True Found Happiness' we all so much deserve. In marked contrast to our way too constantly listening to our mere fear based forms of endless emotional spin. Or other than wise always trying to mere half wit mostly in our heads alone, keep pushing ourselves toward what we merely keep 'thinking' is success - toil!"

"This in turn is exactly fwhat makes it possible for us to much better Whole Being sense, that who we really are! Is both a very special Some-One, as well as just Another One. Who actually by way of this inner attunement, can truly Be our very own most unique sense of fully Lit Up, poetic like Power Ranger(s) of the Uni-Verse. And thus the very sort of Some-One's who by way of us actually becoming fully Miracle making Co-Creatively Empowered, Magical Adults. Will now have the possibility to come home full circle in the much greater sense of us being fully enabled to live our ways forth. As if actually cradled in the arms of Uni-Versal Love It-self. No longer as mere children constantly 'needing' the cradling arms of our mom's and pop's or for that matter anything else outside of our Self's. To help our own sense of our Self's keep on creating positively great ongoing True Happiness oriented solutions in the context of living forth our lives. Simply because we our Self's will now have found, that very underlying beyond lying Loving Hum Embrace - of One-Ness Itself. In such a way as to help our Self's actually be most likely to keep on attracting towards our Self's given this world of constantly ever challenging situations. The greatest possible inner Happiness oriented solutions, not just for our small egocentric only self's. But also In-So-Far as we ourselves keep roaming through-out this constantly ever emerging virtual Loving-Ness Ocean - of endless ever greater true Happiness oriented now actually Co-Creative possibilities. Now for Every-One else's way larger all around us Made in the Image of One-Ness It-Self. And therefore ultimately largest most expanded = actual Tap our Source connected sense - of what amounts to our One & Only. Hugest possible and thus most Holo-Centric without limits sense of our Self."

"In other words in our now way more consciously actually getting to Know this place of our most Magical Effortless - Whole Being Awake Flow Zone. This becomes exactly how every One of us learns to most sensitively listen to what our Heart Core attunement is attempting to attract toward us. Via that great non-local, synchronistic at a distance, well beyond ordinary great life oriented time clock. Which exists within the very everywhere present Still Point Core - of our Uni-Verse. Of course always in relation to whatever great intentions we may be thus by way of our Heart Core Hearing, keep choosing to set before our Self's. In the much larger sense that this is exactly how we support the inner most sense of our most expanded possible core Essence. Into actually being effortlessly guided to be in the right place, undertake exactly the very best possible action, in precisely the right moment. This is exactly how we learn to completely 'Let Go' into the Wholeness of our very own Purest possible Big Picture attuned Awareness. In such a way as to now Let the Force of Love Move Us into One now Huge Heare & Now - total Love of Everything attuned Happening. Every single Cosmic Charlie or Quantum Katie - Sky

Walker of this Singular most Uni-Verse who we all of us really within our very Heart of Hearts, actually most are! Rather than as some sort way too effort-ful, and thus constantly stressful doer. Who will always far too desperately keep 'trying' to make various things happen. From our much narrower fear based / mind locked - egocentric point of view alone only! As though we are somehow wiser than that Singular most Source-Force, which can be heard to Hum Resonate Within. So that we may thus fully Bloom our greatest possible inwardly oriented process of ever greater solution generative 'In-sight', constantly newly invented forward seeing 'Words', and of course total 'Peace Loving oriented Deeds'. Into the vey sort of truly Miracle making Magical Adult Children of this everywhere present Source Force of Love. By way of our learning to completely let go, or totally surrender, into this very moment of our now Big Heart attuned Guidance. Which actually is non-separate from the great Oh My Good God - Mysteriously Loving Everywhere Presence - of One-Ness Itself."

Illustration # 24 - Every One's Now Wholly Natural - Completely small Mind Blowing Actually Truly Most Incredible Uni-Versal – Now Big Mind / Big Heart Now Fully Awake & Therefore Most Conscious Whole-Sum 'I' Integrated - Philosophers Found Wise-Dome Stone - Which Is of the Purest Possible Awareness

Which amounts to No-Thing more or Less than our most Pure Full-On no holds Barred - Beyond All Bounds without Limits. Capacity to keep on endlessly totally Heare & Now Full Conscious Loving - In every Way we may thus keep Choosing to fully Be. Cause From the point of view of Pure everywhere Present Energy - endlessly 'Flower of Love Humming' - IT'S most Uni-Versal Love Song within positively every single thing we ever come to Know. In pure energy truth since we all of us actually appear to be a most intimate Holographic interconnected - and therefore same Source Made in The Image Part - of every singular so called thing that every manifests into form - Here. The way great news is the very moment we learn to open our whole nervous systems fully up enough, into an inner place which is well beyond any more fear based or mere idea attached resistance. We will thus find our Self's able to sense this pure underlying / beyond lying everywhere embedded, Uni-Versal Harmonic Flower of Love manifesting all things into form energy. Totally now Hollow Bamboo like completely free to Hum wave IT'S way both all our way within, as well as all the way through our Self's. In such a way that this Love Energy will at the same time so roar, so soar through the ever expanding - Still Calm Zero Centered Point within Us. And therefore through the actual Warm Whole of our ever more present truly Heart Loving sense of being. We will now within each and every moment start to Heare & Now an inner Heart Core based Messaging. Constantly most effortlessly attempting to guide us toward each next unfolding moment - of our now way more Heart Centered Awake - every ongoing action. To the point wherein we will now find our Self's more and more able, to just trust where our Heart's are attempting to guide us. Within the context of whatever great intentions we may keep choosing to put most up in front - of our own uniquely talent gifted Love to Do Self's.

To such a truly One-Der-Full degree, our days will now seem to just keep humming so lovingly along. It will be as if we are living within what is going to amount to a veritable - completely Big Picture One Ocean-Sea Heaven - here on earth. In such a way as to thus constantly keep finding ourselves as though now most miraculously enabled - to keep-on playing our most Love to Do sense of Self's ever forward - toward the actual Ful-Fill-Ment of virtually all of our most truly whole being oriented goals. Always now awake enough, to keep our Self's constantly under-standing our highest good. Has not so much to do with giving our prosperities and abundances away. As it has to do with helping every 'One' else Yes We-Can - to find their very own sense of whole being empowerment. So that they too can manifest to their very own Hearts attuned content. All the inner most found prosperity and unique whole being fulfillments oriented abundances, at all '7' levels of their very own inner most beings, as they possibly can to their own max. Now in conjunctive harmony with whatever the rest of us, may also love to play at most. Ho, this is the way of complete Ful-Fill-Ment, and thus the only way for us to end up totally loving life. With the very Whole of our now entirely Peace-Ful, totally great solution oriented - Holiest of Whole Being-Nesses. The only question remaining, is what degree of integrity do you really most want to manifest for your very own within At-One-Ment attuned & thus Truly Love thy Neighbor as thy Self - Greatest Possible Sense of your Self?

(Accompanying Explanation – With the whole point Heare Being, that in our so agreeing to learn how to love positively everything, including thy neighbor - actually as thy Self! Not merely only as 'though' - they are thy Self. And then 'only' when it seems to suit the more fear based, mere mind locked non-sense of our much smaller mere ego-centrically focused self - alone. Here through the Golden doorway of our fully open Hearts is to be found our cosmic Uni-Versal pathway. Toward the fulfillment of positively every thing our innermost beings, may now truly sacredly grounded - within our Heart of Hearts - ever truly desire! Always remembering that loving all things made manifest, does not in any way prohibit us from using all things made manifest. It only points to the larger sense of us agreeing to find ways to truly appreciate, in such a way as to now totally Love, positively everything we may ever choose to use. From within a much larger Total Loving-Ness for all that we are most blessed to keep receiving. From within this Now truly Whole-Sumly completely Big Picture Holo-Graphically In-Tegral, which is to say God-Ness In It-Self Embedded - Framework.)

24 Cosmic Consciousness

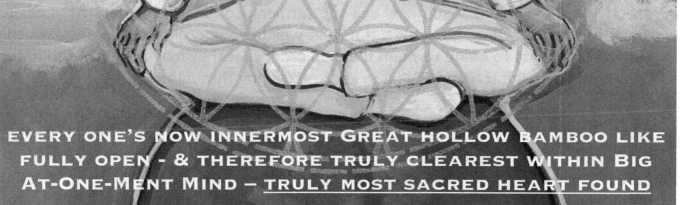

EVERY ONE'S NOW INNERMOST GREAT HOLLOW BAMBOO LIKE FULLY OPEN - & THEREFORE TRULY CLEAREST WITHIN BIG AT-ONE-MENT MIND — TRULY MOST SACRED HEART FOUND

POSSIBILITY TO KEEP FLOWER OF APHRODITE LOVE HUMING ALONG - WITHIN POSITIVELY EVERYTHING WE EVER EXPERIENCE ESPECIALLY INCLUDING INSIDE OUR NOW WELL BEYOND ORDINARY - WHOLIEST POSSIBLE TRUE PHILOSOPHER'S WISE-DOME STONE & THUS MOST ACTUAL JOY-FUL FOUND SENSE OF OUR SELF'S

WE ACTUALLY BECOME THE WORLD - INASMUCH AS IN OUR MOST PURE ENERGY AWAKE TRUTH - IT SEEMS WE ARE A MOST INTIMATE SAME SOURCE INTER CONNECTED MADE IN THE IMAGE PART - OF EVERY EACH OTHER - AS IN 'I' & MY SINGULAR MOST ONE & ONLY FATHER SKY / MOTHER EARTH MAKER - ARE NOW AS 'ONE'

"In-so-far as you should therefore not find your self, in such a way as to be left, saying unto your smallest non-sense of self. You simply can't, don't know how, or claim to not be able to trust your own innermost Heart Centered - great Wise-Dome guiding forth - place within? Ask any truly great brilliant Co-Creator who has found themselves most blessed to bring forth some new level of great wisdom product, or upper end level of performance, in any field of endeavor. And they will tell you, that at some point in their development. They were able to realize, that it was not their outer shell self which was felt to be responsible for their great work. They themselves were not in actuality the great doers, they used to 'think' they were! Merely the well prepared vehicle for some well beyond ordinary level of Co-Creativeness, to be able to come through them! From within some in fact extra-ordinary Source Tapped Into place - Inside of them! Such that in coming to this realization, such brilliant co-creators suddenly find themselves now able to end up bowing the whole of their beings, in total reverence and respect. For all the Co-Creativeness they have been blessed - to receive. In such a way that within the context of this new found humbleness, they are now able to accept that their gifts have not been meant for themselves alone. But to be shared with all who each in their own unique ways, are part and parcel of this very same great Mystery Field out of which all such manifestations can be sensed to arise out of, just as well. Which is exactly why you will hear so many peak performers, continuously offering heartfelt praise in totally gratitude, for the gift of that well beyond ordinary greatness, which has the possibility to come through them. In order that they may thus help facilitate this Great Force Source, continuing to keep on coming through them."

"Is this what is meant by, the statement that 'the kingdom of Heaven can only be found within' - great inner wisdom teacher within? Could this be what it is like to be in actual Whole-Sum-Communion with our Great Gran Father/Mother, or that pure left whirling / right whirling energy Source Force - out which all things manifest? Is this what people mean when they ask us to become fully conscious, and thus to be truly Big Mind - Big Heart - Big Picture awake truly now En-Light-End as to just what is going on Heare. As opposed to letting our selves be far too driven, by our more un-conscious egocentric fears & self doubts - alone? Which are what in turn, seem to keep dragging us down into the pits of being not much more than mere - 'fight or flight' seemingly reptilian driven animals. On the other hand by the same token, we are the only One's here as the non-separate Son's & Daughters of this Mysterious Source Force. Who can ever even hope to find our most fully now conscious - now truly Magical most One-Der-Ful ever forward playing - well beyond bored fully grown up miracle making Wizard's. Which we have all been so blessed to actually have - within - each and every One of Us? To help every One of us manifest the very Garden of Eden we were promised here on earth. Provided the more of us agree to learn just how we may now clearly Heare - that Huge One Love Hum which under pines the truly Big Picture - of It All!"

"And how shall we know whenever any One of Us is actually being as an ever more non-separate, and therefore well beyond ordinary, now effortlessly empowered. Ever growing all up 'Mustard Seed' like Vortex' of the Great Singular most without beginning or end, One & Only Loving everything into form - Super Light Source - In It-Self? By the following combinations of way more Holo-Centrically embedded & thus inner most integral states of Awareness, we will now find our Self's experiencing. For example, instead of us way too constantly trying to small mind only, keep 'thinking' our way through the various difficulties and challenges which the living of our lives will constantly tend to bring. We will suddenly find our more essential sense of our Self's having way more Big Picture attuned patience, to now wait for our very best possible decision making process to fully ripe within us. In such a way as to find our Self's actually being ever more effectively Heart Flow Glow guided. More from our now Holo-Centrailly embedded within One-Ness It-Self, insides-out. Into our ongoing state of way more spontaneously continuously arising in the moment, truly inner Heart Felt found sense of well beyond anymore self doubt - most essentially Peace-Ful-Ness oriented Clarity. Which will now tend to be much more constantly ongoing inspiring, uplifting, full of grace gratitude. And most specially Over-Flowing with the very sort of Peace-Ful oriented Heart sensed Loving-Ness Knowing. That will enable us to now live our life's forth toward the fulfillment of our very best intentions, from within a place of Pure Good God Connected-Ness - in It-Self! Rather than from our mostly me, me, me Ego-centrically focused, outsides-in only!"

"Which is to say, we will now know of our possibility to spontaneously, whole field of awareness inner essence full bloom, even more gloriously than the lilies of the field. Precisely by the very way our very Heart's will now start to continuously glow flow guide us. Into the very sort Super Light Source Awakened Beings, who will thus now find our Self's with our head's alone way more out of our way - and our now Heart Flow Zone Centered sense of our Self's, way more completely in our way. In such a way as to actually find our Self's now best enabled <u>By our Love, By our Love,</u> to keep on manifesting all that we long for. In the much larger sense that based on our very own now new inner found, total Lovingness for all of One-Nesses Creations. We will now forever after keep choosing to focus all of our innermost sense of, 'Life', 'Liberty' and True Happiness seeking, and thus positively all of our Hu-Man/Woman most vital fulfillment motivating energies. Toward helping every singular most One of Us, to actually Be as genuinely Oh My Good God greater solution Caring & Sharing empowered. As yes we now Know we actually Can-Be! In order that we each of us may thus constantly align our Whole Being Found awareness, toward our possibility to keep Vision Seeing our now greater collective good intended, every way forward. Into the Co-Creation of totally Loving Healing solution outcomes, for the All of Us, not just some egocentrically identified - supposedly select phew."

"Always in other words, exactly in relation to our truly greatest 'Hu-Man Kind' found collective potentials, to keep on Co-Creatively inventing the very best possible. Ever greater Whole Heartedly Loving oriented outcomes, it is possible for any of us to keep on generating here. And of course ultimately always within a context of us constantly showing our utmost truly inner Peace-Ful found, Loving most respect for every Hum Love manifested creature, indeed all Love Hum engendered so called things, whether great or small. Re every kind of challenging situation we may ever find ourselves faced with. In such a newfound way that every One we now know, may come to hang out as their very own individually magnificent Love Humming Birds and Bee's. Within the context of all those various prosperity generating Mustard Tree like branch and leaf things, we our Self's have all the inner Quantum level attuned equipment we require. To help One-Ness In It-Self - keep on evolving into ever better new branch & leaf like forms. Insofar as our own most Whole-Sum found Divine At-One-Ment Consciousness, or pure Loving Aware-Ness place within. Will now be getting to Know of It's very best Heart Warming - Co-Creative inventive possibilities. Precisely by way of no-thing other than that most expansive sense of pure, quiet, still, inner core Peace-Ful Loving-Ness for that One-Ness ever manifests forth - we will now have found within. And which we will now o keep choosing to put into whatever One-Ness intention oriented decisions - we may keep choosing to make."

"In marked contrast to those very worst forms of our mere ego centrically focused, seemingly endless Harm-Ful manifestations. Such as tend to keep taking us down into being in Dis-Harmonious conflict, with this Singular most - Seed Source. In such a way as to way too persistently, beyond all greater Whole Being found reason. Keep keeping our mere small ego Identified self's always choosing to rationalize various Dis-Cordant ways of being here, with all Source manifest creatures. Particularly in all those ways that will tend to keep as many people in one's small mind focused life, as helpless and dependent upon one's own controlling whims and self determining interests, alone. As our 'means' to keep us mostly devoid of our possibility to actually be more truly in our Heart of Hearts, egocentrically 'thinking' in our 'split & divided' head's alone. That we are somehow better or holier than any given other - some One else! Far too often based on our way too resistive, backward looking reluctance to vision see, a much more Holo-Centric future for all of Man/Woman Kind. Which in It-Self would seem to indicate to any clear sensing being, that any such half wit felt or other than wise rationalized messages, for us to in any way keep being Harm-Ful. Could only be coming from the utter non-sense of far too many of us, way too often continuously choosing, to keep living in mere ego-centric focused separation, from the Loving Source of all things alone. Which most unfortunately for the greater whole of us, is how far too many of us keep choosing to live ourselves forth. In our so called modern, mostly me, me, me alone focused, lack of greater found Wisdom, way too ultimately Whol-E-Ness destructive - world today. (This may be a good time for our readers, to review the great how to grow our Self's fully up parable, of the Mustard Seed, Matthew 13, 31-32!)"

"Which is to say, part and parcel of this great open ended Co-Creative Magical Mystery Tour, we all find ourselves born into here. Is that ultimately within the context of that Greatest of all Truth's, which has since time immemorial been posited by pretty much every One of our very greatest, great Mystery attuned Spiritual Teachers. Who keep declaring unto us, that we all appear here as a most intimate part of the Great One-Ness or God-Ness, and thus of each other. It ends up being completely up to each of Us - to keep finding ways to discover our very largest possible within At-One-Ment attuned sense of our most Whole-Sumly, actually single I integrated - true found Self! Indeed discover this One-Ness, in such a way that the Force of Love or the Force of our most Integral Heart found Intelligence It-Self - 'May Always Be Within Us'. And thus always enabled to come through us, in every way we may now choose to manifest our own unique senses our greatest possible Self's, ever forth. In the largest possible sense that ultimately the very best way we ever have to evaluate any of our Co-Creations. Is going to have to do with the degree we can sense any given wholly integrated Intelligence based - inventions of ours. In such a way that any such Co-Creative invention will end up being Harmonically Hum Resonant with that sense of Whol-E-Ness or One-Ness we all have the possibility to keep finding here, to begin with. Which is to say, the time has come for our Hu-Man/woman most living within the Great At-One-Ment family, to fully realize that what the Great Whole has always been, and always will be about. Is always about the survival of the Whole, not some mere at expense of everything else, supposedly superior part of that Whole. In the very sense Bruce Lipton attempts to point to in one of his latest DVD talks 'Spontaneous Evolution'."

Other than wise, to the extent we keep choosing to live with these 3 most intelligent aspects of our self, continuously divided and in conflict with each other. I.E. 1.) Our greatest possible sense of 'Life', or our so called right brain full-on vital energy empowering intelligence fully on board within us 2.) Our greatest possible sense of 'Liberty" or our now so called left brain constantly ever forward moving, abstract rational logical inventive intelligence fully on board wholly integrated within us 3.) & Certainly our greatest possible sense of that most Core Central whole Intelligence integrating processing Unit, we all have within us, our Hearts. We will just keep on, keeping on, as if lost in endless circles of the same old, same old pain & suffering ways of living out our life's here! Constantly law of attraction manifesting, all kinds of in varying degree's hell on earth experiences, for our little split and divided self's, exactly as we so much fear. Very much as a consequence of our holding unto whatever fears and self doubts, whatever mere narrow mind ideas and beliefs we will so desperately keep wanting to hold onto inside of our Self's, and thus in front of our self's, in our first place! No matter how many mere glimpses of this Whole Big Hue Unlimited without beginning or end Heaven, we may on occasion find ourselves most blessed to receive!"

"Perhaps the simplest possible way to say it, is that 'All Our Way In' toward the total dissolution of all our fears and self doubts, all of our small mind mere idea & belief based abstract Identifications & Attachments. And thus always onwards and outwards, into that place of our now total unbound expansion, wherein we will suddenly find no more separating boundaries, between us and our One Source Maker! And thus between us, and all our very neighbors! Is the only way for us 'To Be All Out' dissolved into that most Whole-Sumly Integrated, poetic like Wholiest of Holies Uni-Versal Sea of everywhere non-local present Consciousness - which ultimately is of Infinite One-Der. Such that Yes, each & every One of Us actually Can become now as our own Co-Creative partners with the great Mystery of One-Ness Itself. Always able to roam this Great Singular most Ocean with the utmost respect, for that most expanded possible sense of our no-longer separate from One-Ness or Good God-Ness potential - to most fully Be. In such a way as to become most effortlessly capable of Co-Creating the most One-Drous of Holo-Centrically focused, truly great Life improvement Solutions - for every singularity engendered One of Us. In the much greater sense that Holo-Centric Vision Once truly full Under-Stood! By It's very all encompassing Nature always encompasses any felt sense to resort to back Ego-Centrism for a time, in order to help us focus on our own felt wants & desires. Whereas mere ego-centrism alone, by It-Self, can never fully grasp the greater truth of Holo-Centrism! And will thus always if left to it's own mere egocentric ends alone, by way of it's way too limited narrow band focus. Tend to keep self sabotage destroying even it's very best of intentions! Ho, in this much greater sense it appears we have come to a time for all of our dearest potential Miracle generating Quantum Katie / Cosmic Charlie Hu-Man/Woman most - Adults Within - of the One & Only Source! To now find ways to keep playing our most Whole Sum found sense of our Self's - ever forth. All our way out to our very Hearts Utmost Content from both within & into every unbound without limits - Heare & Now! For in our so playing, Yes, this is not only the only way Any One of Us Can ever even hope to find the all various '7' vital energy centered 'True Found Inner Happinesses' - we all every singular most One of us - so richly deserve! But also the only way we can ever hope to manifest the ultimate harmonic Loving Peace-Ful-Ness - we all long for.

Looking to Summarizing Illustration # 25 – Actually Knowing of God's Love

Image Therefore to Show Our Singular Most Source Force's Manifest Positively Every Here & Now Love Hum Thing Way - To Keep On Ever Lastingly Loving Each of Us Back From Precisely Within An Entirely New Imminence of 'God' or 'Pure Love In It-Self' - Presence - Being Everywhere Present Most Especially Including Within The Very Core of Us Made In The Image Beings Ourselves - Insofar As We May Now Choose To Find Our Very Own Fully Open Heart Centered - Greatest Possible Truly Big Picture Connected Perspective

Inasmuch as everything about what we have been talking about here, has everything to do with our possibility to connect or tap link our own pure inner zero point found - unbound with At-One-ment energy essence - all our way Up. In such a way as to now fully sense the pure underlying / beyond lying Power & Glory energy essence - of every single things One & Only initiating everything into form - Same Source Force. That very Source Force of Love It-Self which can be sensed to exist at the very root of all that ever manifest's into creation - including our very own selves. It is precisely this possibility to ground with all of our Innocent most, here and now Mother Earth sensed - One-Der. As well as all out expanded into that most Whole Uni-Verse which of Only One Sky found Infinite Super De-Light. In such a way that we may now actually sense the everywhere underlying / beyond lying Love Hum, of this truly magnificent everywhere to Infinity & Beyond everywhere At-One-Ment Presence! Which we have been referring to as Divinity or God-Ness - in Itself! This linking all up possibility we all have, is then what more than anything helps us all the very most. To become as the most effective, actual Holographic embedded Co-Creator we can possibly be. Way more enabled within this great mystery of At-One-ment, to thus keep on inventing ourselves ever forward in way more total Loving Harmony with our Same Source. Except now in the much greater sense of us actually, being as though we are truly non-separate from this One & Only Source-Force of Love - In It-Self. By way of us agreeing to totally internalize Michael Angelo's famous highly inspiring reach out half way to this God-Ness from within our very own Self's - actually world renowned Image. And this God-Ness or Loving-Ness principle will reach more than half way back into us - to help keep on Inspiring us ever more Forward. Which he went on to paint on the Sistine Chapel in Rome

MICHAEL ANGELO'S FAMOUS PAINTING ON THE CEILING OF THE SISTINE CHAPEL RE-VISIONED - REACHING ALL OUR WAY OUT TO NOW TOUCH THE VERY LOVING-NESS CORE OF ONE-NESS OR GOD-NESS ITSELF - FROM WITHIN A WAY MORE TRULY WHOLE BEING INTEGRAL - & THUS WAY GREATER POSSIBLE – NEW FOUND HU-MAN/WOMAN KIND - PERSPECTIVE

25

TAPPING OUR SOURCE - OR GROWING THAT MOST QUANTUM HUM LOVE AWAKE STATE - WHICH IS OF US BEING NOW ALL DISSOLVED WITHIN THE ULTIMATE LOVING-NESS OF ONE-NESS OR GOOD GOD-NESS IN IT-SELF - IN SUCH A WAY AS TO HELP US ACTUALLY FIND THAT UTTERMOST VIRTUALLY UNLIMITED BRILLIANCE - WE ALL HAVE WITHIN

HERE IS OUR POSITIVELY GREAT HIGHER OR HU-MAN/WOMAN KIND - NEWS! THE MOMENT WE AS MADE IN THE IMAGE BEINGS - DISCOVER JUST HOW TO MELT THE UTMOST WHOLE OF OUR VERY OWN INNERMOST SACRED - BIG HEART AWAKE SPIRIT SHINING SENSE OF OUR SELF'S - WITHIN WHAT AMOUNTS TO THAT ONE & ONLY SINGULAR MOST TO INFINITY & BEYOND PURE GREAT OCEANIC LIKE ONE ENERGY SOURCE OF ALL - SAID TO MANIFESTS INTO OUR WHOLE UNI-VERSE OF THE MOST ONE-DROUSLY DIVERSE FORMS! INSOFAR AS THIS SAME EVERYWHERE PRESENT MANIFESTING INTO FORM SOURCE FORCE CAN BE SENSED TO LOVE HUM IT'S WAY ALONG WITHIN POSITIVELY ALL THINGS - ALL CREATURES GREAT & SMALL - THIS WILL BE THE VERY SAME MOMENT WE WILL THUS FIND OUR VERY OWN NOW TRULY CO-CREATIVE INSPIRATIONAL SPARK - TO COMPLETELY ELEVATE WHO WE ARE INTO THAT PLACE WHEREIN YES WE WILL NOW ACTUALLY BE - FULLY LOVE OF ALL ENABLED - TO NOW FULFILL ALL '7' DIMENSIONS OF OUR INNER MOST SENSES OF OUR SELF'S - EVEN BEYOND OUR WILDEST OF WHOLE-NESS ORIENTED DREAMS!

"Just one more summary note, inner Wisdom now felt motivated to further clarify! Although each of the '9' methods of awareness outlined here, have historically been shown to be complete in their own right. In the huge sense that each method is capable of carrying any One of us into that place within, which has been referred to as being in a state of In-Light-en-Ment. Nevertheless we seem to have come to a place and time in the history of man/woman-kind. Wherein we have the possibility to accelerate this potential we all have inside each and every One of us. To actually enter into this place of En-Light-En-Ment, or that King-Dome of Heaven found place within, at an accelerated pace never before seen in human history. By way of us choosing to combine all '9' methods together, into the very sort of progressively unfolding golden pathway, which can be both far easier and far more likely. To help us all begin to realize this state, for each of ourselves, within ourselves. Inasmuch as these '9' aspects or methods of awareness, are really part and parcel of the very same now whole unified, nervous system based principle, we all already have been blessed to have within us. Insofar as we might all just begin to agree, to seek and find this place of being well beyond ordinary linked up, tapped into, and thus empowered by, this very without beginning or end to infinity & beyond Magical Mystery Source Field. Which can actually be experienced within the very Heart Core of every us, to exist at the very root of all Existence. "

"In this huge respect the great news for us all is, that when these '9' methods are taken all together into helping support us to find a place of unified integration - within us. There is no longer any necessity for us to cloister into some kind of monastery or temple. Dedicated pretty much exclusively to some kind or another of meditative or prayer like awareness, practice. Which could well take several lifetimes to fully integrate within us. Much rather in our knowing how to apply the whole range of these methods or aspects of our pure nervous system grounded, awareness. To help us keep growing this pure awareness place within our selves. Makes it way more possible for us to integrate at least certain portions of these methods. Into any of our very own uniquely chosen, ongoing in the moment, daily routines. And thus as such, given they can be integrated into anyone's normal ongoing daily day life. In this sense, they are far more likely to lead to a much quicker realization, of that which at the very least can be under-stood - to be. The underlying / beyond lying essence of what pure meditative like - or other wise enlightened – awareness is all about. Such that eventually, the cultivation of these '9' aspects altogether, would in due course. Be far more likely to lead to the full realization of enlightenment, within way more of us. Wherefrom within this grater Wise-Dome place, we as a more collective humanity might actually empower ourselves, to live exactly from within, such a more truly enlightened place! With much greater respect this huge Unlimited Divine most Field or Ocean of Love, which we all find ourselves living - With-In! Which in itself appears to involve a constant ongoing, ever forward moving into Infinity & Beyond, state of pure Loving energy in motion. Always thus involved in the constant Re-Creating of what inevitably amounts to no-particular thing other than the ultimate Whole of It-Self!"

"Imagine for example, becoming in this respect so grounded inside of every part of your whole body all at once, within the context of each inhaling and each exhaling breath. In such a way that you would now be able to dive totally without an ounce of any more resistance, completely whole Heartedly into. The pure energy of positively every vital energy based feeling & e-motions that might ever come your way, in every moment of your existence. To the point wherein you would now sense your presence, as such a radiant field of light, within every moment of your existence. That your own energy field would constantly melt into sensing the pure energy essence of everything you might ever find yourself experiencing. Within such a profound innocent One-Der like way of being, that you would now find your inner most essence feeling such an inward state of pure perfect brilliant core Peace-Ful-Ness. It would now simply be impossible not to elevate into a state of being totally in love with everything you might ever experience, within each & every this very moment, of your existence here. In such a completely profound way, that your very love with regard to everything within existence, would now keep on inspirationally guiding you, to keep on inventing your love of all - constantly forward. In such a profound way that all your actions would now be aimed at an optimal love based harmonization, with the utmost truly reverend respect for everything all around you. Including the way you would be motivated to help other human beings find this same state of pure Loving-Ness within every moment of their very own Hu-Man/Woman Kind most Being-Nesses, for themselves."

"See the point, each of the '9' prior practices every One of us has been presented with, by our very own inner Wise-Dome of awareness principle. Are quite simply, part and parcel of the very same single unified state of our purest possible awareness, such as can actually be found within - by every One of us. With the implication being that ultimately, there is no other way for any of us to find the true happiness we long for. Other than for us to take that pilgrims journey which involves finding this state of our purest possible awareness, within us. As to why it is so, we cannot know! As to the reality of this being so, our whole point has been that we already within our innermost Wisdom, actually do already know. The reality of our potential for this greater awareness - to most clearly be so. (Please note, if you your self would like to read more about this huge full consciousness oriented difference, between our possibility to Be in a mostly me, me, me ego-centrically focused and thus to varying extents governed my our most unconscious shadow side, decision making place. And our Hum-Man possibility to grow our Self's full-on up into a more truly Big Picture Holo-Centric or true Love of One-Ness or Kind Dome of Heaven attuned place - within. We highly recommend Geena Lake's book on this very subject - 'Return to Essence' - How to be in the flow and Ful-fill your Life's Purpose.)

Illustration # 26 – An Attempt to Now Portray Uni-Versal or Quantum Love Hum Attuned Cosmic Consciousness - From the Point of View of Every Great 4 Corners of Our World - Spiritual Tradition

Huge News Flash - Given that our very best mystical spirit teachings from all 4 directions our world over. Have been from time immemorial attempting to reveal to mankind essentially the very same thing. Which is that we appear to be a non-separate 'Made in the Image' part of that great singular most pure great Mystery Field Energy Ocean - said to be of One-Ness or God-Ness It-Self. Why then do you suppose we keep agreeing to pretend that our own particular version of this One-Ness, or God-Ness principle? Is somehow way better than any One else's? If not that we still feel some kind of compulsive fear based, as well as small ego-centric mere abstract idea mind based childlike 'need' - out of our own particular histories of self doubt,? To keep feeling/believing we are somehow holier than various other some One's?

Wouldn't it make far more sense, if you were God-Ness or ultimate Loving-Ness in It-Self. That you would want as many people from all 4 corners of our world, to have some pathway to get to know of Your Ultimate - everywhere to be found Loving most Grace. Rather than to try and limit such under-standings, to a mere select seemingly mostly ego-centrically focused elitist my way of the highway -Phew. Clearly inasmuch as modern scientific based under-standings about the non-local nature of what amounts to the infinitely inter-connected - pure energy basis which seems to result in the formation of every dimension of so called reality. Are increasingly supporting the very same realization - which is that we ourselves appear to be fully Made in the Image capable of reflecting this huge to infinity and beyond Grand Uni-Versal Love Humming Hologram. Out of which all things seem to manifest into various forms, in any first place. Such that in these terms we could well now say, it actually does appear to be that 'We Each & Every One of Us - Are the World'. In the much larger quantum level energy Holographic Sense - that every One of Us actually is - a most intimate part of Every Other One. Perhaps the time has come for us to learn from each others found pathways, rather than to keep ourselves assuming such mostly ego-centrically focused statuses - about whose mere beliefs are somehow Whol-I-E-R than any other thou - same Source Made One of Us.

This helps explain why in most ancient so called aboriginal cultures - Shaman or certain gifted tribal healers - who would find ways to access such states of Pure Energy Awareness - Within. Have so often attempted to represent our power to access this state of At-One-Ment by way of wearing costumes in the form of certain special locally relevant animals. They would in this most Whole-Sumly Awake way - actually sense themselves to be in a state of non-separate wholly communion with? Such that to claim an experience of One's Heart being able to Soar Like an Eagle - would end up being among the most Brilliant of Metaphors capable of expressing our ability. To actually be in a state of such true Whole-Sum found Quantum At-One-Ment Energy attuned real Communion. With what would ultimately amount to that great singular most Only One Gran Father Sky - Progenitor Source Force? Out of which all things in this Higher Conscious way – can-be sensed to Manifest into Form?

Such that it would be precisely such a Shaman's ability to access these more pure energy embedded states of At-One-Ment consciousness. Which would end up giving them access to various seemingly psychic levels of well beyond ordinary healing power. As well as visionary seeing helpful insights to help their particular tribe move the most effectively forward. Certainly within the context of helping us get the huge cosmic joke behind our far too usual tendencies, to keep taking ourselves and our various less than full conscious psycho-dramas - way too seriously. Wherein such lesser more unconscious of this ultimate Whole-Ness or One-Ness, driven states! We thus so inevitably tend to keep taking ourselves down, yet once again! Into various forms of ongoing inner held pain and suffering, over and over again! As opposed to us finally being able to get that much larger self healing sense - within which we might actually start to know that positively everything in this greater actuality. Is really a non-separate part of the very Same One-Ness or God-Ness Source we in various ways tend to keep pretending to be Separate from. And thus in various self defeating ways, tend to keep keeping ourselves in perpetual self harming sickness engendering conflict - with both within ourselves as well as all around ourselves? In marked contrast to our possibility to finally be able to in good cosmic humor, completely heal our Self's of all former in separation Delusions. In the much greater sense of actually enabling ourselves to live right within this greater singular most One & Only Source.

Which is to say, Once any One of us truly get's this huge Cosmic Healing viewpoint. Which is that everything that ever happens, or that we may choose to do here, is really just another way for One-Ness It-Self to discover yet another of IT'S endless possibilities! The only question remaining, is how would you your self truly Love to way more Big Picture Consciously Play Out - the rest of your Life? As Some-One who now knows you are Non-Separate from this Source or God-Ness principle? And who therefore has your own possibility to invent your Self ever more forward, as a most integral intimate part of this great One-Ness Mystery! Or as someone who mostly 'fear based keeps feeling' 'or little mind way too constantly keeps thinking', that no-thing we do here in our mere half witted awareness alone, really matters? Does this help you too much better truly Under-Stand just why all of our very greatest of One Spirit Teachers, have always suggested? We make a decision to proceed with the living of our lives as Heare & Now Heart Centered Awake, as it is Hu-Man-Womanly possible for each of us to keep manifesting our way forth. Within what always amounts to this huge most Sacredly blessed – **Whole Mysterious Field of At-One-Ment?**

(**Accompanying Explanation** – With our whole point being that in so agreeing to help ourselves keep learning to totally Love everything, exactly as though we are actually a most intimate part of thy Same Source - of One-Ness in It-Self. Is to be found our golden doorway pathway toward the actual fulfillment of positively everything - our Hearts may ever truly desire. In the much larger sense that the Great Mystery of One-Ness actually appears to Wholly so Love us, so much! It is just a matter of us learning to trust the guidance of our One Source connected pure awareness principle - through the constantly guiding us ever more fulfillment forth messaging medium - of our most Sacred found Hearts - Within! Whatever tradition we may choose to thus help us! In this huge respect, you may want to check out Peter Russell's 'The Global Brain', as well as Howard Bloom's Global Brain - The evolution of Mass Mind - Here. As a means to help you finally get it, that One-Ness in It-Self has through some of the very greatest of us. Actually provided all of us with many diverse pathways, toward our possibility to find the very same Transcendental found state of Whole-Ness or God-Ness Realization - Within.)

Northern Warriors of
the Great Spirit

26

Such as the Legendary Hiawatha -
Black Elk & Rolling Thunder

+ Far Eastern At-One-Ment
Mystics

Like Krishna - Mahavira - Buddha -
Lao Tsu - Bodidharma & Quan Yin

Mid Eastern Only One Sky
Desert Walkers

Such as Moses - Jesus - BaHola
& Mohammed

+ Southern There Is But
One Earth - Love Healers

Like Quetzalcoatl - various SA Pachi
Mama's - including Africa's Shaman

SENSING HU-MANKIND AS NOW READY TO TRANSCEND
BEYOND EVERY OLD SELF LIMITING FORM OF MERE IDEA /
BELIEF - IN THE MUCH GREATER SENSE OF US ACTUALLY
BEING FULLY ENABLED TO BE AT-ONE WITH OUR MAKER

"Which is to say, to take this under-standing of our ability to stand within One's inner most awake Heart Resonance - to One's utmost Koo, Koo, Kajoob we are not separate from anything - especially our One & Only Source - max! It does actually appear my dearest ever more Cosmic/Quantum attuning - Beings, that our hearts in beyond 'Thought', 'Word', & 'Deed' truly do constitute that very place - Within. Which makes it most possible for us to actually now know, that we are not only the Walrus. But also that 'I am You', 'and You are Me', 'and thus we as One, Are All Together every singularity most embedded One of Us. In other words part and parcel of this Same Mysterious Source Force we keep referring to as God. Is that insofar as we ourselves might choose to now engage in the sort of growing awareness journey, which might best help us fully open our Hearts, totally. Into that very 'Quantum Love Hum Vibration', which has been said by all of our very greatest Wise-dome of Awareness Awakened Teachers. To under pine all that ever arises out of this most Sacred Source Field - into every manifest form we can ever - come to know. This all boils up to every One of us having the potential to learn to fly so high, into our now Co-Creative Light Shining Brilliance within. That our hearts will now begin to soar, as though we are each of us, like some now non-local, Fully Love conscious At-One-Ment Eagle. Enabled to fly 'All across the Uni-Verse in such a way, that we will thus feel constantly inspired within this Super Light Source Field of Dreams. To help Co-Create the most truly prosperous and abundant brilliantly Conscious Life's for as many of us, as Yes We-Possibly-Can! Thank you, thank you, thank you, Great Super Light Source for helping every One of us to now way more clearly see this! For in this Greater Light, we are all blessed to be here in ways that can actually fully enable us to now live ourselves ever more Lovingly forward. Completely non-separatively within this truly Un-Limited Uni-Verse - which In-Self appear to Be a Field potentially Endless Dreams In-Spiring - One-Der & De-Light."

"With respect to which Inner Wisdom added one last huge exclamation unto the utmost essence of It's very own - One & Only Self! Why it appears to now Be Innermost Wisdom, that there Is nothing left, but for each of us to keep-on Love Song Soaring along in Purfect Harmony From within the very whole of our very innermost full-on Heart Awake - Heare- ing place With-In? In every possible all together gone, all our way out, into each here and now moment. As Yes we now totally Super Light Soaring to infinity & beyond Tap our Source Present Connected, possibly can! All Hail with One Huge Humungous Miraculous most Reverend Over Seeing Everywhere present 'I' - Wow! To this positively no boundaries Unlimited - Biggest of All Possible Pictures - 'Singular Most Loving Source - Force! Which can now be most Whole Sum-Ly sensed by the very Heart of Us! To actually Be of No-Thing other, than that Pure Loving-Ness which can be Now sensed to actually Be, at the very root of all that ever Manifests into Form. (A variation on the famous Heart Sutra or Heart Teaching by the famous Bodhisattva - Avalokitesvara – first published as early as 2,000 B.C.)"

(Please Note – If you should find yourself at times, having been moved to places of Full-On Heart Open Joy, in relation to the various under-standings put forth in this book. We shall have made our point! In order to help your self fully internalize this inner space of being, as a now more effortlessly Empowered Vortex - of the Great One & Only Super Light! Watch for Dr. Sereda's youtube ongoing presented Quantum You Learning Academy series of greater awareness enhancing Learning Academy Lessons. Plus the endless series of implications for us that will come from the more of us ever more realizing such elevated states of Consciousness!)

NOW for One's Well Beyond Ordinary Totally With-In At-One-Ment - Oh My Good God-Ness Actually Truly most Extra-Ordinarily Joy-Ful V - Ninth Level Super-Light Empowering Vortex of Pure Energy Prayer Unto One's State of most Miraculously Integral

& Therefore Ultimately WHOLIEST Possible Fully Realized Sense - Of ONES TRUE NON-SEPRATE FROM DIVINITY ITSELF - SELF.

"Wowie, Zowie, Halleluyah, Om Shanti Om, Shazzam Kazam, Allah Bam, Ho, You All Yo! Inasmuch as my Heart is Now able to Soar Like the Winged Heart of a Sufi - even North American Kachina Eagle! Thank you, thank you, thank you, Great Miracle Generating Mystery Source Force. Tor this realization you have helped grow within me, is truly miraculous! Inasmuch as my most expanded sense of awareness now implies the Big I-Am, whom my very own unique Me-Really-Ultimately-Is most intimately connected to! Within the most quantum level attuned core of my most Big Heart Awake possible - Me. Is some One who can now be so Hum Love attuned to this Infinite Ocean of pure everywhere Super-Light energy - which exists all around. It is now possible for me to sense that this awareness of my now unlimited no boundaries sense of my self. Helps me like never before to be so filled with this everywhere present Love-Hum! I can now sense that Yes-I-Can now become as a constantly inspired, always in my flow zone. Effortlessly empowered and thus endlessly joy-fully happy, vortex of pure radiant shinning, great solution generative Super-Light! Unto my most essential Whole Heart Found sense of whom I most core found within, really Am!

In such a way as to now find my most essential Heart core Centered Self as if guided, by an ever ongoing stream of constantly moving forward - Single I inner seeing visions. Which my new inner whole being Insight-Ful found capability, will now actually be able to keep putting together before me. Most especially in the direction linking my own non-separateness all up with all those like wise Insight-Fully inspired, other Hu-Man/Woman presences. Whom I now sense within my very own ever growing, well beyond ordinary whole field of awareness, are most willing in their own unique ways. To jump totally on board this quantum level of within At-One-Ment - under-standing! In such a way that we may now help everyone We-Possibly-Can, realize this same place of effortless empowerment within. In order that we may thus play our most essential core Self's, all together ever forward as One. Into that very Garden of Eden which we all so much long for and indeed have long been promised! Provided we each of us might finally agree, to now grow our inner most wisdom of awareness - to our most extraordinary max."

Chapter 11

Clearly It's Time For All Hu-Man/Woman Kind To Develop A Truly Equivalent Both Inwardly In-Vestigative - While At The Same Time Way More Whole Being In-Tegrating & Therefore Far More Fully Oh My Everywhere Good God-Ness Real Actual Heart Felt Appreciative - 'Science Of The Inner'

INASMUCH AS LEARNING TO OPERATE THE WHOLE OF OUR OWN NERVOUS SYSTEMS WITHIN - HOLDS THE KEY TO HELPING OURSELVES ACTUALLY BE THE SORT OF SOME ONE'S - WHO MIGHT NOW SENSE OURSELVES AS BEING FULLY ENABLED TO KEEP ON INVENTING THE POSITIVELY GREATEST POSSIBLE FULFILLING LIFE'S FOR ALL OF OURSELVES - WE CAN POSSIBLY MUSTER

It is important to note, that each of the '9' methods contained within the prior chapter presented '9' greater wisdom oriented methods, for developing our clearest possible state of here and now present awareness. Are based on us learning to use the very same awareness principle that we have learned to use in relation to our usual scientific way, of investigating the world outside of ourselves. Inasmuch as the greater reality is, we have only 'One' same - awareness principle within ourselves. What's more this same awareness principle always happens for us through the medium of our own 'internal nervous systems'. Which is exactly why more and more of us are increasingly beginning to sense, just how important it might be for us to turn this same awareness principle inwards, as a means to investigate just how this awareness system seems to work - inside of our own selves. Particularly in relation to our possibility to optimally open - the very nervous system through which we get to know that world which exists outside of ourselves. In the sense of us learning to both inquire into as well as much better attune as holistically as possible within this nervous system we all have been given. In such a way as to encourage our selves to thus be optimally inwardly clear and thus more fully here and now present.

Certainly most of us can acknowledge that when it comes to the world outside of ourselves, it seems to take a certain responsibility to enable us to build a great life for ourselves. Yet no matter how much we keep pushing, constantly trying to manipulate, cajole, control, the world outside of ourselves in relation to our attempts to invent ever better standards of living for ourselves. We rarely seem to find the true Peace-Ful-Ness and whole being complete Love of Life we keep seeking, within. Indeed One might well be led to say, that it is precisely this tendency of ours to keep pushing, manipulating and controlling, which seems to result in our lack of inner found Peace-Ful-Ness & thus complete Love of Life within ourselves. Why then is it so difficult for so many of us to finally get it, that perhaps, it may be even more important for us to find ways to take response-ability to find this core Peace-Ful Loving-Ness within ourselves, first? As the very best gift we have to help ourselves manifest the true found Loving Peace-Ful-Ness we keep longing for, in the world outside of ourselves. Which is to say, perhaps it is time for us to take the very sort of collective - greater masses of us inwardly oriented response-ability? By way of us finding a way to come into a way more harmonic, truly now fully at home within ourselves partnership - not just with every aspect of the world that we might thus find - within ourselves? But also in the very same heart beat, with every aspect of the world we live in, outside of ourselves? In such a now much more internally clear way, that we might now be able to Radiate Shine with Light, help In-Still truly way more Holistically Inspired Solutions for ourselves, and finally bring ourselves into a state of so totally Loving everything about Life, and all that It has to offer. We would end up inventing this total Love of Life, into everything we might now ever choose to intend into form!

In other words the old we live in separation model, has kept allowing us to merely believe in some kind of higher force outside of ourselves, as the means to save ourselves. Whereas the new model wherein we might agree to learn to live in non-separation, seems to require that we find ways to be willing to take fully response-ability like never in the history of humankind! To keep ourselves ever more growing into this state of non-separation with our maker! Before proceeding further into this notion of more inward In-Vestigation, which in all probability would end up being human kinds greatest hope. Toward our collective possibility to invent truly Peace-Ful Loving ways of being with the Maker of All Things, All Creatures Great & Small. Let's take some time to reveal the huge basic difference between how outward investigation is designed to help us. And how more inward in-vstigation might be sensed to work, in ways that might help us way more.

• 	When it comes to a science of the outer, we agree to take some so called dependent variable in the world outside of ourselves, with respect to which we would like to be able to predict most probable outcomes. And then we proceed to measure some sub set of so called independent variables, which we deem most likely, to convergent into the influence some desirable measured dependent variable outcome. In such a way that we co-relate these independent variables in relation to our possibility to predict some so called looked for dependent variable outcome. In other words our science of the outer is very much oriented toward the prediction of some sort of other of - desired outer world oriented dependency.

• Whereas when it comes to a science of the inner, we end up choosing as we have already indicated by way having presented our '9' nervous system related methods of awareness. To now focus our in-vestigation entirely in-ward upon various dependency fostering variables within us. In such a way as to help ourselves dissolve or vaporize these various internal conflict resultant dependencies we have taken on over the course of our lives. Always in order to enable ourselves to become far more divergently expansively empowered now capable of inventing / creating. Entirely new now completely multi-variable independent, alternate solution generative possibilities. In relation to our prior intention set, most desired for our selves outcomes. In this much greater sense we say, that inward in-vestigation is designed to help fully liberate us, from all forms of dependency. In directions that enable us to create ever better future effective ways, of living ourselves ever forward with respect to both ourselves, as well as the world outside of us.

• Which is to say, more inward investigation involves focusing ourselves forward. Toward just the mirror opposite purpose of mere outward investigation - alone. Inasmuch as the whole intent of these kinds of more inward In-Vestigation, are all about enhancing our much larger inner sense of take action oriented, creative / inventive independence, from all forms of dependency. In such a way as to enable us to keep on best inventing our lives ever more effectively forward. Past all senses of us being mere passive victims of our more outward oriented sense of dependent possibility, alone. Wherein we keep feeling bad experiences just keep happening to us - beyond any sense of our possibility to become completely independent invertors of a positively Great way more Loving World.

So let's take a few moments to review these '9' testable science of the inner - independence enhancing awareness procedures. Based on what we might expect to happen given the internal application of these '9' already outlined methods of inner dependency reducing awareness - way more inside our selves. In relation to 3 distinguishably different nervous system based aspects of ourselves, which all together make up our internal experience. First, those of our first '3' methods or aspects of our Awareness which have to do with us making an agreement to use this very awareness principle. To now learn to inquire totally inward all our way into, both our more embodied present sense of our being. And thus at the same time into our essentially entirely unavoidable feeling & emotional nature such as tends to constantly go on inside our bodies. Our human bottom line is that the more we practice these methods, the more and more we are going to begin to notice, that who we really are. Seems to involve us much better sensing our potential, to be way more fully radiant alive awake to our inner force of 'Life' in itself. In other words awake to the awareness that we are not so much just seemingly solid entities only, as we are in fact the most incredible energetic systems, we might have ever before imagined. I.E. Hence Aspect: # 1) 'Being Whole body grounded embodied' - The more we encourage ourselves to in-vestigate what it is like to be more fully here and now sensorily present embodied, within the whole of every bit of our bodies all at once - every moment we can. The more inwardly here now grounded pure light energy present aware, and thus less dependently tense, we will now feel our own inner vital energetic presence's actually being. In other words the more we begin to notice that who we really are, is a pure energy generating system. aspect # 2) 'Feeling every Emotion that ever comes our way - Fully' - The more we in-vestigate totally into, in such a way as to thus feel totally through the vital energetic currents of whatever formerly pain body reactive negative emotions we may be still holding unto - inside of ourselves. The more and more independently vital energy expansive and thus emotionally radiant positive, we are going to find our vital energetic presence's becoming. With respect to our possibility to optimize our sense of all the very vital energies we require, to help ourselves move ever forward into the inner most fulfillment of our lives. Aspect # 3) 'Total House Clearing All Inner Held Self Doubt & Self Loathing' - The more we dive with our in-vestigative awareness directly into and thus all the way expansively through out, the various self doubts and self loathing's we still tend to hold in relation to whatever great intentions we may be choosing to set before ourselves. The less and less self doubt and self loathing - we are going find hanging around anywhere inside of us. To thus keep self sabotaging ourselves into way too constant co-dependent downer states - anymore.

Next, those subsequent of our '3' methods, which have to do with making an agreement to In-Vestigate into the ways yes we can develop our rational/logical capacity. To form abstract ideas and concepts about the world outside of us, such as we all inevitably find ourselves living within. To the point wherein we support our ability to now totally 'Insight See'. Not just that the greater world outside of us - is much more inter-connected and holistic than any of our mere mind based abstractions, can ever convey. But also, that this world both outside of us, as well as within us, is actually made of one unitary singular whole field of Pure quantum level energy - In It-Self. In such a way that this next level of in-quiry into our rational / logical potential has the capacity to completely total 'Liberty Free' us from being overly 'Identified With' or other than wise way to o 'Attached To'. Any mere abstraction which we ourselves are the ones who end up inventing into our various ideas & beliefs, out of this essentially Unified Field. In such a way that our new found Freedom can enable us to move ever more optimally inventively Co-Creative forward, toward the actual Ful-Fill-Ment of whatever various unique constructed by us - great intentions. Such as we may keep choosing to set in front of ourselves, in any first place. Which is exactly why the more we can encourage our own inner pure energy awareness, via Aspect of our greater Awareness # 4) - to keep our sense of Self's 'Expanding To Infinity & Beyond'. In such a way as to enable our more expanded sense of our Awareness to penetrate right on into the pure energy base which underlies the formation of all other things, in the world outside of our selves. The more we will find our selves having truly actual peak Oceanic like, total no boundaries complete inner freedom oriented - so called real religious experiences - with much greater respect to the world outside of ourselves. In such a way that will ultimately begin to help us fully realize that our Purest here and now most Present possible Awareness Principle, is not really separate from the Singular most Source Force Field of all Energy. In the very sort of direction which will thus tend to help us become ever more fully free liberated capable, in the sense of our actually being far more creative ideationally enabled to keep inventing ourselves into ways of living within this Source Field. Which are ultimately going to be way more holistically harmonic integral, than we ever so called conventionally 'think' possible. Insofar as we remain overly small mind frozen locked into, our old ideational identifications and attachments, only.

Aspect # 5) of our Greater Awareness Re-Claiming Our State of Innocent One-Der! When it comes to this next level, the more we can encourage ourselves to look at reality from within our potential to be in a state of Pure Energetically Attuned – In-Nocient like true One-der. In such a way that we now begin to help our Self's ever more truly see - the incredible inter-connected magnificent beauty - which exists at the very root core of all existence. The more truly excited we will find ourselves becoming, about all those endless ideational inventive possibilities we all have within us. In relation now to our now way more expanded possibility to be fully participatively, totally involved. In our very own everyday ongoing open ended, truly now creatively completely independent, great life oriented inventive process. In such a way that we enable our Self's to enter into this place wherein we have the possibility to truly See this most One-Drous beauty - which resides at the very root of all existence. Each new day and indeed every entirely new ongoing moment of our life's. The more we will begin to encourage Aspect # 6) of our Greater Awareness which can be said to involve the actual In-Still-Ation within ourselves, of the very sort of inner state which is going to be now way more 'Totally Peace-Ful. The more our state of inner Peace-Ful-Ness is going to help us to actually be far more optimally Co-Creatively Brilliant, on a daily ever more ongoing basis. Inasmuch as we are now going to be much better enabled to sense that this great field of One-Ness In It-Self, seems manifest everything it ever does into form. From within such a place of Perfect Brilliant Stillness - In it-Self. Which is to say, regular access to this place of Perfect Brilliant Still-Ness within, is going to accelerate our solution generative capacity to our optimal max - by the power of at least 10. In the much greater sense

292

that we are going to now find ourselves actually enabled to be so whole brain lit up all at once, awake to our now Whole Field of Awareness. Our possibility to now 'In-Sight Vision forward Invent See' our way much more holistically great solution generative, ever forward is actually going to become way more optimally enhanced. Always in relation to whatever positively independence oriented, have a way great life intentions, we may each in our own individual freedom given right. Keep choosing to set in front of our selves in terms of our own unique goals to totally Ful-Fill the very insides of our Self's. As opposed to us so much either/or piecemeal only, constantly trying to keep ourselves spit and divided narrow band little mind, 'thinking' our way forward, alone. In constant isolation from what amounts to a much greater sense of the Huge Whol-E-Ness - we all find ourselves most blessed to be living within.

And finally the last of our '3' nervous system based methods or aspects of our Greater Awareness. Which have to do with supporting ourselves to align with the most essentially Peace-Ful / Loving nature - of the pure essentially unified quantum level energy field - In It-self. To such a core centered open degree, we will now begin to sense our own inner / outer attuned pure energetic nature, able to now come into a much more full-on awake place. Wherein we will no longer experience ourselves as being in separation, but much rather totally connected into the very sort of place within. Which we will now enable us to fully realize a totally unified Tap Our Force place of communion - with the very Source of all of Creation within ourselves. In such a way as to inwardly align our very core essence, with the very qualities of Peace-Ful Loving-Ness - which this quantum Source Field seems to Hum along with - within It-Self. Insofar as this Huge Unlimited Source Field will now be sensed to keep on Love Flowering It's Way - into all of IT'S various forms of here and now present - manifestation. These last 3 methods of more inward inquiry then, could very well be said to constitute the most core center Sacred Potent - of all our inwardly In-Vestigative methods. It's time therefore for Aspect # 7) of our Purest Possible Awareness. Which has to do with the 'Practice Full Heart Open Great-Ful-Ness' for all the Source manifest presents we are so continually blessed to receive. Such that the more we choose to investigate, just what it is like to be fully Heart Open Grate-Ful for the incredible gift of total Loving-Ness we all come in Heare with. The more and more totally Whole Being Energetically Love Source connected In Love and thus positively independently self sufficient Empowered Co-creative, with the constant living forth of our lives. We will now find our inner core energy connection to all we have already been blessed with, able to Bloom totally forth from within Us. Insofar as this is the most inspirationally motivating place we all have In-Side, to help us keep manifesting forth - even more. Now for 'Tap Our Source Connecting our sense of our Self's Whole Up - with the Well Beyond Ordinary Power of Love' aspect of our Purest Possible Awareness # 8). The more and more in love with life, and thus in love with finding positively great holistically harmonious solutions - to every challenge we may ever face we keep encouraging our greatest possible sense of ourselves to become. The more we will begin to feel like we have the completely independent total love of life, actual Free Will Power Within Us. To help all of our selves Co-Create forth anything our heart's connection to Source - may ever truly most desire.

To conclude this great life journey, now for that aspect of our Purest possible Awareness # 9). Which involves our possibility to keep encouraging no thing more or less than our clearest possible Pure Energetic Dual Torus Manifold endlessly here and now Whirling into form sense of our Self's - Our Hearts. To actually 'Become Now as not more than an Effortlessly Empowered Still Point Centered Hollow Bamboo like Vortices - of the Great Underlying/Beyond Lying non-local 'Super Light Source'! In-As-Much as it appears the more and more well beyond ordinary pure Energy attuned to the very Center of our own Dual Torus - we choose to help ourselves become. In such a way that when all of these inwardly investigative methods are taken all together, the better and better we become at learning to actually Heare the most clear ongoing in every moment. Subtle energy messaging guidance of the energy of the Uni-Verse coming through our Hearts! Constantly attempting to tell us whatever we would most love to do in each next unfolding moment of our lives! Especially in relation to whatever great heart felt fulfillment intentions, we our own unique us may keep choosing to set in front of ourselves. Then the more and more able to keep inventing ourselves forward, in ways that are likely to enhance the harmonic good of the whole both within us, as well as around us. We are going to find ourselves actually being. In ways within which we will now sense ourselves to be ever more enabled to manifest the positively great even beyond our wildest dreams. Now way well beyond ordinary actually Whole Being Ful-Filling lives, we all of us most long for. Not just for ourselves, but for all those we within Our Heart of Hearts most come to Love, including our neighbors as thy self. Of course please under-stand, that there are many variations to these inner dependency reducing methods, which have been evolved by us in various parts of our world over our many centuries. With respect to this process of discovering our ultimate state of most Heart of Hearts centered - and thus optimally whole being awake now effortlessly Empowered Consciousness. Including the reality that insofar as we keep choosing to move ourselves ever forward, toward ever brighter positively brilliant - truly radiant shining futures. We will no doubt discover even more effective methods with respect to our possibility to optimally Empower these '3' principle dimensions of our innately given - now way more whole being integrated Nervous System Potentials.

In other words # 1.) insofar as we agree to use our most developed awareness principle, to keep In-Vestigating fully into our body and it's feeling & emotional nature. What we end up discovering is that our feelings & emotions are made of the sort of pure vital energy. Which has the potential to lift our most essential Spirit

Nature into a state of way more radiantly connected to the energy of everything - here and now fully Alive sense of our Being-Ness. # 2.) Insofar we might agree to use our awareness principle to actually In-Quire into the very essence of what amounts to our more conventional rational/logical based 'thought process'. What we end up discovering is that our 'thoughts' are merely figments of the gift of our highly unique Hu-Man/Woman most abstractive process. Designed via our mere abstractions, keep giving us the very sort of highly useful imaginal tools, that can best help us keep Co-Creatively inventing our way ever forward, into what amounts to a Unitary most pure Energy Field of At-One-Ment. 3.) Finally Insofar as we might agree to fully open our Hearts, what we discover. Is that our Hearts constitute that most unique integrative aspect of our potential for whole being Intelligence. Which can not just best help us to unite both halves of our brain power into a single Unified Whole. But which can also help us to so attune to the underlying / beyond lying loving Harmonic Hum Resonance, which can be sensed to exist at the very root of all existence. Such that via this attunement, we end all our way up helping ourselves to actually be best enabled to keep manifesting our selves forth, in complete Visionary Harmony with this truly Mystical - Biggest of All Pictures - Holiest of Wholes. Or what we historically have been referring to as the everywhere presence of that ultimate Whol-E-Ness - which is of One-Ness or God-Ness - In It-self.

See the huge point being made here, any truly In-Vestigative Science of the Inner. Is going to be all about finding our place of being so attuned to the Huge Unlimited Unbound Field of Pure Quantum Level Super Light Energy, which can be sensed to exist both within ourselves as well as infinitely beyond ourselves. Such that our ability to align ourselves totally up with our greatest possible sense of filled with 'Life' energy, fully 'Liberated' great life oriented now super rational / logical inventive energy, and last but not least a truly heart open, full-on totally peaceful loving and thus actual 'True Found Happiness' oriented energy. All of which ultimately have the possibility to lead us into what is going to amount to a much grander way more Miraculously and seemingly Magically Inspired Vision, with ultimate respect to our both our inward and outward Tap Our Source connection. Or, potential to be in a state of real holy communion with that truly One & Only Big Picture Source Force - which can be experienced to be at the very root of all so called objective reality. The positively great news for us is that it is precisely this sort of more inward In-Vestigation, which most helps take us into place of being far more Wholistically truly Big Picture solution empowered. Than mere outward investigation alone, can ever even hope to bring about for us.

Which is to say, our most blessed reality appears to be, that we have the possibility to keep supporting our selves to attune so thoroughly through out all these aspects, of our inner most nervous system grounded selves. In such a way that we will now discover that this underlying / beyond lying hum vibrating Field of Super

Light, It-Self. Out of which all things, including our selves, can be sensed to manifest into form, in our first place. Such that Yes-We-Can actually to grow ourselves sufficiently up into that place wherein we will now find ourselves becoming effortlessly empowered vortices of this Super Light. Now fully enabled to manifest our greatest of dreams in such a beautifully internally full-on & up empowering way! We will now end up resonating with this very same sense of Love and Peace-Ful-Ness, out of which everything has been said to manifest into form, in the first place. In such a completely now open to this Force Field way, that we will thus end up being motivated to actively Co-Create ourselves forward - in way more holistic harmony with this same underlying / beyond lying Loving Force – such as we will now be able sense to be at very root of all existence. Every moment we do thus find ways to open ourselves all up into being in total inward free flow, with all these dimensions of our inner most - unitary attuned sense of ourselves! Can you now so Heare?

To help every One better understand just how the basics of our own whole being integrated nervous system, both our ANS or so called Autonomic Emotional Nervous & our CNS or so called Central more rational/logical oriented Nervous System. Have been most exquisitely designed / evolved in such a way to operate all together as One, in harmonic conjunction with each other. To help us by way of the full-on awakening of our Hearts - to actually realize this fully empowered possibility - we all have within.. Let take a few paragraphs here, to elaborate here more on the basic's of S-R or stimulus / response based psycho-biology. Inasmuch as what we have been saying with respect to this basic S-R differentiation. Is that to the extent we encourage ourselves to grow the more sensitive, receptive S or Yin side of both our Central & Autonomic nervous systems to the max. Via the first 5 methods we have outlined for enhancing our awareness principle. In such a way that we thus help ourselves find our philosophers, or natural wise-dome 'stone' within. And I do mean 'stone' in the sense of learning to be as totally naturally high as we possibly can, based on our possibility to learn how to open our sensory receptive side, to our most optimal max. In other words learn the very kind of Whole nervous system Open-Ness, which can carry us into experiencing that sense of non-separation. As though the very essence of us is actually living within every single thing, which appears to exist in the world outside of ourselves. In this respect, even though I myself see no problem with using natural herbs such as arise out of Source, as natural nervous system balancing forms of nourishment. To help us foster our ability to grow our entirely natural, no longer dependent upon anything outside of us, now whole nervous system awake 'Stone'. Nevertheless I do strongly feel, that we have the capacity to grow this natural 'stone', based on the full-on mobilization of gift of our nervous system based awareness principle, itself. In ways that can get us entirely past us anymore feeling any kind of 'need', to ingest such herbs. In other words, the real philosophers stone that was talked about in the Al-Chemical or

Higher Chemical, tradition, has everything to do with getting ourselves into the sort of entirely natural state of nervous system open awareness. Which would be completely past being dependency addicted - to any such herbs or man made chemical formulas. Or for that matter, any other forms of fear based dependently addictive behavior.

Of course, given the internal gift of that other R or response capability aspect of nervous system function, which we all have within. Which has to do with the more responsive, or active participant Yang or change the world side, of our whole being operating nervous system. As Ram Dass so aptly put it, in his recent dvd Fierce Grace. It is "One thing to discover how to stay 'stoned' or high on life, all day long. But, what then?" "Well" he went on to say, "at a certain point, after several years of getting high pretty much every day! Our group noticed we were starting to get bored, with just being 'stoned' - all the time! It was then we started to question, what we might like to actually do, or accomplish with our 'Stone'." This then is what the first part of the 3rd lesson, in the greater sense of the importance of setting positive intentions in front of our selves. Along with last 4 lessons, which focus on what fully mobilizing or blooming our take action side, or most co-creative R based response-ability capabilities, are all about. In the much larger sense of us actually finding ways to help ourselves manifest ourselves forth, exactly in terms of the positively great lives we most long for. In other words, in terms of this great Magical Mystery Tour we all find ourselves living within. It seem we must first find ways to become optimally sensitive in a context of being more optimally aware of just what is already so. With the utmost respect to what would we might most like to co-create next, in terms of our endless possibilities to invent ever more comfortable and truly love of life interesting way of living, for ourselves. And then go on to find ways to fully mobilize the whole of our most empowered sense of ourselves, toward the full realization of whatever creative / inventive goals, we may keep on choosing to set in front of ourselves. Both by way of us learning how to actually 'sustain' this kind fully nervous system awake and thus whole being found state of fully intelligently mobilized consciousness within - on a regular ongoing daily basis. By means of continually practicing something like the whole range of the '9' greater wise-dome oriented lessons, we have just provided.

Simply because, the moment we truly get this fundamental truth about the Mysterious Unified Field nature of our so called Reality. Everything about how we will now choose to go about inventing ourselves forth, is going to change for the Oh My Good-God, now I really get It - Way, Way, Better! Which is to say, the awakening our inner most awake sense of now actually Co-creative empowerment. Will end up giving us the possibility to alter howsoever we may be experiencing our mere at the mercy of, mostly passive receptive senses of ourselves only. In the direction of us finding: 1.) A much greater sense of our flow zone enabled, inner vital energetic availability: 2.) Our possibility to much better enter that s tate of truly magnificent

One-Der which comes along with our possibility for pure energetic attunement within the world that exists outside of ourselves; 3.) A way greater sense of complete freedom from mere conventional, so called pre-determined mostly object oriented forms of small mind boxed in bias & compulsion; 4.) And thus the ultimate enhancement of our sense of true liberation from so much dependent, at the mercy of, predictability; 5.) All so that we may of course open ourselves way more into our inner most sense of our greatest possible empowered sense of ourselves, wherein we start to experience that yes we-can keep on inventing ourselves ever forward. In the face of what is going to amount to a much more pure energetically open, and therefore now actual endless possibilities, Co-Creative participant view of our so called - Reality. 6.) Always in the name of thus empowering the most glorious solution generative, take the most effective action possible, aspect of ourselves. In the direction of our having a sense of us now being enabled, to continuously re-invent alter our experience of outward reality. More and more in line with those ever expanding potentials, we have been given to best ful-fill the complete range of what amounts to our own inner biologically motivated, wants and desires. 7.) As well as in much better so called psychic, or whole being wakeful alignment, with what our now far more effectively attuned sense of inner wisdom might keep revealing to us. In relation to just how it is we may best orient our ultimate Co-Creative inventive capabilities. In ways that will have the possibility to keep bringing us into ever better harmonic attunement with that huge positively Biggest of All - truly Holiest of Holographic Whole - Sacred most Pictures.

Certainly this sense of inventiveness, is something those born within the context of our modern industrial, new wave technological age, should well understand. Inasmuch as we have just born witness to an age of invention, the likes of which our small planet has likely not ever seen, before. In other words, we have already introduced such a huge variety of new variables in relation to our possibility to keep inventing an ever greater standard of living for ourselves. We have lost the conventional mere outwardly oriented scientific capability to predict, much less control, the likely dependent effects of our multi-varied co-existential inventions. Such that what we would seem to require now, is the development of an equivalent science of the inner. In order that we might sense ourselves as now way better enabled to invent ourselves forward in much greater harmony, within what amounts to that much greater Big Picture Whole, we all find ourselves living within. In other words in view of these understandings, perhaps the time has come for us to develop both methods of inquiry In a direction that might help us to way more effectively 'marry' or 'unite' both forms of investigation. Into a much more singularity integrated science of highly sensitive At-One-Ment attunement. With respect to our possibility for a much more independently empowered, far greater inwardly under-stood sense of Co-Creativity.

Besides, from the work of Max Planck forward, we now know that there may be no such thing as - so called truly objective reality alone. In the huge sense that our much deeper reality appears to be, the moment we choose to engage ourselves within any form of inquiry, no matter how actively or passively. Howsoever we choose to engage based on whatsoever mere abstractive-ly invented forms, we may thus decide to See any given so called thing from, in our first place. Seems to change the very nature of whatever we may keep 'thinking' we are experiencing. In this larger sense then, it would seem that we cannot even exist in any so called purely objective way, without us influencing whatever we may 'think', we are experiencing. So far better we learn to influence whatever we 'think' we are experiencing, in ways that are going to be way more integral to the greater whole. Than to keep deluding ourselves that we even have any possibility to be so called fully objective. In other words, the huge collective intention for mankind would appear to be for us, to keep supporting the most freely liberated creative end of ourselves. In the direction of our possibility to keep inventing a true Garden of De-Lights for our selves. Rather than remain as the mere dependent victims of our lowest strictly animal driven, and therefore least possible empowered sense of our selves. Or what amounts to our least conscious potential to invent ourselves - way more in harmony with One-Ness It-Self. Which I would posit, is not even possible lest we get to actually know of this One-Ness - such we have been given the possibility to experience within. Hence our call for a truly equivalent In-Vestigative Science of the Inner!

What this all boils down to, is that the most significant aspect of the truly amazing intelligence, which we have all been given. Seems to In-Volve, our uniquely Hu-Man or higher man/woman ability to be in the sort of inner awake place. (Look up the meaning of the prefix Hu and you will find it refers to Higher) Which is going to best afford us the possibility to be optimally great life inventive, in the most truly Heart Sensed endless ever greater possibilities, now totally open ended ways! Yes we possibly can! Especially in the sense of our being enabled to invent ourselves forward, into exactly the great lives we ourselves, most truly long to experience, for ourselves. Rather than in the non-sense of us believing that we are mere passive victims of some kind of pre-determined God-Managed reality. In relation to which we must merely obey, and do our best to try and keep adapting to. Such that the moment any 'One' of us truly gets that we appear to be a most intimate non-separate 'Made in the Image' part - of all that ever does manifest into creation. In such a way as to thus help ourselves finally realize this huge possibility we all have to Co-Creatively invent each of our own unique sense of our self's. Ever forward into exactly whomsoever we in our Heart of Hearts most long to be. This will be the moment this self inventive adventure we all find ourselves living within, will become the most exciting of all adventures that any given earthling of us can ever hope to embark upon, here on planet earth. In the huge sense that this is exactly what can make life so exciting, we can hardly wait to jump out of bed every morning. In such a way as to 'get ourselves all up' in the direction of each of us now being enabled - to keep playing inventing ourselves ever optimally forward. Into our possibility to fully truly realize the greatest possible lives - we can ever thus help to Co-Create for all of our selves! In-So-Far as you yourself can now most Hope-Fully much better Heare - of your very own Made in the Image - endless Tap Your Source possibilities. To keep on inventing the very life - every you may ever most Find your Self - longing for?

In this huge respect you could well say, that our own sense of 'Life' appears to be like some grand, endlessly open ended, Great Magical Mystery Tour. Within which the consciousness of One-Ness or God-Ness It-Self, gets to experience It's own endless possibilities to keep on evolving into way more consciously harmonic - ways of manifesting It-Self - forth. Via our own Made in the Image Hu-Man most Being-Nesses who have already been blessed with a Garden of De-Lights to keep playing ourselves forth - within. Here in this ultimate respect, is the rub all my dearest Cosmic Charlie's, or Quantum Katie's, who already exist within You! The only question remaining, is whom would you your very own self my great potential Miracle performing, most Great Mystery attuned Adult's within, most love to invent your self into? Someone who has come to totally love life, and all that it has to offer. In such a way that you would now want to invent yourself self forth as a truly caring, totally heart open loving attuned to the greater force - integral most Hu-Man/Woman being. Or merely as someone who hates so much about life, that you would do anything, including selling your very own life spirit, into a place of having fallen from the grace of this much greater De-Light. In order to get what you merely 'think', you at any cost, most want. In your huge swollen me, me, me, alone, separated out from the rest of your larger whole self, and thus from the rest of existence itself, mere tiny pin head lack, of any true sense of your much greater potential Big Mind awake sense of your Self!

Clearly, we have come to a huge evolutionary convergence point with respect to the development of our human species. We can either choose to root, hog & fully alive integrate, much more inward investigation methods into our schools, colleges and universities. In much the same way we have focused upon teaching systematic processes, for investigating the world outside of ourselves. Or, we can die, go extinct, dis-appear, as a truly whole being integrated, and thus truly wise truly functional - species! Certainly the greatest wisdom sages of the ages, have constantly and consistently pointed to the significance of us first and foremost, valuing such inward investigation. In one tradition, this is summarized in terms of us becoming willing to take on the very sort of attitude, which focuses upon us developing our most intelligent possible 'In-Quiring Mind'. Which is to say, use our awareness principle to inquire inwardly in such a profoundly attuning way. As to help us discover how to truly liberate our largest possible sense of Self, into a place of being enabled to now keep inventing our selves ever forward. In much greater harmony with that which we find existing, well beyond our much more limited sense of me, me, me alone, mere fear based small mind. Or lack of any greater sense of one's much larger Tap one's Source connected and therefore way more Whole-Sum - sense of One's Self!

Most importantly what we are saying here in the context of these '9' guiding ourselves ever forth lessons - which we have just outlined for you. Is that in order to support ourselves to get to this place within which we empower ourselves to be optimally, truly from within our Heart of Hearts! Total great life Ful-Fill-Ment inventive, way great Mystery connected – Total Love of All Beings! Is that it seems to require the sort of persistent, consistent effort of inwardly directed awareness. Which inasmuch as none of these inwardly oriented aspects of our awareness, need be separate from our ordinary existence. These inwardly In-Vestigative methods actually amount to nothing other, than the very sort of subtle effort, which can be easily integrated into our everyday routines. Indeed, the beauty of us agreeing to practice these '9' methods, is that they do not ask of us to in any way cloister or abstract hermitage our self's out of the living of our everyday life's, as did so many of the older methodologies. Rather they simply ask us to become an ever more subtly active aware participant, in such a way that will enable us to facilitate the growth of our own innate ability to become. 'As more and more effortlessly empowered vortices of this great 'Super Light' out of which all things manifest into form in the first place. That we may in this way help our self's to be now much more enabled to Co-Create in optimal harmony, with the very Source of all creation, It-Self. Just exactly whatever sorts of great life experiences, we each of us in our own unique inner most senses of self, might truly most 'love' to Co-Create for all of our Self's.

Hopefully you can now much better comprehend, that our world is actually filled with many wisdom teachings from all kinds of traditions, which admonish us to become as active participants in our greater wisdom quest. Which is to say, go beyond merely believing in such a way that we agree to become as active participants in the continual un-fold-ment, of our very unique own potential brilliance - within. That we may thus experience ourselves as being enabled to invent, whatever forms of ever greater whole being Ful-Fill-Ments, we ourselves have the potential to keep envisioning forth for ourselves. Not as mere endless passive 'believers and hopers' alone, that we will someday be saved by some Force outside of ourselves, only. But much rather in terms of the greater reality, that we ourselves, are the very One's who must take those response-abilities required, to invent forward save ourselves. From what in truth can be to amount to our much lesser aware, constantly divided and conflicted way lesser sense of our selves.

Fortunately in this much greater respect, more and more of us are coming to actually know, that we are not separate, from what we have been referring to as God! In other words clearly within the context of everything we in our modern context of inquiry, have come to know about ourselves. The pathway to salvation would seem to reside within our own willingness to discover just how we have the possibility to be truly holi or holistically inventive enough, to be thus enabled from within to actually save Our Self's. As to why a certain effort of awareness seems to be required, I cannot say. Except that insofar as we keep believing that no effort is required, only fervent belief in some higher Force by it-self. We never seem to come to fully appreciate - the Fullest possible whole being Sense of just who we have been designed / evolved to be! That this is so, to this I can testify! Just as have pretty much all of our great wisdom teachers from our past - have also so testified!

Please note clearly therefore, all my very dearest Quantum Katie's & Cosmic Charlie's of the world. The clear admonitions as were suggested to us by way of the various hi-lighted 'verbs', in the following well known biblical passages! Toward all us Made in the Image Beings, which includes you your very own sense of Self, to keep taking various kinds of Greater Awareness oriented Action. In other words engage in a process of fully growing your greatest possible sense of Self, all your way Up!

'Seek' and ye shall find! - The King-Dome of heaven 'is to be found' within! - 'Make thine 'I' single', and thy body shall be 'filled' as with light! - 'Be still' & ye shall know that I-Am God' (or the One Source out of which All things made manifest appear into various forms)! - 'Ask' and you shall receive! - 'Help me remove' from my heart, any fears & doubts', that may still remain hidden! - Lest ye 'become' as little children, ye shall not know of that King-Dome which is of Heaven! - 'Love' thy neighbor, as thy self! (Not merely as though they may be your self, and then only when it suits you to some advantage, but rather as thy actual most Whole found sense of your highest possible Self!

Even - 'The kingdom of heaven(within) is like a mustard seed, which a man 'may take' and 'plant' in his field (of awareness). Though it is the smallest of all your seeds, yet when it 'grows', it is the largest of garden plants and 'becomes as a tree', so that all the birds of the air may 'come' and 'perch' in its branches! (Is it just possible, that this King-Dom of heaven has to do with cultivating our very own most brilliant shining Source given, full-on grown up integral, 'Tree of Life' or nervous system based intelligence, we all have the potential to fully realize within. Such that in finding this inner most Tree of Life within, every One all around us will be able to perch in our many branches. To thus enjoy the fruits of this 'Kind Of' inner most Wise-Dome of made in the Image Awareness - we will now have found within.)

And of course my very favoriteS, 'See' the lilies of the field and how the bloom, though they 'neither toil', 'nor spin', (please note both of these verbs imply we take opposite - to so called normal split and divided mind action - action) Yet Solomon in all his glory 'was never arrayed' as any of these! (So what do you suppose the opposite of toiling or spinning is? Perhaps to 'become' as an in full bloom, effortlessly empowered vortex of super light? And thus the sort of Some-One who is now fully present able, to flow this Super Light which exists at the very core of everything all around One. All the way through into One's now most expanded sense of beyond all boundaries, and thus now truly unlimited sense of Self? Such that the Light of this natural Force, literally ends up filling the very Lily like Bloom of every inventive action, such a One may ever choose to undertake!)

Finally, 'I' (which is to say One's very own most fully grown up I-Am within) '& My Father' (or the One Source of all so called Things), 'Are now as One, As if (actually existing) in the King-Dome of Heaven'! As well as 'forgive them Lord' (of the Uni-Verse), (for in not knowing of this great At-One-Ment truth). Insofar as they keep choosing to harm any aspect of Your most blessed One-Ness - 'They know not of what they do'! Wake up, wake up every Dear One, do you have any idea as to how many of our world's Greatest Mystic's from all '4 corners' of our world, have said most essentially, this very same thing? Which is that we are not actually separate from One-Ness, or that which we keep referring to as God!

Om Shanti Om, Buddham Sarinam Gachami, Dhaman Sarinam Gachami, Sangam Sarinam Gachami, Lehiam, Halleluyah, Allah Akbar! My Whole Heart Now Soars Like An Eagle, Ho! In The Greater Sende of Actually Humming Much Like A Bright Inner Shinning - Star!

Clearly every One of these Real Spiritually oriented admonitions, could be considered precursor calls for the building of a truly In-Vestigative science of the Inner. For it is only by way of each of us our self's, being willing to make an agreement to enter as deeply and fully as possible into that incredible singular most energy magic, which makes up every manifestation that ever appears into form - in very here and now. That we have the possibility to find the great wisdom of our very own nervous system based 'Philosophers or natural Wise-Dome of awareness Stone', which is to be found within. So how about we all of us invite our inner most self's by way of whatever related take action processes, we can find within our own spiritual traditions. Agree to now grow our very own inner wisdom to the max. For the power and the glory of One-Ness is simply to grand to be contained in any one narrow band viewpoint - alone. Rather the great blessing within the much Bigger Picture Whole, I suspect. Is that there as many pathways to wholeness, as there are human beings on planet earth. Inasmuch as each unique one of us, can be said to come here with our very own possibility to discover how to best fully unfold. The full blooming power and glory of that most blessed unique aspect of God-Ness getting to know of It's endless One-Ness possibilities through us. Which every One of us has the possibility to reveal back onto One-Ness It-Self, provided we might choose to become fully conscious of this most powerful possibility!

(Note the images above yet once again, as we have in this greater respect attempted to illustrate before! The 2 oldest spiritual traditions on our planet doing their very best to help reveal to all of Man/Woman Kind, the very same Heart Centered possibility we all have within. So that we may in turn best help our very own unique individual Self's fully Bloom, even more gloriously than the Lilies of the Field. One image via our possibility to attune to that Hum Resonant Om Sound, which can be sensed by us to emanate from within the Uni-Versal quantum level to Infinity & Beyond At-One-Ment Source Field of all things - in It-Self! And the other by way of our innate given possibility to sense that most Sacred Every-Thing engendering Uni-Versal Force Field. Which by way of the great Mystery of Sacred Geometrical Fractal Pattern Formation, keeps manifesting every single thing into every differential form we can ever come to Know!)

See the point, when will we ever learn? Inasmuch as You, Yes You by the Great Singular Wise-Dome of unlimited expanded awareness, pointed to by all those teachings put forth by every singular 'One' of Man-Kinds greatest Big Picture attuned Seers. By the power of the very yellow brick road golden illuminating pathway, which leads to the discovery of our very own most One-Der-Ful Heart attuned - Giant unlimited great solution generative Wizard Within. And by the collective support of our like minded brothers and sisters, who link in true fellowship to help each other actually find, this magnificent Kingdom of Heaven which can be found within. It appears we have all actually been designed / evolved to Co-Create in true 'Wholly Loving Communing' & thus actual Loving Harmony, within this great One-Ness Field. Which 'In-Plain-Sight', 'Beyond Word', & 'In-Every-Deed' amounts to that very 'Everywhere All About Us' both underlying as well as at the same time beyond lying - 'Loving most Whole Field Mystical Presence'. Such as can actually be experienced within to be no-thing more or less, than 'Every One's same Source connection to One's One & Only Maker'. With the provisio of course, that we under-take those subtle efforts of awareness, which seem to be required to help ourselves truly realize this filled with Grace King-Dome of Heaven found Blessing - we all are most blessed to have the very same access too - Within.

In this huge respect, it is most important to fully get it, that we are not asking any One anymore, to merely believe in the notion of At-One-Ment. Rather we are suggesting that the time has come for each One of us. To now engage in the very sort of totally inwardly In-Vestigative oriented journey, that will help every One of us to actually experience, this Made in the Image state for our very own Self's. Exactly within our most Magical Adult awake sense - of just Whom or What we have all been Made in the Image to most fully Be. Inasmuch as the history of mankind to date, clearly suggests that believing alone, no matter how much we may keep choosing to invest in our beliefs? Has so far made very little difference in our ability to manifest truly Peace-Ful, completely Loving ways. With respect to us being able to actually be positively great life forward moving inventive - in relation to every each other. Even though, heaven knows, we already in the form of our Magical Child Within - actually do know so much better. It's just that our history of fear based patterns and narrow band small mind conditioning, inevitably begin to overtake us, unless we at some point agree take some form or another of actual self clearing Response-Ability. Which in turn is exactly why it is incumbent upon very single One of Us, to undertake of our very own, INNER WISDOM MAGICAL ADULT ORIENTED JOURNEY! Inasmuch as within the ultimate mystery of who it appears we have been designed / evolved to be! It seems there simply is - no other way for us to discover just how to be the fully Whole beings we all have the Source designed / evolved potential to be!

Fortunately for all of us within the context of new modern understandings about the nature of more expanded states of consciousness. Which in turn seem to be leading us in the direction of more and more us actually wanting to more fully develop this more inwardly investigative kind of inquiry. Many of us like never quite before in the history of Man-Woman-Kind, are finally coming to fully 'Grok' that what we have heretofore been referring to as God-Ness? Appears to be not so much just an external entity, per se only. But much rather more a presence that is in some huge mysterious way, is both transcendental to. As well as at the same time imminent within all things, perhaps especially including our selves. Which in turn makes it possible for us as potential Made in the Image of God or Love - Beings. To now via our processes of more inwardly oriented In-Vestigation, actually come into much more whole sum, or wholly empowered state of communion. Within our very own most expanded senses of our very own truly unique most Whole sense - of our most One-Ness or Divine connected Self's. This in itself represents a quantum leap in our potential for more human conscious - Self Realization. In the huge sense that the more, more and more of us begin to fully internalize this huge potential we all have within. It going to change everything about how we are going to now want, to keep on inventing ourselves ever forward into this great infinite Mystery Field of Whole-Ness or God-Ness we all find ourselves living within - in It-Self.

Illustration # 26 – To help you better under-stand this last Investigative Science of the Inner - chapter! You may want to find some way to watch the Power of 10 Movie - Here

Please Note - In relation to this viewing , we ask you to create your very own image of the Quantum Katie or Cosmic Charlie which resides within you. In such a way that you might now actually use your inwardly oriented investigative microscope, to help you zero ever more deeply inward into your very own micro core self. To where you would end up discovering nothing other than pure everywhere non local quantum level energy, constantly flowing throughout every part of you. While you at the same time by way of using your more outwardly oriented macro scope, help your self now see that this pure energy within you is connected all the way out of you - to infinity & beyond. Inasmuch as your possibility to sense this ultimate connectively to the Source of everything, is the very best means you have. To help your self actually be enabled to now realize, the positively great life that you might most long for. And in continuous 'in-sight', 'intended word', and 'take action oriented deed', so much in greater truth, really do deserve! In the context of this great ultimately Mysterious At-One-Ment Field, we all find ourselves living within!

To Conclude - A Short Note Re: Every One's Possibility to fully Develop One's core most - Now 'Quantum Hum Level' attuned Processing Unit - Such as we all have to be Found by each & every One of Us - Within'

It is being said, the next generation of computer processors are going to be called 'Quantum Computers'. And as such they will have the incredible ability to project 3-D holographic images, in an instant. Much like in the last Star Wars episode wherein the Jedi's found themselves able to communicate with each other in Holographic image form at a distance. With the additional capability that we will now be able to enter these now 3-D Holo-Grapchic images with our very own inner motivated joystick. And then make whatever changes with respect to some field of interest hologram, we may be choosing to play forward within, pretty much immediately/instantaneously with one move of our joystick. In such a way that the whole holographic matrix, will now adjust to whatever changes we may choose to use our joystick to help us make, in pretty much the same moment. With our whole point within the framework of this 'Quantum Attunement' process that we have put forth here, being that we already have the most One-Der-Ful quantum level Wizard computers - within ourselves. Which can actually enable us to enter that large Big Picture Holographic matrix, we refer to in terms of that multi-dimensional world outside of us. Now known within the leading edges of quantum energy level under-standings, to already be instantaneously non-locally inter-connected. In such way that our inner awareness guided joystick, has the instant ability to jump the whole of ourselves totally into this non-local multi-dimensional reality. With a most incredible given ability to help ourselves very quickly inventively change our sense of reality, in relation to whatever great life intentions we may keep choosing to put in front of ourselves.

"Wow, as one young adult I shared this understanding with, so aptly put it! You mean the great whole of Who I-Myself-Most-Am - within me? Is like having my very own joystick to help me most fully operate the giant quantum level computer, that I already Am. Such that the more I-get It - I now See that Yes-I-Can actually choose to use the instantly Co-Creative - constantly ongoing reality changing joystick - I already have Within. In such a way as to learn just how to now fully operate my very own huge Holo-Graphically embedded, gigantic quantum computer matrix of information, which I have by way I have been guiding my joystick, thus chosen to store within me. Always in the context of whatever interests and talents I may be most choosing to be most intentionally involved with. Then the more I can actually help myself fully 'get', just how to play my self ever forward to the max. Within the framework of this Big Holographic - At-One-Ment Field Matrix we call reality. No matter what stance I may choose to take within the context of my playing myself forward. Whether I choose to play totally passive wimp repressive, way too depressed half dead! Or alternatively, far too aggressive harmful, constantly energy losing macho fighter tough! Even into a whole matrix of such frozen idea attachments and belief identifications. My life never seems to live up, to what I most long to be able to invent for my Self. And of course most preferably, all my way out into being maximally lovingly expanded, and thus optimally great holistic solution aware! Then every joystick guided movement or non-movement I may ever choose to take, no matter how poorly or well attuned to whatever is emerging on - the ongoing screen of my awareness. My joystick guided behaviors are actually going to totally change the very nature of just what it will be, I will now find myself in this way experiencing. In the huge sense of my ongoing possibility to actually participate in the actual manifestation of whatever inwardly motivated, forward moving toward total Ful-Fill-Ment states of feedback, I may be most looking for. Always with respect to whatever great intentions I may most long to keep creating my Self forth into - in any first place?"

Yes, Yes, In-Deedy Do! The moment any One of us truly get's this, about the nature of the giant super brilliant quantum level computer, we all already have within us. We suddenly realize, we are the One's who end up creating whatever we may find ourselves experiencing, based on how we keep choosing to move our own internal Joy-Sticks or sic in far too many cases, our Cursors. Into this giant Whole Field matrix, we all find ourselves living within. Such that we may as well learn how to activate our own inner now Joy Stick's in all those best intention set ways. Which are going to be most likely, to best enable us to keep inventing our way ever forward, toward the fulfillment of our most inwardly intended dreams. As opposed to staying stuck feeling like we-are merely the passive victims of whatever so called negative experiences, we keep finding ourselves law of attraction having. Based on our more unconsciously driven ways of moving our Cursor. Re our much greater Joy-Stick potential to keep playing our selves forth, way more Co-Creatively consciously into whatever actual Ful-Fill-Ments, we may find ourselves most longing for. "Holy inner wisdom, nobody quite ever said what my life is all about, quite like this to me - ever before," this young man went on to say! "Thank you for this huge small mind blowing insight - about myself! I never even thought of my self, and the way I choose to use my own awareness to help guide my behaviors forth, in the context of the huge hologram that I live within every moment of my life. As some great potential Joystick vs my own Cursor! Yes, in thought, word, and deed, now that 'I get it'. I can 'See' that learning to play with my very own quantum computer within, to my max. Via the way I choose to use that joystick which is my ability to use my awareness, in such way as to direct my reality changing behaviors precisely within those fields of endeavor, within which I most love to play within. Is the very best tool I have within myself, to thus help myself choose to behave my self forth, in ways that are going to actually help me to fulfill the very Heart Core of my greatest possible sense of my Self. "WHAH, this positively huge In-sight about my self you have given me, has helped me to now much more fully realize, that learning to play my own quantum level computer within to my utmost max. Is truly the most exciting quantum computer game adventure, on the whole of our planet earth! Which as you say, there really is!"

Imagine then I would ask all out there who might really be listening, that insofar as the more of us might choose to keep orienting ourselves in this way more consciously aware - pure quantum Source Energy attunement direction. If we were to start building quantum attunement computer games in the world outside of ourselves, in such a way that would actually help us to play ourselves through these '9' levels of awareness, exactly more on the very inside ourselves? In such a way that would finally help to learn to operate the Whole of our Nervous System based intelligence, more as an Integral Whole. Rather than in terms of our various intelligence potentials being way too constantly held in mere piecemeal, constantly divided in internal conflicts with each other, and thus way too self dis-functional ways. Until such time as we might become positively brilliant at playing our quantum level computers within our Self's to our most brilliant whole solution generative capacity - max. Simply because learning to play 'this inwardly oriented, and thus ultimate full-on empowerment enabling, quantum level computer game'. Exactly within our very own sense of our most core essential whole being integrated sense of our Self's. Is all about how Yes We-Can actually become the now way more fully Conscious Joy-Stick controller's of the very best ways to keep choosing to live ourselves forth. From within the very core essence of our most awake sense of our Whole Being Integrated Self's. as Yes-We-Possibly-Can. In such a way that via the very process of fully engaging in this inner awareness game, within ourselves! This sort of engagement inevitably, is going to help us not just influence the very nature of that more holographic reality, we are going to now experience to exist in relation to ourselves. But also the very way more Integrated ways we will now keep choosing to play our Self's ever forward. In relation to this Great to Infinity & Beyond without limits true Whol-E-Ness Mystery - we all find our Self's most blessed to be living Within - every to infinity & beyond Here & Now!

Such that in the larger sense of us learning to play forth our quantum level computer's within, to our optimal max! Why not learn to play at using our inevitably reality altering joysticks, as opposed to our cursors? In ways which within the context of our larger dreamed for intentions, are going to help us to actually realize, whatever it might be that we would most love to fulfill - for ourselves? Very much as consequence of how we may now way more consciously choose to play, at this great life actualization game, we are inevitably going to be playing our way into anyway? Whether we choose to play full consciously or far too unconsciously continue to knot? Since this is exactly how we learn to become ever more higher level – truly Holistically effective! At playing ourselves toward whatever intended results within this Grand Hologram, we might choose to use our own inner most One-Der-Ful Wisdom Wizard – such as we all can find With-In! To thus help us actually play ourselves into, whatsoever we may most Wisely choose to play all our selves into! In the much greater sense of helping all ourselves to fulfill all those way more inward '7' vital energy whole being Ful-Fill-Ments, we all of us keep seeking! Can you now see how this kind of more inwardly oriented computer gaming within our selves? Would be far more way total interesting fun, than merely playing at some silly only outwardly, merely entertaining just for a brief moment - sort of result? In terms of our much greater potential to actually way more core inwardly, actually play at totally fulfilling, the way greater whole of our most conscious sense of our greatest possible Self's?"

Fortunately for all of us, this new 'Growing One's Inner Wisdom - to our Max book, has been written for both younger people and older adults. To offer guidance on how to way more fully operate and thus way more optimally actualize the next generation level quantum computer processors, that we all already have within us. Which in greater truth, we all innately already actually know we have, deep inside the very core of our Being's. It's just that we have been fear programmed, or hypnotized away, from the greater internalized realization of these basic truth's, with respect to our much greater potentials. Whereas this book, inasmuch as it is based on the very sort of principles of awareness, such as have been designed by our very greatest wisdom teachers, over countless ages of human inquiry into our much greater potentials! Has been evolved to help every singularity most attuned 'One of Us', bloom even more gloriously than a King or Queen such as Solomon or Salome, or even than that of a Lily in the Field. Into whomsoever we each of us in our Heart of Hearts ability to vision ourselves forward, truly might most long to flower into being. By way of helping our innermost essence discover, just how to much more fully operate the quantum computer that we already have within each of ourselves - to our most empowered max. That we may through such true found Wisdom, all support our inner most core pure energetic essence, to now blossom forth the most gloriously possible, even beyond our wildest dreams! All it takes is a willingness for each of us to take those grow our innate awareness response-abilities, such as seems to be required for us to learn how to so internalize these greater more expanded awareness processes - we all have within. To the point where they become second nature - to all of whom we already - really are! Ho, this is what's so! Other than wise, we are likely to remain much less than whole, and thus constantly lost to whomever we really in our Heart of Heart's, may most truly want to most fully Be.

In this huge respect, is it not so that huge numbers of us have been willing to spend months and years learning to effectively operate such external devices as planes, trains & automobiles, not to mention all kinds of video equipment, audio equipment and computer programs. To help us keep manifesting ever better lives for ourselves? So why should we be surprised that a certain effort of our awareness, might be required? In order for us to learn how to fully operate that most Sophist-I-Cated info processing Unit - we all already have within ourselves. Insofar as this internal processing capability is really the best instrument we each of us actually have. To best help us manifest the positively greatest possible life's, we all of us most long for. In these terms then this book can also be understood to constitute a draft outline proposal for a never quite like before, holographic image based inwardly oriented computer game. Complete with built in bio-feedback linked instrumentation, with respect to helping us both develop as well as integrate each of these 3 levels of our nervous system based intelligence, we all have within every One of us - to our ultimate Max. I.E. Our feeling & emotional nervous system based intelligence, our supra rational logical nervous system based intelligence, and our most core heart cosmic or most One-Ness attuned intelligence. Re helping ourselves to sense our self's as fully enabled to Co-Create the best possible life's for ourselves.

In the huge sense that it would help show our children, just how to play the most exciting possible of all adventure games - ye devised. With respect to helping develop our innate potential to actually be best enabled. To actually manifest our Self's forth - to our optimal fulfillment capable max.

Toward this end, we also see this as the basis for a world wide best selling 3 D movie, centered around our 2 Innermost Wisdom oriented characters Quantum Katie & Cosmic Charlie. Such as would have the possibility to help guide us with respect to our much greater human potentials, for which the first treatment draft is already written. We welcome therefore all the support we can muster to help us bring these visions for a much more whole being fulfillment possible, truly Higher Made in the Image and thus way more Conscious Ha Nu Man-Woman-I-Ty. In such a way that would now enable every singular most One of Us to fully Bloom into way more truly Whol-E ways of Being Heare. In all 4 directions with respect to this relatively small belonging to Us All - planetary most Home we call Earth. To make such a contribution you can contact us via our Quantum You website quantumyou.com as well as via an alternate link to our Quantum You Learning Academy found on youtube just below my name under my Lynn Sereda postings on youtube. This Learning Academy link will then show you all the free video lessons re the 9 methods or aspects of awareness such have been outlined in this book - to help you access that state which is known as Pure Unlimited Loving Awareness.

Notes

_____

_____

_____

_____

_____

_____

_____

_____

_____

_____

_____

_____

_____

_____

_____

_____

_____

_____